A WONDERFUL BOOK . . .

"Theroux's gift for painting Third World characters . . . is equal to that of Graham Greene or Somerset Maugham."
—*Los Angeles Times Book Review*

"Engagingly intimate . . . The chapters in this novel devoted to Andre's years in Nyasaland and Uganda display Mr. Theroux's now patented ability to describe the foreign, the alien, the strange, with both an insider's affection and an outsider's eye for incongruous detail."
—*The New York Times*

"No one has written about the inner life of the American male lately with more comic, poignant candor than Paul Theroux in his new novel. . . . He writes brilliantly about people."
—*Playboy*

"Jenny is one of Mr. Theroux's great female creations. . . . MY SECRET HISTORY has a kind of artistry all its own."
—*The New York Times Book Review*

"A strikingly vivid picture of a writer. . . . Theroux's trademark place descriptions are as vivid as ever, but with MY SECRET HISTORY, he takes us on a journey unlike any other."
—*The Houston Post*

MY
SECRET
HISTORY

MY
SECRET
HISTORY

PAUL THEROUX

FAWCETT COLUMBINE • NEW YORK

A Fawcett Columbine Book
Published by Ballantine Books

The author gratefully acknowledges permission from the following sources to reprint material in their control:

Henry Holt and Company, Inc. for lines from "Into My Heart" by A. E. Housman. Copyright 1939, 1940, © 1965 by Holt, Rinehart and Winston. Copyright © 1967, 1968 by Robert E. Symons. Reprinted from *The Collected Poems of A. E. Housman*, by permission of Henry Holt and Company, Inc.

Warner Bros. Inc. for lyrics from "Moonlight Bay," lyrics by Edward Madden, music by Percy Wenrich. © 1912 Warner Bros. Inc. (renewed). All rights reserved. Used by permission.

http://www.randomhouse.com

Library of Congress Catalog Card Number: 96-96618

ISBN: 0-449-91200-0

This edition published by arrangement with G. P. Putnam's Sons, a division of the Putnam Berkley Group, Inc.

Manufactured in the United States of America

First Ballantine Books Mass Market Edition: April 1990
First Ballantine Books Trade Paperback Edition: August 1996

10 9 8 7 6 5 4 3

CONTENTS

ONE: ALTAR BOY [1956]   17

TWO: WHALE STEAKS [1960]   95

THREE: AFRICAN GIRLS [1964]   191

FOUR: BUSH-BABY [1968]   271

FIVE: LEAVING SIBERIA [1974]   359

SIX: TWO OF EVERYTHING [1984]   417

AUTHOR'S NOTE

Although some of the events and places depicted in this novel bear a similarity to those in my own life, the characters all strolled out of my imagination. My wife Anne, for example, does not in the least resemble Andre Parent's spouse. As Evelyn Waugh wrote in a similar context, *I am not I: thou art not he or she: they are not they.*

PAUL THEROUX

Into my heart an air that kills
  From yon far country blows:
What are those blue remembered hills,
  What spires, what farms are those?

That is the land of lost content,
  I see it shining plain:
The happy highways where I went
  And cannot come again.

—A. E. HOUSMAN

MY
SECRET
HISTORY

ONE

ALTAR BOY

1.

I was born poor in rich America, yet my secret instincts were better than money and were for me a source of power. I had advantages that no one could take away from me—a clear memory and brilliant dreams and a knack for knowing when I was happy.

I was at my happiest leading two lives, and it was a satisfaction to me that the second one—of the dreamer or the sneak—I kept hidden. That was how I spent my first fifteen years. Fifteen was young then and I knew this: The poor don't belong. But one summer out of loneliness or impatience my second self did more than wake and watch, and more than remember. He began to see like a historian, and he acted. I have to save my life, I used to think.

Early that summer I was walking down a lovely crumbling little street lined with elms, called Brookview Road. The city of Boston, with its two tall buildings, was visible from one end of the road looking east along the Fellsway. The brook was a shallow ditch at the other end of the road, where the Italian families had tomato gardens. There were rats in the ditch, but it was a pretty part of town when the wineglass elms were heavy with leaves.

It was a perfect day of blue sky and the hot summer hum of insects, which made a sound like the temperature rising. I had my rifle over my shoulder—a Mossberg twenty-two—as I passed Tina Spector's house. She was sitting on her piazza, which was our word for porch. I had planned it this way.

She said, "Hey, Andy, where are you going with that gun?"

"Church," I said.

"It's Tuesday!"

"But I've got a funeral."

I was still walking, and now Tina started off the piazza towards me. I knew she would: it was part of my plan.

"How come you're bringing your gun to church?"

"Target practice, up the Sandpits," I said. "After."

She said, "My mother can't stand guns."

Everybody said that. I kept walking.

"And you're not even sixteen," she said.

I could feel the warm pressure of her eyes on the back of my neck.

She said, "Can I come with you?"

"Okay," I said, probably too eagerly—but I didn't want her to change her mind. I had planned to agree very slowly and reluctantly. I had blurted it out, because I was so glad she had asked. The thought of being alone with Tina in the Sandpits on a hot summer afternoon was very erotic, and having my rifle with me made it still more erotic, for a reason I could not explain. I did not know what erotic meant; wicked was the word that went through my head.

"Meet me outside Saint Ray's."

"My mother doesn't want me near that church."

Her mother was a non-Catholic.

"What's in that bag?" she asked—she was still following me, three steps behind.

"Ammo," I said. "Bullets."

That was a lie. My cartridges were in my pocket. In my bag I had a starched surplice—a white smock with starched sleeves and a stiff plastic collar. I was an altar boy, on my way to serve at a funeral.

I heard her sneakers crunch behind me. I knew she had stopped but I didn't look around.

"See you later," she said.

"Okay," I said.

We were both fifteen years old. I did not know whether she would be waiting for me. Things always happened suddenly, without much warning. Some days nothing happened and other days everything.

* * *

The rule at St. Raphael's—St. Ray's—was that if you served at three funerals you got a wedding as a reward. Funerals were gloomy, and it was an elderly parish, so there were plenty of them. But there was money in a wedding. The altar boys usually got two dollars, and the priest got ten. The money was handed over by the best man or the bride's father. It was always in a white envelope, always in the sacristy. "Here you are," they'd say to us, and then turning to the priest, "This is for you, Father."

"God bless you," the priest would say, as he folded the envelope into his vestments. Meanwhile we were tearing ours open.

There was no money in funerals, and it could be terrible, especially if it was Italians—the shouts and nose-blowings of big competitive families, and the loud abrupt sobbing, or *"No!"* or the screaming of the dead person's name. *"Salveeeeee!"*

I unslung my Mossberg and held it muzzle down, walking stiff-legged to conceal it. I sneaked into the sacristy and saw Chicky DePalma pulling on his cassock.

"I hosey the bells," he said, before I could speak. Ringing the bells at the consecration was considered one of the enjoyable duties of an altar boy, and the boy who rang the bells also got to hold the plate at the communion. That was a flat gold pan that was placed under a person's chin to catch any falling flecks of the consecrated host.

Chicky had started buttoning his cassock—a finicky job, thirty buttons or more.

"Hey, shitface, you're not supposed to bring guns into a church!"

He fought the buttons with his big fingers.

"It's not loaded. And I took the bolt out."

"It's still a gun! It could go off, asshole!"

"You don't know shit about guns," I said. "Anyway, this is the sacristy."

The sacristy was a safe place—not sacred, but a sort of neutral area, like a lobby where we altar boys met and waited until it was time for mass. In the meantime we were growing up. Whenever a priest tried to explain what limbo or purgatory was I thought of the sacristy. Who would know if there was a gun here?

I slipped the Mossberg into the closet behind the hanging cassocks, and then looked for a cassock my size.

Chicky said, "I saw you with Specks."

"She was following me." I decided not to tell him I was taking her to the Sandpits—he would laugh or else mock me.

"Her sister got knocked up—she had to get married." Chicky was now working his arms into his surplice—it was pure white and pleated and fringed with lace. Italians always had the best surplices, because of their mothers; and they even brought them on hangers. "She was a real tramp. She once took on six guys. She used to give hand-jobs. She let Moochie eat her out."

"Quit it," I said.

"You fairy," Chicky said, and smoothed his surplice in the mirror. "I was making out last night. I'm not going to say with who. After about two seconds she was letting me have bare tit. I was really getting her hot."

"I'll bet you weren't," I said, to encourage him. I was eager for more. I buttoned my cassock and pretended I wasn't listening.

"He doesn't believe me," he said, in a confident way, and then teased me with silence.

"How did you know?" I whispered, looking around. The priest had still not arrived, although the vestments were out, folded neatly on top of the altarlike cabinet, the stacks of linens and the bright chasuble; and his cope, his cincture and stole.

He said, "I could feel it."

I was staring at him, holding the skirt of my cassock.

He said, "When a girl gets hot her hole gets bigger."

I could picture this very distinctly, the dark opening and the way it widened in a round welcoming way. My mouth was very dry. No one had ever said those words to me before, but it made perfect sense.

Chicky was fixing his plastic collar—twisting it to fasten the collar button into it.

"She was really hot," he said. "I got three fingers into her."

The sun was streaming through the stained-glass window over the vestments, and the alb and the white linens blazed. The sacristy was warm and smelled of floor polish and soft candlewax.

"Who was it?"

Now I had my cassock and surplice on, and I was tying the black bow in front of my collar. It was impossible for me to hide my fascination with what he had told me.

He grinned to tease me with another delay, and then he said, "Magoo."

It was a girl named Eloise McGonagle, but no one called her anything but Magoo.

Chicky was still grinning, but now his lips were purple. He held out a bottle of mass wine and said in a man-of-the-world way, "Want a swig?"

I tried not to look shocked. It was not that he was drinking mass wine—I had seen him do that before, and had even had some myself—but rather that he was doing it so near to the time the priest was to arrive. His tongue was purple, he had a purple mustache. He sloshed the wine in the bottle and said, "Go ahead." His face was Italian yellow, he had long eyelashes and a birthmark like a bruise on his cheek. When he smiled he looked like a monkey.

I took a swig. It tasted harsh and bitter—it tasted dreadful. I had another. It tasted even worse.

"Have one of these," Chicky said.

He was holding out a handful of communion wafers, small papery disks, and some spilled to the floor as he offered them.

"They're not consecrated, so what the fuck," he said recklessly and stuffed the hosts into his mouth.

Just then the priest came in, walking fast.

"In the name of the Father, the Son, and the Holy Ghost," the priest said, blessing himself as he strode from the sacristy door to the sideboard where the vestments were neatly folded, and there he genuflected.

"Let us pray," he said, and paused, before he added, "for the conversion of Russia."

His face seemed to swell up when he closed his eyes to pray. He murmured—the little whimpers that suggested that the prayers were for a lost cause—and Chicky gulped down the last of the hosts and made a face that said, "Who's this dink?" which was a remark he often made.

"Amen," the priest said, and began the slow business of putting on his vestments, murmuring more prayers and kissing each garment before wrapping it around himself.

I had never seen him before, and I knew at once he was unlike any of the other priests at St. Ray's. The Pastor was white-haired and tall and had a stern chalky forehead and small pitiless eyes and pale lips; and the other priests—Father Skerrit, Father Hanratty, and Father Flynn—were young, thin, and Irish. They had knobby joints and large Adam's apples and the popping eyes that usually go with them, and blush blotches on their cheeks. They smelled of clean laundry and talcum powder; the Pastor had no smell at all.

But Father Furty (I saw his name in the Mass List on the sacristy wall) was a big man—thick arms and an overhanging belly—and although not old he had grayish hair cut very short in a sort of Julius Caesar style. He was bottle-nosed and had a meaty face and sausagey fingers. I could tell he was strong—the way he filled his vestments, the way his loafers squeaked. That was another thing: I had never seen a priest wear anything as sporty as loafers—and to a funeral!

He seemed unusual, but I could not figure out what it was about him that made him different. Then I realized what it was: he was human. He looked like a normal man. He was a man in a priest's clothes. I had never thought of priests as men before—and I had certainly never thought of nuns as women.

He smiled at me and said, "Yoomit." He took a hanky out of his sleeve and wiped the perspiration from his face.

It was a moment before I knew he meant humid.

He said, "You guys better light some charcoal. This is a requiem mass."

He said "guys" and "requiem" in the same way, out of the side of his mouth. For some reason I felt he had been in the navy—he certainly looked more like a sailor than a priest, and perhaps for that reason I found him a reassuring priest.

Chicky and I brought the thurible onto the lawn outside the sacristy and put a match to the charcoal disk. The cross on it fizzed and then we took turns swinging it around until the disk was fiercely alight.

This, like ringing the bells, was another enjoyable routine of being an altar boy. During the mass the priest would sprinkle incense onto the glowing charcoal and a powerful and pungent odor would be released in billows.

I had never questioned being an altar boy. It was something that was expected and inevitable when a boy turned eleven. It was part of being a Catholic boy—an honor and a duty. And becoming a priest was also a possibility. "You might have a vocation," my mother used to say. I hoped I did not have a vocation; I did not believe I had a choice. When my mother said, "God might choose you for Holy Orders," I imagined something like marching orders—a beckoning finger, a stern summons—and off I'd go to be a priest, whether I liked it or not. But so far I had heard nothing.

"I've never seen this priest before."

"Furty," Chicky said. "He's an alkie."

"Bullshit."

"He's a boozehound. I can prove it."

It was a beautiful July day, with a bright sky and a loud drone of bees on the flower beds and the clack of lawnmowers across the Fellsway. We knelt in the shade, playing with the smoking thurible, which looked more than ever like a lantern, and then we went in to the funeral.

The routine of a funeral meant waiting until the casket was wheeled into position in the center aisle, and the pews were filled. We could see this from where we now stood, two altar boys in front, priest holding a monstrance like a gold mirror against his chest.

"Let's go," Father Furty said, and Chicky yanked the chain to warn the congregation we were coming, and we could hear them clattering to their feet as soon as the bell sounded.

The rich aroma of flowers I always associated with death, and the incense and the beeswax candles always meant a solemn high mass and a long service. It seemed the more odors there were the longer it would all take. At this funeral there were snuffles and sobs, and one person weeping very loudly.

I was fifteen. I had never known anyone who had died: the emotion of grief was disquieting to me, but alien; yet it was no more disturbing to me than hearing someone laugh and not knowing the reason. My first funeral had bewildered me—not the idea of the body in the casket but the crying, the intensity of it—I had never heard anyone crying like that, so sad and continuous. It was always loud and pitiful, but it also seemed to me insincere, because the person was dead. But I had never known anyone who had died.

When we walked down from the altar to the center aisle and the casket, passing the hot rack of burning vigil lights, Chicky motioned for me to look at him. He was carrying the long-handled cross. He had a very ugly, rubbery, funny face—and the candlelight made it yellower. He often tried to get me laughing, especially at funerals. I faced him, to show him that I could take it without laughing. He wrapped three fingers around the shaft of the cross and shaped the word "Magoo" with his lips.

I was more likely to laugh at a funeral than in an empty church—the people screaming and sobbing only made me laugh harder. But I resisted. I was thinking about what he had told me—bare tit, hand-jobs, three fingers. "Her hole gets bigger."

The casket was closed, but I knew what was inside: in the center of white ruffles, like a clown's collar, was a dead old man—the pale powdered face with sunken cheeks and eyes bulging under the lids, and farther down, in more ruffles, a rosary twisted around knuckly fingers; like Walter Hogan's Uncle Pat, whom I had seen at Gaffey's.

We started the requiem mass. I had learned my Latin from a pamphlet that had set it out in easy-to-say spelling.

Intro-eebo ad-ahltaree-dayee ah-dayum-kwee-lah-teefeekat yoo-ven too-tem mayum.

That was how we began. It made no sense at all to me, though I knew it by heart and I could win races reciting certain prayers.

It was a sung mass—a fat lady and an organist in the choir loft—*Dies Irae, dies illa!*—and Father Furty intoning the Latin in a falsetto, as if he knew exactly what he was saying. Then he gave a sermon—it was about football and life and being a team player even though you knew you were alone. He said "frannick" and "sem-eye professional" and instead of aunty, "anny." He said, "yooman beings." I was thrilled by this. He was like a man from a foreign land.

He finished and the mass continued. The "Confee-teeyor" turned into a race between Chicky and me. Normally we tried to say it very fast, like the "Soo-ship-eeyat," but when I saw Chicky bent over and hammering his chest at the "mayah kool-pah" I decided to beat him and, swiveling and muttering, I finished first.

"I beat you," I said, just before the consecration. We were at the side table to the far right of the altar, picking up the cruets of wine and water.

"You skipped the middle part," he whispered.

"Your ass I did," I hissed at him.

But he wasn't listening. He whispered, "I'm going to prove he's an alkie," and tossed his head.

I looked back at Father Furty, who was coming towards us with the chalice.

Normally a priest held out the chalice to receive a little wine and water, and returned to the stand in front of the tabernacle to drink it. It was a simple operation. But today Chicky did something I had never seen before. When Father Furty extended the chalice for the wine, Chicky emptied the cruet into it—tipped it upside down until all the wine dribbled out.

The chalice trembled, Father Furty seemed to object, but too late; he let out a noisy breath of resignation, considered the full chalice, then moved it sideways for me to add the water. But he lifted the chalice before I could pour more than a few drops in. He returned to the tabernacle, and we studied him.

He straightened up, and then leaned forward and rested his elbows on the altar and glanced into the chalice, tipping it towards him like a big glass. He pushed out his lips, seeming to savor it in anticipation, and then he grasped the chalice more affectionately, shifted his weight onto his back leg, raised the cup, drank it all, and let out a little gasp of satisfaction.

He staggered a bit after that, just catching the toe of his loafer on the altar carpet, and when he was supposed to sprinkle holy water, clanged the gold rod into the holy water bucket and tossed it at the casket. By then his prayers had become growly and incoherent. There were blobs and beads of holy water on the shiny wooden lid.

Men gathered near the casket. There was a shout of pain from the congregation, and more sobbing. Then we stood at the foot of the altar and watched the casket rolled nicely on silent rubber tires towards the doorway, where summer was blazing, and there were trees and traffic.

Back in the sacristy, Chicky doused the incense and took his cassock and surplice off quickly. He said he had to run an errand for his mother. He knew he had done something wrong, and yet his last glance at me said, "What did I tell you?"

Father Furty seemed bewildered, as if he were having difficulty phrasing a question. Finally he said, "This cabinet is empty. That's very strange."

It was the cabinet where the mass wine was kept; but Chicky

had hidden the only other bottle—before mass, when he was sneaking a drink.

"There's a bottle in here," I said, reaching into the cassock closet, where Chicky had put the bottle he had been fooling with.

"Ah, yes. I thought I was going mental for a minute there."

As he took it from me he saw the Mossberg.

"The hell's that?"

"Mossberg. Bolt action. Repeater."

He hoisted the bottle to see how much wine was in it.

"It's mine," I said. "It's not loaded."

He smiled and poured the wine into a glass—the wine went in with a flapping sound, bloop-bloop-bloop, purply blue with the light passing through it as if it were stained glass. And with a similar sort of sound, Father Furty drank it, emptying the glass and gasping as he had on the altar.

All this time he was smiling at my Mossberg, but he said nothing more. I felt stronger—I was strengthened by his under-standing; and from that moment, the period of time it took him to drink the wine, I trusted him.

As I pulled my surplice over my head I heard the sighs of Father Furty still digesting the wine. He was at the sideboard, among the vestments, in his suspenders, leaning on his elbows and belching softly.

Then he staggered back and sat down and sighed again—more satisfied gasps—and said, "Don't go, sonny."

I was trying to think how to get my Mossberg out of the sacristy.

Father Furty was still smiling, though his eyes were not quite focused on me. He looked very tired, sitting there with his hands on his knees. Then he grunted and started to get up.

"I'm going to need a hand," he said. "Now put that gun down and point me in the right direction." He was mumbling so softly he was hardly moving his lips. "Funerals are no fun," he said.

2.

Father Furty limped beside me, steadying himself by holding on to my shoulder with his right hand and sort of paddling with his left hand. I kept my mouth shut; I was his cane. His face was redder and it was as swollen as it had been when he had knelt in the sacristy and prayed for the conversion of Russia. I had set off worrying about my Mossberg in the cassock locker, and about meeting Tina—I was already late; and worrying too about everything Chicky had said, the sex talk. But Father Furty's big soft hand was holding down my worry and calming me—we were helping each other out of the sacristy.

Instead of going to the rectory which was only fifty feet away, we passed it, cut behind the church and down the parking lot, crossed Fulton—he was still limping: where were we going?—and headed towards a blue bungalow. It was called Holy Name House. I had never seen anyone enter or leave it, and I did not think it had any connection with Saint Ray's.

"Easy does it," Father Furty said. "We're almost there."

He seemed to be saying it to encourage me, because I was slowing down. Did he want me to follow him in? He was rather feeble, and I was sure there was something wrong with him. I did not imagine him to be drunk—after all, he had only downed one cruet of wine and less than half a bottle in the sacristy. It was not enough. No, he was sick—I was sure of that.

An "alkie" was a different kind of person altogether—the kind of crazy stinking bum that slept on Boston Common and mumbled as you passed by and always had a bottle in his hand. But even staggering and breathing hard, Father Furty had a look of understanding and authority—and I had the sense that he was both funny and friendly. He had seen my Mossberg and only smiled!

The porch of Holy Name House was screened-in and breezy but the interior of the house was very hot. The shades had been pulled down to cut the glaring sun, but the shadows looked just as hot as the bright patches. The day darkness of the house made it seem like a hospital ward, smelling of rubber tiles and clean paint and decaying flowers.

"This is where I'm staying," Father Furty said in an announcing way that I was sure he meant as a joke. "I can't exactly say I live here. Pretty spartan, eh?"

It was different from his mass voice, the one that had intoned the Pater Noster, and I liked it much better.

He had begun to slow down, though he was still leaning hard on my shoulder. And moving more carefully, he looked into each room as he passed it, poking the door open with his free hand and putting his head in.

"I guess we're going to be all right."

The house was empty, and the bright light of the summer day outside glaring through cracks in the venetian blinds only made it seem stranger and more deserted. I was not at all afraid to be alone here with him; I was actually glad that he had chosen me to help him home—I had never been here! And I was so absorbed in this task that I had forgotten my anxiety about meeting Tina and picking up my Mossberg.

Father Furty groaned.

"I could call a doctor," I said.

"What do doctors know about flat feet?" he said, staggering a little more.

We turned a corner. There was a mop stuck in a bucket in the middle of the corridor.

"Someone left that there for me to trip over," Father Furty said and halted and swayed sideways.

I moved the mop and the bucket, and Father Furty continued. When he came to the last room on the right he caught hold of the doorway and hung on to it and panted, as if he had reached the end of a long struggle and was too exhausted to feel victorious.

Just then the doorbell rang.

"Let Betty get it. That's Mrs. Flaherty. The housekeeper. Oh, bless us and save us." He was still panting.

The bell rang again, the same two tones, stupid and insistent. I left Father Furty hanging on the door to his room and went to answer it.

A big distorted silhouette, head and shoulders, showed in the frosted glass of the front door. It was the Pastor. He scowled at me horribly when I opened the door, then he unstuck his lips and lowered his head and leaned towards me.

"What are you doing here?"

His sharp question made me uneasy and defensive; I felt instantly guilty, and uncertain of the truth. I did not know why I was here.

"Mopping the floor," I said, because I could prove it, and I was not sure I could prove anything else.

"Alone?"

"I guess so."

"You guess so."

He always repeated what you said when he wanted to be sarcastic, and it never failed: every time he repeated something I had said it sounded stupid, and it gave me another reason for thinking I was dumb and that nothing good would ever happen to me in my life.

He repeated it again, making it stupider. I tried not to blink. Then I remembered my Mossberg in the sacristy, and I felt much worse and almost confessed to it.

"I'm looking for Father Furty," the Pastor said. "Have you seen him?"

The last time I had seen Father Furty he had been hanging on the door to his small room and panting, "Oh, bless us and save us." He wasn't well, he needed protection; I knew the Pastor to be very fierce.

But instead of saying no, I shook my head from side to side. I held to the innocent belief that it was less of a lie if you did not actually say the word.

I hesitated, waiting for the thunderbolt to strike me down in a heap at the Pastor's feet—and he would howl, "Liar!"

"Don't just stand there," he said. "The floor will never get mopped that way."

I looked at the scarred rubber tiles.

"Mop it for the glory of God," he said. "Dedicate that floor to Christ."

When he said that, the floor looked slightly different, less filthy, and it even felt different—more solid under my feet.

The Pastor did not say anything more. He turned and left, and I realized as he went down the path that I was terrified: the thunderbolt had just missed me.

"Who was it?" Father Furty said, not sounding very interested. He was sitting heavily in his chair beside the bed, his arms on the arms of the chair, and his hands hanging.

"The Pastor."

His hands closed and he sat up. "Where is he?"

"He went away. I told him you weren't here."

He settled into the chair again and smiled.

"That was a close one," he said. "But why did you fib?"

"I thought you wanted me to," I said, though I was very glad he had used the word "fib" and not "lie." "I thought you were sick."

"It's not fatal," he said. "What's your name, son?"

"Andrew Parent."

"Shut the door when you leave, Andy," he said. "God be with you."

Then he made a little sound, like a hiccup or a sob. I left him in the hot shadows of his small room.

Tina was walking away from the bus stop as I crossed the Fellsway and when I yelled at her to come back people turned around.

"Kid's got a gun," someone in front of the drugstore said.

Tina said, "Hey, I've been waiting for over an hour."

She wore a blue jersey and white shorts and sneakers and had two pony tails, one sticking out on each side of her head. Her lipstick was pink, the same shade as her small fingernails, and she fooled with a plastic bracelet, twisting it, as she looked at me.

"They're never going to let you on the bus with that thing. You could kill somebody."

But when the bus came, all the driver said was, "Take the bolt out of your rifle."

"It's out," I said, and showed it to him.

We sat in the rear seat, listening to the shudder of the tin flap on the back of the bus. We did not talk. Tina went on twisting her bracelet. Near Spot Pond we passed the New England Memorial Hospital.

"They're all Seventh-Day Adventists," I said, trying to make conversation. "They don't smoke or drink coffee. They're not allowed to dance. They can't eat meat. Hey, they can't even eat tunafish!"

Tina did not say anything. I became fearful.

"Hey, are you a Seventh-Day Adventist?"

She shook her head—she did not say the word "no," and so I wondered if she was lying. As far as I knew, she never went to any church, and I had no idea of her religion. I guessed that her mother was a protestant because she wasn't a Catholic. Not having a recognizable religion added to Tina's sexual attraction.

Beyond the hospital was a large gray building, like a court-house with magnificent windows—the waterworks, on Spot Pond; and then the woods closed in. We passed the zoo and went another mile on a road that had become flatter and nar-rower.

"They don't have sidewalks here," Tina said.

We were the last passengers on the bus. We got off at Whipple Avenue and walked down a dirt road, through some dusty pine-woods.

The sky had gone pale gray in the heat, and there was a sea gull overhead, very high and drifting slowly.

"I once saw a guy shooting at a sea gull with a thirty-thirty."

Tina squinted at me as if to say, "So what?"

"It's against the law to kill sea gulls," I said. "Because they eat garbage."

A dog tumbled from behind a boulder and barked at us in a stupid desperate way.

"You can protect me," Tina said.

"I'd never shoot a dog," I said. "I wouldn't even shoot a squirrel."

"What have you got a gun for, then?"

"To break bottles," I said.

We walked through the woods and entered the Sandpits. Part of it was a miniature desert—flat scrubby ground and dunes and cut-out slopes of sand. The quarry was the best place for target shooting; there the ledges were high and the sides funnel-shaped and cliffy, like Hell in Dante's *Inferno*—I had recently bought the paperback and found it unexpectedly pleasant to read—and full of stinks and sights. The Sandpits had the same angles as Dante's Hell, the same series of rocky shelves and long pits. But it was all empty, as if awaiting sinners.

I had sometimes seen sand trucks here, but there were none today. It was very hot. I could see small dusty birds and all around us was the screech of grasshoppers. Being there alone with Tina aroused me, and made me nervous, and gave me the idea of feeling her up—squeezing her breasts. The most I had ever done was kiss her, in the dark, at a party.

I arranged a row of beer bottles on a log and told Tina to stand behind me, and started to shoot.

At the first shot, Tina said, "Hey! My eardrums!"

She was startled and afraid. That gave me confidence. I kept firing and emptied the chamber, then filled the tube again.

"Your turn."

"I'm not touching that thing!"

"You're afraid," I said.

She said, "My mother would kill me if she knew."

There was something about the way she said it that made me want to impress her; and her fear steadied me, because I knew there was nothing dangerous about my Mossberg as long as you followed the rules. I broke six bottles apart—six shots—and then went back to where Tina was squatting under a sandy cliff.

"So you're afraid," I said.

Her elbows were pressed to her sides, and her face was squeezed between her hands. I sat beside her, holding the Mossberg.

"Huh? Afraid?" I pretended to adjust something on the gun and pushed closer to her.

She took a ball of Kleenex out of her sleeve and pinched it over her nose, and blew and twisted. The end of her nose was red.

"I'm not afraid."

I stood up and raised the Mossberg and fired three shots. Bits of the broken bottles were flung aside with puffs of dust.

Tina blew her nose again.

I put the gun down. I did not know what to say. I wanted to kiss her. I wanted to know what she was thinking, and I wanted it to be: Kiss me, touch me, do anything you like.

She said, "I'm going to have to wash my hair when I get back home."

While she was saying this I put my arms around her. She closed her eyes and let me kiss her, and she kept her eyes closed, so I kissed her again. Her lips softened and still she did not open her eyes. That encouraged me; it was as if by keeping her eyes shut she was being obedient.

Kissing her harder and closing my eyes I moved my hand onto the stiff cone of her breast, feeling the seams on her bra and rows and rows of stitches.

"Don't," she murmured into my lips.

When I tried it again she snatched my hand away hard and said, "Quit it!" That was tormenting: kissing her soft lips and at the same time feeling her quick fingers snagging my hand. Finally, I stopped kissing her, and then she opened her eyes.

"If I don't get home pretty soon my mother's going to yell at me."

But I felt frustrated, so I delayed by shooting the remainder of my cartridges, finishing the box of fifty, while she pouted into the mirror in her wallet and put on more pink lipstick.

On the bus she said, "Hey, what was the funeral like? Don't tell me!"

I thought a moment. She was teasing. But the funeral and its aftermath was very vivid to me, and it seemed to have a meaning I did not yet understand.

"The priest got sick."

"Oh, they're always getting sick," she said.

We did not speak about the kissing or my trying to feel her up. But we had never talked about it. The other time I had kissed her she had been worried about her history project—The Louisiana Purchase. Kissing was unmentionable; it was something we did with our eyes shut. If she had said something I would have been embarrassed. As it was, saying nothing, I felt older and experienced.

As for the other thing—touching her breast—I was relieved now that she hadn't let me, because I did not know how to tell it in confession.

That night at supper—meatloaf—my father said, "Where were you today?"

"Nowhere," I said.

"What did you do with yourself?"

"Nothing."

"He had a funeral this morning," Louie said.

Louie had stopped being an altar boy the previous year, when I started—later than most boys. He had coached me on my Latin.

"Charlie Plotke," my mother said.

Saying his name like that made it seem as though he were still alive; but I knew the body in the coffin was dead and empty—like

Hogan's uncle. I had imagined the pale dummy head in the bunches of ruffles and thought: Nothing—no one.

"Charlie was a daily communicant," my father said. He always used these Catholic expressions, like Shrovetide and Septuagesima and Lenten and Triduum and, always solemnly, ejaculation. He jerked his head at me and said, "Who celebrated mass?"

"Father Furty."

No one said anything.

"He's new," I said. "He's not from Boston."

Everyone looked at me.

"He says 'anny.' For aunty."

Now my parents began staring at each other in a querying way.

"He lives in Holy Name House," I said.

As soon as I had said that I sensed something go back and forth between my mother and father—over my head. It was like a beam of heat, but it was a certain pressure too, shooting right and then left, just touching the ends of the strands of hair in my crew cut. It was an inaudible buzz, and then a hovering bubble of suspense that broke and left a hum; and I realized that I had made it happen. What about that house? What about Father Furty?

"If you pray very hard," my mother had always said, "God might choose you to be a priest."

Before, I had always thought of the Pastor, or Father Ed Skerrit, and being a priest meant stepping out of life and standing on the sidelines—just waiting there with skinny ankles and a big Adam's apple, and red hands sticking out of a black cassock. But now "priest" meant Father Furty, and that did not seem bad. They seemed to know something about him, but they would not tell me—they never told me secrets.

"Two more funerals and you get a wedding," Louie said.

3.

My part-time job that summer was at Wright's Pond: locker-room attendant, three days a week. I sat at the entrance to the tin building next to the parking lot and read Dante's *Inferno*. When people said, "What are you reading that for?" I said, "Listen to this."

> *Between his legs all of his red guts hung*
> *With the heart, the lungs, the liver, the gallbladder,*
> *And the shrivelled sac that passes shit to the bung.*

Not many people used the locker room. It was dark, the lockers were rusty, the floor was always wet—I hosed it down in the morning and it stayed wet all day. I had the only key—one key for three hundred lockers. No job could have been easier. I sat in the sun, I played whist with the lifeguard and the policeman, I rowed the boat, I read Dante. Now and then someone said, "Hey, lockerboy," and I locked his clothes in a rusty box. That was the Men's; the Women's was attended by a fat tearful woman named Mrs. Boushay who used to sit with her arms folded and staring at her new Buick and saying, "I wish I'd never seen it."

There was a rumor that you could get polio at Wright's Pond. It had been closed the previous summer for a week, while they tested the water; and even this summer the inspector visited regularly and took a jar of water away. People said Wright's was dangerous and dirty, and laughed when I said I worked there. Tina's mother wouldn't let her go there, and in fact I had never seen Tina wearing a bathing suit. In some ways I was glad that Tina didn't swim at Wright's. We had a rough crowd, always swearing and yelling, and she was so pretty the boys would have teased her and splashed her.

I was at Wright's a few days after I had served the funeral—it was a Friday—when I saw the girl we called Magoo walking through the parking lot. She was with her younger brother, who was a smaller version of her. They had very white freckled skin, buck teeth, and limp brown hair that lay very flat against their heads. Their noses were pink and peeling, and their ankle socks were very dirty. They both walked in the same sulky way; they were pigeon-toed. Magoo was my age, the brother about ten or eleven, although he had the face of an old man.

The brother saw a dog he recognized and chased it down to the water, and seeing Magoo alone I went up to her, swinging the key on my finger.

"Want to go for a walk in the woods?"

She said, "I thought you're supposed to be working."

"After work," I said, but already I felt discouraged. She was fattish and pale, her fangy teeth gave her the look of someone who doesn't believe anything, she had a rubber band twisted around a bunch of her hair. I did not dislike her; I pitied her for being so ugly and was irritated by Tina, who was making me go through this.

"Just you and me," I said. "We'll walk around the pond."

She looked very bored and then opened her mouth slightly and let her teeth protrude. Then she said, "I have to mind my brother."

"He can stay here. He'll be all right."

She made a face. I hated her for forcing me to ask her these questions.

"Come on," I said. "It won't take long."

I was thinking of Chicky saying *three fingers*.

"Nah."

"Why not?"

"I don't want to, that's why."

I hated her deeply for a minute and wanted to say *Then why did you make out with Chicky?* She walked away and I hated Tina, and finally I hated myself. Then I was glad—saved: I hadn't sinned. I had come so close to committing a mortal sin.

The next day was Saturday—confession. As always, I went alone in the late afternoon, after worrying the whole day. I waited in the cool darkness at the back of the church behind a pillar, and watched closely, then chose the confessional with the shortest lines—the fewest people in the pews nearby—because that meant the priest was fast: if he was fast he was easy—he listened, asked one or two questions, and then gave absolution. The hard

priests gave severe lectures and sometimes sent you away without absolution. "You don't sound sorry enough—come back
some other time when you really mean it." The Pastor had once
said that to me, and I had avoided him after that—I learned to
spot his shoes showing beneath the curtain.

I had been rehearsing, mumbling to myself, all day: I was
more than apprehensive—I was afraid. It was the strangest day
of the week; I lost my body and became a soul—a stained soul.
I had no name or identity, I was merely the sum of my sins. I felt
close to Hell before confession, and afterwards not close to Heav-
en but happy, unafraid and oddly a little thinner and lighter.

The confessional in the corner behind the Seventh Station
had only a few people waiting to go in, so I walked over and slid
into the pew. I rehearsed my confession, pretending to pray.

A hoarse small-boy's voice came out of the confession box.
"And I yelled at my brother." I had never heard that sin before.

He left; another person entered and left; then it was my turn.
I pulled the curtain tight behind me and knelt with my forehead
against the plastic partition. It was a square hatch with riblike
corrugations and was strung like a tennis racket. Late afternoon
light shone through it, coloring it orange. I heard murmurs from
the other side, and then my hatch opened and I saw a priest's
bowed head behind the tennis strings. I had started whispering
very fast as soon as I heard the slap of the hatch.

"Bless me, Father. I confess to Almighty God, and to you,
Father, that I have sinned. My last confession was one week ago.
My sins are—lied, three times, disobeyed my parents, two times,
impure thoughts, seven times, committed acts of impurity alone,
three times, committed acts of impurity with other people, once,
and yelled at my brother four times. That is all, Father. For these
sins and other sins I cannot remember I am very sorry."

I stopped, breathless, with a hot neck and burning eyes my
mouth so dry my tongue had turned into a dead mouse, and I
trembled, fearing what was to come. I could only see the priest's
face as a shadow. His head remained bowed, as if sorrowing for
me, praying for my soul.

He went straight to the sin that mattered. They always did, no
matter where I inserted it.

"This act of impurity with other people," the priest said softly.
"Was it one person or several?"

"It was a girl, Father."

"A Catholic girl?"

"Her parents have a mixed marriage."

"What exactly did you do?"

"Touched her," I said and the mouse in my mouth became dustier.

"Where did you touch her?"

"Up the Sandpits, Father."

"On her body or her clothes?"

"Clothes, Father."

"Pannies?"

I paused on that word before answering.

"No," I said hoarsely. "On the chest." This did not seem as sinful as *on her breast.*

There was a short silence. I listened for a sigh, or any indication of what was coming—I dreaded more questions. But there were no more questions.

"You knew you were doing wrong," the priest said. "Somehow you were tempted by the devil. Remember, you can fool the devil by avoiding occasions of sin. If you sense an impure thought coming into your head, say a prayer to Our Lord and Savior Jesus Christ. For your penance, say three Our Fathers and ten Hail Marys. Now make a good Act of Contrition, son."

Eagerly, and grateful that it had gone so well, I said the Act of Contrition, while the priest prayed with me in Latin.

"Oh, my God," I said, "I am heartily sorry for having offended thee. I detest all my sins, because I dread the loss of Heaven and the pains of Hell—but most of all, because they offend Thee, my God—"

The priest was moving his right hand behind the shadowy panel in blessing. Already I was feeling lighter, happier, cleaner, thinner. I had stopped noticing the rock-hard kneeler and the smell of the plastic hatch on the partition.

"—who art all good," I went on, "and deserving of all my love. I firmly resolve, with the help of Thy grace, to confess my sins, to do penance, and to amend my life. Amen."

"Amen," the priest said, drawing it out a bit, making me linger.

I waited for him to slide the hatch shut. He seemed to be hesitating.

"God bless you," the priest said, and I bent closer to the tennis strings. He wasn't blessing me—he was scratching his ear. "Is that you, Andy?"

For a moment I could not speak. Then I managed to say, "Yes, Father."

I felt trapped. I had never heard my name spoken in a confessional.

"Thanks very much for guiding me back to the house the other day."

So it was Father Furty.

I never knew what to reply when someone thanked me. And in a confessional!

"That's okay, Father."

"Want to go for a boat ride next week? Say, Thursday?"

"If I'm not working."

"Swell. Stop by the house around noon. I'll provide lunch. Some of the Sodality will be there."

"Thank you, Father."

"It'll just be, oh, baloney sandwiches, potato salad, that kind of thing."

"Yes, Father." I wondered whether anyone in the pews outside could hear this.

"Now go do your penance."

When I left the confessional I tucked my head down and hurried to the communion rail, so that the people waiting to go into the box wouldn't recognize me. Even if they had not heard they knew that I had been in for a fairly long time, and that always indicated a sinner.

Father Furty was in shirtsleeves, a Hawaiian shirt, with his black priest's trousers and his squeaky loafers. He was loading his car in the parking lot of Holy Name House when I arrived—"I'm kind of glad you didn't bring your gun," he said—and then we set off for Boston Harbor.

"Did I mention that some of the Sodality are coming along?" he said. "They're a great crew."

The correct name was Our Lady's Sodality, but as it was all women I usually saw it written in my mind as Our Ladies' Sodality.

"Beautiful day for a boat ride," he said, and switched on the car radio.

My father's old Dodge did not have a radio. Father Furty's was a fancy-looking one, and I was grateful for it, because it took the place of conversation.

"Come-on-a my house," it played.

It seemed messy, sinful, human.

"What kind of a tie is that?"

I had worn it to impress him. I had bought it in a joke shop on School Street with my birthday money.

"Look," I said, and squeezed the battery pack in my pocket. "It lights up."

"It's fabulous," Father Furty said, and laughed—his face swelled up when he laughed, as it had when he prayed. "I want one of them for myself."

We moved slowly through the sunny streets, the car filling with heat, and the radio still going.

"I love this tune," Father Furty said. And he sang, "Skylark— Have you seen a valley green with spring?"

The radio replied, "Where my heart can go a-journeying—"

He was more tuneful singing this than he had been singing the high mass. I sat listening, enjoying it. We were in Charlestown, in heavy traffic, and the car was growing hotter as we crawled along, the metal and paint and even the yellow veiny plastic of the dashboard giving off the scorched odor of heat.

"What do you need a gun for?" he said suddenly.

"Breaking bottles. Target practice."

"And what sort of work do you do?"

This questioned embarrassed me, because he was continuing the conversation we had started in the confessional.

"Paper route?" he said, pronouncing it *rowt* instead of *root.*

"I'm a lockerboy, up at Wright's Pond."

"You brought a book, I see."

He twisted his head around in order to get a look at the paperback in my lap.

"Danny," he said. "Like it?"

I riffled the pages of the *Inferno,* not knowing what to say. I saw my underlining and stopped riffling. If he saw the ink he might ask me what I had marked, and why. *That passes shit to the bung,* one said, and another *Spews forth his stinking vomit.*

"Hell's shaped like a funnel," I said at last.

"That what Danny says?"

His hand went to the radio.

"It's a classic," he said, and then a song seemed to come out of his forehead, "Blue Skies—smiling at me—"

Afterwards he lit a cigarette and kept driving, exhaling through his clenched teeth. I loved the smell of tobacco smoke—cigarettes especially; it lingered in my face and found its way into my head and made me dizzy. Father Furty's brand was called "Fatima"—a yellow-orange pack with a woman's thin face on the front.

"I know what you're thinking," he said, seeing me staring at his pack of cigarettes on the seat. "No, it's not Our Lady."

Father Furty's boat was named *Speedbird*—white with blue trim, and before we cast off he shut his eyes and put his big hands together and said, "Let us pray."

His sleeves flapped, he looked gray and sorrowful, the wind stirred his short hair; but when his lips stopped moving and he blessed himself and said "Amen," he began to smile and seemed intensely happy.

He was tidy and fussy in a boat-owner's way, and he had the skipper's habit of coiling every line and clearing the decks and putting things away—"Let's stow this," he said, and he also said "starboard" and "port" and the rest of them.

What made all of this somewhat unusual were the women, six or so, from the Sodality—they were dressed as if for church, they wore hats and pearls, they carried black plastic handbags.

Father Furty said, "Stow the baloney sandwiches aft," and the women giggled. He said, "We'll keep the sodas fo'rard."

The women laughed even harder at this.

"We don't call it soda," I said, because I hated to see him being laughed at by those women. "We call it tonic."

"*Tonic?*" He laughed so hard he started to cough. Whenever he coughed he lit a cigarette, always a Fatima.

When we were under way, plowing through the harbor under a blue sky, Father Furty had a peaceful, distant look on his face. I was happy, too. On this boat everything seemed possible, the world was simpler and brighter, and Boston was not a hot dirty city but a much bigger place, rising out of the sea—with a huge and busy harbor, and islands; it was visited by vast ships. I saw that the city was also the water around it—so it was freer and had more space.

Father Furty said, "There are so many islands in this harbor—that's another reason you get so many strange currents running around here."

I thought he was going to say more. Any other priest would have. But Father Furty did not say of the islands and the currents *They're like life.* They were no more than they seemed; they represented only themselves—which was plenty. They did not need any other significance.

He said you had to be careful here, what with all the shipping, but that there was nothing to be afraid of.

"She's a sturdy boat. She's all mahogany." That made him more human too, calling the boat *she.*

The Sodality women had also brought food; and it was clear that there was too much of it. Each woman had a basket or a bowl with salad or chicken or a homemade cake or cookies. Mrs. DePalma, Chicky's mother, had a parcel of cold cuts and pickles which she arranged in a fan on a plate. Mrs. Prezioso had stuffed peppers. Mrs. Corrigan had tunafish casserole, and on the top, she said proudly, instead of crumbs she had sprinkled crushed potato chips. Mrs. Palumbo brought celery sticks with cream cheese pressed into the grooves.

"From my own garden," Mrs. Prezioso said, and fed a stuffed pepper to Father Furty.

The other women urged him to have a bite of their food. They did not eat anything themselves—they said they weren't hungry.

Father Furty said, "Aren't I a lucky guy?"

He said it as if he really meant it, and he was chewing something the whole time. The women stayed in or near the cabin, admiring him, as he steered *Speedbird* through the outer harbor.

"Shipping lanes," he said. "Very tricky."

He inhaled smoke, drank some Moxie and then exhaled the smoke. "See. I keep it in my lungs, so I can swallow." He tried to blow smoke rings at Mrs. Palumbo's request, but couldn't. "Too much wind," he said.

The women giggled when he did something funny, and they screamed when the spray flew up and wet them. They wore good shoes, but tottered on them. They wet their blouses, and Mrs. Corrigan got spray on her hat and the salt dried and sparkled on her veil. They offered to help, but Father Furty would not let them.

"This is my first mate," he said, meaning me. "His tie lights up." He made me flash the bulbs for them. "Andy, get me my other chart of the harbor."

The women did not like this, I could tell, and they resented my being there. Several times I was in the cabin, and Mrs. Hogan or Mrs. DuCane pushed me aside and said, "Show me how to steer, Father!"

Each time I backed up and started climbing the ladder, but before I took two steps I heard Father Furty's voice.

"Stick around, Andy. You're my right-hand man."

I could sense waves of anger coming at me from the women, like an odor in wiggly lines.

"He's reading Danny," Father Furty said.

They didn't care. They showed no interest at all in my book.

We moored the boat for a while near an island and during a lull in the conversation, Mrs. DuCane said, "Tell us about the sacrifice of the mass, Father. It's so complicated."

"It's simple," he said. "It's the body and blood of Christ. Real flesh. Real blood. It's not bread and wine."

He said "wine" hungrily, making it a round ripe word, and I remembered him drinking it out of the chalice in a glad thirsty way.

The women sat in a circle around him, feeding him and protesting that they weren't hungry. He looked like a king on vacation, with some of his subjects.

On the way back he said, "Next time we'll do some swimming."

"Can I bring a friend?"

He said, "Sure. Swell. As long as it's not that other altar boy. He's lethal."

4.

God was always glaring at me out of a hot sky. He was as pitiless and enigmatic as most of the adults I knew—they all spoke for Him anyway—and He said no just as often. But after that boat trip, when my mother said, "God might choose you to be a priest," it did not seem like the end of the world. It was God's choice, not mine, yet if He chose me I could be a priest like Father Furty—with a car radio, and a speedboat, and baggy pants, and a pack of Fatima cigarettes in my shirt pocket.

On Father Furty's boat, everything had seemed possible: being a priest, getting married, going to college, earning money, having a future—it would all unroll. Until then, my feelings had been uncertain and whenever I became hopeful and looked ahead, the sky blazed and I thought: It will never happen. The boat made everything larger and different—Boston was bigger, the Sodality seemed truly sillier, the summer was breezier, I felt older and useful. I was proud to know this man. Sometimes I forgot he was a priest!

Knowing him made knowing Tina easier, though I could not tell exactly why. Things seemed less urgent. I wanted to touch her, but I could wait. I did not feel as if I had to hide—anyway, what was there to hide? I stopped sneaking and stopped trying to think of ways of impressing her. A month ago I had pictured us at the Sandpits and I was in the open, wearing my sunglasses, blasting bottles with my Mossberg, and Tina was waiting for me in the shade, so thrilled by my marksmanship she wanted me to hold her and squeeze her. Now that picture seemed a little silly. We took walks instead.

On one of these walks in Boston we went to the Public Gardens—rode in the Swan Boats, strolled around the pond. Tina didn't know that although the Common was right across the street, the laws were different. You could lie on the grass on the Common—or even sleep on it all night—and have picnics and parties and baseball games and do whatever you liked. In the Public Gardens everything was forbidden—no picnics, no games, no sleeping.

"You can pick flowers on the Common," I said.

"That's why there's no flowers to pick," Tina said.

But people hugged and kissed on the grass of the Common. Tina said that because of the laws the Public Gardens were pretty and the Common was a mess.

"That's a funny thing for a non-Catholic to say," I said. "I thought only Catholics worried about laws!"

There were often speakers on the Common—the black man telling how he had found Jesus; the little group with flags from the Socialist Party; the vegetarian; the ranter who said he was from the mental hospital in Mattapan; the couple from the Anti-Vivisection Society. Each speaker attracted a handful of listeners and a few hecklers.

"Why don't you go back to Russia!"

"Hey, you think they should use people instead of rats?"

I used to stand and listen to the shouts—back and forth—and I wondered whether anyone meant what he said.

That day, with Tina, there was a new group, all in black, men and women.

"They're priests and nuns," Tina said.

I said no, priests and nuns never ranted on the Common—because privately I thought all the speakers on the Common were a little crazy. This group was dressed as priests and nuns, and yet I did not believe they were the real thing.

The speaker was a short, gray-faced man in a stiff dog-collar. His hair was thick on top of his head and he was very angry—yelling so loud that the listeners stepped away and made room for him.

"Our Lord Jesus shed His holy blood and died for our sins!" he yelled. He twisted his face and reached out with his hand. "And yet there are those among you who won't enter His church to be saved!" He seemed to be looking straight at me when he shouted, "Unless you enter that church and cling to the Catholic faith you are damned for all eternity—you will burn!"

I stepped back, and someone said to the priest, "Wait a minute—do you mean—?"

"I'm not afraid to tell you the truth," the priest said. "That's why I can stand here and tell you that Harvard College and the whole diocese of Boston are being strangled by Jews, who—"

Someone said, "Don't listen to him."

"—robbing them blind and crippling them. Collecting money! Promising salvation and offering institutionalized atheism. They are selling damnation! One of the leaders of the Jew-Communist conspiracy is Albert Einstein—yes, the same Albert Einstein. But there are others—"

He named six or seven people, practically choking as he said their names, and some of the audience laughed and others protested. In between attacking Jews and communists and Russians, he talked about Jesus, the Catholic Church, and how everyone who stood aside was going to burn in Hell.

It was bad when he shouted but worse when he whispered. He was popeyed, and at the end of his speech he made threats against the government and the Archbishop. He was a very ordinary-looking man, but when he spoke his face changed and became ugly and fierce. I would have been frightened except that the rest of the people there either laughed or shouted at him—they weren't afraid.

Then he blessed himself and said a loud prayer, and a woman beside Tina joined in, repeating the prayer.

"Come back, Father Feeney!" a man called out.

The priest did not reply. He stepped off his wooden box and disappeared in the middle of the priests and nuns.

The nuns went through the crowd with felt-lined plates collecting money. Even though I was fifteen years old I was struck by how young the nuns were, and in spite of their black cloaks and stiff headdresses, how attractive they were—what pretty faces. All the nuns I knew were ferocious and elderly, with huge bonnets that looked like starched sea gulls on their heads. But these were like the sort of veiled muslim women I had seen in harem pictures, with small white hands and dark eyes.

After the collection, one of the priests lifted a blue silk banner of the Virgin Mary and they all set off in a procession, singing.

No one followed them, but I could sense that they had left a certain atmosphere in the little crowd of onlookers, as if their dust was still sifting down on us. The people were quiet and serious; it had all been bluff and bluster before, but perhaps now they were afraid.

I had heard the notorious name of Father Feeney before, but this was the first time I had seen him. He didn't come up to my expectations—he looked very ordinary, pasty and small. But I was excited by his shrill voice, by the gangster faces of his priests and by the beauty of his nuns, begging with their collection plates.

Tina had not said a word. At first I thought she was afraid of Father Feeney; then I realized that she was afraid of me. I kept asking her what was wrong, and she kept saying nothing, nothing. When we were alone, walking through the Common to Tremont Street, Tina started to cry.

"That guy scared me," she said, and sniffled.

I said he had not scared me, or made me believe anything. I had been scared, but I had also been thrilled by his anger and conviction.

"If I tell you something will you promise not to tell anyone? Will you swear?"

I said God could strike me dead if I blabbed a word.

Tina scuffed the sidewalk and said, "My mother's Jewish."

I was startled—I couldn't hide it.

"You're going to tell!" she said. She had seen the excitement on my face.

"No, no," I said.

"I mean, she's Russian," Tina said.

Did she think that would calm me? Being Russian seemed worse than Jewish, and her mother was both!

I said, "Well, we're French. Our name's actually Perron— that's the way you're supposed to say it."

But the blood was beating in my head and making my eyes throb. It was a wonderful secret. If Tina had been a Catholic I might have given up on her. She was half Jewish—it didn't matter what the other half was. This revelation made her seem pagan and possible. Nothing was a sin to her. But she couldn't help it—she was already damned.

At the altar boy meeting in the sacristy a few days later, the Pastor read out the roster for the following week's mass list. I had three seven o'clocks and another funeral—Mr. Kenway, from Brogan Road. I was serving all of them alone—that was strange. I turned to Chicky DePalma to get his reaction, but he was whispering to an altar boy named Slupski.

"She stuck a light bulb up her pussy, I'm telling you," Chicky said.

"Did it light up?" Slupski said.

"I don't want to see anyone wearing sneakers on the altar," the Pastor was saying. His mouth hung open as he scrutinized us, and it made him seem very temperamental and impatient, like a big dog on a hot day. "I want to see clean faces and hands. No dungarees, no whispering. None of this Elvin Presley stuff."

It was a warm summer night, with yellow moths flattened against the sacristy screens, and we sat and sweated and listened to the Pastor.

"What's so funny, Bazzoli?" he said suddenly.

"Nothing, Father," Bazzoli said and began swallowing his smile with difficulty, as though sipping it.

The rest of us knew why he had been smiling: "Elvin" Presley. Nothing undermined a warning quicker than a mispronunciation.

The Pastor resumed—he repeated himself, he criticized us some more—and then he said, "Get on your knees and pray for forgiveness."

My mind had wandered. I had been thinking of Tina Spector and *Did it light up?* I had not heard the reason we were praying for forgiveness, but still I prayed as hard as I could.

"Name of the Father, and the Son, and the Holy Ghost," he said, making a slow sign of the cross with his stiff fingers. "You're all dismissed except Andrew Parent."

The altar boys left quickly, noisily, scraping their chairs, and some of them smirking at me.

The Pastor did not say anything immediately. He stared at me, he tortured me with the slow contemptuous heat of his colorless eyes, he let me suffer.

"Why were you smiling?"

I had been thinking about Tina—he had guessed at that: it had been plain on my face. I frowned in order to stiffen my expression and make it serious.

"Do you think immorality is funny?"

"No, Father."

He let his mouth hang open and he panted at me in his doglike way. Then he said, "Immorality is a mortal sin. Your body is a temple of the Holy Ghost—"

He had known exactly what I had been thinking.

"—If you have impure thoughts you defile that temple. It's as if you've smeared mud and filth on a lovely white sheet that your mother's just washed. That's nothing to smile about!"

"I wasn't smiling, Father."

He winced: he was insulted that I had replied to him—that I had spoken at all.

"Backtalk," he said sourly.

"I was just thinking, Father," I said, and there was a terrible twanging in my head. I was still kneeling, with my face upturned to the Pastor.

"Smart, aren't you," he said. "You're very bold"—bold was one of the worst things anyone could be. "I don't know where you get it from. Your mother and dad are good kind people. Your brother Louie was an excellent altar boy—always well-behaved and very clean-cut. But you just stare and smile, bold as brass."

It was always disastrous for me when someone described the expression on my face, and it was—though I cannot explain why—a very common occurrence. As soon as the person said it, I assumed that expression—their saying it made me guilty and silenced me. Now I was ashamed, but I was not offended: I expected to be criticized—I knew I deserved it for my impure thoughts.

I dropped my gaze and saw, looking behind me in deep embarrassment, that I was wearing sneakers. Another rule broken—and they were very torn and dirty. I had worked the morning shift at Wright's and spent the afternoon at the Sandpits. Alone, among the steep slopes and ledges and secret places, I had thought intensely of Tina. Isolated places always gave me impure thoughts and anyway I had begun to think of the Sandpits as Hell—like the great naked teasing Hell in Dante.

"What's that in your back pocket?"

I pulled it out and offered it.

"A book, Father."

Instead of taking it from me, he moved his hands behind his back and left me holding it in the air. He twisted his head around to read the title.

"Dante. *The Inferno.*"

"It's about Hell," I said. "And different types of punishments, for the various sinners. It's all separate circles."

He narrowed his eyes at me and said severely, "Does your mother know you're reading it?"

"I think so, Father."

"He thinks so."

But he said no more for a moment, and I had the feeling that he was at a loss for words.

"Kneel up straight," he said sharply.

I had let my bum rest against my heels. I straightened and raised my hands prayerfully under my chin.

"I've given you another funeral," he said, and when I did not respond he added, "Don't you know how to say thank you?"

"Yes, Father. Thank you, Father."

"One more funeral and you'll have earned yourself a wedding."

Ah, that was why he wanted to be thanked—for the wedding that lay ahead, the short happy service, the white roll of cloth down the center aisle, the kiss, the confetti afterwards, the two dollars.

"And three early masses. Make sure you're on time. And no sneakers."

"Yes, Father."

"That's all. Now pray for forgiveness. Pray for your immortal soul."

"I was going to ask a question, Father."

He winced again and looked at me with hatred. *Bold as brass,* he was thinking. *Backtalk!* I wanted to apologize and tell him I couldn't help it.

He nodded—twitched once—for me to continue.

"Is Father Feeney a real priest, Father? I heard him speaking on the Common."

The Pastor chewed his tongue for a moment, and then said, "Father Feeney received the sacrament of Holy Orders. That can never be taken away, even though he is not a Jesuit anymore, nor a Harvard chaplain. He still celebrates holy mass—it is his sacred duty."

"But what about his sermons? I was just wondering."

"Only Almighty God knows the answer to that," the Pastor said, and then he added, "Father Feeney had a very difficult time. He was a brilliant man, and a lot of what he says makes sense," as if the Pastor knew a little of what Almighty God might say.

"Thank you, Father."

"And did your mother know you were hanging around Boston Common?"

"No, Father."

"Well!" he said triumphantly, and the matter was settled. "Now pray!"

Yet I was still not satisfied. At the first of my three seven o'clocks I asked Father Furty the same question.

"Him!" he said, waking up. "Feeney!" And out of the side of his mouth, "He's a crackpot!"

It was funny hearing him say this with all his vestments on. I said, "I sometimes think I'm a crackpot."

"Oh, no. You're an ace, Andy. I like you. We're intimate friends."

This made me beam eagerly, and perhaps he guessed that I wanted to know more. Yet I was angry with myself for noticing that he had said *innimit.*

"You fibbed for me. You're a great altar boy. You're bashful. And I love the way you told me how much your gun cost you."

"Forty dollars?"

"Fotty dawlas," he said. He thought I talked funny, too!

5.

That was the strangest thing about the altar boy roster—all my masses were being said by Father Furty, and they were all early, and I was the only server. I could not explain it, but I was glad about it. It meant that I would be on time for the morning shift at Wright's Pond, and my afternoons would be free—to shoot bottles at the Sandpits, or to see Tina. And there was the bonus of the funeral. I had not wanted to appear too grateful for fear of seeming too greedy; but I looked forward to another funeral, and finally a wedding.

All this also meant that I would be seeing Father Furty. I had begun to depend on him, not just seeing him but confessing my sins to him. These days I was much more truthful in the confessional and felt better afterwards. I had stopped feeling that I was probably going to Hell, and I sensed that I would most likely end up in Purgatory. The punishment in Purgatory was that you did not see God. It was a punishment I felt I could bear, and in fact on some days I was relieved by the prospect that I would not be seeing God in Purgatory; I had so often felt punished—ashamed and afraid—in the glare of God's sight.

This change in my mood I attributed to Father Furty. He made me feel I could face things. I was worthwhile and mature. Sometimes I was funny! He could be stern in the confessional, but he criticized the sin and made me see how it was avoidable. He always left me with hope, and just as he had surprised me by telling me I was his friend, he urged me at confession to pray for him.

I hoped he was my intimate friend, as he had claimed. He had the sort of good-humored friendliness that sometimes seems to hide real feeling—he was simply too generous and openhearted and gentle a man to reveal his doubts. He was never unkind or offhand; I loved him for that, but it prevented me from knowing him well. I must have disappointed him often; but if so he had never let me know it. He always made it seem as though I were doing him the favors, not the other way around.

"Sorry to get you up so early," he said when he came into the sacristy on those mornings for the seven o'clock mass. He had puffy eyes and looked as though he had not slept. He sometimes looked punished, like a prisoner serving time, which was why his cheery nature was so surprising.

"What shall we pray for?" he said, before he began putting on his vestments.

I said, "The conversion of Russia?"

"I'm beginning to think that's something we might leave to Saint Jude," Father Furty said, and winked at me. "Let's try for something we might verify fairly soon—a lovely day and good weather this weekend."

He often looked frail. He was one of those people whose physical appearance is different morning and evening. He altered throughout the day, starting out weak and trembling. He strengthened and grew pinker as the hours passed. By late afternoon he was healthy and talkative. His hands were steady. The next morning he was small and trembly again.

"Got to see the dentist today," he said after the first seven o'clock. "I've always been plagued with dental problems."

Dennist, he said; and *dennal.* Pronounced that way they did not sound quite so bad to me.

"Still reading Danny," he said before we entered the church another day.

I had the paperback in my back pocket. I suppose he saw the bulge in my cassock.

"I'm up to Panders and Seducers," I said.

"Abandon hope, all ye who enter here," he said.

When I turned around, he winked at me.

"Pull the chain," he said, and out we went, on the bell.

Intro-eebo ad-ahltaree-dayee ah-dayum-kwee-lah-teefeekat yoo-ven too-tem mayum.

Early mass on a weekday was restful—very few people in the congregation, a half a dozen or so, scattered here and there, just shadows and occasionally a groan. They were anonymous people, they never sat in the front pews, they took communion but always with their faces averted. They knelt and prayed with their heads bowed.

"Not many people this morning," I said one day after mass, just making conversation.

Father Furty said, "Enough of them to show us the way."

He implied that he needed them—and all the other priests I had known seemed to imply the reverse of that: You need us! The Pastor's line was usually: I'm leaving you sinners behind!

At early mass there was no sermon. Father Furty whispered the prayers, the few people in the congregation groveled and muttered in the humblest way, and I breathed the responses.

Soorsum corda.

Habeymoos a Dominoom.

At the congregation there was only the briefest tinkle of cruets and the lightest ring of bells. It was all muffled and peaceful, but also like a secret ritual. I always remembered what Father Furty had said on his boat: "Real flesh, real blood."

I kept the wine cruet in one hand, the water in the other: he took a drop of each, and they ran down the inside of the gold chalice like two tears.

When he offered the host and then leaned over the altar to say, "This is my body," he closed his eyes and became so still that it sometimes seemed as though he had died.

He was always saying, "Stick around—what's the hurry?" And the second morning he took me to Holy Name House for breakfast. There he introduced me to Father Hanratty and Father Flynn, who were very skinny—Adam's apples, popping eyes, narrow ankles—and they were full of talk.

"More toast, Betty," Father Hanratty said to Mrs. Flaherty. "Father Furty tells us you've got a great appetite. But what does he know about anything? He's a foreigner!"

Father Furty was sipping coffee and smoking his first Fatima of the day.

"He's from New Jersey," Father Flynn said.

"God's country," Father Furty said.

"Ah, you reminded me!" Father Flynn said, and laughed and shook his finger in excitement. "The Boss received a postcard yesterday from his brother in Ireland—you'll never guess the message!"

"Don't tell me you read it," Father Hanratty said, but he was more interested than angry.

"If you weren't meant to read postcards they'd be in envelopes."

Father Furty said, "You're keeping us in suspense."

"Postmark, Cork. Message, 'Greetings from the land of faith.' I swear it! Have you ever heard such a thing?"

Father Furty laughed, but gently—it was still early morning and he was not yet himself. He said, "That's enough. You'll confuse the boy." He turned to me. "You won't get any intellectual stimulation here, son. They've never read Danny. Father Flynn here reads the racing sheets, while Father Hanratty struggles with the *Boston Globe*. And of course they read the Boss's postcards."

"And what do you read, Billy?" Father Flynn said.

"Eldridge's Tide and Pilot Tables," Father Furty said. "And I see that High Water in the harbor this Saturday is at the civilized hour of twelve noon. You'll be coming along, won't you, Andy?"

My mouth was full of toast, but I nodded eagerly yes.

We sat, and I listened to their banter, and I was the more excited for not understanding it, because I was so flattered to be included. I had the strong impression from their comedy, which was always a little forced and desperate, that they were outcasts, and that I was one of them. So at last I had a place at Saint Ray's.

"Too bad you have to go," Father Furty said, when I got up to head for the pond.

He sounded as if he meant it!

"Why not serve for me tomorrow?"

It was the only day I didn't have a mass.

"I'll add your name," he said. "Listen, I'd appreciate it!"

That made it a full week of serving early masses, but I began to see a point in the routine. Instead of the masses being an interruption, the other hours in the day seemed an interruption; the masses were regular, dignified, austere and orderly on those cool bright summer mornings: the muffled church, the few people in the pews, the whispered prayers, the two tearlike droplets in the chalice; four masses, and then my second funeral.

We went to an afternoon movie, Tina and I, because I wanted to touch her. It was *All That Heaven Allows,* with Rock Hudson and Jane Wyman, and we held hands until they were so hot and sticky I was glad to let go. That year the girls wore several petticoats that filled their skirts, and Tina must have been wearing two or three because they crunched in the narrow movie-seat, I suppose it was the starch, and aroused me. I reached for her leg but her hand was there already and snatched mine away. I put my arm around her and kept it there until it went to sleep, and when I yanked it back, we knocked our heads together. The movie ended at five-thirty and we went out and were blinded by the sun on Salem Street. I had a headache, my feet were tingly from sitting. We bought ice-cream cones at Brigham's, then I went home and had meatloaf. It was always meatloaf. I was glad that Tina had not let me touch her: there was nothing to confess except the impure thought. She had saved me.

"You've been smoking," my mother said, putting her face against my hair and sniffing hard.

I denied it—it must have been the musty stink at the Square Theater.

"Where have you been?"

"After work I went to the library."

Wasting a glorious day in God's sunshine! she would have said if I had been to a movie. *And where did you get the money?* If I had told her I had gone with a girl she would have squinted at me and said *Why?* And she would have kept asking why until I admitted that it was a waste of money, a waste of time, and very foolish—*And who is this girl?*

I never dared to give the truthful answers to her questions. I lied and pretended I was telling her the truth. She glared at me like God and pretended she believed me. But she knew.

"I was looking up some information on Dante—and seeing if they had the other two books."

Louie said, "I don't believe you're really reading that book."

"Test me!" I said, and put the paperback on the table. The cover was cracked and peeling from being stuffed into my back pocket. It had the mangled look of having been read.

No one said anything—perhaps I had been too shrill. But after all my lies they had chosen to challenge me when I was actually telling the truth!

"It's not fire at the bottom of Hell, you know," I said, because out of curiosity—and fear—I had skipped ahead in order to know the worst. I had read the last three cantos. "It's ice, it's all ice—murderers are frozen in it. It's not fire!"

They were a little impressed and a little apologetic, and I felt all the more guilty about having lied about the library.

My second funeral, Mr. Kenway's, was eerie. I found myself thinking: One more and I get a wedding—and I warned myself not to think it.

"I didn't know he was a Catholic," my mother said. "He never went to mass."

I took it that he might not have died in a state of grace. He had been old and alone. He had no family. The pallbearers were from Gaffey's Funeral Home—I could tell by their gray gloves and black coats and pin-stripe trousers. They had brought the coffin and were waiting to take it away, to Oak Grove.

There were no tears, no sobs, the church was almost empty. I recognized the other people as those who went to most of the services—early mass, the Novenas, the Stations, and the funerals of people they didn't know. Yet that day Saint Ray's was sadder than if every pew had been filled with weeping, honking relatives. Father Furty and I were the chief mourners, and were not mourning. When the coffin bumped over the threshold, the sound rang throughout the church, like a loud *ouch!* Then the pitiful clatter of the wheels, and the organ groaning into the emptiness.

Father Furty seemed frightened. He was very silent and trembling in his midmorning frailty; his shoes squeaked in a way I associated with timidity—most of his moods were revealed by the different squeaks of his shoes.

Once again I was the only altar boy. In the still church, with the solitary coffin, I went through the routine and noticed how Father Furty's hands trembled. He was very unsteady and walked in a toppling way. When he came over for water and wine his chalice rattled against my cruet of wine. I was in the habit of only dispensing a drop, and though he seemed to be waiting for more—clank, clank—I mechanically resisted tipping the cruet. He got his two drops and went to the tabernacle, still trembling.

It was a hot day, but he was perspiring more than usual, and his white sleeves and his collar were limp and dark with dampness, his wet hair shone in prickly points on his forehead and his neck. (My own plastic collar was slippery with sweat and kept springing out of its button and clamping itself over my shoulder.)

Father Furty's voice quavered when he spoke directly to the coffin in Latin. He incensed it, and holy-watered it, and blessed it; but still it had a sad unpolished look and I kept thinking that Mr. Kenway's soul might be in Bolgia Five of the Inferno, among the Grafters and Demons.

The men from Gaffey's got up and rolled the coffin down the aisle towards the blazing doorway, and then the church was empty and smelling sadly of vigil lights and flowers.

"There's nothing to be afraid of," Father Furty said, when we were in the sacristy.

Was he talking to himself? He was removing his vestments, kissing each one and mumbling a prayer as he took it off and folded it. He did this slowly, in a resigned way, and I felt like a savage, yanking my surplice over my head and tearing open the snaps—so much easier than buttons—on my cassock.

"Are you going up to the pond?"

"Yes, Father. And I'm late."

"In that case, I'll give you a ride."

"I'm not *that* late."

He raised his hand. It was a characteristic gesture. It meant: No problem.

He played his car radio the whole way, and at the pond he insisted on buying me a hot dog and a root beer. He said the beach looked very nice, and bought himself another lemonade. I introduced him to the policeman and the lifeguard and the matron of the girls' locker room, Mrs. Boushay. "That's my Buick," she told him. "I wish I'd never seen it." He didn't call himself Father Furty. He stuck out his hand and said, "Bill Furty."

"You've got a nice crowd here," he said to the policeman, and he talked to the lifeguard about Fort Dix, New Jersey, where he was about to be stationed.

I hoped that they would not bring up the subject of people getting polio at the pond, and they didn't.

Father Furty stood in his civilian clothes and gazed across the murky pond, seeming not to notice the kids in their bathing suits—swimming, splashing, running, howling, hanging on the floats, throwing sand.

He said, "If I go in, will you watch me?"

I must have looked bewildered. I did not want to ask him why, but he sensed the question.

He said, "Because I can't swim."

He changed in the locker room—I gave him a locker—and he returned to the beach. He did not swim. He waded in and lay back and floated for a moment; and then he stood up and the water streamed down his body and his black trunks. It wasn't swimming, and it wasn't a dip. It was more like a baptism.

"A lot of fishermen don't know how to swim. It's deliberate. There's less agony if their boat sinks. They just go down with it. That's the way I'd want it."

His eyes glittered as he spoke. He looked happy again, and a little healthier—it was past noon.

"Oh, I'm just wasting your time," he said.

I laughed at the way he put it—wasting my time!

When he was gone, I told the lifeguard and the policeman he was a priest. They said, "Cut the crap, Andy."

It made me admire Father Furty all the more to think they did not believe me.

6.

Father Furty had a whiskery off-duty look, and his Hawaiian shirt flapping over his black priest's trousers, and the way his loafers squeaked today, made him seem relaxed and thankful. A hot day in this part of Boston—we were just getting out of his Chevy on Atlantic Avenue—was made hotter by the soft tar bubbling around the cobblestones, the dazzle of car chrome in traffic, and the smell of red bricks and gasoline. *Speedbird* was tied up at Long Wharf, among the fishing boats and other cabin cruisers. The high sun was smacking and jangling the water.

My mother had said, "Who'll be on the boat with you?"

I didn't mention Tina. I had told her that I did not know, which was a good thing, because there were ten ladies from the Sodality, and if my mother had known she would have felt left out.

They wore dresses and blouses and hats and big blue clumping shoes, as they had before. Besides Mrs. DuCane, Mrs. Corrigan, Mrs. Prezioso, Mrs. DePalma and Mrs. Hogan, with the same picnic dishes they had brought on the last outing, there was Mrs. Palumbo with Swedish meatballs, Mrs. Bazzoli with a basin of coleslaw, Mrs. Skerry with a fruit basket and a loaf of Wonder bread, Mrs. Hickey with a homemade chocolate cake, and Mrs. Cannastra with two bottles of purple liquid that looked like Kool-Aid.

Mrs. DuCane asked what it was.

"Bug juice," said Mrs. Cannastra.

"Poor Edda Palumbo," Mrs. Hickey said. "God love her. She lost her husband to a tumor."

"What's your name, honey?" Mrs. Hogan said.

"Tina Spector."

"You got a mother here?" Mrs. Hogan was confused.

Tina just shook her head and blushed.

"Give me a hand separating these cheese slices." And Mrs. Hogan showed her bony teeth. "You like Velveeta, dear?"

Tina was recruited: she became one of the women, and because she was there I noticed how smooth and pink her skin was, and how the rest of the women were furry-faced, and had downy cheeks, and some had bristles.

I had not mentioned Tina to my mother. She knew Tina was a non-Catholic; she would have misunderstood and been suspicious, and after a while she would have resented it and blamed me and said, "There are so many Catholic girls."

Never mind religion, I didn't even think of Tina as a girl. She was a desperate feeling in me that made my heart gasp and my throat contract: I loved her.

Meanwhile, Father Furty was saying out loud that he hoped we would have a safe trip and good weather, and then he blessed himself and I realized that he had been praying.

"Cast off," he said next, and directed me to untie the lines from the cleats on the dockside.

The Sodality ladies all shrieked and laughed as we started away, like small girls. Tina was not among them; she stood in the shadow of the cabin, looking old and sick with worry.

"What if my mother finds out?" she had said before we boarded. "What if the Father asks me if I'm a Catholic?"

"We'll ad-lib," I said.

It was a Furty expression.

I was very happy. That was so rare. I had known contentment but until then not this kind of happiness. And what was rarer—I knew I was happy.

I had been raised to believe that I was bad, that most of what I did was bad, that the things I wanted were bad for me. It was not an accusation—no one barked about my badness. It was rather an interminable whisper of suggestion that I was weak and sinful, and the sense that I was always wrong. And it seemed I could never win. It was *Hurry up!* and then *Don't run!* It was *Eat!* and then *Don't eat so fast!* It was *Speak up!* and then *Don't shout!*

What have you been doing? could only be answered truthfully in one way: *Being bad.* There was something natural and unavoidable about being bad. Being hungry was bad, going to the movies was bad, sitting and doing nothing was bad, being happy was bad; and bad turned easily into evil.

On Father Furty's *Speedbird* I had the unusual feeling that I was not doing something bad, and that to me was pure joy. It was Father Furty's influence, the way he smiled at Tina and welcomed us on board. He had a graceful way of implying that we were helping him: we were doing him a favor by being with him, and he was depending on us rather than the other way around. But I was also happy because Father Furty knew me. I had confessed to him, and though of course he would never break the seal of the confessional, he had seen my heart, and it was not the messy and sometimes imaginary bad that I was nagged about at home. No, he knew my sins and had absolved them, so it was Father Furty who was responsible for my being in a state of grace.

"Is that one of them two-way radios?" Mrs. Bazzoli said.

"Nope. That's a one-way radio."

She said, "Are you sure?"

Father Furty made a face. "Questions, questions," he said. He might have been joking or angry: it was impossible to tell. " 'Are you sure?' 'Do you really mean it?' Questions like that and incessant talk are a crime against humanity."

Mrs. Bazzoli had tucked her head down—shortened her neck—not knowing whether Father Furty was attacking her, but also taking no chances.

" 'Why' is a crime," he said, and for emphasis he shook his jowls. " 'Why' is a serious crime."

Mrs. Bazzoli cleared her throat in an appreciative way, as Father Furty reached for the radio. He turned up the volume of a Peggy Lee song and began to sing with it. He always knew the words. Something about knowing songs made him seem to me very worldly and very lonely.

"You give me fever," he sang.

Mrs. Bazzoli shook her head and returned to the stern section of the boat, where the women had asked me to set up folding chairs.

"Is this it?" Mrs. Skerry said. "Is this all?" And she looked around, widening her eyes and touching at her bristles. "I thought there was something else about boats."

"There's sinking," Mrs. Cannastra said, and sipped from her Dixie cup. She smiled and said, "Bug juice."

Mrs. Corrigan was knitting, Mrs. Palumbo pushed her face towards a tiny mirror and pressed lipstick onto her pouty mouth. Mrs. Hickey tried to control the *Herald*, but the pages lashed at her head. Mrs. DuCane sat smiling with her hands in her lap.

"I didn't realize there were so many islands out here," Mrs. Skerry said.

We had left the inner harbor and were plowing through the speckled, oil-smeared water—boats all around us, and islands on the left and right. Plump white-bellied planes were descending overhead, making for Logan Airport. Mrs. Corrigan could see the Customs House, Mrs. DePalma could see the John Hancock, Mrs. Hickey thought she could see the Old North Church.

"I can see two Faneuil Halls," Mrs. Cannastra said.

"Are you sure that's bug juice?" Mrs. Corrigan said.

Mrs. Cannastra grinned at her with purple-stained teeth.

"I'll bet you're starving," Mrs. Bazzoli said to Tina.

Tina said no, she wasn't.

"I would be if I were you."

Mrs. Bazzoli must have weighed two hundred and eighty pounds.

"I've just been down with renal colic," Mrs. Hickey was saying.

All this time, Father Furty quietly steered us to the outer harbor, and when we began to approach another island—Deer Island, he said—he asked me to kneel at the bow and make sure there were no rocks in the way.

"All clear so far," I said.

At last we reached a ruined jetty and moored *Speedbird* to the still-standing posts.

"Let's set up them card tables," Mrs. Prezioso said.

They pushed three together on the afterdeck and covered them with a paper tablecloth, which was held in place with all the bowls of food.

"Shouldn't we say a prayer?" Mrs. DuCane said, and looked triumphant as the others froze in the act of loading their plates.

Mrs. Cannastra had been saying to Father Furty, "Go ahead. It's bug juice, Father."

He held it but did not sip it. Instead he turned to Mrs. DuCane and said, "This is a form of prayer. Be happy. This is a way of praising God."

"I hope you like onions!" Mrs. DePalma said, heaping a plate with salad. "This is for the Father."

"I was doing one for him," Mrs. Hogan said, with a note of objection in her voice.

Mrs. Bazzoli said, "I know he likes coleslaw. That's why I got this one ready. Hey, it's an Italian helping!"

They all still wore their big earrings, and their small hats were skewered to their piled-up hair, and some wore tight gloves— the kind they wore to church. They bumped arms at the tables— it seemed each woman was taking charge of Father Furty's lunch by readying a plate for him, making a mound of food.

"I can't eat all of that," he said. "But it's swell of you to think of me. Listen, this one will do me fine."

He took Tina's plate. She had not intended it for him, so there was very little on it—a Swedish meatball, a sesame seed roll, and a few spoonfuls of green salad.

"Eat," he said, and pulled the roll into three hunks. And raising his paper cup he said, "Drink."

He had dragged his captain's chair to the end of the row of tables, and the women fitted themselves in, five on each side. They sat down and hunched forward, so their long slanting breasts lay supported by their upthrust bellies.

Tina and I sat on the rail—there wasn't any spare room at the tables. In fact, the tables and the women filled the whole of the stern section of the boat. But though they were hemmed in, and the breeze made the tablecloth flap and tear against the women's knees, it seemed much more formal than a picnic. It was more like a ritual—polite and pious.

"This is a real sit-down dinner," Mrs. Prezioso said.

"Pass the pickles, Mrs. Pretz," Mrs. Hogan said.

Father Furty said, "Let's hope the Boss doesn't find out."

No one understood except me.

"That's what we call the Pastor," he said. "Sometimes we call him the Keeper."

The secret words seemed scandalous to them, and they laughed hard, congratulating themselves that they had heard it from Father Furty himself.

"I think someone's going to be a stool pigeon," he said. He was grinning. "Who's the fink?"

Mrs. DuCane said, "Certainly not me!"

But the others looked quickly at her and didn't say anything, so the mere fact that Mrs. DuCane opened her mouth seemed to single her out as the guilty party.

Father Furty didn't mind—he was still smiling. He took his paper cup in two hands and lifted it as if in praise. Then he swallowed in anticipation—holding the cup away from his face—and finally gulped some, and chewed a hunk of bread.

"I love to see you digging in," he said. He really did seem to be enjoying himself, and yet he had only drunk the bug juice and had eaten practically nothing.

"Just feeding our faces," Mrs. Skerry said. "Isn't that a sin?"

"Oh, no, nothing like that," Father Furty said. "This is innocent pleasure. This is glorifying God. Hey, let's have a smile, Hazel—God's not your enemy!"

Hazel was Mrs. Corrigan's name, but it was odd to hear it spoken in such a friendly way by a priest. Yet he didn't look like a priest. He looked human—like a man, like a manager who had decided to turn the company banquet into a picnic.

"At least it's not a sin," Mrs. Bazzoli said, and moved a drumstick to her mouth. "I'm never sure about sin."

"I've seen plenty of bad, but I've never seen evil," Father Furty said. "Bad yes, evil no. And I'm from Jersey!"

"More bug juice?" Mrs. Cannastra said.

She leaned over to pour it out. Father Furty protested but he took it all the same. His face had begun to swell and grow pinker.

I could tell that Tina was shocked—the way non-Catholics reacted when they saw a priest acting human: eating and drinking and calling women by their first name. Yet I was grateful to him. By being human he made me feel pious—not holy but doing my duty, and maybe still in a state of grace.

"This is my last one," Father Furty said. "But I want the rest of you to drink up and dig in!"

He winked at us but looked a little ill, and when he got to his feet he seemed unsteady.

"Let's have a song," he said.

"A hymn?" Mrs. Hickey said.

"A song," Father Furty said, and began to sing.

> *I was sailing along, on Moonlight Bay,*
> *I could hear the voices singing*

They seemed to say:
You have stolen my heart
So don't go way—

He kept on, with the women joining in, then he sat down and smoked Fatimas and flipped the butts overboard.

"How's Danny?"

"I'm up to Circle Eight. Thieves."

"That's swell," he said and seemed genuinely pleased once more.

"They're in a pit, all tied up," I said, encouraged by his interest. "But instead of rope, it's snakes twisted around them."

"Oh?" And now he seemed surprised.

"There's a man called Vanni Fucci in the pit. His sin was stealing a treasure from a sacristy—snakes all over him! He's not even sorry. In fact, he—"

Father Furty was very interested, and I saw that I had gone too far to stop. He squinted at me to continue.

"This guy, um, gives God the finger," I said, and to cover my embarrassment at having said this went on, "By the way, the bottom of Hell isn't hot, Father. It's all ice."

He thought a moment, then turned to Mrs. Cannastra. "Hell on the rocks," he said.

"Sounds like a drink," she said.

"Sounds like all drinks."

He was still smiling, and I thought: This is all I want for now. I was happy being with Tina, the sun crackling on us and the water lapping the boat with a bathtub sound. For once I felt I was doing the right thing, and enjoying it, too! I was also glad that none of these women were paying any attention to Tina or me. I had never loved her more. It was because we were here.

There were more songs. Mrs. Skerry sang "Galway Bay," and Mrs. Bazzoli and Mrs. DePalma sang an Italian song that they said was about the sea, and I kept hearing the words *medzo mar.*

There were rumbles of thunder from the direction of Revere, and a black cloud enlarged like a stain over Nahant.

"We'd better start back," Father Furty said, and then the sun was gone. He felt his way along the rail to the cabin, his shirt lifting and flapping.

Passing me, he squeezed my knee and said, "Bad yes, evil no," and winked at me. He had not squeezed me hard, but there was something in the pressure of his fingers that told me he was not well.

We thumped the jetty posts twice, and flaked off some of our paint, while I was untying my clove hitches—for some reason, Father Furty was gunning the engine. Then we started away, the boat shimmying a little. At the wheel, Father Furty was wearing a crooked grin—perhaps it was because of the Fatima in his mouth. He was singing along with the radio.

The women were clearing up the plates and folding the card tables.

It did not seem to me that Father Furty was really steering the boat. It was more as if he was holding tight to the wheel to keep himself from falling. He sagged on it, rather than keeping it in a light steerer's grip with his fingertips, as he usually did. He looked wildly happy.

"Are you all right, Father?" I asked.

He said, "I'll bet she's a joy to be with."

The harbor water began to smack and slop against us. The splashing over the rail I took to be a bad sign, and the girlish screams of the women made me anxious.

"What's that?" Mrs. Palumbo asked.

"Probably Moon Island," Father Furty said, and turned slowly—first his eyes, then his head—to watch it pass on the portside.

I said, "Careful of that tug."

Accelerating, Father Furty said, "What tug?"

But it was too late.

There was no panic. Even as the side of *Speedbird* was being stoved in by the tug from *Blue Neptune Towing,* and the rails twisted off the decks, and the cleats sheared cleanly off by the shoulders of the tug—as all this was happening, the women of the Sodality shrieked and laughed, as they had when they'd been hit with spray that morning. They did not know it was a disaster—they may have thought it was part of all cruises, the really funny part. That was how much they trusted Father Furty.

7.

Afterwards, the way people talked about it made it seem dramatic and dangerous—two boats crashing in the harbor, some near-drownings, heroism, chaos. But it was not that way at all. It was an embarrassing accident, we were towed into harbor by the very boat we had hit. It was humiliating, it was bruises and hurt feelings.

Then I saw that there is a neatness about tragedy—it looks perfect, as false things so often do: fake blood in all the right places, pretty victims, stately burials and then silence. It is all glorious and conceited. But nothing is worse than disgrace. It is lonely and irreversible—a terrible mess. The loud snorting laughter it produces is worse than anguish. Having to live through a disgrace is worse than dying.

All your secrets in a twisted form belong to everyone else— and you are in the dark. That was how I felt then, guessing at what was going on; and I didn't know the half of it. Nothing truthful was revealed, but a version of events emerged. It was like a badly wrapped parcel coming apart—slowly at first, just stains producing rips and leaks, and then more quickly collapsing until it was all loose string and flaps and crumpled wrapping, and something dark and slimy showing through, and finally flopping onto the floor in full view, while people said, "Oh, God, what's that?"

It began, as so many disasters did, when I heard my mother speaking on the phone.

"Don't be silly," she said. "I don't believe you."

No, she believed it all, and wanted more: this was her way of encouraging the person at the other end.

"That couldn't be true," she said.

She became more interested as she became disbelieving.

"Well, we all know that's his cross," she said. "He'll just have to carry it."

The last thing I heard as I hurried out of the door was her calling my name.

But I kept going—to the bus, to the Sandpits; with my Mossberg. In that frame of mind, nothing was more consoling to me than the sound of beer bottles breaking on a crate as my bullets smashed into them.

I had thought that by managing to get ashore we would be safe. No one was hurt. Mrs. Bazzoli had a bruise above her knee that was like a faint smear of jam, and she kept raising her skirt with a kind of dreadful pride to show it. There were wet blouses thickened over bras. Mrs. Cannastra could not stop laughing. The leftovers had turned to garbage. Mrs. Palumbo proposed saying a prayer of thanksgiving that it had ended safely.

Father Furty did not join in on that prayer.

"We're going to hear about this," he said, yet he did not look sad.

He watched *Speedbird* winched onto the wharf. Its whole portside was gashed, and its nose splintered; panels and rails dangled from it; it hung like a huge fish that had been hacked to death.

When I helped Tina onto the pier, Father Furty was standing a short distance away, looking very relaxed with a Fatima in his mouth.

"Wet feet," I said.

"You'll be all right," he murmured, speaking through the cigarette and barely parting his lips.

I was heartened by that—whatever he said to me was always a boost—but when he helped me up his hand trembled on my elbow and I had the impression that he was very elderly and feeble.

All day I had been building up to kissing Tina. It always seemed a long and complicated procedure. But when *Speedbird* struck *Blue Neptune Towing* my plans fell apart, and I saw that I was as far from kissing her as ever. We were not even holding hands.

But on her front steps that evening after I walked her home, she said, "Oh, Andy, I'm so worried." I put my arm around her and without thinking kissed her lightly on her lips. At the time it seemed natural; but my mind kept going back to it and seeing it as amazing.

"Where did you go with Father Furty?" my mother asked.

"Nowhere," I said.

"What did you do all day in the boat?"

"Nothing."

"Did you have a good time?"

I shrugged. "I guess so."

The next morning the phone calls started, and *I don't believe you* and *That couldn't be true.* But I was out the door.

When I came back, my mother said, "Kitty DuCane called. Sit down, Andy. I want to talk to you."

She said she knew everything. Half of what she knew was wrong, but how could I tell her the truth without making things worse? Anyway, she would have believed Mrs. DuCane before she believed me. She was angry that I had taken Tina and not mentioned it. But she had spoken to Tina's mother.

"We think it's better if you don't see each other."

Father Furty walks into Holy Name House and tosses his skipper's hat on the hall table.

"Had a little accident," he says.

"Anyone hurt?" Father Hanratty asks.

"Some wet feet," he said. "Some soggy chicken salad."

And then he goes through the business of lighting a Fatima— tapping it on the back of his hand, knuckling it into his mouth, and setting it on fire.

"We smacked into a tugboat."

And then he winks and heads for his room, where he kicks off his sneakers and grins into the mirror and says, "You've really made a mess of it this time, skipper!"

That was how I imagined it. I could not picture him taking it hard, and that was the worst thing about the gossip: he was depicted as a fool and an incompetent and probably worse—I wouldn't listen to the stories, not even from my mother.

I had a Father Furty seven o'clock the next week, but he did not show up. It was Father Skerrit. I waited for the next mass list. Father Furty's name did not appear on this one at all.

I went to Holy Name House.

Mrs. Flaherty came to the door. "What do you want?"

"Father Furty."

"He's not seeing anyone."

An hour later, on my way to Wright's Pond I met Magoo.

"Where are you going?" she said. I didn't reply—I was thinking hard about Father Furty, my hands in my pockets, walking fast. Magoo said, "I might as well come along."

She wanted to take the shortcut into the woods!

I got nervous and said, "I've got renal colic."

She looked angrily at me.

"You could get into trouble," I said.

"I didn't do nothing!" she said, very loudly, and there was something about her bad grammar that made her seem innocent. I was afraid of her ugliness—she was fat and white and had green teeth.

Everything looked dangerous to me now, especially sex.

That night I tried again at Holy Name House. The windows were dark, and no one answered the door. But I sat on the wall nonetheless—sat there, and prayed, and felt insignificant.

At home—late for supper—I had a sense of desperation: wanting to do something and not knowing what. My mother asked me if there was something wrong. I said no.

"You've been smoking!" she said.

"No!"

"Don't use that tone with me," she said. "I sometimes think you don't have a vocation at all. A priest wouldn't talk that way to his mother."

It seemed to me that what she said made sense. The way I talked to her probably meant that I didn't have a vocation.

"What if God calls you?"

But no one called—God was like the rest of them. I was in the dark, thinking of Father Furty, missing Tina. The darkness was silent.

I dreamed of Tina standing in her underwear in front of a mirror. She was barefoot, combing her hair. I could not imagine her naked, and I doubt whether even if I could I would have found it thrilling. I liked this—sex to me was satin panties and strips of lace, it was all elastic and straps.

The following day I served another mass (Father Flynn) and thought: If God calls me I'll go. Being a priest did not seem bad. Father Furty's example was the proof that you could be a priest and still have a wonderful time, smoking, singing, listening to your car radio, and bombing around in a speedboat. And I had seen him at the altar during the consecration, with his eyes tightly shut, praying hard. That was the test—with his back turned to the congregation and his face in front of the tabernacle. Only the altar boy could see his face. He was a good priest.

And I also thought: If I'm a priest I won't have to worry about those other things.

Tina in her Sears Catalogue underwear was a problem that left me feeling flustered and impatient. It would have been a relief, I felt, if someone I trusted whispered in my ear: Impossible.

All that was during mass.

Back in the sacristy, Father Flynn took off his vestments without speaking.

I coughed to give myself courage, and then said, "How's Father Furty? All right, I hope."

Father Flynn turned slowly. I saw his hesitant thoughts flickering on his face.

"I'll tell him you were asking for him," he said.

"Yes, please."

Whispering, the priest said, "Say a prayer for him, son."

This was the Father Flynn who had shouted, *The Boss received a postcard yesterday from his brother in Ireland!*

The worst of it was that Father Furty was my confessor as well as my friend. I had come to rely on his being in the confession box behind the Seventh Station on Saturday afternoons. He was not there last Saturday; he might not be there next; and my soul was growing muddier. Because he had not quizzed me much I had been able to be honest with him and tell him everything. I had stopped padding my confession with trivial sins ("Used the name of Our Lord and God in vain—three times") and made the serious ones plainer. I had begun to feel hopeful about Holy Orders. But where was he now? My sins were mounting up—so many in fact that by being denied Father Furty as my confessor I knew only Father Furty could possibly absolve me of this many.

I had finished Dante's *Inferno,* and I knew the detailed punishments that awaited sinners in Hell—whirling around, heads on backwards, stinking air, black frost, jumping reptiles, boiling blood, fiery tombs, and ice, and being chewed. I wished I had never read it.

Say a prayer for him, son! I was the one who needed prayers. I knew I was not in a state of grace. I felt guilty, and sneaky, and because I was in sin, very vulnerable.

I went on asking the priests and my folks about Father Furty. No one told me anything. I was not surprised. I felt that to be taken seriously was a privilege I had not yet earned.

Chicky DePalma and I served the ten-fifteen that Sunday.

"Where's your gun?" he said.

"I forgot it."

No, I had begun to feel guilty about that, too, because it was pleasure. Everything enjoyable made me feel guilty. I was trying to do penance—I did not deserve to have any fun. But it was no good; I had sinned; and I was losing count.

"I got bare pussy off Magoo again last night," he said.

My face went hot as I pictured this dangerous sin. It wasn't Circle Two, The Carnal: torture by tempests and high winds— that had something to do with love. Magoo's ugliness, her shrunken anklesocks, made it a more serious sin, down among the flying reptiles.

Chicky had got to the sacristy first and had nabbed the cassock with snaps. He stood up—done already.

"Hey, did you hear Furty's in the hospital?"

I felt numb, my fingers wouldn't move, but I said, "Yeah," because I did not want him to know how startled I was.

"He's going to be all right," I said. "It's not serious."

Chicky grinned at me. His grin meant: You're kidding yourself.

"He just happens to be sick," I said.

"Sick means drunk," Chicky said. As he spoke, he reached into the cupboard and took out a green bottle of mass wine. He swigged some and started to laugh.

During mass I was so weak I thought I was going to faint. I felt panicky, my skin went rubbery and began to buzz; I needed help, from Father Furty. He had to save me.

There were famous altar boys. You became famous by doing something memorable on the altar—showing the enormous holes in your shoes when you knelt down—or holes in your socks; wearing cowboy boots with big heels; having an erection and telling everyone; having a laughing fit and being yelled at by the priest while he was saying mass. Franny Cresta threw up once during mass, and everyone had to sit down while a janitor mopped it up. Augie D'Agostino was famous for tripping on the altar carpet—two or three times—and actually falling on his face. My brother Louie was serving with Robert Libby the time Libby shit his pants, the most famous altar boy incident of all—how his face changed, how he panicked, how he shook a turd out of his trouserleg.

But all these would seem unimportant when I became famous for passing out on the altar—just fainting dead away at the thought of Father Furty sick in the hospital.

Trying to keep my composure, I decided to listen very carefully to the sermon.

It was one of the Pastor's more terrifying ones, and it was about Hell—but a part of it that Dante had missed. It bothered me that the Pastor could give a sermon on Hell without mentioning Dante. It seemed that Saint Teresa of Avila had a visitation from an angel—her guardian angel. The angel said that if she continued to sin she would go to Hell, and not only that, but there was a place in Hell reserved especially for her. The angel scooped her up and rushed her to the edge of Hell and showed her. It was a box, like a slightly larger than normal oven. Every bit of it was red hot, and there was only room to kneel in it, or crouch—so she would not be able to stand up or sit down. The angel said that she would be hunched in it—stuffed in this box in the most awkward posture imaginable—and go on burning for all eternity.

"Sit up straight!" the Pastor shouted from the pulpit, and everyone in the church turned to look at me perspiring.

I said to my mother, "I've got to see Father Furty."

"After all that's happened I think you should get down on your knees and say a prayer."

Say a prayer. Get a job. Those were her usual responses when I despairingly wondered how to meet the world. *Get a haircut. Take a bath. Be glad you're not feeling worse.*

"I'm worried about him."

"You should be worried about yourself."

"He's in the hospital," I said. "Chicky DePalma told me."

My mother looked at me sharply: I had told her something she didn't know. She sent me away and went to the phone.

"Not just in the hospital," she said, in a triumphant tone of going me one better. "He's on the Danger List."

This in my imagination was a long piece of paper tacked to the hospital wall, and names printed in black, one under the other, and some crossed out.

"What hospital?"

"Morris Memorial."

I tried to hide my desperation.

My mother said, "They certainly won't allow you in. Not if he's on the Danger List."

"I'm not going there," I said, and went to my room and took my Mossberg off the wall and filled my pocket with cartridges.

"Where do you think you're going?"

"The Sandpits."

"I hate guns," she said.

But instead of taking the Hudson Bus to Stoneham, I walked through the Morris Estates, the Mossberg over my shoulder. At the hospital a gardener yelled, "Hey, you!" but then thought better of it. Seeing me entering the hospital, people hurried to their cars. Father Furty would laugh when I told him that the only way I had been able to see him was by taking my Mossberg out and pretending I was going to the Sandpits to break bottles. He'd call it a fib—it was a wonderful word.

"You can't come in here with that thing!" the receptionist said.

"Don't worry," I said. "The bolt's out." I rested it against the wall of the lobby.

"I'm here to see Father Furty."

"Was he a friend of yours?" she asked in a whisper.

8.

It was a requiem mass, all bowing and singing, two priests and six altar boys. I was one of the acolytes, holding a four-foot candle. I felt shaky and weak, as if someone had screamed "Wake up!" and slapped my face, and badly damaged it. I had woken up, and it hurt. Until then I had never known anyone who had died—no one in my family, none of my relatives or friends, not even my grandparents—all four of them were alive. This was my third funeral, but it was my first death.

From the moment I heard the bad news I was very silent. I did not speak to anyone at home—they found out the same day, so I did not have to tell them. I didn't talk, and yet I found it easy to pray. God was still glaring at me out of the hot sky—perhaps listening, but did it matter?

"You are all-knowing, God, so you know that Father Furty was a good kind man, and his happiness was love. His happiness was a way of praying. He must have been good, because he liked me and took me on his boat. Before I met him I felt worthless and unimportant, and I—"

But I had to stop myself. It was not that I was rambling, but rather that whenever I talked about Father Furty I began talking about myself. I saw that this was an unfair connection, but I nearly always made it. It was not that he was a priest—he was the first person to make me feel as though I existed in the world; he made me feel I had a right to live. He made me laugh and he laughed at things I said. I was fifteen years old, and he treated me as though I were a whole, large mature person; he listened to me; he gave me compliments and praise. That was why it was such a shock to lose him—because he had been on my side, and now there was no one.

I had never believed that such a priest was possible, and so until I had met him I had never imagined being a priest. He was better than me, but he resembled me. I had thought that I was sadder and more tormented, and that my life was more difficult than his. But he made me believe in myself as a priest; by making happiness look natural and right. I had always thought happiness was a venial sin—that it was selfish. Now when I imagined the priesthood I saw myself with a wiffle and a flowered Hawaiian shirt and black slacks and sandals, smoking Fatimas and singing along with the radio in the car.

All this was news to me, and it helped, but remembering that he was dead still made me feel sick—sick, rather than hopeless.

Chicky DePalma was in the sacristy that day talking to Walter Hogan.

He said, "I'm bombing up Brookview to the church, thinking I'm going to be late—and who do I see in a tight sweater, with knobs like this? Yeah! Hey, Parent, are you listening?"

"No," I said.

"And a tight skirt, and I think, *mingya!*"

"Cut it out," I said.

"Parent walks around with a boner all day."

Chicky had thick lips and spaces between his teeth and hooded eyes and a heavy Sicilian jaw. Whenever he said something obscene he made his monkey mouth.

"So what do you think of Tina the Wiener coming to church with her knobs—"

I heaved myself at him and pushed him against the lockers, banging his head and yanking his cassock. "If you say one more word I'll kick the living shit out of you!"

My threats didn't matter, but he had hit his head very hard, and I had torn three or four buttons off of his cassock. He was startled, and hurt, and he saw that I was very angry.

"He's apeshit," Walter Hogan said softly.

That was a form of praise. But my reaction had startled me too and taken all my anger away. I also felt righteous—my swearing didn't matter: I was on the side of sanctity, insisting on reverence and fighting for it. That calmed me down.

Meanwhile, another altar boy—Vito Bazzoli—had walked in. Walter whispered to him, but they said nothing directly to me. I think they were afraid of me—or respected me—at last, and I was glad.

The mass was said by the Pastor, and as it was a requiem he was assisted by Father Skerrit. Requiems always seemed to me like plays—dramas with two characters. The Pastor had the main part, and Father Skerrit had a subsidiary role, scurrying around and responding in a nervous voice to the Pastor's pompous lines. We altar boys were on the sidelines, a thurifer, and four acolytes, and Chicky with the seven-foot crucifix.

"It's going to be a closed coffin," my mother had said of the wake.

There was a meaning in her voice that I did not understand. I had never thought about it before—a coffin closed or open. The dead looked so lumpy and absent with the life drained out of them. But I was sorry I could not see Father Furty again, and I kept imagining his face against the lid of the coffin.

Standing beside it with my candle I felt weak again and I knew I was conspicuously pale and trembly. This suffering was not wholly due to the fact that Father Furty was dead (but how had he died? and when exactly?—I was troubled by the vagueness of it all, and ashamed because I was too young to be told). I suffered, too, because I was not in a state of grace. I had sins on my soul: without Father Furty I could not confess.

But I could discern a logic in being a sinner and wanting to be a priest. In fact, it seemed to me that one went with the other. It wasn't piety, but sin, that made someone want to enter the priesthood: it was the only possible purification. Your choice was either that cleansing by the sacrament of Holy Orders, or else you left your soul black and lost your faith. And either way it was a sacrifice—your body or your soul.

The church was more than half-full. I had never seen so many people at a funeral; I had never recognized so many. No one was crying—that was strange; but I heard faint screws of sound, a kind of mewing and soft coughing that was almost as sad as silence.

As we circled the casket—priests and acolytes, Chicky and the thurifer, Father Skerrit with the holy water bucket, the Pastor with the sprinkler—I glanced towards the back of the church and saw Tina sitting by herself. She was sitting, I guessed, because she was not used to kneeling. She wore a blue sweater, and a white handkerchief was pinned to the top of her head. Now I was glad I had banged Chicky's head in the sacristy.

We went back for the consecration—Father Skerrit did the bells—and then the Pastor waved us to the side pews and walked slowly—still playing his pious role—to the pulpit for his sermon.

In that moment of silence—no litany, no music—I heard some nose-blowing and some sobbing. I was certain they were the women Father Furty had taken out on his boat. Although they had seemed very plain and matronly on the boat, at the funeral, dressed in black, with veils and white faces, they looked almost beautiful to me, the way Father Feeney's nuns had seemed. Their crying was not loud, there were no shrieks; it was all a soft agony of mourning, and in its muffled way it seemed to me the worst grief.

The Pastor hooked his hands onto the front of the pulpit and hung on and leaned back, staring hard at the congregation. His severe eyes seemed to still the sobbing. Then it struck me that

I had modeled God on the Pastor—God's glare, and God's scowling face, and even his paleness and his white upswept hair; and both God and the Pastor had narrow Irish mouths that they held slightly open to show doubt or scorn or self-importance.

His silence silenced the congregation, but I knew it was a gimmick. As an altar boy, I had seen all the priests giving sermons—from Father Flynn, who trembled and forgot what he had just said, to the Pastor, who glared like God. Father Furty always opened with a little joke, and he often based his sermons on common expressions, like "throwing the bull" or "down in the dumps."

The Pastor began today with a sudden shout and I could see people jump and straighten up, and a man in the first pew snapped his hymnbook shut. Usually, during sermons, people read the miracles in the back pages of the Novena book, to kill time. *My ironing board caught fire . . . My son fell out the window . . . On a recent trip to New York City . . . Riding my bike on a busy street . . . My riveting machine exploded throwing heavy chunks of metal in every direction. I could easily have lost an eye or even my life. Miraculously, I was not hurt—not even a scratch. I owe this to the intercession of the Mother of God, the Blessed Virgin Mary. I had attended the Novena for nine Mondays in a row and asked especially for protection at work . . .*

No one was reading the miracles now.

"We then that are strong ought to bear the infirmities of the weak, and not to please ourselves," the Pastor said in a quoting voice—a sort of halting falsetto. "For even Christ pleased not himself. But, as it is written, the reproaches of them that reproached thee fell on me."

He let this sink in. "Paul's Epistle to the Romans," he said, and then, "What does 'strong' mean? It means strong in faith." And what did weak mean? It meant weak in body and soul. And what did infirmities mean? Infirmities meant giving in to occasions of sin. And what did we mean by "written"? And why did we say reproaches?

I remembered Father Furty saying, "Questions, questions! 'Are you sure?' 'Do you really mean it?' Questions like that are a crime against humanity . . . 'Why' is a crime . . ."

"And not to please ourselves!" the Pastor declaimed.

He repeated this, and defined simple words and made them

so complicated they were hard for me to understand, and he went on asking why. The people listened intently because the Pastor's voice—it was another of his sermon gimmicks—was loud and then soft: shouts and whispers to keep their attention.

I listened. I had never really listened to a sermon before, but when had a sermon ever mattered so much?

He seemed to be saying that Father Furty was weak and that he, the Pastor, was strong. And we were strong, too! It was our duty to pray for the weak, to help save their souls. It was what Christ did—gave himself to other people and propped them up and helped them enter Heaven. He had done more than that—he had died for the sins of the world. Christ took that burden upon himself, and therefore we should follow his example and take this burden upon ourselves—Father Furty! In so many words, that was it.

"And not to please ourselves!" he kept saying. And this refrain meant it wasn't pleasure—no fun, no enjoyment, not even any conscious satisfaction. It was suffering. He said: Pray. He said: Forgive. He said: Do penance.

And all this because Father Furty was a sinner. The Pastor didn't use that word—he said "weak" and "almost lost" and "struggling"—but it was clear that he meant that Father Furty was a sad case. Because the poor man had needed help when he was alive (what help? That small dark room in Holy Name House?), now that he was dead the help had to continue, for alive or dead the weak were still weak and needed prayer.

Every time he said dead I died.

The idea was that Father Furty was in Purgatory, but we had to do the work to get him out.

I saw from this sermon how much the Pastor disliked him, and how he had turned poor Father Furty into a test of faith. But none of this really bothered him, for the emotion that was clearest in what he said was relief. Father Furty had been a problem as a live and lively man, but now that he was a soul in Purgatory—and not in Heaven or Hell—he was less of a problem. ⁓

Father Furty's sermons were so different. "He went to the dogs," he used to say. "Let me tell you what happens when you go to the dogs. Think of it—the dogs!"

I laughed when he said that, thinking of a pair of cocker spaniels my uncle owned. Father Furty laughed too. It was a good sermon. The message was: Don't give up—Keep the faith—You're not as bad as you think you are!

"On your knees," the Pastor was saying. There was a sort of terror, like a black flame, hovering over the congregation. Father Furty had been a problem. He was better off dead—death in fact had come just in time. He was lucky to be dead, because he had been a failure, and now it was up to us to get him out of Purgatory and into the sight of God.

It was awful, it was horrible, I wanted to cry; but if I had the Pastor would have bawled me out from the pulpit.

There was a little more about penance, and then as suddenly as he had begun, the Pastor blessed himself—"*And* the Father, *and* the Son, and . . ."—and the sermon was over.

Eetay mee-sigh est.

Dayo grah-see-ahs.

I picked up my candlestick and as we filed slowly in front of the altar, and as the casket was rolled away, I realized that my mind was made up: I wanted to be a priest. It must have been God's will, for how else could the thought have been planted there? I was glad that Tina had been at the funeral, because now it would be easier to explain my decision.

"Hey, Parent," Chicky said in the sacristy.

His voice was gentle and friendly: it was his way of showing there were no hard feelings.

"Hey, that's your third funeral."

I had not thought of it as a funeral. It had been something much gloomier, more intense and final and private than anything I had ever known. I gave Chicky a blank look. I had lost my voice.

"Hey, you got a wedding coming to you."

9.

It was too painful after that to pray for Father Furty, because as soon as my prayer produced his friendly face my memory told me he was dead, and I missed him more than ever. I thought hard about becoming a priest. Did God want me? And I thought about Tina. I wanted to be the sort of priest who would have a friend like Tina, and it seemed a good life—being a priest, with close friends. Father Furty had been human in that way, and his example gave me hope.

There were my sins. I was still not in a state of grace, for whenever I thought of Tina—whenever she shimmered into my mind—I undressed her. Not all the way, but to her satiny slip, with little straps, and lace at the bottom edge, and the light showing through it and outlining the contours of her panties, the way she was packed into them. She always stood up in my imagining, with her arms at her sides, and slightly smiling, like a model in a Sear's catalogue. This vision made the blood in my head pound, yet I knew it was wrong, it was Circle Two, and I had to hurry out and run, or break bottles, to get rid of it. But of course it was too late: it was just another terrible sin overlapping the others stuck on my soul like black patches.

Not seeing her made everything worse. I wanted to see her, but her mother and mine had come to some agreement to prevent our meeting. And of course, wanting to see her was not the same as having the willpower to see her, and I often thought I would be content just to go on imagining her in her underwear.

Then, two days after the funeral, the telephone rang.

"It's me," she said.

"Hi." I was afraid to say her name.

"I saw you at the church."

"Yeah," I said. "How come you went?"

"Because I liked him, and I wanted to say goodbye. That sounds stupid. I mean, I didn't want to stay away."

"How did you know when to stand up or kneel down?"

"I just guessed."

"Did you pray?"

"Sort of," she said. "I saw you carrying that candle. Was it heavy?"

"Not really."

"You looked cute in that altar boy outfit."

I did not know what to say. I let a moment pass, but she spoke quickly and filled that silence with her whisper.

"Andy, my mother just went out to a sale at Filene's and I'm all alone in the house, so why don't you come over?"

The hammering began in my head, my mouth went dry. I said, "I don't know." I could sense her lips against the phone.

"We could listen to records," she said.

"I'm pretty busy," I said—a terror was taking hold of me. It was not dragging me away—it was thrusting me nearer to the danger of saying yes. Tina's warmth came through the phone like heat through a pipe. "Let's see, what time is it?"

From the next room, my mother said, "It's half-past one."

She had been listening!

"I just remembered something," I said.

"Who's that?" my mother called out. "Who are you talking to?"

"I've got to go," I said, and hung up.

"Who was that?" my mother said. She was ironing in the kitchen, a laundry basket on the floor, a stack of neatly ironed clothes on the kitchen table. She was shaking water out of a tonic bottle fitted with a nozzle, and sending up hissing steam by pushing her iron over it. She always looked older and tireder when she was at the ironing board. *Your shirts,* she sometimes said in an accusing way, making me responsible for having to do this work. "Tell me."

"No one."

"I think you enjoy tormenting me," she said. "Was it a girl?"

"No," I said, because I was afraid of the questions that would follow my saying yes.

And yet they followed all the same.

"Andy, do you have a girlfriend?"

I shook my head: it seemed to make the lie less vicious.

"Is it that Tina Spector—the girl you promised me you wouldn't see?"

When had I promised that? My denying grunt was "Uh-uh." Again, a grunt seemed milder than an outright lie.

But my mother persisted, demanding the lie. "Are you sure?"

"No!" I said, and was surprised that I was not struck to the floor by a thunderbolt.

"What do you want a girlfriend for?" my mother went on, assuming that I had lied, and that I had meant yes.

"I don't have a girlfriend!"

"Do you really mean that?" she said, knowing that I didn't. "You've got a bike, and you were making that boat with Walter Hogan. And you've got a gun—though I hate guns. But you've got plenty to keep you busy without spending your time with some dizzy girl."

"I know, I know."

"You could get into a lot of hot water. Some of these girls—"

I didn't say anything. I knew my voice would incriminate me. I looked down at my toes and waited, wondering if a storm would break over my head: sometimes she screamed at me, sometimes she cried.

She said in a piercing voice, "Are you telling me the truth?"

"If you can keep a secret, I'll tell you something," I said, in a desperate effort to head her off. "But it really is a secret."

Her nostrils moved: she was taking a long snort of air, perhaps wondering what was coming. She knew I never told her secrets; she knew I never told her anything.

"Please don't tell anyone," I said.

"Of course I wouldn't tell anyone," she said, both interested and insulted. And then in her impatience to know she became stern. "What is it?"

"I think I want to be a priest," I said. "I have a feeling that God wants me."

She smiled and put down her iron and beckoned me to the ironing board. She hugged me, she said, "Andy," and that was the end of her girlfriend questions.

But at that age I belonged to no one, and then to everyone, because I didn't matter. There was no such thing as my privacy. If someone didn't spy on me it wasn't out of respect, but because they thought I had no secrets. And that was probably why I always thought of the future with foreboding, because I knew I was nowhere, and that I would have to start from the beginning, and that I would have to prove everything, and that I would never forgive anyone for making it so hard for me.

"The Pastor wants to talk to you."

My heart sank. I said, "What about?"

She said she didn't know, and I couldn't ask whether she had told him about my wanting to be a priest, because of course she had, and she would have hated me for making her deny it.

He was seated at a dark desk in a hot room in the rectory, and I thought how miserable it was to have to be inside shuffling papers on such a lovely day. It was bad enough having to wear socks and shoes! I associated hot airless rooms and dusty carpets with the tyranny of old unhappy men.

"Sit down," the Pastor said, and just the tone of these two words told me I was in for it.

There were no papers on his desk, nothing in the room but a skinny Christ writhing on a wooden cross on one wall, and a vigil light in a red glass cup under an oval picture of the Virgin Mary. The Pastor was staring hard at me, and he put his finger-tips together and worked his big clean hands apart and studied me with his mouth gaping like a fish.

"Where is your book?"

"Dante's *Inferno?* I finished reading it, Father."

"What are you reading now?"

"*Campcraft,* by Horace Kephart."

He squinted at me. "Did you say *Campcraft?*"

"Yes, Father." He looked displeased. I said, "And also *He Went With Marco Polo.*"

I did not want to tell him that I had borrowed more Dantes from the library and that I had found *Purgatory* dull and *Paradise* unreadable. I had liked the noise and motion of the *Inferno,* and I could easily imagine the funnel full of people. It was not just the blood and gore—and the reptiles and the ice—but that the people in Hell seemed real; the ones in Purgatory and Paradise were wordy and unbelievable. The *Inferno* was like life, and some of it seemed familiar. Father Furty had laughed out loud when I told him that the *Inferno* was full of Italians, like Boston. The words "shit" and "vomit" did not thrill me anymore; secretly I held on to six lines that Ulysses spoke to Dante,

> *Neither fondness for my son, nor reverence*
> *For my aged father, nor the debt of love*
> *That should have cheered Penelope*

Could conquer in me the lust
To experience the far-flung world
And human vice and bravery.

"Is that how you're preparing yourself?"

"Yes, Father." He blinked. I thought: What was the question?
"No, Father."

It was another trick of priests—not Father Furty—to say nothing, and for you to squirm until you guessed, somehow, what
they meant.

"Well, what *are* you doing to prepare yourself?"

To prepare myself for what?

"Praying, Father."

He stared: he knew I had just given him an all-purpose answer. And he knew I was lying. I wasn't praying, I was only
worrying whether I would ever experience the far-flung world.
But wasn't praying worrying out loud?

"And asking for God's help."

His smile was worse than his stare, his silence more terrible
than anything he said. And I was trapped in the tick of his clock.

"And doing penance, Father."

He pounced on this.

"What sort of penance?"

"Doing things and offering them up. Helping my folks. Drying
the dishes. Working up at Wright's Pond"—I was failing, and I
knew it—"and going without things."

He seemed bored, the air seeping out of him.

"Like candy, and—"

He glanced up.

"And camping equipment," I said lamely, and added in desperation, "And bullets."

This made him wince. He said, "So in fact you're not doing
anything to prepare yourself."

"No, Father."

"How old are you?"

"Fifteen, Father," I said in a defeated voice.

"Got a girlfriend?"

"No, Father." It was bad enough that I was telling a lie, but
it seemed so much worse that I was denying Tina's existence. My
lie made her pretty face spring into my mind and made me sad.

He knew I was lying. He was smiling, watching my lies accumulate. I could hear the scrape of his breathing, like a comb in his throat.

Behind his head, a large tufty cloud moved past the window and made me wish I was outside. The cloud climbed, leaving blue sky, and I felt trapped down below.

"What makes you think you could be a priest?"

I said nothing at first. His eyes were perforating my soul. I said, "I don't know."

"I'll tell you something. You don't simply say, 'I'm going to be a priest' the way you say, 'I'm going to be a doctor or a lawyer.' "

Though it struck me that it was much harder to be a doctor or a lawyer, I said, "No, Father."

"You don't volunteer. 'Here I am—might as well have a try!' " He made it sound thoroughly foolish. "You are chosen! You are called. To receive the sacrament. To perform the holy sacrifice of the mass."

"Yes, Father."

"Almighty God does the choosing!"

I wanted to get out of that room.

"You must think you're pretty darned important," the Pastor said.

I looked down, to appear ashamed, and saw his thin socks of black silk and hated them.

"Did you ever think you might be motivated by pride?"

There was no point in saying no. I knew I was beaten.

"Now we're getting somewhere," he said, and smiled his terrible smile. "The Church has no use for slackers. You don't know how lucky you are!" He looked aside, then turned back to me and said, "A non-Catholic once said to a Catholic, 'Do you believe that Christ is present in your church?' The Catholic said yes. 'Do you believe that, when you receive communion, God is in you?' And the Catholic said yes. 'Do you believe that when you die you have a chance to spend eternity in Heaven with Almighty God?' 'Yes,' the Catholic said. And the non-Catholic said, 'If I believed those things I would go to that church on my knees!' "

"Yes, Father."

"I would go to that church on my knees!"

I thought: But he didn't—didn't believe, didn't take communion, didn't go to church. It was easy to say that, like saying, *If I believed men could fly I would jump off the John Hancock Building.* Or, *If I believed what you believed I would die for it.* It was only an if—and a selfish boasting if. All they were really saying was, ". . . If, and pass the mustard."

"That's a pretty powerful example of faith, don't you think?"

I lied again, and I thought: Powerful example of a lack of faith, you mean!

"Let me ask you a question," the Pastor said, making a fresh start, as if the conversation had just begun. "If you were chosen by God to be a priest, and if you had enough sanctifying grace—what sort of priest would you be?"

I was stumped. But he went on staring. His stare said: I've got all day to watch you squirm.

"I don't know, Father," I said in a pleading voice.

"Have a try." He seemed friendlier saying this—it was the first kindly encouragement he had given me. I decided to tell him the truth.

I said, "I would try to model myself on Father Furty."

The Pastor began slowly leaning back as if trying to get me into focus by making me small.

I said, "I was his altar boy. I used to watch him."

But my words were dropping into a void—into the space that had opened up between us. I knew I had already failed. Nothing I said really mattered, and yet I could tell from the flick of his eyes that I had triggered something in the Pastor.

"Wouldn't that be the easy way out?"

I didn't know what to say.

"Father Furty—God rest his soul—was alone when he died. He was alone physically. He was alone emotionally and spiritually. Weakness is a terrible thing—it's a kind of cowardice. It can make you a very easy target for the devil. Father Furty abused his body. Do you think a person can abuse his body without abusing his soul?"

"No, Father."

"Are you sure?" he asked.

It was a cruel question; it was one that Father Furty hated. But I had already failed—and way back, lying about penance and prayer; so I lied again.

[89]

"When evil gets a grip on you," the Pastor said, with a kind of horrible energy, "it never lets go. Never! And you burn for all eternity." It was what Father Feeney had said, ranting on the Common. The Pastor's voice was quavering again and the scrape of his breathing began. "That's why we have to pray for the repose of Father Furty's soul."

His chair creaked and he was facing me.

"You don't want to model yourself on Father Furty."

I lied once again.

"I think you can do better than that," the Pastor said.

He meant Father Furty's disgrace—much worse now that he was dead, because he wasn't around to repent. He had died and left us with the mess to clean up, getting his stained soul out of Purgatory.

I said yes, I could do better than that; but it was the worst lie I had told all day—not only was it a denial of Father Furty, but it was a claim that I could do something I couldn't. I was in despair: in belittling my dead friend I had destroyed my vocation. Then I thought: I don't really have a vocation.

"I think you're going to work out fine," the Pastor said, for I had agreed to everything he said. He had me on his terms.

He ended by speaking of the Church. When he mentioned the Church I thought of a church building and saw it very clearly. It was a tiny boxlike thing with a stumpy steeple and very few pews; it was hard to enter and uncomfortable inside, which was why most of us were outside.

"I hope I've given you something to think about."

"Yes, Father."

He opened a drawer and took out a sheet of paper with typing on it.

"This is the new altar boy roster," he said. "You've had your three funerals. You've got a wedding on Saturday. Make sure your shoes are shined," and put the paper down with his left hand and raised his right. "In the name of the Father, the Son, and the Holy Ghost. Amen."

10.

"Where are you going with your gun?" Tina said, as I passed her house.

"A wedding." My Mossberg was over my shoulder, my cartridges in my pocket. I was on my way down Brookview Road.

"Who's getting married?"

"I don't know."

"He doesn't even know!"

Tina rose from the glider and walked to the rail of her piazza. She encircled the piazza post with her arm and lifted her leg to the banister. There was a lovely inch of lace showing at her knee. She was in the breeze now, her long hair blowing against the side of her face.

"Maybe we could go to the Sandpits later," I said. "Do some shooting."

"I've got to go shopping," she said. "When my mother gets back. She's out—so's my father."

It was a sort of invitation, I knew; but it meant now. And now I had to go to St. Ray's—the wedding, the nuptial mass that everyone said I had earned.

She said, "If my mother knew I was talking to you, she'd kill me."

I said, "Yeah," and kept walking, glancing back to see her leaning against the rail. The slender poplar in front of her house blew and leaned, too, with masses of spinning leaves—the whole tree whirling madly.

The wedding cars had jammed the parking lot—crowded it worse than any funeral I had seen; and one of the cars, the largest, a Caddy, had white ribbons tied across its roof and its hood, with a bow on its trunk. I lingered, standing behind a tree on the Fellsway, watching the wedding party go in, all in suits, waving to one another, laughing loudly; the women wore corsages and hats and white gloves, and the men were smoking their last cigarettes before entering the church. Two little flower girls in tiny gowns were quarreling, and a small boy in a sailor suit was crying under the statue of St. Raphael.

I tucked my Mossberg under my arm and crossed the Fellsway to the church lawn, and I hid near the grotto that the Pastor had built in May—it was the Blessed Virgin in a cave, because May was Mary's month. Watching from the edge of the cave, I saw Chicky DePalma run into the sacristy. He would be first, he would grab the cassock with the snaps, and have a swig of mass wine.

Chicky looks around, and seeing no one takes another swig of wine and thinks: I'll tell him about Magoo, how she let me do something or other, and he begins fastening his cassock.

I've got the bells, he thinks. I'll do the biretta. I'm moving the book.

Father Skerrit or the Pastor enters and says, "Let us pray," and Chicky tumbles to his knees and stuffs the bottle under his surplice and prays for the conversion of Russia. The priest kisses his vestments under the stained-glass window of Saint Raphael—the saint has swan's wings and a halo like a crown and a slender cross.

"Can I come in?"

It is the best man, in a new suit, a carnation in his buttonhole, new shoes, smelling of after-shave lotion, red-faced from nervousness and heat.

"Hope I'm not intruding!"

"Not at all."

Envelopes are produced. "A little something. I didn't think I'd have time after the mass."

"Very thoughtful of you."

"Hey, thanks," Chicky says.

There is a moment of awkward hesitation when the best man looks around and says, "Where's the other altar boy?"

"Not here yet," Chicky says.

And the priest tugs his chasuble aside and claws at his alb to see his wristwatch, and says, "It's Andy Parent, and he'd better get a move on, if he knows what's good for him."

Motionless, attentive, listening, I stayed where I was. Then I walked away and was aware in those seconds that my life had just begun—like a wheel slipping off an axle and rolling alone, and already it was spinning faster. I thought: A wedding is just a happy funeral.

* * *

The old heavy Mossberg was propped against a tree. In the course of the bus ride with Tina I had outgrown the gun, and now it seemed a silly thing, noisy and dangerous, something for a kid or an immature man.

We lay in the shade, on a bank of grass that was like an altar, rectangular, with a stump in the middle like a tabernacle. Beyond us were the cliffs and ledges of the Sandpits. The wind spun some dust up and it traveled in tall hobbling cones through the quarry. We were talking about some gulls we saw, did they ever land here, and about the clouds through the branches, about nothing, and I was glad when we stopped talking, so that my nervousness was less apparent to her.

"My mother's going to kill me," she said eagerly.

"What about me?" I said. "Missing the wedding!"

I had no choice but to sound brave and reckless, because I knew I was lost. We both were, and were thinking: What now?

I put my arm around her, and when she didn't object I hugged her. After a while, I got to my knees, so that I could see her better. She lay crouched on the grassy mound, very quietly and a little fearful, like a sacrifice. I touched her arm and she got smaller—sort of shrank, without a sound, like a snail. Her eyes were wide open, watching me and making everything difficult. Then she shut them and I took this to mean that she trusted me and was giving me permission. I could see her bra and panties outlined beneath her blouse and her skirt. My hand went to her knee. I moved it higher, to where it was warmer, on her thigh.

She said, "No, don't," but made no move to stop me.

Leaning over, I kissed her, and as soon as our lips touched she opened hers and began sucking on my tongue. I was too happy to think of anything but my happiness. We had gone there alone and ignorant, and lay stupidly under the trees; but now we knew a little more. I could not tell where my flesh ended and hers began.

Wickedness entered me. My soul darkened and I felt a shameful thrill as it tottered and began to fall. It caught fire, and Tina was crying softly but holding me, and then we were both burning.

TWO

WHALE STEAKS

1.

With a name like the Maldwyn Country Club I knew it had to be one of these fake-English places with a look that said Keep Out. I was right, and the reason for the Englishness was that it was all Armenians. And it took over an hour to get there from Medford Square. But I needed the job.

Walking up the long driveway to my lifeguard interview, I thought: No girlfriend, no car, no money, no job—nothing except funerals dragging past in a procession in my soul, and sorrowing hopes, and the tyrant Pain planting his black flag in my skull. I had been reading Baudelaire on the bus.

Big cars went past me. It was not the *Nixon* stickers in the windows, and not the speed; what made me feel small was the way they swished by, missing me by an inch, as if I didn't exist or didn't matter. They didn't see me, or else they figured a pedestrian had to be a bum. Their business sense was: Money talks, bullshit walks. They didn't know that I was in college, and that I was plotting their downfall, putting a curse on them. They had everything. Pretty soon they might even have me.

On my left was the ninth hole—one man hunched over his putt, the other golfers watching. I hated them for being fat, for being happy; hated the look of them, the breeze blowing their plaid pants, the way they were doing just as they pleased. I gave the putt the evil eye and the ball slid past the cup. When the foursome moved off they seemed to be browbeating the caddies—two kids carrying doubles in this heat. I thought: Why not kill them?

"I'm a communist," I told my brother Louie, when he said he had joined Students for Kennedy.

"You don't like him because he's a Catholic," Louie said.

"I don't like him because he's a bad Catholic," I said. "I'm voting for Gus Hall. American Communist Party. It's legal!"

It was wonderful to see how this little pronouncement shocked him. I tried it again with Mimi Hardwick at Kappa Phi. She had said she couldn't go out with me. She made excuses, and when I badgered her she said, "I'm afraid of you." It was simply that she didn't want to sleep with me.

I said, "I'm a communist," because I knew I would probably never see her again, and I wanted to leave her with a worry.

"I don't believe you," she said. "What do you mean?"

I was looking at her and thinking: Girls get up in the morning and wash themselves carefully and put on four different types of underwear, not including a girdle, and choose a certain color sweater and clean socks and a matching skirt. They take the rollers out of their hair. They put in ribbons, they do their eyes, they rouge their cheeks, put on perfume and lipstick, earrings, beads, a bracelet on one wrist, a tiny watch on the other, and all day they go on checking themselves in mirrors. It was an amazing amount of trouble, but it worked. Why were they so surprised when we wanted to squeeze them and feel them up? Mimi Hardwick smelled of lavender and I wanted to push my nose against her.

"We have meetings. Secret meetings. We're all socialists."

"But what do you stand for?"

"Destruction," I said.

On another occasion, to get her to sleep with me, I had told her that I had twice tried to kill myself. And I said that I took drugs—cough syrup with codeine in it, the Family Size bottle, chugalugged the whole thing. I told her I had hitchhiked to Florida, getting rides with maniacs. Anything so that she would remember me. But it just frightened her.

Telling her I was a communist was my way of saying goodbye.

"Can I help you?"

That woke me from my reverie. It was a security guard. His question meant: What's a kid in an army jacket and sunglasses and torn sneakers think he's doing here at the Maldwyn Country Club?

I said, "I have an appointment with Mr. Kaloostian."

"Go ahead."

But I was angry with myself for giving him this information. I should have said, *It's highly confidential* and let him figure it out.

The clubhouse ahead of me at the top of the driveway was a white building with a roof of green shingles. It was surrounded by fat trimmed bushes, and geraniums in plump pots, and in the bulgey bay window there were fat golfers going *haw-haw!* This was all supposed to be English. Another fat car went past and almost clipped me. I felt small and skinny. I smelled roasting meat. I was hungry, and being here made me feel hateful. I imagined starting a fire in the clubhouse and watching the golfers run out with burning hair. *Help!* they'd scream as I turned my back.

The secretary's signboard said MISS A. BERBERIAN.

She said, "Is it about the lifeguard job?"

I was annoyed that she guessed it and so I said, "That's partly the reason. The rest is highly confidential, I'm afraid. You can tell him I'm here."

There were two men in the office. Mr. Kaloostian was the purple-faced man in the suit. He introduced the man next to him in the sports shirt. "This is Mr. Mattanza, our pool superintendant."

"Vic Mattanza," the man said and squeezed my hand too hard.

Standing up added very little to his height. He was short and dark. His black hair was pushed straight back. He was one of those Italians who looked to me like an Indian brave—dark, brooding, and with tiny eyes very close to his big nose. He was short, yet I could see from the way his shirt was stretched that he was muscular. But he was too muscular for his size. He reminded me of a clenched fist.

"Sit down, Andrew."

"Andre," I said, and they frowned at me.

"It says here you live in Medford, you go to UMass, nineteen in April, you're a medical student—" He was reading from my application in a way that embarrassed me. All these trivial facts made me feel small. I had the urge to tell him I was a communist.

"Pre-med," I said.

"Hey, that's great," Mattanza said, "but we're looking for someone who can swim."

"I can swim. And I thought a knowledge of first aid might be an asset." I smiled at Mattanza. His close-set eyes were fixed on me. He was thinking: Wise-ass.

"That's a very good point," Kaloostian said.

"Except we need a lifeguard."

Mattanza's teeth were very white and large and doglike.

"That's why I'm here." I could tell he hated my smile.

"It says here you worked at Wright's Pond."

"Right. I was a lockerboy. Then I got my Red Cross lifesaving certificate and became a lifeguard. After the intermediate I got the advanced."

"You mind if we see your badge?" Mattanza said. "It's not that we don't believe you."

"My mother sewed it on my bathing suit."

Mattanza looked at Kaloostian. "His mother sewed it on his bathing suit."

"That's where it's supposed to go," I said.

He flashed his snake-eyes at me.

"Is that the only proof of your proficiency?" Kaloostian said.

"I've got the certificate," I said, and pulled it out of my book and unfolded it.

"You're a reader, I see," Kaloostian said, and he leaned over to look at the title. He couldn't see.

"The Flowers of Evil," I said.

"Gatz," Mattanza said under his breath.

"What did you do to earn this?"

"Swam a mile. Learned the rescues. Rowed. Surface dived. Picked up weights from the bottom. Jumped in with my clothes on and made a flotation device with my pants—you knot the cuffs and inflate the legs. And the first aid." Kaloostian had asked the question but I was speaking to Mattanza. "That's the advanced certificate."

Mattanza said, "Great. But what kind of practical experience have you got?"

"Two years at Wright's Pond."

"We're talking about a swimming pool."

"It's tougher at a pond," I said.

He moved his mouth at me. His lips said: Prove it. His teeth said: I'm dangerous—I bite.

I spoke to Kaloostian. "In a pond you've got poor visibility, deeper water, noise, greater density of swimmers, and weeds. Last summer I pulled three people out. One of them went about two hundred pounds. I used a cross-chest carry on him."

"So why aren't you still there at Wright's?" Mattanza said, in a challenging way.

I could just imagine this little twerp strutting in a tight pair of trunks.

"This seems a nicer place," I said, and when Kaloostian smiled smugly at this I said, "More congenial, and a kind of English atmosphere."

"We're very proud of our club," Kaloostian said. "It's like a family here. The members, the employees. We're all part of a winning team."

What bullshit, I thought. But I needed the job.

"I guess I want to be part of the team."

Mattanza winced and put his finger on my application. "It says here your hobby is shooting. You got a gun?"

"Not on me," I said.

"I hate guns," Kaloostian said, and shook his face so that his eyes rattled at me.

Everyone said *I hate guns* in the most virtuous way, as if all guns were murder weapons.

"I shoot beer cans," I said. "I think some of your members might be interested in marksmanship."

"Why do you want to work at Maldwyn Country Club?" Kaloostian said, putting his elbows on the table. I could not understand why his face was so purple—was it a tan or high blood pressure?

"Why did you advertise?" I said.

"We need a lifeguard."

"I need a job," I said.

"But we need more than a lifeguard," Mattanza said.

"It takes a lot of humility to be a lifeguard," Kaloostian said. "Humility and perception and strength of character. Do you know what I mean by those words?"

I don't want this job, I thought. I'll work in a bakery. I'll sell papers. I'll get a job with the state at an MDC pool. I'll cut grass. I'll steal cars.

"He means you keep your eyes open. No reading. No blabbing. No backtalk. No college stuff." Mattanza was getting so angry I decided that I wanted the job, just to spite him. "We don't want a candy-ass."

"I've got references," I said.

"A very good one from Mike Bagdikian."

I almost said *He's an old friend of my father's.* He had told me to apply. Good hours, good money, a nice class of people. Had he met Mattanza?

"You're nineteen?" Mattanza said.

"That's right."

"Sheesh," he said, exasperated. "We're looking for someone who can take responsibility."

I said, "I pulled three people out of Wright's, like I said. One I had to give artificial respiration. They would have died if I hadn't fished them out. It was in the *Medford Mercury.* But I don't know—maybe you don't call a matter of life and death responsible."

"We'll be in touch," Kaloostian said.

Instead of going straight home I took the bus to Cambridge to kill time. I walked to Mount Auburn Cemetery and looked for the grave of Mary Baker Eddy. I had heard that she had a telephone in her tomb, so that if she woke from the dead at some point she could call the Mother Church at Mass Ave. and say, "Listen, it's Mrs. Eddy—I'm back from the dead. Dig me up." But I couldn't find the tomb.

I stretched out on a grassy knoll and read Baudelaire, a poem about a dead sheep with its legs upraised "like a lustful woman." And I saw a couple kissing near a tree and the girl's legs were like the sheep's in the poem. I watched them, pretending to read, and felt like Baudelaire myself, wicked and watchful.

After that I walked to Harvard Square. There was a restaurant on the street corner beside the Coop. The menu was taped to the window, *Special Today—Whale Steak $1.29.* Never mind the coleslaw, french fries, dessert and coffee. I imagined a whale being harpooned, and a vast thrashing tail, and blood on the waves. In *Moby Dick,* one of the characters—Stubb or Daggoo—made a big deal out of eating whale steaks. And there was a whole chapter about eating whales. I made a mental note to look it up. But what I wanted at that moment was a whale steak. I hadn't had any lunch and I didn't have any money. So this hunger and inspiration just insulted me. I thought: This moment will never come again. Who should I blame for denying it to me?

I looked in the bookstores, and then wandered around the Harvard Coop and, passing through the men's department I stole a beret. I put it on outside and took the bus back to Medford.

"What if you don't get the job?" my mother said. "What are you going to do?"

I didn't have the slightest idea, but I was thinking that this house did not feel like home anymore.

"I've got lots of irons in the fire," I said.

"Just don't ask me for any money."

"I've got enough."

All I had was my bus fare back to the Maldwyn Country Club. But that was handy, because the next day Kaloostian called and said, "You've got the job. We'd like you to start tomorrow."

They could have told me that before. By making me wait they were trying to intimidate me: that's what you did with employees—you made them wait. You did not realize they were reading Baudelaire and writing poems that began *Snake-eyes, you dago dwarf with dog-like teeth* . . .

"It's a new pool," Mattanza said. Just as I had predicted, he wore a tiny bathing suit. He was short and broadshouldered and had a bunch of bulging balls and a hairy back. "Every morning it's your job to seat the filters. You know how to seat a filter?"

"I think I can learn."

"Sure you can," Mattanza said. "You're a wise guy. I hate wise guys. Ever been in the army?"

I said no.

"You're lucky, because if you was in the army they'd break your balls for being a wise guy."

"What do we do with this filter?"

"I don't like the way you talk," Mattanza said. "If you don't get into line I'm going to have to let you go."

He was trembling as he said this, and he was avoiding my eyes. He seemed very strange—nervous and angry; so I decided to calm him.

"Okay, Vic, you're the boss."

"Yeah, don't you forget it."

He showed me how to pour the white chlorine powder into the spool-like filters, and how to screw them into the holes beside the pool. He showed me vacuuming and brushing and how to scoop leaves. That was all, and I could tell from the way he did it that he wasn't very good at it himself. He was too self-conscious and neurotic to be mechanical-minded. He made a mess of the filters and shook the head off the vacuum. I could tell that it annoyed him to see me calmly pushing the contraptions to and fro, but there was nothing he could do.

The swimmers were mostly women and children. There were no boys my age and only a few girls. It was a new pool. The main characteristic of a new pool was that people actually swam in it, and jumped and splashed. I was sure that next year these people would be sunning themselves near it, and that probably no one would be in the water.

"Hello there," a woman said. I noticed that she had been drinking all morning. "I'm Mrs. Toomajian. You know my husband, Kevork?"

I said I didn't know him.

"The Chrysler dealership on Commonwealth Ave.? With the big sign in front? Everybody knows Kevork. He gives deals on new cars."

I said, "Is that your daughter on the diving board?"

I had seen the girl—who was about sixteen, and pretty—talking to this woman earlier. Guessing right made her cross.

"Never mind her," Mrs. Toomajian said. She swallowed some more whiskey. "She's got a friend coming up from New Haven in a couple of weeks. Maybe you'd like to meet her. You could come over."

"And meet your daughter?"

"Her friend," she said, correcting me. "Also she does a little house-work for us."

I said, "I'll think about it."

I did, and it occurred to me that this woman had an objection to my being friendly with her daughter, but was trying to pair me up with this friend, who was their part-time servant. It was a crude kind of Armenian snobbery and when I saw the woman near the pool after lunch I had an urge to push her in.

Mattanza said, "You're talking. You're not supposed to talk. These people are members. You're not a member. Eyes front."

He walked away before I could reply.

We had lunch together in the kitchen—Mattanza; the security guard; several waiters; the assistant golf pro, Miss Berberian; and me. The cook's name was Reuben. He hated serving us, but there was no one else to do it.

Mattanza said, "Hey, how about more pot roast? I hate vegetables. I've got to have meat. See that?" He poked his plate with his knife. "Pure protein. Meat."

The only time I saw him smile was when he said *meat.*

After lunch I worked until five, when children were not allowed into the pool. The mothers went home with their kids and the men—their husbands—came back from work and took a dip. They were hairy overworked men, very agitated from the day's business—talkative and irritable. They had no pleasures, they looked stupid, they laughed like bullies, they never read. I was glad to leave.

That was the pattern. It should have been an easy job but the people made it hard. I paced the edge of the pool and kept my mouth shut. I was not allowed to eat or drink near the pool, I was forbidden to read, and I could talk to members only if they spoke to me first. They seldom did. They were not unfriendly, just uninterested.

"You're not here to make friends," Mattanza said. "You've got a job to do."

Mattanza had problems. He said he had two kids. "I get married. I sleep with my wife. She gets pregnant. She shuts me off—no more sex. She has a baby—Julie, lovely little kid. We start again—hey, it's natural! She gets pregnant again. She shuts me off again. I says, 'What is this?' So if I want kids I can get laid, and if I don't want kids I gotta play with myself."

He was silent, watching beautiful Nina Balakian preparing to dive and snapping her bathing suit over her buttocks as it rode up.

"I used to have all kinds of broads," Mattanza said. "I went into the North End. I told them my name was Joe Falco. I had all the broads I wanted. Want my advice? Never get married. The sex isn't worth it, and all they do is talk—yah-yah-yah," and he opened and closed his hand to indicate gabbing.

Afterwards I think he was sorry that he had told me all that because he snapped at me when he saw me talking to a woman.

"Eyes front," he said. "How many times do I have to tell you? Jesus, I hope they get you in the army."

The woman was about fifty and very friendly. She was reading a book by Norman Mailer. It was unusual to see anyone reading here—and Norman Mailer! The book was *Advertisements for Myself.*

"It's a ragbag," she said. "Some of it is kind of cute, but he's too tough for his own good. Did you ever hear about how he stabbed his wife? It was after a party. She said, 'He had a strange look in his eye.' Then he knifed her. She didn't press charges. What a ding-a-ling!"

At that point Mattanza had interrupted.

"I have to go back to work," I said.

At the end of the first week, Mattanza said, "I don't like your attitude."

"What's wrong with it?"

"See? Just the way you said that! Listen to yourself. You've got a bad attitude." He brooded for a while, then said, "If you don't shape up I'm going to have to let you go."

2.

I had never worked in a place where I couldn't read. Only reading made work bearable. I brought Baudelaire to the Maldwyn Country Club and sneaked looks at it, but when Mattanza saw me he told me to put it away.

"What is it with these books?" he said. "Hey, know what I think? All this reading makes you crazy. Not only ruins your eyes. I mean, it's no good for you." He wagged his scaly fingers at his head, an Italian gesture meaning cracked.

"So when your kids go to school you won't let them read books, is that right?"

"School books. That's different."

"How do you know this isn't a school book?"

"The way you got your nose in it. You like it." He winced at me. "You're going to make yourself *pazzo.*"

"I see. So school books don't drive you crazy, because they're no fun to read. It's only enjoyable books that turn you into a mental case. Is that right?"

We were doing the filters—Mattanza pouring the chlorine in while I screwed them into their holes. Mattanza put the bag of chemicals down. His tiny eyes were black with anger.

"You think I'm stupid, don't you?"

"I don't know," I said, and I became very vague, as if it was impossible for me to determine whether or not he was stupid. I faced him and tried to look baffled.

"Hey, if you don't like this job I could find lots of guys to take your place."

I decided not to reply. I didn't want to tell him what I thought of the job.

"I've got them pleading with me," Mattanza said. "I could show you the applications. Know why there's so many?"

I smiled at him.

He gathered his fingers and shook them at me in another Italian gesture.

"Because this place has class."

I said, "You mean money. That's all you mean. Money."

"Fucken right that's all I mean."

I didn't mention taste or intelligence or generosity, I didn't say anything more. I was fairly sure he was crazy. He was certainly unpredictable. We went on doing the filters—Mattanza shaking the chlorine while I did the fitting—and then he spoke again.

"I used to go in disguise," he said. "I was Joe Falco. I had this special suit that I just wore in the North End, nowhere else. I used to comb my hair different. Know something? A lot of broads like to be slapped around. You wouldn't know that because you don't know shit. But I can tell when they want me to hit them. I just fucken slam them and they love it. They get this"—he weighed his little fist—"right on the mouth. Only it wasn't me. It was Joe Falco." Mattanza looked at me and made his mouth into a smile. "Falco was a crazy bastard."

* * *

No reading, no talking, and Mattanza didn't like me looking away from the pool. A job that seemed to me to have pleasant possibilities quickly turned into a grind. How could a lifeguard job be hard? But at the Maldwyn Country Club it was hard. And if I was only a few minutes late, Mattanza ranted.

"I'm docking your pay! You're losing an hour! You're late!" he said. "I should give you your walking papers. Know my problem?"

"I can't guess."

"I'm too nice. Suit up and get your ass out here."

"The bus was late."

"Don't blame the bus. Don't give me no excuses."

I hated the bus—hated the hard seats, and the way they smelled; hated the condescending bus advertisements that were designed for the down-at-heel bus passenger. *Ever thought of completing your education?* or *There is a future for you in TV and Radio Repair!* I wanted a motorcyle, but how could I buy one on forty-four dollars a week—they withheld seven-fifty in tax. I gave my mother fifteen, kept fifteen and banked the rest. I needed nine hundred by September: I would never make it. Working to make money made me distrust work and despise money.

What demoralized me was that all the members had money: they drove Cadillacs, they played golf, they had huge lunches, and if they wanted a drink they ordered it. They lay spread-eagled by the pool, tanning themselves; they drank. And I stood watching them, which was my job, and I resisted the urge to read.

They had sporty clothes and I had army-surplus. The only advantage I had was that all I was required to wear was a bathing suit. I was healthy and a good swimmer, but so what? I deeply resented the fact that I was a servant and regarded as inferior. And it was a trap: because they were stupid I would never be able to prove to them that I was intelligent.

One hot day in the second week at the club I stood in the sunshine feeling dizzy, and, fearing that I was going light-headed, I decided to plunge in and cool off. Mattanza was waiting for me at the top of the ladder when I came out.

"No swimming," he said. "Hey, don't you like this job? Because if you keep goofing off like this I'm going to have to let you go."

But less than an hour later he had put on his tiny bathing suit and begun diving into the pool. He swam poorly but he was a good diver. I was glad to see that he was the sort of show-off who sometimes goes too far. I hoped that he would overdo it and bash his brains out on the edge of the pool.

There were girls my age who spent the whole day there. I watched them but I did not speak to them. They had wide Armenian faces and were heavy, and had big brown thighs and broad feet and square shoulders. In spite of all their money they would always look the way they looked, which was a kind of warning. They lay sleepily in the sun and got even browner.

The boys my age made me feel like an outsider. They were not intentionally rude, but they were too selfish to know how to be friendly and too stupid to hold a conversation. The girls were all daughters and the boys were all sons—special for that and protected. Their whole lives were taken care of. They were fat and slow and they would become fatter and slower; they had money. Even the younger ones were hairy, and a few fourteen-year-olds had mustaches. I could tell from the way they jumped into the pool and splashed everyone that they would be hell when they grew up.

"That's my kid, Kenny," a man said to me one day. The boy had done a cannonball from the end of the pool, nearly landing on a woman's head. But the man was laughing. He loved seeing aggression in his son. He pointed to himself. He said, "Deek Palanjian."

I smiled at him. I saw Mattanza watching. He was thinking: No talking. But Palanjian was talking to me.

"Elia Kazan—know who I mean? Big movie director? He's an Armenian."

"I didn't know that."

"Michael Arlen? Wrote a lot of best-sellers? Know what his real name is?"

I shook my head because Mattanza was watching.

"Dikran Kouyoumjian."

"No kidding."

"That guy in Russia—he's Armenian."

"Which guy in Russia?"

"Anastas Mikoyan," he said, and waved to his son, who had climbed onto the diving board. He was a short heavy brown boy with a shaven head, and he moved nimbly with his arms down, like an ape. "Hey, Kenny, show me a dive!"

"How do you stand this job?" the woman said. It was the same woman who had been reading Norman Mailer. Today she was reading *The Henry Miller Reader*—the man's sly devilish face on the book jacket looking up at me from between the woman's breasts.

"The job's all right."

"You don't have to be polite to me. I've been watching you," she said. "I think you hate it here."

It astounded me that she was able to read my mind, and I was embarrassed because I guessed she might have an inkling of all the ingenious ways I had devised to destroy the Maldwyn Country Club: making a minefield of the golf course, poisoning the water cooler, bombing the clubhouse. And lately I had been thinking that, just for the cruel fun of it, I would jam a potato in everyone's exhaust pipe—all those limousines in the parking lot—so that they wouldn't be able to start the engine. Then they would have to walk, like me.

"I do hate it," I said. "But I need a job."

"What would you like to be doing?"

I thought: I would like to be lying here in the sun, drinking cold lemonade and reading a good book. I would like to be doing pretty much what everyone here was doing, which was another reason I hated this job. It was like being very hungry and working in a restaurant, bringing people food; like standing on the sidewalk reading *Whale Steaks $1.29* and not having any money.

"I'd like to be reading," I said, because it seemed rude to tell her what I pictured—myself on the chaise lounge, with my feet out. "What do you think of that book?"

"It's lovely," she said. "He's so funny. Have you read Henry Miller?"

"No. I thought he was banned in the US."

"His best books are banned. But someday we'll be able to read them, and we'll probably find them very boring. Imagine preventing people from reading something—as if reading is going to make us into monsters!"

I looked up expecting to see Mattanza: that stupid man had

a book-banning mentality. No sane person could ever find a book dangerous, and it struck me then that an unmistakable sign of beetle-browed paranoia was seeing a book as a threat. The fact that I couldn't spot Mattanza made me suspect that he was spying on me.

"Lawrence Durrell thinks Miller's a genius. He wrote the Introduction."

"I've read *Justine,*" I said. "And *Balthazar.* I'm waiting for the others to be published in paperback."

"You know the characters Narouz and Nessim? I'm their mother."

"I don't get it."

"Same name—Leila. My other name is much too difficult. You must find our names ridiculous."

"Mine's pretty ridiculous. Andy Parent."

"I'm Leila Mamalujian—my husband's the contractor. The John Hancock Building? He put it up. Big deal."

"I don't think I've seen him here."

"We never come here together. We never do anything together. That's probably why it works. Would you like to have lunch sometime?"

I said, "I'm not supposed to fraternize with the club members. It's a rule."

"That's why I asked. It's more exciting if you're breaking a rule."

"Mattanza would kill me."

"He has a problem. His size, I think. Did you know that his wife won't sleep with him unless they're planning to have a baby? She thinks sex has something to do with having children."

She didn't laugh. She lit a cigarette, reddening one end with her lipstick and looking at me through big bulbous sunglasses.

"Mrs. Mattanza could use a little Henry Miller," Mrs. Mamalujian said. "So how about lunch?"

"I work every day."

"You have a day off. I've been watching you."

"On my day off I'm usually hustling."

Mrs. Mamalujian said, "Lunch is just a figure of speech."

It wasn't a figure of speech to me. It was a meal in a restaurant. You went in, had a drink, ordered prawn cocktail to start, and then a whale steak with mashed potatoes and string beans, and apple pie à la mode for dessert, and two coffees; and afterwards you went for a walk and smoked a White Owl to digest the meal. It was something I longed to do. I liked the weighty word "meal" and nowadays meal meant whale steaks.

Mrs. Mamalujian's close attention was making me self-conscious. I said, "I've got to get back to work."

That evening as I was getting ready to go home, Mattanza stopped me and said, "I've been getting complaints about you."

"What kind of complaints?"

"Serious ones. Like you're neglecting your job. Like you've been goofing off. Like you talk too much. And somebody saw you with a book."

"What was I doing with the book? Something weird?"

My sarcasm enraged him. "That's right—keep it up! Piss me off. See where it gets you."

For a moment I was going to tell him to shove the job. But I needed it. It was more money than I would be earning at Wright's, and fewer hours. The State was hiring lifeguards for the MDC pools, but I knew they were zoos.

"These complaints," I said, "are they verbal or written?"

"You are such a smart-ass," Mattanza said.

"Who complained about me? What did they say? I've got a right to know."

Mattanza narrowed his tiny eyes at me. "You writing a book?"

I stared at him until he blinked. Then I said, "Yeah."

"Then leave this chapter out."

He started to walk away, a little bowlegged Indian brave from Sicilia. He suddenly turned as I was watching him, and he said, "Don't mess with me. I was in the army. Korea. I seen action."

For a few days I didn't speak to anyone. Were any of these people complaining about me? I felt Mattanza was making it all up, but what if he wasn't? On my way to work one day, cutting through the parking lot, I saw a big blue Lincoln leaking gas— the full tank expanding in the heat, and gas all over the bumper. Why not fling a match on it and blow it up? The only thing that kept me from doing it was the thought that I might be blown up with it. I hated these huge cars; but I knew how to sabotage them—sugar in the gas tank to foul the engine, a potato to plug the exhaust pipe. I saw Mrs. Mamalujian drive in—she had a white Buick—and I crept away.

She never swam. She wore a big billowy gown with poppies on it, and a white sunhat and sunglasses. Her straw shoes had fake fruit stitched to them. She drank gin and read *The Henry Miller Reader.* She looked clownish but I knew that while she was sober she was intelligent. She never spoke to anyone else.

After a few drinks she stopped talking about books. Then it was just that business about lunch.

"What we should do is simply meet and have a bite of something. It doesn't matter what."

I found *It doesn't matter what* very strange.

"Do you like Chinese food?"

"It gives me pimples but I like it."

"Or we could meet anywhere and talk about books. And maybe this place where we meet could be out of town, or somewhere special. You like talking about books, right?"

"Yes. At the moment I'm trying to get Ovid's *Metamorphoses.*"

"That sounds heavy going."

"I need it for something I'm planning to write."

"About ancient Rome?"

"No. It's a play set on the Notions Counter of a big department store like Filene's. You know Filene's Basement?"

She nodded. "And when I say this place could be somewhere special I have lots of ideas."

"The thing is I don't have a car."

"You can use mine anytime you like."

"Thanks very much," I said. "I wish I had a motorcycle."

"You want a motorcycle? I'll give you a motorcycle."

Just her saying that made me stop wanting it.

"God, am I bored," she said. "Aren't you bored?"

"I'm working," I said. "So it doesn't matter."

"These women are always looking at you."

"Mattanza's had complaints."

"I feel like complaining about him," Mrs. Mamalujian said. She was drunk but at least she was on my side.

I looked up and saw his big Indian nose and tiny eyes peering at me through the shrubbery.

Every night after work I took the bus to Medford and walked home. I changed. I went for an ice cream at Brigham's and ate it outside in the cool night air. Or I sat in the public library across from Saint Joe's, and read. Or I watched television, the progress of the presidential campaign. I went to bed after the *Tonight Show*. One night Jack Paar said he was going to introduce a living saint, and a little Irishman with glistening eyes stepped onstage—Dr. Tom Dooley.

Dooley talked awhile about his hospital and his wonderful work, and then he stood up and put his hands together in a praying gesture and said, "God bless you all. As long as I have strength in my body I will go back among my people and work. But I need your help. Give, for God's sake—give."

The way his voice broke gave me the creeps. I thought he was crazy, too, and the fact that everyone applauded like mad also gave me the creeps.

"He has cancer," my mother said the next day. "He does God's work—it's a miracle. You used to talk about being a missionary."

Once I had seen a missionary wearing an Arab headdress and talking about the desert, and I thought: That's for me—but it wasn't the preaching part, it was the travel. I'll get out that way, even if it means being a missionary, was my idea.

"I'd still like to go to Africa or Turkey, or somewhere."

"And do God's work?"

"No, just do my work," I said. That was my new idea.

But it annoyed her to hear me say so. What a summer. It was almost July. I still had no girlfriend, no money, no motorcycle. I was trying to save for the fall, so I avoided everything that cost money. I hated the bus. I hated my job. I delved deeper under the black lid of the big cauldron where imperceptible and vast Humanity was boiling. Baudelaire.

"Want to borrow it?" Mrs. Mamalujian said to me. This was the end of my second week at the Maldwyn Country Club. She handed over *The Henry Miller Reader*. Miller's roguish face leered from the cover. It was hardback, brand-new, smelling of Mrs. Mamalujian's perfume.

"I'll take good care of it."

"I think he's basically a comedian," she said. "He's funny, he uses funny words, the sex is a farce. That's the whole point."

At lunch, in the kitchen, when Reuben served us coffee, I took it out and began to read it.

Mattanza said, "Hey, what's that supposed to be?" and snatched it.

"Give that book back," I said and stood up to intimidate him.

" 'I pulled my cap over my eyes and muttered, "Fuck you, Jack." And that's the way it was that summer, a bloody fucking nightmare in which—' Hey, that's nice. That's very nice. What would your mother say if she knew you were reading this shit?"

"It's not shit."

"It's *gatz*. I wouldn't have that in my house. Hey, where did you get this fucking thing."

I tried to grab it from him, but before I could he flipped it open and saw scribbled on the flyleaf *Leila Mamalujian*.

"Hey, you stole this book!"

"She loaned it to me."

"You're not supposed to talk to the members. Hey, you got something going with her? Hey, you know what I think of this book?" He held it over a pot of stew that was bubbling on the stove.

Reuben said, "Get out of my kitchen" and took the book from Mattanza and handed it to me.

I read some of it that night. It was wild, it was funny, it thrilled me. I had never read anyone so foulmouthed who was at the same time so bright. It was energetic and coarse. I went to sleep smiling, thinking of *o glabrous, o glab and glairy,* and I was still reading it on the bus the next day.

Mattanza was waiting for me when I arrived at the club.

He said, "Don't bother to change."

He stood in a break in the hedge, blocking my way.

"I'm letting you go."

"What do you mean?"

"You don't work here anymore. So take a walk."

I wanted to hit him, but if I did he would have had an excuse. I said, "I'm going to talk to Kaloostian."

Miss Berberian, seeing me, handed me an envelope. I opened it, thinking it was a letter. It was a check for thirty-one seventy-six.

"Where's Mr. Kaloostian?"

"He's not in today." She was very intent on her typing.

"I've just been fired. Doesn't Kaloostian know that?"

"Yes. See, he signed the check. I'm really sorry, Andre."

"Mattanza's crazy, you know. He's really nuts."

She didn't say anything.

I lurked for a while. I went to the kitchen and asked Reuben for a coffee. He gave it to me and said, "I hear that little wop canned you. Don't worry. There's plenty of work around. Know what I think? Get an education and then you'll never have to work." I drank the coffee and when Reuben left the kitchen I heaved a bag of potatoes onto my shoulder and headed for the parking lot.

Every car, except for Mrs. Mamalujian's, received a potato in its exhaust pipe. I jammed them as far as I could, so that they wouldn't show and would be hard to remove. And I laughed to think of them all stranded here, when they wanted to go home.

Instead of going straight home, where my mother would ask questions about my losing my job—why else was I home so early?—I went to Medford Square for lunch—a submarine sandwich, at Salem Street Subs.

A new man was making them today. He looked slightly drunk, his paper hat crookedly fitting his head. He was Italian, which was odd, because Italians seldom got drunk in the Boston area.

"What can I do for you?"

"A large meatball sub."

"What do you want on it?"

"Everything."

He measured off a foot of Italian bread from a long loaf and cut it and then slashed it lengthwise. He began ladling meatballs into it.

"So what do you think of Henry Miller?" He had seen my book.

"He's good. He's funny," I said. "He's got a great vocabulary."

The man smiled. "He employs sesquipedalian verbiage," he said, and eased the meatballs into the bread with the heel of the ladle.

I was fascinated that a drunken Italian in a paper hat would say something like this.

"But his best books are banned because of our procrustean laws," he said. "Know what I mean?"

"Something like procrastinate?"

He shook his head—no. He was spooning chopped onions and tomatoes.

"Procrustes was a robber in Greek legend who had an iron bed. It was a certain size. He made people lie on it and if they were too tall for it he cut their legs off. If they were too short he stretched them to fit the bed. Procrustean. It means ruthlessly inflexible."

"What if they were the right size—what if they fit?"

"No one ever fits," the man said, and handed me my meatball sub. "He was killed by Theseus. You owe me thirty-five cents."

He said he was a writer and I was sure he was telling me a secret. He was writing a play set in Leipzig. Had I thought of writing plays? I said yes, telling him one of my secrets. He said he hoped to see me again, the next time I wanted a sub. His name, he said, was Sal Balinieri.

That night I wrote a Henry Miller letter to the Maldwyn Country Club and used the word "procrustean" in it.

3.

The next day I went to the MDC pool on the Charles River, across the road from the Mass General Hospital, and I was hired as the third lifeguard. The other two were Larry McGinnis and Vinny Muzzaroll.

Larry said, "A position just became vacant this morning. It's kind of a strange story. See, Arturo Lopez, the other lifeguard, was a member of a street gang on Harrison Avenue. About five of the guys jumped a woman around midnight and dragged her up to the roof of a building, where they took turns raping her. When it was Arturo's turn, and he was about to bang her, he saw it was his mother, and he jumped off the roof. Which is why we have a vacancy."

I was on the point of saying *It's like a Greek tragedy* when Vinny Muzzaroll piped up.

"Don't believe him," Muzzaroll said. "Lopez joined the army. It was the only way he could get back to San Juan."

Still, I kept thinking of the story. It made no difference to me that it hadn't happened. As he had spoken I had vividly imagined it, and I knew I would never forget it.

We took turns on the lifeguard chair. The pool was a stew of thrashing swimmers. Larry said, "It's impossible to watch them all. Every night when we clear the pool I expect to see a stiff on the bottom that's been there all day." The pay was better than at the Maldwyn Country Club, the hours were shorter, and no one minded if I read on the job, providing the book wasn't obvious.

"The only reason Muzzaroll doesn't read on the job is he can't read," Larry said.

I found it very relaxing here. It had been a strain to work among people who had money and no brains. Except for Mrs. Mamalujian, they had seemed dreadful people; and I did not know which was worse, the way they had ignored me or the way they had stared. Thinking about them often made me angry. One lunch hour I called Kaloostian. Reuben had baffled me one day by telling me that this man was an Assyrian.

I said, "You didn't reply to my letter."

"I didn't realize you wanted one. It's not the kind of letter that's easy to answer."

"That would have been the polite thing to do," I said. "I guess it's not an Assyrian custom."

He went silent. It was probably a mistake to refer to his origins.

"I think Mattanza's out of his mind," I said. "I think he's a feeb."

"We understood that from your letter, but we can't give you your job back."

"I don't want the fucking job back—I want an explanation."

"So do we. For example, we were wondering what happened to a twenty-five-pound bag of potatoes that vanished from the kitchen."

"Don't ask me."

"And how they ended up in the parking lot, stuck into the exhaust pipes of the members' cars."

I had been so angry about his not replying to my letter that I had forgotten about that. I was glad we were on the phone, so that he could not see me smile.

"Noreen Dorian had a sick mother. Naturally she couldn't visit her. I understand the poor woman was beside herself. Putting a potato into someone's exhaust pipe is a pretty heartless act."

Hearing him say it that way made me laugh, but I put my hand over my mouth.

"Some of those cars are still not working properly."

"It's got nothing to do with me," I said. "I'm not interested in those cars. All I want is an answer to my letter."

Kaloostian wasn't apologetic. He said, "Know what I'd like to do? I'd like to keep that letter and show it to you in about twenty years."

"What for?"

"Just to see what you'll say. I think you'll be ashamed of it."

"I won't! I'll be proud of it. In twenty years I'll say the same thing."

"About 'pernicious little tyrants in Bermuda shorts'?"

"Yes, all of that. I won't forget it. I want you to know one thing. I will always remember that you and your friends will never get hemorrhoids, because you're perfect assholes."

I hung up, banging the receiver hard.

There was a snicker behind me—a girl suppressing laughter; but when I saw her I laughed too.

"I'm glad you weren't talking to me," she said.

"That was the president of the Maldwyn Country Club. He let me down. I have no mercy."

She was slim, pinch-faced and blonde. She had a biggish nose and small breasts. Her dark blue bathing suit made her seem paler than she was, and she had alert intelligent eyes. I liked her lips and the way her hair was tangled. She had the bad posture that I associated with shy girls—sort of pigeon-toed as she stood there. She was carrying a book. Anyone with a book interested me. Hers was *On the Road,* the hardback.

"Can I use the phone?" she said.

"Go ahead," I said, and realized that I had been staring at her.

I went back to my post, which was a tall steel chair at the edge of the pool. I put my leg up and tucked *The Henry Miller Reader* just behind my knee. I had thought the crowd and the noise—all the running and screaming—would make this pool a hard place to work. But my reading took the curse off it. The swimmers didn't create problems, but the others did—they fought, they tripped and fell, they bruised themselves and cracked their skulls. Muzzaroll did the bandaging and then kicked them out. That made it easy: if someone didn't behave we sent him home. If only I could have done that at the Maldwyn Country Club.

There were solitary men here who never swam, but only lurked and watched the little girls with hot eyes. Some kids did nothing but chase each other. Others hung on the fence like monkeys. On good days the nurses from the Mass General came over for a dip.

My back was turned to the Charles River. Sometimes I glanced around and saw the people in sailboats, the racing eights, the lovers in rowboats, the yachts making their way to Boston Harbor. But the view from the lifeguard chair was of the pool, and behind it the bathhouse, and across Memorial Drive the Mass General—people in pajamas at the windows, staring with chalky faces, looking upset.

I discovered that I could read amid the screams, the honking traffic, the running feet, and Muzzaroll's announcements on the loudspeaker: *We have found a purse. Will the owner please come to the office and identify its contents?* They played radios, they yelled, they sang. The factory whistles blared across the Charles, and the MTA trains rattled on the bridge to City Square.

At the end of the day, Muzzaroll said sharply, *We close in half an hour. All swimmers should leave the pool immediately. This means you—*

They had specific rules that everyone had to follow. It was not like the Maldwyn Country Club, where no one knew the rules and people did whatever they wanted, because they had money.

That day I climbed down from the lifeguard's chair, feeling relaxed from an afternoon of reading.

"Hello."

She said it in a friendly singsong way: it was the pale girl I had seen near the telephone.

"We're closing pretty soon," I said.

"I know. I'm going."

But she wasn't going. She was standing in front of me.

"You were really mad," she said, smiling. "I've never heard anyone say those things in real life. I thought people just yelled like that in movies."

"I wasn't yelling. I was being coldly abusive, reducing that guy to a physical wreck."

"It was nice," she said.

"Where do you live?"

"Pinckney Street," she said. "Just over there."

I liked her for not saying Beacon Hill.

"I'm walking that way," I said. "I could walk you home."

"Sounds good," she said.

I went to change and by the time I had locked up she was outside waiting. I was glad that neither Larry nor Vinny had seen her: I wanted her to be my secret. We crossed the street, and I thought: If I had some money I could take her to Harvard Gardens and have a few beers. She said she worked in a bookstore on Charles Street, but this was her day off. I could tell from her accent that she was from the South Shore. She went to BU, she was an English major; she was renting a room here for the summer. I told her my name. She said hers was Lucy.

"Want to come in?" she said, as we turned into Pinckney Street. "The thing is, if you do you have to be careful. The landlady's deaf but she's got very good eyesight. If you're quick she won't see you."

"I'll be very quick."

She turned her key and eased the front door open, and listened; then she nodded and I followed her to the end of the hall. Her room was only half a room, just a bed and a closet and a narrow space. There was nowhere to sit except on the bed.

"She didn't see us!" She seemed very pleased that we had outwitted her landlady.

I sat next to her and she leaned against me.

"So we're perfectly safe," I said.

"Sure. As long as we don't leave. If we stay right here, we're fine."

In that tiny room, with the window shut, and the shades drawn, and the closet door closed, sitting side by side on the bed.

"Then why don't we stay right here?"

I put my arm around her and she drew nearer to me. Then I leaned over and kissed her and she put her mouth on my lips and licked them. I reached under her blouse and ran my hand over her breasts and let my fingers graze her nipples. She didn't stop me, and so I did it again. She sighed, and her sigh was the sweetest kind of encouragement. I put my other hand between her thighs. She moved her legs to accommodate me. And then I jammed myself against her and pleaded for her to let me in. I thought she was resisting, but she was pleading for me to begin.

It all happened quickly, and a few minutes later we were panting in the dusty heat of the small room, our skin stuck together. The tension had left me. I did not know what to say. I felt somewhat awkward to be here with her, and the air stifled me. I wanted to get away so that I could think about it—walk down to the bus, buy an ice cream and head home; and maybe see her tomorrow and do it again. But I stayed where I was, stuck to her, out of politeness.

She said, "That was nice. I was thinking about that today."

"When?"

"At the pool—looking at you."

"You were thinking about *that?*"

She laughed and said, "Yes!"

I was slightly shocked that a girl would sit down and stare and think about screwing; but I was glad, too.

I said, "It's hot in here, Lucy."

"I'll open the window," she said.

"That's okay. I have to go pretty soon."

She didn't object. She just said, "And I have to eat."

Amazing. We had just made love passionately and furiously—and in a few minutes she would be eating spaghetti or something and I would be on the bus to Medford Square, as if nothing had happened.

I said, "As soon as I get some money we can go out to eat. I know a few places. I'd like to see you again and have some fun."

She said, "Sure."

I thought: I don't want anything more than this. And then I was walking down Pinckney Street alone, and whistling. The sun was behind the houses and the air was cool.

I kept glancing up from my book, expecting to see her in her blue bathing suit. But she didn't turn up that day, nor the day after, which was July Fourth. We always worked on holidays. Kennedy came to Boston, and Larry and Vinny ducked out to see him. They were very grateful to me for taking over, but it was no sacrifice. Kennedy was a bad Catholic and a millionaire. I had grown up with the sense that the rich were dishonest.

At about eleven o'clock Larry and Vinny came back saying that they had seen him and that he had class.

"What's Jackie Kennedy like?"

"I'd fuck her," Vinny said in a praising way.

A little later I was looking for Lucy and saw a man staring at me.

"Excuse me—you got a minute?"

I had always found that a forbidding question.

He was skinny, with very short hair and piercing eyes that were two different colors—one gray, the other blue. That made me think he had been hit very hard on the side of his head. His mouth hung open, making him seem both thoughtful and stupid. He breathed through his mouth in a laborious way that suggested he had low intelligence. His bathing suit was too tight, and I began to wonder whether men who wore very tight bathing suits were strange.

He said, "Does it bother you that we're sending tractors to Cuba, I mean actually shipping them to that dictator Fidel Castro?"

I didn't know what he was talking about. I said no, it didn't bother me; and I looked around the pool for Lucy.

"I wrote him a letter. I called him names."

"Castro? Did he write back?"

"Would you write back if someone called you names?"

I could only think of my letter to Kaloostian, which was actually a letter to the entire Maldwyn Country Club. Was there anal symbolism in shoving potatoes into their exhaust pipes?

"Then I wrote to the President," the skinny man said. "Of the United States. 'Ike,' I says. 'How can you be so stupid?' That's all."

"Any reply?" I was still glancing around.

He laughed. "I was telling him something!"

I saw Larry tapping his watch: lunchtime.

"I have to go, pal."

"I wanted to talk to you."

"You already did. I think it's very interesting that you wrote to Fidel Castro. Maybe next time you should write in Spanish."

"See, the thing is," he said, not listening to me. "I've got one of these tiny little cameras. Japanese. I can take pictures of anything."

I thought I was walking away from him, but he was following. I could hear the air going into his mouth.

"I want to take your picture. I mean with your clothes off. You'd probably be too shy, huh?"

When I stopped and turned he bumped into me. He was apologizing as I said, "You like it here, pal?"

"My name's Norman. You can call me Norm, or Norman. I'm here for my nerves. I can't work. It's my nerves. The doctor told me to swim."

"If you want to swim here, then swim. But don't make strange requests. Understand?"

But the man had startled me and made me uneasy. And that crazy talk had given me a strong desire to see Lucy. She was what I wanted—I needed a girlfriend. And she worked in a bookstore. I thought of sex and I also thought how she might get me a discount on books.

"Aren't you having a beer?" Larry said at the Harvard Gardens.

We had taken our sandwiches there, to the bar, because it was air conditioned and there was a jukebox. He was drinking a Budweiser.

"This is going to sound batty," I said, "but I don't have any money. About five bucks, that's all. It has to last me until payday."

"A fin until next Thursday!"

"And I wanted a take a girl out." I didn't tell him who it was. I didn't want him to know that I had met her at the pool. "I could use about thirty bucks."

"I know where you can make an easy twenty-five." He was eating a meatball sandwich and just then a meatball fell out of one end as he bit into the other. He was chewing and picking up the loose meatball as he said, "Over at the hospital. We can go after lunch. It's a tit."

"And just pick up twenty-five bucks?"

"That's what they pay for a pint of blood," he said. He was still eating, chewing the meatballs, so I knew he was serious.

* * *

We were still wearing our bathing suits and our red T-shirts lettered LIFEGUARD, but no one took any notice of us. We walked through the hospital, went up to the third floor in an elevator that held a whimpering woman in a wheelchair, and then down a corridor to a waiting room with posters saying BE A BLOOD DONOR. A nurse at a desk recognized Larry and began talking to him. She was about twenty and had dark eyes. She was pretty but had hairy arms.

"Loretta, this is Andre Parent," Larry said. "He wants to give blood, and so do I."

"As long as it doesn't hurt," I said.

"Not a bit. Ask Larry. He's been here lots of times."

"It's nothing," Larry said. "It might even be good for you. Like I noticed this strange thing. The more times you give the easier it is. The first time your blood is sort of thick and ketchuppy. But after a few times it gets thinner."

"How do you know, if it's in a bottle?"

"It gushes out faster."

His saying *gushes out* made me nervous. I said, "We have to get back to the pool."

"Muzzaroll's on the chair," Larry said. "And you covered for him this morning." He turned to Loretta and said, "We went to the parade. Saw Kennedy. He was about as far away as I am from you. He is definitely going to win. He has class. I mean, he's Irish. And his wife's a piece of ass."

"Please watch your language," Loretta said. She was smiling, but she became brisk. She stood up and said, "This won't take long."

"It's a business proposition," Larry said.

"If you want to be paid we'll give you twenty-five dollars afterwards. And a cup of coffee." She smiled. "But some people do it for nothing."

Larry said, "You charge patients for it, so why shouldn't we cash in."

"Step inside," Loretta said.

It amazed me that we were talking about bottles of blood.

Loretta pricked my finger and tested it on a glass slide. She said, "You're B-negative. We always need that group."

I lay down on a high-legged bed and she suspended an empty bottle beside me. I looked away when she poked the needle into my arm, but I saw her connect it to a tube that led to the bottle. I started to perspire, so I concentrated on staring at a machine at the far end of the room. A sign over an opening said DO NOT INSERT ANY PART OF YOUR BODY INTO THIS MACHINE. I could only think of one part, and that gave me a twinge.

Loretta gave me a rubber ball to hold. It was black and a bit smaller than a baseball. "Squeeze it slowly and watch what happens."

I gave the ball a squeeze and a plop of blackish blood ran down the side of the clear glass bottle. I looked at the machine and kept squeezing.

After she connected Larry, he said, "I'll race you."

When my bottle was full I stood up and felt weak and lightheaded. I had a coffee and collected the money and we went back to the pool. I still felt woozy, and so I climbed the lifeguard's chair and stayed there without reading for the rest of the afternoon. I hoped the feeling would pass. I was also watching for Lucy.

At closing time—still no sign of Lucy—Larry said, "Want to try something great? After you give blood it's very easy to get drunk, because there's less of it. Let's go over to the Gardens."

I had money in my pocket and nothing else to do. And Larry was right. After one beer I felt drunk, but I had another one just the same. Then I began to miss Lucy, and got sad because I couldn't tell any of it to Larry. Eventually I was too drunk to go home.

We staggered outside and Larry said, "Let's get something to eat. What do you feel like?"

I said, "Whale steaks," and imagined chewing one.

He said, "You're shitfaced," and laughed in an unfunny drunken way, and in the Chinese restaurant—I could not remember how we got there—he was still laughing.

I said, with my brain buzzing in my head, "See, it's not Jonah inside the whale. It's the whale inside me. That's what I want my life to be like."

He said, "God, are you shitfaced."

This Chinese place was supposed to be cheap, but it cost us seven dollars each, and an ice-cream sundae was another dollar, and afterwards I threw up at the bus stop. Larry said, "Put your head between your legs" and left me there. Thinking it was a police car I waved my arms, and when I realized it was a taxi I took it home—another seven dollars.

"You look sick," my mother said.

I didn't say anything about giving blood, or the Chinese food or the taxi—she would have asked me where I got the money.

"Where have you been?" she said.

"Nowhere."

That was my Fourth of July.

In the morning I felt fine, but I only had ten dollars left and that wasn't enough for a date with Lucy. But where was she?

4.

"There was someone looking for you, Andre," Muzzaroll said one morning. "She was kind of disappointed."

"What did you tell her?"

"That you're late for work."

I said the bus was late. But he wasn't angry. He didn't care.

He said, "When I see a pretty girl waiting for a bus I always get horny, because I know that all I have to do is stop and she'll get into my car. I can plank her, because she wants a ride."

"Maybe she doesn't," I said. "Maybe that's why she's waiting for the bus."

It was a lovely day. Norman was writing a letter—probably to Eisenhower, or maybe Khrushchev. I steered myself away from him and reflected on how typical it was that he was sitting against the fence scribbling. Weirdos never went into the water, except to yank down kids' bathing suits, or fondle them underwater. They lurked, they lingered, they stared and muttered. Public swimming pools attracted the strangest people. Mrs. Mirsky wore a corset under her old-fashioned bathing suit and used to sing; Mr. Schickel ate his lunch in the changing room and said, "I'm still very hungry" to naked boys; the boy who stood outside the fence holding his radio against his head; the man who swam in sunglasses and wearing a baseball hat.

The normal ones screamed and splashed, and went home with wet hair. They were mostly kids. The rest were mental cases, or else very lonely. The pool was for everybody, which was why I found it interesting.

Just as I was leaving that day, Lucy stopped by the office.

"I've been tied up at the bookstore," she said. "I just wanted to say that I'm free at the moment if you wanted to do anything."

We immediately went to her room and made love. Afterwards I felt very shy, because she seemed shy. It was so odd to make love to her like that in her bed. We had hardly spoken before then, and so there was not much to say afterwards. Just a moment ago she had been gasping and saying *Oh God!* and showing the whites of her eyes. I felt I owed her something.

"Maybe we could go to a movie sometime," I said.

"There's a French movie called *Breathless* that I want to see. Jean Seberg and Jean-Paul Belmondo."

They were always the expensive ones; and a meal after the show. I would have to wait until payday.

"Let's go next week," I said.

"Can't we meet and do something before then?"

Do something meant one specific thing to me now.

"Sure," I said, and picking up her copy of *On the Road* I said, "Can I borrow this?"

It was also my way of telling her that I was going home.

I stopped at the pool to pick up my bag. Muzzaroll and McGinnis were playing cards in the office.

"That wasn't her," Muzzaroll said.

I stared at him.

"The woman who came looking for you this morning. That wasn't her."

I was in the lifeguard chair reading Lucy's copy of *On the Road*, and liking the book. I thought: I'll hitchhike home tonight instead of taking the bus. And next year I'll go out west. When I thought of travel I remembered the sentence I had underlined in Baudelaire, *Anywhere out of this world.* But Kerouac was familiar—he came from Lowell. My aunt Eva was from Lowell! Sometimes his writing was truly terrible, and that gave me hope for myself. Again and again, I read the same line about "the charging restless mute invoiced road keening in a seizure of tarpaulin power" and I could not make up my mind whether it was baloney or genius. It was probably a little bit of both.

Larry said, "You're going to ruin your eyes, Andre."

The little Puerto Rican kids were screaming and jumping into the deep end. Above me, the Mass General was like a fortress, with the faces of patients looking out. I saw myself as a Kerouac character who was capable of feeling a holiness in this confusion: holy children, holy sick people, holy weirdos.

Then Lucy's voice said, "What are you having for lunch?"

She was smiling at the fence, still in the pretty dress she wore to work.

"I've got my mother's meatloaf sandwiches," I said, climbing down from the chair.

"Why don't you eat them in my room, in style?"

Larry asked me where I was going. I said, "I've got to take a wicked leak." I didn't want to tell him about Lucy. "I'll be right back."

At her room, I showed her how the meatloaf just dropped out of the sandwich if I tilted the bread. A crumbly hunk of wet hamburg slid into a pool of ketchup on the plate.

Lucy said jokingly, "Some people think it's more polite to say catsup."

"It's a Chinese word, so it doesn't matter."

The room was too small to hold a table. It was a little cube for living in. She told me it was perfect for one person.

"This is my garden," she said, showing me the flowerpots on the windowsill—African violets, and geraniums, and herbs such as mint and thyme. "This is my bed—as you know," she said. "And this is my library"—a bookshelf with about fifty paperbacks jammed onto it. She showed me where she kept her letters ("My extensive files") and where she hid her money ("My bank"). Her kitchen was a shelf with a hot plate and some cans of soup, and her clothes were in a shallow closet. All these things she showed me by stretching out her hand. It was such a tiny room I could not move without knocking something over. Just being there with her was like a sexual act.

When she said all these things in her sweet funny voice, I realized I knew nothing about her. I felt sorry, because she was

a good person, and intelligent, and she liked me. I knew also that
it was a risk for her to have me here. I suspected her of being
a bit desperate, but I was grateful because so was I.

"I love that Kerouac book," I said.

"He's almost forty, did you know that?"

"God, he's old," I said. "I thought he was young."

Lucy said, "He was born in nineteen twenty-two. My favorite
is *The Subterraneans*. Want to borrow it?"

But leaning over for the book I brushed against her, and
kissed her, and then there was no going back.

"Oh, God," she said, when I entered her, and she threw her
head back and gasped. I felt like a bystander until she got her
breath; and then she was whispering and encouraging me, until
my last gasp.

The room was very warm. Even though the window was open,
there was no breeze. We lay there, stuck together, and she said,
"I like you. I like being with you. I was dreading this summer,
but it's turned out really nice."

"What year are you in?"

"I'm a junior."

That meant she was at least twenty, and probably twenty-one.
I said, "Me too," which was a lie, because I didn't want her to
know how young I was.

She put on a silky robe, which I found sexier than her nakedness.

"I've got the afternoon off," she said.

"I'm supposed to be back at the pool at one, so the other guys
can have their lunch."

"Don't go away," she said, and held me. She hung on. "I want
you to stay here."

A loud noise made me jump. It was a knocking at the door,
and it was twice as hard as it should have been, because it was
Miss Murphy the landlady, and she was deaf. I realized that I had
banged my knee when I had jumped.

"Just a minute!" Lucy said, and held the door shut.

"Are you in there?" Miss Murphy said, rapping again.

Lucy pulled open the closet door and motioned me to get in.
She threw our clothes in after me and tied her robe and brushed
the bed. Then she shut the closet door. I crouched in a woolen
darkness of Lucy's coats, with her clothes in my hand. The dress
she wore was still warm from her body and smelled of her skin.

"Do you have a minute?" Miss Murphy asked.

"I have to go pretty soon," Lucy said.

But Miss Murphy didn't hear her. She simply saw the girl wearing a bathrobe and figured there was no hurry.

"I want to show you something," the woman said.

I had never seen her, but I imagined wiry hair and dark circles under her eyes, because she sounded like Miss Sharkey, an old teacher of mine from the fourth grade. As Miss Sharkey bawled me out I used to cringe and look down, but I was equally terrified by the sight of her cruel shoes. I imagined them on Miss Murphy's feet.

I heard Lucy's bedsprings creak as the old lady sat down. I put my face in my hands and sweated. I tried not to breathe.

"These are the albums I was telling you about," Miss Murphy said, and in a monotonous reading voice went on, "Nineteen ten. Nahant Beach. Memorial Day."

"Very nice," Lucy said.

"My father always said that you should take your first swim of the year on Memorial Day. My uncle had a lovely house in Nahant. You can just see the roof in the background—and that window with the shutters. That's me with my little pail. And that's my brother Patrick—"

"Miss Murphy, I have to go."

"And that's my mother. Isn't she beautiful? They all wore bathing suits like that."

"Miss Murphy—"

But Miss Murphy was deaf. She droned on, talking too loud and turning pages, describing pictures. A cramp in my leg came and went, a desire to cough passed through me. I sneezed but she didn't hear me—didn't even pause.

She went through the entire album—it must have taken half an hour.

"Nineteen eleven," she said. "Wait until you see the snow—"

She kept talking. It was the worst kind of snapshot monologue, giving the background of each blurred person and each indistinct object; and describing, in minute detail, things that weren't shown in the pictures.

After a while ("There's Patrick again—"), she said, suddenly, "What's wrong?"

"I have to go," Lucy said very loudly.

"I'll come back some other time," the lonely woman said.

But all this while I was considering in the darkness how much I liked Lucy, and when Miss Murphy had gone and I stepped out of the closet and kissed her I knew that something had happened in me. In that space of time, while I crouched beneath her dresses and she was outside murmuring, I fell in love with her.

"Not so hard!" she said, when I hugged her. But I didn't want to let go.

No one seemed to mind that I was late for work.

"She was here again," Muzzaroll said. "That woman. With the hat."

I said, "I was taking a leak."

"Who are you trying to kid?" Larry said. "You've probably been in the saddle."

I hated that, and it wasn't true; but I couldn't tell him about Lucy, or that I'd been stuck in her closet.

When we closed the pool that day, I went over to the Mass General and up to the Blood Donor department. Seeing Loretta I wondered whether the girls I desired could be put into different categories: the Nurse, the Whore, the Child, the Cheerleader. But, no, it didn't work, because Lucy wasn't any of these. She was someone like me. Or was that another category: the girl who resembled me?

Loretta was nodding. She said, "B-negative, right?"

"That's me," I said. I wasn't surprised that she remembered. My father, who sold shoes, knew people by their shoe size. *He's an eight e,* he'd say, or sometimes using a shoe-man's jargon, *He's an eight Eddie.*

"You look great," Loretta said. "You and Larry are so lucky to be working at the pool. You've got a fantastic tan. You just sit there and get the rays."

"It's brainless work, and there's no money in it. Anyway, I'm trying to save for school. That's why I'm here."

She just smiled at me.

"I want to sell you another pint."

"You're a stitch!" She shook her head and was laughing as she said, "You have to wait at least six weeks before you can give it again."

I said I didn't know that.

"You can't keep taking blood out of your system. You'd get anemic. You'd probably die."

"I feel all right. I'm broke, that's all."

"Come back in a month or so. I could probably take you then. Gee, if I had any extra money I'd loan it to you."

I told her that was a very nice thing to say; but even so I wouldn't have borrowed it. What I wanted to do with it was walk into a restaurant with Lucy and order whale steaks for us both, and afterwards tell her I loved her.

When I left the hospital I became very self-conscious imagining Loretta telling the other nurses how I had come back less than a week after giving blood and said *Want another pint?*

It was raining, the pool was empty, and we were playing whist in the office—Vinny, Larry, and the janitor we called Speedo—this was about two days later.

I said, "I'd like to give blood again—I mean, sell it. But you can only do it every six or eight weeks."

"What else is new?" Larry said, and put a card down. He had a cardshark's way of snapping them onto the table. Then he said that he had heard of places where you could sell sperm—they injected it into women who wanted kids.

"Hey, I could do that," Muzzaroll said.

Speedo grinned, thinking the same thing.

"They'd turn you assholes down," Larry said. "They don't want a bananaman. They want class. You gotta take tests."

"Jerk-off tests," Speedo said.

"Psychological tests, to make sure you're not crazy. Intelligence tests. The whole bit. You think it's just a hand-job. It's not. It's science. After you get the okay, you jerk off into a test tube and they give you about twenty bucks. You think I'm shitting you. The place is right here in Boston."

"You can sell your body," Muzzaroll said. "For science. For experiments and shit like that. You can get about three hundred bucks for it."

That sounded like a fortune to me.

"Or in Speedo's case, about thirty clams," Larry said.

"What happens?" I said.

"Andy's interested," Larry said. "It's like this. You sign something and they give you the money, and when you die they claim your bawd. Then they cut you into hamburg for their experiments."

"Who are we talking about?" Muzzaroll said.

"Students," Larry said. "Harvard students."

Speedo said, "How do they know when you die?"

"They find out. See, when they give you the money they put a tattoo on the sole of your foot. It stays there. No matter when or where you die, your body gets shipped to Harvard Medical School."

"I'd do that," I said. And I imagined showing someone like Mimi Hardwick, or Lucy, or any girl, the tattoo on my foot that said *This body is the property of Harvard Medical School.* "What difference would it make? I'd be dead."

"What if your foot got chopped off?" Speedo said. "Like you got run over or something—"

"Play the fucking game," Muzzaroll said, scraping up the deck of cards and dealing.

Then Larry said, "Here she comes."

It was Mrs. Mamalujian, in a big cartwheel hat and a flower-printed dress. She looked very stylish and out of place, carrying a blue umbrella and walking up the path to the MDC pool. She lifted her sunglasses and looked at me.

I had put my cards down and run out to intercept her. I didn't want the others to hear anything.

"Where have you been hiding?"

I wanted to tell her that I didn't have any money, and with no money I felt I did not exist.

"I've been here. How did you find me?"

And I walked over to the fence so that she would follow me and so that the others wouldn't see us.

"Your mother told me," she said. "This is my third visit, for crying out loud. I'm glad to see you. We miss you up at the Maldwyn Country Club."

"They can come down and swim here. This is for everybody. Only they probably wouldn't want to. It's all maniacs here."

There was laughter in the office. They couldn't play whist with three people, so they were horsing around, and I could hear Speedo shouting and protesting.

Mrs. Mamalujian said, "I thought we were going out to lunch."

"We were, but I ran out of money."

"Don't be silly," she said. "I've got lots of money."

That made me feel sick with envy and confusion.

She said, "God, you're funny," and looked past me at the pool.

Vinny and Larry were carrying Speedo through the rain to the pool. Speedo was wearing his janitor's blue overalls, and he was yelling and struggling. They propped him up at the edge of the pool, tormented him for a while, and they pushed him in.

"Who are they?"

"My colleagues," I said.

Mrs. Mamalujian laughed. She had a good, deep, appreciative laugh that was somehow improved by her heavy smoking.

"I have to go back to work," I said.

"Some work," she said, sarcastically. "When's your day off?"

"Saturday."

"We'll have lunch then. Do you know the Copley Plaza? Peacock Alley? I'll meet you there Saturday at noon."

That night after work I went back to Medford Square, not so much to buy a sub as to talk to Mr. Balinieri again.

But there was a new man behind the counter.

"I was looking for Mr. Balinieri."

"He don't work here no more."

And I knew he had been fired by this ignorant procrustean guinea wop, because he didn't fit.

5.

I brought my copy of *Moby Dick* so that I would have something to talk about with Mrs. Mamalujian. I had underlined the paragraphs in chapters 64 and 65 that were about eating whale meat, which was what I wanted to have for lunch. I was very nervous.

Coming out of the Boston Public Library I had often looked across the square they called the plaza, and marveled at the grand hotel on the south side, and wondered what the rooms were like. I had never felt that it was forbidden to go in, only that it was better to have a reason, and an inkling that you needed an invitation of some kind. The idea of going into any Boston hotel seemed strange to me. They were for businessmen and honeymooners; for strangers, for people from out-of-town. I had a notion that hotels were for people who did not quite belong: they had nowhere else to go.

It was a mystery to me. I was nineteen years old and had never traveled anywhere; had never stayed overnight in any hotel. That took money and I didn't have any.

Another reason for my nervousness was I had told Lucy I would call her. But I was hesitant. I didn't know what time I would be free, and I felt guilty about making her wait.

I thought fondly of her watering her flowerpots. *This is my garden,* she had said. *This is my library.*

And I thought it might frighten her if I told her I loved her. It seemed simpler for things to remain as they were—for us to be passionate when we were in bed, and in between times be close friends. I was also afraid myself that she would depend on me, and I imagined every time I turned around I would see her and she would say, *What shall we do now?*

Was that Irish-looking doorman staring disapprovingly at me? He had white hair and a red face and a graceful way of reaching for the door. When I saw people doing lowly jobs like opening doors and hailing taxis I tried to picture them as presidents or kings by mentally giving them different clothes; and usually it worked. I made that doorman a presidential candidate and then breezed past him.

What Mrs. Mamalujian had called Peacock Alley was a long cor-ridorlike entryway, with oriental carpets the length of it, and mir-rors on the sides. Between the mirrors there were ornate chairs.

"There you are," I heard.

Mrs. Mamalujian was sitting in a big soft chair, her legs crossed, and kicking one up and down.

"I don't think I've ever seen you with your clothes on before," she said.

That made a passing couple smile.

"It's impossible to tell whether you're blushing, you have such a good tan."

She stood up, wobbled a little in her shoes, and gave me a wet kiss.

"Oh, I've left lipstick all over you," she said, and then made a business of wiping it off, which she did with a very fragrant handkerchief. "Shall we go?"

She had made me unsure of myself. It was the confident way she spoke to me, and the fact that she seldom said anything that called for a direct reply. She just uttered odd statements and she seemed to be making them as much to people who might be eavesdropping as to me.

"I've seen trees come up faster than that elevator," she said, and behind us some men chuckled.

She smiled, enveloped in a cloud of strong perfume.

"What's the book?"

"*Moby Dick,*" I said, trying to whisper.

"I've always liked that title," Mrs. Mamalujian said.

One of the men cleared his throat.

"You look good in clothes, Andre. You should wear them more often."

Someone snorted behind me.

"What floor is it on?" I asked, when we got into the elevator, just to have something to say.

"Six," she said, and poked the button with one of her bulging rings.

When we were outside the door I asked, "Is this a restaurant?"

She just laughed and jangled the key and fumbled with the lock. It was not that she was unmechanical, but rather that she was too vain to wear her glasses. At last the key turned and she pushed the door open.

"Do you like it?"

I stepped inside and looked around.

"Is it a living room?"

There was no bed. I saw a sofa and some wing chairs, and a table with a new copy of *Look* on it (Kennedy on the cover), all of Boston out the window.

"The bedroom's in here."

It was my first hotel room. I did not have to be told it was a suite. I was impressed—by the luxury, the silence, the coolness on this hot summer day.

Mrs. Mamalujian said, "Sometimes when I'm feeling really awful I check into a hotel. This one or the Ritz-Carleton, or the Parker House. And after a few days I feel much better, and then I check out. Do you ever do that?"

"I don't usually feel awful."

"It's wonderful to be young," she said. "Sit down and have a drink."

She handed me a menu with a list of drinks on it. I wanted a beer but there was something wrong with drinking a beer in this suite at the Copley Plaza. I looked down the list: *Pink Lady. Sidecar. Grasshopper. Manhattan. Tom Collins.*

"I'll have a cocktail," I said, stalling.

"Which one?"

"A Grasshopper."

"That's exciting," she said. "I'm having a dull old gin and tonic. But tonic's healthy, you know."

As I was wondering where the drinks would come from, Mrs. Mamalujian lifted the phone and said, "Room Service? This is six-oh-eight. We want three Grasshoppers and three gins and tonic." She hung up and said, "I can't wait to see what a Grasshopper is."

I had no idea what it was. I said, "Is the restaurant on this floor?"

I was sitting deep in the sofa, and Mrs. Mamalujian smoked in a wing chair across the room. She was swinging one leg over the other with her shoe dangling.

"Room Service," she said, blowing smoke. "Hungry?"

"A little," I said, to be polite. I was very hungry and I knew the drink—whatever it was—would make me hungrier.

She said, "I wish I were hungry. I love the idea of food, but the sight of it affects me, and when I start eating I lose my appetite."

The drinks came—three for Mrs. Mamalujian, three for me. After she signed the bill, the bald man in the tight vest said, "Very good, Madam," and left the room walking backwards.

"What would you like to eat?"

"Whale steak," I said.

She looked at me strangely and said, "Are they on the menu?"

"They must be," I said. We looked. I was very surprised that they weren't.

She dialed Room Service again and said, "Do you have whale steaks? No? Well, what do you have?"

To simplify matters I said I'd have a hamburger. She ordered crab salad. She smiled at me and said, "Grasshoppers. Whale steaks. *Moby Dick.*" She winked. "You've got a sense of humor."

A Grasshopper was a minty green drink in a wineglass, mingled with alcoholic chocolate and topped with a layer of thick cream. It was sweet sticky goo, and the liquor in it made my eyes water.

"Is that drink all right? It looks like creme de menthe to me. I don't know how you do it. You're so thin!"

"I always drink these," I said. Did that sound debonair? I didn't think so.

She had already started her second gin and tonic. "It's good if you have malaria," she said. "By the way, they miss you at the club. It hasn't been the same since you left. That idiot Mattanza still walks around in his stupid bathing suit, thinking he's so wonderful."

"I'm still pissed off about that job."

"You don't need them," she said. "You've got me."

I wondered what she meant by that. Why was I here? It seemed the most inconvenient place to have a meal. You ordered a drink and waited twenty minutes. You ordered food and a half an hour later you were still waiting.

She said, "What sort of people stay here, do you think?"

She seemed to be genuinely wondering.

"People from out of town," I said. "Society people."

"Oh, society people," she said, and made a disapproving noise in her throat. "Have you been reading the papers?"

I said no, I never read the newspaper. I was too busy with books.

"The scandal about that so-called debutante—Olivia Harrison? The one who was jilted by that Brazilian? The one they just locked up? Know what they locked her up for?"

I didn't know what she was talking about.

"After the greaseball jilted her for another so-called deb, she went to Brazil—just got onto a plane and flew there. She saw the guy and shot him dead. But she wasn't finished with him. She cut his penis off and took it back to Boston in a box, and gave it to his new girlfriend." Mrs. Mamalujian took a sip of her drink. "Society people."

The food came on a wheel-in table. There was an upside-down silver bowl over my hamburger and Mrs. Mamalujian's crab salad was in a dish balanced on cracked ice.

"I'm really impressed that you're reading *Moby Dick.*"

"I'm rereading it."

"Any particular reason?"

She put her fork down and wiped her mouth carefully so that she wouldn't smudge her lipstick. Was she through after two mouthfuls?

I was too embarrassed to tell her how I imagined eating whale steaks and reading her passages from the chapters "Stubb's Supper" and "The Whale as a Dish." I wanted to eat whale, so that I could say that whale was my favorite meat.

"You've finished your hamburger," she said. "I wish I had your appetite. Can you eat any of my salad?"

I ate all the crab salad, and all the rolls, and even chewed the thin slices of orange and the sprigs of parsley that decorated the plate. But I had only drunk one Grasshopper.

Mrs. Mamalujian had finished her gins. She took a small gin bottle out of her bag and said, "Be prepared," and poured herself another drink.

"You're a great reader, aren't you?" she said, raising her glass.

"I guess so."

"But you can get lost in books. Remember you once told me you were writing a play set in a department store—something about a notions counter?"

I nodded, too humiliated to speak, hearing the thing described to me. I had said that in order to keep what I was really trying to write a secret.

She said, "I got so sad thinking of you indoors staring at a blank piece of white paper on a beautiful summer day."

That was exactly what I loved doing.

She was too drunk to notice that I hadn't said anything.

"I love books, but sometimes you have to put them down and go into the next room. Art is wonderful, but—you know what's in the next room?"

I said I didn't know.

"Life," she said.

The first time I heard that I was deeply impressed: it was an experienced woman's wisdom.

She said, "You're very bad—you're making me drink too much!"

"Isn't it supposed to be healthy?"

"It has a nice clean taste," she said. "That's why I like gin." She plopped a little more gin into her glass. *"Moby Dick,"* she said, and giggled.

She still wore her hat. She stood up unsteadily and sat down beside me on the sofa. I wondered whether anyone would find her attractive—her face was somewhat lined, probably more from sitting in the sun than from old age. She was big-breasted and had skinny legs and her high heels made her seem tall. She was well-dressed—the sort of woman who had her picture taken: an important man's wife.

"I bet you have a fur coat," I said.

"I have three fur coats." she said. "What a thing to say on a hot summer day! You're a scream."

She became very quiet and nodded a little: I had the impression that time was passing very quickly for her, though it was passing very slowly for me.

She said, "Sometimes you have to put your books down."

I finished the thought in my head and this second time it sounded corny.

"Look at the time," she said, putting one eye against the dial of her watch. "I'm too drunk to go home. I'll have to take a shower."

She plumped her hand on my knee, and then my shoulder, struggling to her feet.

"Excuse me," she said.

"I don't mind."

"I'm just going to get into the shower." She tottered a little as she made for the bedroom.

I didn't know what to say.

"I'll be in the next room."

"That's all right," I said.

She went into the bedroom, leaving doors open and talking to herself, repeating things, sort of narrating what she was doing. "Right in here . . . Pull the drapes . . . Put my bag down . . ." In a muffled and straining voice she said, "Get these clothes off."

After a while I heard water running very loudly. The bathroom door was open. I heard the hiss and crackle of the shower curtain being hit by spray.

I picked up *Moby Dick*.

That mortal man shall feed upon the creature that feeds his lamp, and, like Stubb, eat him by his own light, as you might say; this seems so outlandish a thing that one must needs go a little into the history and philosophy of it.

I read on and became so absorbed in it, and in the subsequent chapters, that I was startled when I heard "Have you seen my dress?" Mrs. Mamalujian was standing over me, very wet, and dripping, and wrapped in a small towel.

Fear made me jump up and find her dress in the next room.

"My eyes are terrible," she said. "I can't tell whether you've got your clothes on or not."

"They're on," I said.

It was four o'clock. I had been reading for half an hour or more. When Mrs. Mamalujian dried off and got dressed and put on her lipstick, it was after four-thirty.

She said, "Will you do me a very big favor?"

I was afraid to say yes, but I managed it.

"I have to go home now, but I want you to pay for the room."

She paused, making me choke for a moment at the thought of my paying for the room with the three dollars I had in my pocket.

"I'll give you the money." She took out crushed and crumpled bills, not seeming to count them. "That should be enough," she said, adding another one to the pile.

It was over a hundred dollars.

"If there's any left, you can keep it. Buy some books." She kissed me. "I have this feeling you never want to see me anymore."

"No," I said. "I had a good time. Really."

She smiled and kissed me again, and her lips moved as though she were speaking to me.

"You don't have to go home," she said. "Sit here. Stay as long as you like. Stay overnight. I can think about you sitting here, reading—what?"

"Moby Dick."

She laughed in her deep-throated way. "That title kills me!"

"It's the whale," I said.

Then she left, mumbling a little. I read a few pages, and put the book down. I couldn't read. I went into the other room—her smell was here, of perfume and clothes, and the shampoo or

soap. The bathroom was unpleasantly wet and the towels soggy.
The bed was the biggest, the widest, I had ever seen.

I picked up the telephone and called Lucy.

"Darling," she said.

"I'm sorry I'm so late in calling you."

"I don't mind," she said. "I knew you'd call."

I loved her for that.

Very soon she was with me in the room. She said, "You're
amazing. What are you doing here?"

"It's a secret," I said, and when I looked up again she had her
clothes off. Now what Mrs. Mamalujian had said did not seem
so silly. We were in the next room and this was better than
anything. She had been right—this was living. Lucy arched her
back beneath me as we made love, and she gasped at how deep
I had gone, as though she had just then lost her virginity.

6.

That was the oddest day I had ever spent—the afternoon in the
hotel; lunch with Mrs. Mamalujian; her shower and my *Moby
Dick;* and then a long night with Lucy. We checked out at five
in the morning, and with the thirty dollars left over I took a taxi
home. If I had blundered in at midnight my mother would have
asked me where I had been. But because I arrived just before
breakfast and didn't wake them they assumed I had been in bed
all night and had just got up early. I was in the yard, ankle-deep
in dew, marveling at my luck.

There was more. The rest of July was like a new life to me: I
had a girlfriend, I had money, I had a job, and I had Mrs.
Mamalujian. I suspended my reading of Baudelaire.

Mrs. Mamalujian was lonely. She told me that she had met her
husband, the construction man, when she was eighteen. Her
children were my age, but she was vague about how many she

had and didn't like talking about them. She preferred to talk about herself as a girl and said, "I was spoiled rotten," and smiled. She had never gone to college. Because of that she had never stopped reading, and she read everything, Norman Mailer, Freud, Somerset Maugham, Kahlil Gibran, Frances Parkinson Keyes, *A Night to Remember*, Tennyson, Salinger, *I Jumped Over the Wall*, Jacques Barzun, and sex books. I was the same, only I varied it a bit more by reading Ovid, and books about camping, gun catalogues and *Isis Unveiled* by Madame Blavatsky.

She did not treat me like a son. She made me understand that I was her friend and that she was grateful for my company. We had lunch and talked about books. Now and then she would be talking about a sexual episode—the man in the Norman Mailer story sodomizing his girlfriend, for example—and she would call it "spicey." The word would remind me that she was thirty years older than me, and I thought *God!* We didn't go to a hotel again. It was always restaurants.

"Is there anything you want?" she usually said after lunch.

She didn't mean food. She meant anything else. She urged me to want something.

"How about one of those blazers we were looking at on the way here?"

Passing Brooks Brothers in Harvard Square I had said I liked the striped blazer in the window. Mrs. Mamalujian had a very good memory for wishes and desires.

"Let me buy it for you."

I had never bought things I wanted. I had been made to believe that they were beyond me and that I did not deserve them. Work was the proof that I could have them, but being a lifeguard was not work—not real work. I saved the money I earned and cheated myself with what my mother called pin money. I bought secondhand military clothes in the Army and Navy Store. I still wore a khaki shirt and fatigue pants, combat boots, and sunglasses.

I let Mrs. Mamalujian take me to the shops—Brooks Brothers, J. Press, the Ivy League Shop, or the Coop, and I would try things on. What surprised me was that they fit me so well. But I was shocked by how expensive they were, and if you added the price of lunch it was fifty dollars or more.

The salesmen were always sly, and they would pressure Mrs.

Mamalujian because they could see she was paying and she was eager to please me.

"It's excellent quality," they said. "That cloth wears like iron."

"What do you think, Andy?" she would say to me.

The salesmen never listened to me.

"Everyone's wearing that style," they said.

That did it. As soon as I heard that I didn't want the thing.

So when Mrs. Mamalujian said, "Is there anything you want?" I thought: *Yes, what no one else has, what no one else wants or can even imagine.* People with money bought things to be like everyone else. If I had money, I thought, I would try to be as different as possible.

But the idea of wealth was so remote that I could not imagine having any money myself. And I could not think of anything I could do to become wealthy. It would never happen.

That made me value Mrs. Mamalujian and it made me hate the rich even more than I already did. The sight of Kennedy's face—his lovely teeth showing behind his smile—made me want him to lose the election. It was an unfortunate irritation because wherever I looked he was smiling—gloating—at me. I realized that I could never have lasted at the Maldwyn Country Club. I despised those people too much. And I was proud of the fact that I had been fired. I reasoned: If you couldn't succeed with the rich you had to be their enemy.

Yet I needed money badly—for tuition fees, for my rent at college, for books, to take Lucy out. I had about four hundred dollars in the bank; if I didn't have a thousand by September I would have to find a job in the second semester. I kept thinking of Vinny Muzzaroll saying *You can sell your body.* How did people get money? How did a banker become a banker? How did a man become a landlord? These people who drove Cadillacs—how did they get them? There were boys my age at the Maldwyn Country Club who had Thunderbirds and Bulova watches and some had their own golf clubs. They got them from their parents. I had the idea that people who had things—money, cars, tennis rackets, beautiful shoes—had been given them. I could not imagine that they earned them. What on earth could a person do to earn a Caddy? My father worked hard and drove a jalopy.

[145]

There was a secret that I suspected, did not know, that I would never know. That suspicion made me secretive—if I don't know theirs why should I tell them mine?—and it made me grateful to Mrs. Mamalujian. If I wanted something she would give it to me. That was a helpful thought, but it was only a thought. I did not want anything conventional.

When I politely refused these gifts—a suit, a jacket, a pretty tie—she said, "You shouldn't be so modest—"

She didn't know that it was arrogance. Something special, that no one else had—that's what I wanted.

But she had a talent for gift-giving. It is a rare talent, fitting a gift to a person, since most gifts are an obscure burden or obligation. No one had ever tried to please me with a present. Did she know that I disliked having lunch in expensive restaurants? It wasn't a favor. I felt these places confining. I hated sitting in the dark watching her drink. Perhaps she knew that, which was why she was likewise grateful to me. There was no sex, so it had to be a profound friendship.

She gave me a wallet with my initials on it; a jackknife with six blades; an electric razor; a belt with a fancy brass buckle; a leather keyring; a Japanese camera; a Timex watch; a pair of ivory chopsticks, a leatherbound *Tom Jones;* Italian sunglasses; a cigarette holder—just handed them over, "That's for you." When I protested, she said, "You've got to have it," as if this trinket was one of life's necessities, like shoes. I accepted them because they weren't expensive, and because I could have bought them myself.

She gave me earrings and scarves. "That's for your mother." I passed them on to Lucy, and it amazed me that Lucy liked them. Why hadn't I been able to think of such gifts? But it made Lucy wonder why I could afford earrings and not two tickets to *The Seventh Sea* at the Exeter Theater, or *Smiles of a Summer Night,* which was famous for having a nude scene.

Sometimes Mrs. Mamalujian said, "You're lucky."

I hated that. It was when she was drunk and we were the only ones left in the restaurant. The waiter would be standing nearby and rocking on his heels—wanting us to pay up so that he could go home.

"Very lucky."

Was I supposed to say yes or no? I just politely murmured

through my nose, because I did not want to insult her by saying that I did not feel lucky at all most of the time. Sometimes I felt like a servant—her servant or anyone's—because I had no other place in the world. I was a good servant—well-mannered, tactful, discreet, gliding in and out. Mrs. Mamalujian did not treat me like a servant, which was another reason I liked her. But when she told me how lucky I was, and I had to sit and listen, I felt trapped.

"You're young—"

That wasn't luck. I hated being young.

"You're good-looking. You're intelligent. You've got your health. It's amazing you don't have a girlfriend."

That was what I had told her.

"But in a way I'm glad you don't. A girl would just waste your time."

When she said that I saw Lucy very clearly, sitting on her bed, at her window, smiling. *This is my garden.*

Mrs. Mamalujian only had a few conversations that she could hold when she was drunk. One began *You're lucky,* and another *Gin and tonic is good for you;* and sometimes it was how she had been spoiled rotten in New York.

At the end she always did the same thing—reached across the table and took my hand. Her grip was bony and damp, but I let her hold on because I knew it was what she wanted me to do.

In ways I could not explain, knowing Mrs. Mamalujian helped me with Lucy. Was it a question of confidence, or belief? I needed Mrs. Mamalujian's friendship to have Lucy's love. I didn't want to understand why. Understanding things made them go away. I wanted a mysterious tangle of secrets and, without putting it into precise words, I felt that no one must know me. In order to be strong I needed to have secrets. Neither Mrs. Mamalujian nor Lucy knew of one another. That was very important to me.

Lucy didn't know what to make of the presents I passed on to her. But I loved her for not asking me where they came from. She was perhaps like me—thinking that if she asked too much the things would disappear.

Her father was dead, her mother lived just south of Plymouth, and having seen her driver's license I now knew that she was almost two years older than me. I wasn't old enough to drink in bars legally, but she was always asked to show her ID on the assumption that if she was twenty-one so was I.

I loved her because she was patient and never asked questions and because she liked sex. Sex most of all. In bed we talked about it, but only in bed. She said she didn't know when she had lost her virginity because she was too drunk at the time. She had passed out and had just assumed it had happened.

"I'm terrible when I'm drunk," she said in a naughty-girl voice. "Sometimes I break bottles or throw things out the window. Or I turn to jelly and sort of collapse."

I had never seen her drunk and didn't want to. I hated hearing people's own versions of themselves: they were either much worse or much better than they ought to be.

Many times, after we had made love, I simply wanted to go home. I felt there was nothing more to do, nothing to say. Often it was the sense that we might make love one more time—after the bar or the movie or a walk around the block—that kept me from getting on the bus.

Lucy was at her most talkative just after we had made love, when I was still and silent. She said surprising things.

"When I started BU I was going out with a guy, and I kept asking him to make love to me. I didn't love him and the sex was no fun, but I was, um, small, and I wanted him to stretch me."

That shocked me, the way she said it.

"After a while I got bigger, and it was more fun. It used to hurt. Do you think I'm awful?"

"No," I said, and I wondered whether I really believed it.

She said, "You can do anything you want with me."

I couldn't think of much and that was maddening.

She said, "That Henry Miller stuff."

What did that mean? I reminded myself to have a closer look at the book. All I could remember was Miller with a pathetic prostitute, who was crying, and Miller saying *Has no one been kind to you?* Which sounded untruthful to me.

With Lucy I was so impatient I often made love to her before she took all her clothes off, and then I preferred it that way, remembering my the fantasies looking at the underwear section of the Sear's Catalogue. I was in such a hurry the room seemed very small and hot. We were very careful not to make too much noise—breathe too hard or kick anything. There were other roomers at Miss Murphy's. But I liked the thought that we were making love under Murf's nose. It made me feel like a burglar, and when I left Lucy's at eleven-thirty I pretended I was a thief sneaking successfully away from a house I had just robbed.

One day I tried out her sentence myself and said, "You can do anything you want to me."

She pretended to be shocked, but she was smiling. She knelt and kissed my stomach. I could not control my penis. It throbbed and fattened with desire, and swung sideways and came to rest against her chin. In one movement she twisted her head and took it into her mouth. I was fascinated by the way she treated this stupid thing seriously: I had often looked at my penis and thought: *You moron.* She was sort of speaking silently to it for a while, and then she slurped it like a noodle. I was desperately afraid she didn't like doing it, and that spoiled my pleasure at the beginning. But she did it again and again, and I didn't want her to stop.

We had no word for that. I was too shy even to mention it. It was something we did in the dark.

I used to think of it when I saw her licking a Popsicle, or when she mentioned food she disliked—boiled carrots, or lima beans, or raw oysters—and said, "I could never eat that!"

Lucy knew I wanted to be a writer. She never saw what I wrote, but she used to ask me to tell her stories. Talking to her gave me ideas.

"It's about a man who goes to a foreign country and keeps making mistakes," I said.

"Like a Martian landing on earth."

That was a good idea.

"When he wants to mail a letter he very carefully puts it into one of those trash cans that have a narrow opening at the top."

"That's wonderful."

"And when he wants to throw away a scrap of paper—"

"He puts it into a letter box," Lucy said.

"He squeezes a tube of oil paint onto his toothbrush, because it looks like toothpaste."

"I like it," she said.

But telling her took the place of writing, and it helped to see the merit of a story. This one was a dud, I was sure.

I saw Lucy three times a week, in the evening. We went for walks, we saw movies, we went to Harvard Gardens and drank beer. But every evening ended the same way. We went back to Pinckney Street and sneaked into the house, and into her room, and made love. Then I sneaked out, which was harder than sneaking in, and I walked to the bus stop. I always felt energetic after being released from her small room.

I saw Mrs. Mamalujian twice a week, in the daytime. One of the days we drank, the other we ate.

The women did not know about each other. But they mattered to me, and I needed them both. I often felt that Mrs. Mamalujian was overgenerous with me but that I justified it by passing it on to Lucy; so Mrs. Mamalujian was Lucy's patroness, not mine. And if it hadn't been for Lucy I probably wouldn't have sat all those hours with this fifty-year-old woman; just being with Mrs. Mamalujian made me feel lucky to have this pretty girl, whom I could squeeze and kiss and tell stories to.

So far I had only dreamed of whale steaks: I was saving that pleasure.

7.

Then I had my first whale steak.

Mrs. Mamalujian showed up at the pool early in August looking strangely eager and panicky, as if she was trying hard to remember something she had just forgotten. She had an it's-on-the-tip-of-my-tongue expression, the kind that makes you feel totally helpless. All the wild screaming kids worried her, I knew—she was uneasy around poor people. I had noticed that they made her feel trapped and her reaction was to be too reasonable. She smiled too much and overtipped them.

When she was very worried she agreed to anything, just to get away.

But today she seemed as though she were studying the people at the pool, trying to understand, trying to remember.

Larry had said, "It's your friend," and I found her out by the turnstile.

"You're not free by any chance, are you, Andy?"

This was not one of our regular days.

But I was free and I told her so. Larry had begged to take my shift in the afternoon if I would cover for him in the evening. He was taking Loretta, the nurse from the Blood Donor Department, to the Boston Pops Concert at the Hatch Shell just down the Esplanade.

He had said, "I want to impress her—listen to the old masters, and then plank her."

"I could probably knock off now," I told Mrs. Mamalujian.

"That's perfect. I want to take you somewhere special, because today's a special day."

"There's a restaurant I'd like to eat at," I said.

Mrs. Mamalujian was delighted: she liked giving me what I wanted, and always complained that I didn't ask for enough.

"The Waldorf, near the Coop."

She made a face. "That's a greasy spoon. It's all students. But if it's what you want we shall do it. Let's take a taxi—I'm planning on getting too drunk to drive."

I did not tell her why I had chosen the Waldorf—which didn't seem like a greasy spoon to me, and far from it, rather nice. But when I ordered she knew.

"At last you're getting your whale steak," she said. "Have two of them. Have three!"

"They are pretty good-sized," the waiter warned.

"He's got a huge appetite," Mrs. Mamalujian said.

"One's enough," I said.

"And how would you like it?"

The question baffled me.

The waiter tried to help. "Medium? Well-done?"

I had no idea that whale steaks were cooked like other kinds of meat.

"Medium," I said. "Regular."

"This isn't such a bad place," Mrs. Mamalujian said.

She was already on her second drink. She kept her swizzle sticks as a way of keeping track. She often ended up with a fistful of them.

"This tastes so good," she said, sipping her gin and tonic. "You could probably live on these." She had stopped looking anxious: the drink had stopped her looking forgetful. "I hope you like shrimp salad. I know I'm not going to want much of mine. You'll have to help me."

Perhaps fat people didn't get fat from eating their own meals but rather from also eating everyone's leftovers, as a sort of greedy favor. I wanted to ask Mrs. Mamalujian this, but she was downing her second drink and with her free hand waving to the waiter for a third.

"That whale steak is all I want."

The other thing that pleased me was the cheapness of this place. I had not braved it before, but now I saw that at these prices I could afford to take Lucy here. I began to think of an evening when I might do it. And it was only four stops on the subway from where she lived, so there would be time to make love, too.

"You didn't ask me why today's a special day," Mrs. Mamalujian said.

"Is it your birthday?"

"When you say dumb things like that I realize how young you are."

"What's wrong with birthdays?"

"Oh, my God," she said, and really seemed distressed, as if I had mentioned something dreadful, like sickness or death.

She looked around desperately and then seeing the waiter approach with a drink on his tray, reached out and took the glass and swigged from it. There were also two plates on the tray.

"Shrimp salad for madam. Whale for the gentleman. Enjoy your meal."

I had planned a whole conversation around this dish—how Stubb craved it and woke up the cook to prepare it; and their discussion; and the long chapter on eating whalemeat.

It was gray-brown and scorched, about the size of a boy's shoe, with burned onions on the side, and a scoop of mashed potato next to it. But it looked like an ordinary steak, except that there was no bone.

[152]

Mrs. Mamalujian lit a cigarette. She often did that when she saw food, and smoked instead of eating. She moved both hands to her mouth—smoke, drink, smoke, drink. She had begun to look distracted again.

I cut my steak with the sharp knife and was surprised by the wounded-looking redness of it and the bloody inside. It was a discovery but I said calmly, "Red meat."

"I've decided to leave my husband, that's why it's special," Mrs. Mamalujian said.

I had put a piece of meat into my mouth, my first taste of whale. It was not like any other meat I had ever eaten. It was tough, it was oily, and most striking of all it was salty—sea-salty, with the tang of fish. What the hell had she just said?

"He was completely flabbergasted."

I was blinking from the taste of the whale.

"Don't look so worried," Mrs. Mamalujian said.

Melville had never defined that taste: the one thing he had failed to say about whales.

"It was the last thing he had expected me to do."

Then I remembered what she had said.

"You mean you just went up to him and said," and I chewed the whale, " 'I'm leaving.' "

"Yes, isn't it thrilling?"

I could not hide my real feeling. I said, "No, I think it's terrible."

"How can you say that, when you had something to do with it, Andy."

I managed to ask her what she meant by that by eating some more whale steak and hiding my embarrassment in my chewing. It was the strangest meat in the world. I had wanted it to be different, and it was. There was plenty to talk about in it, which was another reason I was discouraged that Mrs. Mamalujian had chosen today to reveal to me that she had ditched her husband.

"I didn't realize how dull my life was until I met you," she said. "You're fun to be with. You read books. You laugh. You're alive. And you're a terrific listener. I want to spend more time having fun."

This worried me very much—praise always did, but this was worse because this was praise mingled with expectation. What could I offer her? I hated this change, I was frightened by her announcement, and I knew I would not be able to cope with it.

I said, "What about your family?"

"They can take care of themselves," she said. "Anyway, they think I'm a joke."

"But you must have thought about this before you met me," I said, trying not to be responsible for her decision.

Why did she choose now to tell me? I wanted to eat this whale steak, but after that first taste I couldn't concentrate. It was like someone talking when you're trying to listen to music.

"No, sir. Before you showed up at the club pool I assumed my life wouldn't change. I'd just continue going through the motions. Now all that's changed. You don't seem very happy for me, Andre."

It is impossible to say "I'm happy" at someone's request and sound as if you mean it, and when I said "Really" it sounded totally false.

There was a phase in Mrs. Mamalujian's drinking when she became petulant, usually after four or five. I knew by her tone and the number of swizzle sticks that we had reached that mood. A few more drinks and she would be jolly; then scandalous; then sad. She often finished in tears. They were like her kisses, big wet ones. They smeared her makeup, but they didn't go on long and she always went off smiling in an exhausted way—well, no wonder. But I didn't want this today. I wished I were back at the pool instead of here.

"I'm going back to college after Labor Day," I said, because her saying *I want to spend more time having fun* seemed to implicate me. "I won't be around much."

I could not eat this strong briny meat quickly, but I was nearly done. I wanted to dispose of it, think of an excuse and get out of here. If she started crying I was stuck: I could never leave her in tears.

"I can drive up and see you. We can go for picnics. There must be lots of good restaurants up there. Bon appetit!" That was jolly.

Making plans for the future like this made me feel like a prisoner who has no choice but to follow that narrow track until he has served his sentence.

"Your husband must be really upset," I said.

"Stop talking about my husband. You don't even know him. Some of the things I've found in his drawers. You wouldn't believe!" That was scandalous. She drank again and said sadly, "I was hoping you'd go to New York with me some weekend. Maybe take in a show. Wouldn't you like that?"

No, I thought, but I said, "Sure. The trouble is I don't get any time off. If I don't work—"

"I've got lots of money," she said, and gulped another drink defiantly. "You're eating too fast. You're going to make yourself sick."

"I have to get back to the pool."

"You don't care about me," she whimpered.

Then I was determined to go. She'd be tearful in two seconds.

I stood up and kissed her and said, "I'll give you a call—I want to hear more about it." But I didn't want to hear anything about it, and I hoped she would get drunker and forget about me. I thought I would no more go to New York with her than I would do this again—spoil a good whale steak with a fruitless argument. Mrs. Mamalujian was smoking with all her food in front of her when I left. Almost an inch of cigarette ash was suspended over her shrimp salad. I did not want to see it fall.

That lunch with Mrs. Mamalujian made me lonely and restless. Reading didn't help. I had to see Lucy. I called her the next day at the bookstore.

She said, "I was trying to get you all day yesterday, Andy," and that made me feel better. "I want to talk to you."

"How about having dinner with me tomorrow night? There's somewhere I'd like to take you."

She said, "You weren't at the pool" in a monotonous way. It was very unusual of Lucy not to listen to me.

She hardly looked at the menu the next night.

I said, "I usually have the whale steak. Ever had it?"

She didn't reply, she wasn't looking at the menu, she wasn't listening.

"Lucy, what would you like to eat?"

Her eyes were staring at nothing in a blind wide-open way.

I was silent, but after about fifteen seconds my question reached her.

"I don't know," she said. "I'm not hungry."

Then she looked straight at me.

"I mean, if I eat anything I'll throw up."

She had not smiled once.

"They have whale steaks here," I said.

She looked at me as if at a moron, with a kind of hopeless pity.

I said, "You think whale's going to be gray blubbery stuff with square edges and about six inches of white fat. But remember the line in *Moby Dick* where Stubb says something about the 'red meat'? That's not Melville's usual hyperbole, that's a literal fact. The whale steak is red like a sirloin, and very sinewy. There's a strange contradiction between the look of it and the taste"— Jesus Christ, it was so hard talking to someone who didn't reply—"it looks like beef but it has a fishy taste."

It occurred to me that the odd salty fishy taste was the taste of Lucy herself, for after she did the nameless thing to me and took me into her mouth and lovingly noodled with me, I did a nameless thing to her. I knelt down and lifted her legs and, as if making a deep dive, put my face against her and madly moved my tongue. My ears rang from being squashed between her thighs. And now I knew that her wetness on my twisted tongue was whale. So I had tasted it before I knew its name.

I wanted to tell her, but we never talked about sex. It was all done by touch. In bed we shut our eyes and were very silent and active. When it came to sex we were blind and deaf and mute. It was as if we were adventuring in a prohibited place, in a landscape so forbidden none of it had a name.

And I thought that if I told her she tasted like a whale steak she might become very shy and self-conscious, and that would be the end of it. We were different people in bed from the people we were on the street. In this restaurant it was almost impossible for me to imagine making love to her.

She looked very sad. I asked her whether anything was wrong. She let a long moment pass and then she sighed.

"Why do they kill them?" she said, not answering my question. "They are beautiful creatures. They're enormous. They're very friendly. They're intelligent, too. And they sing—haven't you heard that record?"

I said, "No."

I hated the direction this conversation was taking. It was like showing someone a target with a cluster of holes you had brilliantly shot into the bull's-eye, and the person making a face and saying *I hate guns,* undermining the whole subject.

Lucy screwed up her face and said, "It's very haunting."

You always had to take someone's word for that. When someone said *haunting* I was never haunted, I was only annoyed.

I said, "If you stick up for whales you get a pretty distorted impression of *Moby Dick.* The whole sense of it is ruined. I mean, Jesus, the whale's supposed to be evil."

"Please don't yell."

That plea was always a provocation to yell, and I was on the point of it when the waiter came over.

We ordered—a whale steak for me. Lucy languidly said that she'd have half a grapefruit and a bowl of soup. I thought she was deliberately ordering those dull things to get back at me for eating whale. She didn't know she tasted like whale meat.

I said, "It's like hating that Hemingway story, 'Francis Macomber,' because you're against killing buffaloes."

"What's wrong with that?"

"Then you miss the whole point of the bad marriage and the symbolism in the story."

"I hate that story. I hate Hemingway. He's a bully and a brute. I know you're not supposed to say that because he won the Nobel Prize and he's so important and all that. But I can't stand all this animal killing. It's murder."

"Jesus, what are you a vegetarian or something?"

"What if I am?" she said, sounding tearful.

But I was so exasperated I kept on, and said, "And you only read vegetarian stories—no hunting, no fishing, no meat-eating, no trespassing. That leaves out Hemingway and Melville. What about that great Faulkner story, 'The Bear'? Would you like it better if it were called 'The Cabbage'?"

"You're angry. Please don't be angry."

"Or 'The Head of Lettuce'?" I said. "Actually there is one called 'The Dill Pickle.' I'll bet you like that one a lot."

"You're making me feel like the woman in it," Lucy said.

I tried to remember what it was about. Was it a woman seeing an old lover and being very disappointed because the man was such a crumb?

Lucy said, "It's just that I heard that whale record recently. We had it in the record section of the store. I was moved by it—the haunting sound, sort of echoing and calling out in a watery and yearning—"

It was very unfortunate that she was rhapsodizing about whales at that moment, because as she was talking, with a plaintive half-smile on her lips, the waiter put my plate down and a whale steak was bleeding on it.

That stopped her. She loosened a grapefruit segment and spooned it into her mouth, and frowned as she chewed. I wanted to say *You never hear vegetarians eating and saying "Yum!" and "Boy!" and "That sure hits the spot!"* Eating this stuff was her way of punishing herself for being hungry—she was a real Yankee. And the grapefruit gave her the exact expression of disapproval she wanted, I was sure, and every time she spooned some of it into her mouth I was put into my place.

She said, "I think it's as bad as killing human beings."

"You've got to be joking," I said, and chewed the whale steak in an ostentatious way to make my point, which was: There is no use pursuing this argument. Chomping the meat was my rebuttal.

I was also thinking: We're incompatible, she's nagging, she's nuts, this is no good. And I decided that I didn't want to see her again. This was it. We couldn't agree on the simplest thing. I believed that vegetarians were irrational. A person who refused to eat hamburgers I regarded as insane, because that was someone who took a hamburger seriously.

When she was served her soup—it was vegetable soup—she hunched her skinny shoulders and put her head down and submerged her spoon in a pathetic way. I almost felt sorry for her until I remembered how she had tried to make me feel bad for eating the whale steak.

Being angry with her gave me indigestion, or perhaps it was the fact that I was eating too fast in my eagerness to get out of there. I wanted to take her home. Mentally I was on the subway, and then getting out at Memorial Drive, walking down Charles Street and up to Pinckney, kissing her goodnight, saying, "I'll call you" and not meaning it. Just the feeling I had had with Mrs. Mamalujian two days ago.

"Let's go," I said, and called the waiter for my check.

She said, "I'll be right back," and hurried toward the sign that said REST ROOMS.

Her absence first made me dislike her; then made me worry and hate myself for thinking I disliked her; and when she returned after fifteen minutes—but it felt like an hour—I actually did dislike her for making me wait and worry for nothing. I thought: Good night, goodbye, I will never see you again.

We traveled back to Pinckney Street in silence. I loathed her for looking sick, and I told myself she was faking.

"Want to come in?" she said.

"Nah."

Did she know what I was thinking? But when I kissed her I was aroused and I thought *What the hell.*

"If you want to come in," she said, "we can sneak past Miss Murphy and you can do whatever you like with me."

That made me break the promise I had made to myself in the restaurant, but inside her room she seemed weak and inert. She lay back and stuck her legs out and she was as pale as a sacrifice. She did not move when I touched her, which spooked me, and when I saw her cheeks were wet I went no further. Tears always stopped me.

I said, "Never mind," and started to go.

Her room was so small she was able to stretch out her hand and stop me. "Andy, I missed my period," she said. "It's two weeks late. I keep praying, but—oh, God, I don't know what to do—"

That was my second whale steak.

8.

We went to New York City separately—Mrs. Mamalujian took a plane, and (under the influence of Kerouac) I hitched. We met at the Plaza. Another Plaza. Each time I saw her it struck me that she had an original face—red puckered lips and big rouged cheeks, each cheek a distinct muscle. Her eyes were pouchy and smeared with green. I had never seen a face like it.

She said, "I've been here for hours—shopping. Mainly buying underwear."

That depressed me. Any mention of underwear or sex or nakedness made me gloomy. I did not tell Mrs. Mamalujian why I had come. As far as she knew, it was for the candlelight dinner we had a few hours later at the Marquis Carvery, where the coat-check girl had to find a necktie for me to wear with my khaki shirt and army jacket. The tie was stiff with soupstains.

"Eat my avocado, Andy—before the waiter takes it away."

Gloom made me hungry. Eating was sometimes my way of worrying.

"I've got tickets for *West Side Story,* and there's another play Sunday night. We can go to the Museum of Modern Art some afternoon. Isn't it fun to be here? Don't you feel free?"

I felt like a jailbird. I said, "It's nice. But I've got to see a few people tomorrow."

"That's all right, as long as you get back here before show time. Did you know *West Side Story*'s based on Shakespeare? The one on Sunday is Tennessee Williams. Very spicy"—and she winked—"queers and cannibalism. We can have dinner afterwards. It was so sweet of you to come."

Just to set her straight I said, "No, it was great of you to give me a place to stay."

"Don't put it like that," she said.

"I mean, it was a lucky coincidence that I had this stuff to do. The, um, thing. These people."

"You're so busy. I wish I was busy."

I wanted to kill myself I was so busy. I pushed food into my mouth so I wouldn't say anything crazy.

She said, "New York has it all over Boston. You can do anything here."

That had better be true, I thought.

The room at the Plaza had twin beds, I was relieved to find, when we went back after dinner. Mrs. Mamalujian took a long sloppy shower, leaving the bathroom door open, as she had that first time in Boston. I could hear her elbows hitting the plastic shower curtain.

I lay on the bed reading Ezra Pound—*The Pisan Cantos*.

Mrs. Mamalujian came in dripping, and holding a towel against her front.

"Aren't you going to take your clothes off?"

"I've got to get up early," I said.

She smiled at that and I immediately realized what I had said was stupid.

"And the thing is, I always sleep with my clothes on in hotels. I have a morbid fear of fires. I want to be dressed if there's trouble."

The mention of fire took the smile off her face. She stood in the half-dark and slipped on a silky nightgown.

She said, "If there's anything you want to talk about, just come over here. Sometimes the best place to talk is in bed. I mean, you can say things that you can't say anywhere else."

She switched her light off and sighed.

I lay there rigid in the darkness expecting her to touch me. Her powerful perfume made her seem as though she were very close to me.

"But, um, Andre."

"Yuh?"

"If you come over to me, take your shoes off, will you?"

Mrs. Mamalujian was quietly snoring and smacking her lips in the next bed the following morning when I slid to the floor and crept out of the room and went to find an abortionist. That was my only reason for being there. New York was where they were.

I knew they were not listed in the telephone book. The practice was illegal. They were known by word of mouth. A doctor could go to jail if he was convicted of performing an abortion. But I knew such doctors existed. The question was, Where should I start looking?

I was prevented from crossing Fifth Avenue by a Kennedy rally making its way with banners and drums to Central Park. And I began to imagine that these wealthy-looking women with their badges and funny hats had all had abortions; but for them it was like having a tooth pulled—a morning's work. I could also see how these people, women and men and kids my age, all somewhat resembled Kennedy—good families, good clothes, good teeth. They were happy, because they knew that America was going to be theirs for the next eight years. It wouldn't be

mine—that was the sorry feeling I was left with as the rally took
its chanting and music up the avenue.

I walked east, across Park Avenue, and kept walking, thinking
that I might find a neighborhood bar. But there were no bars.
There were hot August streets and big department stores and
apartment buildings. I saw signs—B. M. LEFKOWITZ MD and J.R.
STONE OBSTETRICS AND GYNECOLOGY; and I thought of going in
and asking. But I didn't know how to phrase the question—I
couldn't even begin. The thing was to have a doctor's name. You
paid him a visit. He knew why you'd come. He simply named his
price and made an appointment. I guessed that an abortion
would cost about two hundred dollars, and I had fifty on me for
a down payment.

This part of New York was impenetrable. I walked south and
then had the idea that Brooklyn was where I should go. Brooklyn
had a reputation for illicit activities. It was easy to imagine gam-
bling and prostitution and murder in Brooklyn, and abortion
was somehow related to those crimes.

I had no doubt that it was a crime. But what else could I do?
I had promised Lucy that I would help her. I was responsible for
the fix she was in, and she had become hopeful when I told her
I was going to New York to find a doctor. We had not even
spoken of marriage the thought was so frightening, and in fact
as soon as she mentioned missing her period my love for her was
consumed in worry.

I kept walking. I imagined it this way: I was standing in a bar,
having a drink. I got friendly with the bartender or maybe the
man drinking next to me. What's up, kid? Oh, you're new
around here. Then I asked whether there was a doctor nearby
who knew how to get a girl out of trouble. The way I imagined
it, someone always knew.

"Can you tell me the way to Brooklyn?"

The man selling hot bagels from a pushcart didn't look at me,
but he said out of the side of his mouth, "Cross over, downtown
to Fourteenth, change to the BMT"—and some more that I
didn't catch.

I had not even noticed the subway entrances—small signs
over stairways that led underground. I went down the dirty
stairs, bought a token and boarded a train. It was rackety and it
went so fast, missing stations, that I got off after a few stops

because I was afraid it would take me too far. I asked the way to Brooklyn—about twelve times, just to be sure, and finally discovered that every subway car had a map in it. When I worked out where I was I saw that Brooklyn was huge. I chose Borough Hall, imagining a square with a stately building lined with pillars aboveground. It was a glary shopping district filled with traffic stink and bus horns, and so I walked.

I was encouraged by the brownstones here, and none of the buildings were as intimidatingly tall as the ones in Manhattan.

NICK'S BAR AND GRILL on the corner fitted my image of the bar I had envisioned. I went in and ordered a beer. I had been so impatient I hadn't realized the time—only nine-thirty in the morning. The bar was empty except for an old woman at a table who looked like an alcoholic.

"Quiet today," I said to the bartender.

"Yeah."

"I suppose it really gets lively here later on."

"You kidding me?" he said and walked away.

A man came through the door, sort of pushing it with his stomach in a comic way. He wore a Hawaiian shirt and a straw hat and two-tone shoes. He said hello to me and climbed onto a stool. Without being asked the bartender brought him a shot of whiskey. He downed the whiskey like medicine, making a face, then took a swig of beer and looked around.

"Going to be a hot one," he said.

"I don't mind."

"You'd mind if you were carting around two hundred and sixty pounds of blubber."

I laughed, but inside I was asking myself how I could turn the conversation from the weather to abortions.

He asked me where I was from—something about my accent—and when I told him, he said that Kennedy was from Boston, too, and we talked about the election. He said he was for Kennedy and I told him so was I, because I wanted to ingratiate myself. He said he had been a Democrat his whole life.

"I fought in the Pacific with Jack Kennedy," he said.

I wanted to tell him that the Pacific Ocean was a big place and that he was kidding himself.

"And I think it's about time we had a Catholic in the White House. It'll straighten this country out."

This gave me a very dreary feeling, because I knew this fat man was a Catholic and I also knew that he wasn't going to give me any help.

"Kennedy would never legalize abortions," I said.

"Why should he? It's murder," the man said.

I found an excuse to leave soon after that.

I was a little unsteady from the beer in my empty stomach, but after a few blocks I went into a crowded place, The Broad Street Bar. I sat next to a man in shirtsleeves who didn't reply to anything I said. I tried another man and couldn't shut him up. At last I saw a very sinister-looking man in a torn jacket and said, "Do you live around here?"

"Who wants to know?" he said in a nasty voice.

"I was just wondering, because I'm looking for a doctor," and I dropped my voice. "There's this guy I know who knocked up his girlfriend and he told me to come down here as a favor to see if the doctor's still in business. He lives in this area, apparently."

"The only one I know is Shimkus."

"That might be him."

"I think he's over on J Street."

I thanked him and dashed out of the bar and looked for a telephone. There were two doctors called Shimkus and one called Simkiss in the book. None of them answered the phone. Why did I think that these doctors would be in their offices on a hot Saturday in August?

I tried a few more bars, started conversations with strangers, but got nowhere—didn't even ask the question that was the sole reason for my search.

By midafternoon I was drunkish and hot and had a headache. Walking towards the subway I saw a doctor's shingle and went straight in. The doctor himself was with the receptionist when I entered, and he looked at me in an unwelcoming way over his glasses.

"Can I see you a minute, doctor?"

"Do you have an appointment?"

"No. I just have one short question."

His face was very severe, but he sighed and it softened. Perhaps because his office was empty—or perhaps he was headed home—he said okay unwillingly. I had never met a doctor who was polite, because their politeness was just another way of being rude.

I was so desperate I blurted out the question as soon as he shut the door to his consulting room: My friend's girlfriend needed an abortion—

He placed his fingertips together, making a basket of his hands, and he smiled at me.

"Doctor John can help you. He's right across the street."

"Really? Oh, that's great!" I said, not caring that I was revealing my anxiety and that my secret was probably out.

But as I turned to go, he said, "On second thought, no. Doctor John's in jail." He eyed me, looking triumphant, and added, "That's what I always tell people who ask that question. You're asking me to break the law."

"Fuck it," I said.

That night I saw *West Side Story* with Mrs. Mamalujian. She had seen it before, and had the record, and she knew all the songs. She sang them in her chain-smoker's voice and even when a man behind us complained out loud she kept it up.

Back at the hotel, she took another shower—the usual one, with the bathroom door open, for an hour. I read Ezra Pound in the sitting room and thanked God there was a sitting room. But I was still very worried. *Pull down thy vanity,* I read. After Mrs. Mamalujian got into her bed I yawned and walked around and took my shoes off. Then I lay down on my bed with all my clothes on.

"You're a very funny kid, Andy. I had no idea."

I yawned again, pretending I hadn't heard her.

"I mean strange. If you ever want to talk about it—"

"Tomorrow I have to see some friends of mine," I said.

"I was hoping we could go to a museum. See the Picassos. Have some lunch. Take in a show."

I pretended to be asleep by snoring softly, and soon she stopped talking. But I lay awake almost all night, and in the morning I slid off my bed and went to the door on my hands and knees.

She was staring at me.

"It's in the door," she said, meaning the key she thought I was hunting for.

She made me nervous, because when I was around her I could

not think clearly about my problem; and I knew I was running out of time. I spent the whole of that day, Sunday, walking up and down the sidewalks with my hands in my pockets wondering what to do. I liked the city because the city ignored me, and I felt that it was so large and such a mess that I had as much right to be there as anyone else.

When I got back to the Plaza at about six, Mrs. Mamalujian was sitting in the parlor room of the suite having a drink.

She said, "I could live like this," and from the way she said it I knew she was drunk. Her head wobbled. "I mean, waiting for you to come home from work."

"I haven't been to work," I said, and yawned.

She said, "The trouble with you"—and she gestured with her drink—"is that you don't know how to enjoy yourself. Where is your pep?"

"I'm tired from walking."

"You said you were with some friends."

"Walking with them."

It was very hard to lie or invent when I was so distracted.

"What are they like, these so-called friends of yours?"

"Nice bunch of guys," I said. "But there's one who has a problem. He wanted me to help him, but how could I?"

Mrs. Mamalujian looked at me drunkenly and I wondered whether to tell her.

"I love problems," she said. "Know why? Because I usually have the solution. Know what the solution usually is? Money."

She took sips of gin between sentences.

"The stupid idiot knocked up his girlfriend."

There was a certain way she had of swallowing that meant she was thinking.

"Isn't that the girlfriend's problem?"

"He promised to help her," I said. "He's looking for a doctor to get rid of it."

"There's plenty of those doctors around," Mrs. Mamalujian said.

"That's what people say, but where the hell are they?"

"Right over there," she said, and pointed out the window.

I went to the window. I said, "Where?"

"Park Avenue," she said in a halting voice.

When I turned around she was crying. I asked her what was wrong.

"I know someone who got an abortion from a doctor there," she said.

"What was his name?"

"It was a woman," she said, and sobbed. I believed I knew who that woman might be.

I said, "No—the doctor's name."

It sounded something like Zinzler. That was all I wanted to know. I was so grateful I almost relaxed enough to take my clothes off and eat and sleep properly.

Mrs. Mamalujian went on drinking and around ten o'clock she let out a little giggle and passed out. I put her to bed with her clothes on—she was wearing so many. She looked very small after I took off her shoes and her hat. We didn't go to the play.

I slept fitfully in one of the armchairs and at six I wrote Mrs. Mamalujian a note thanking her for the lovely weekend. I found *D. K. Zinzler, MD*, in the phone book, with a Park Avenue address and then went out and located the building, fifteen blocks away. I had breakfast to kill time and at nine o'clock made my move. The doorman, a goon in a blue uniform, tried to stop me as I headed through the revolving door. I swallowed my pride and told him I had an appointment and asked him whether there was any information he required from me. He was so bored by my eagerness he let me go.

Zinzler was on the eighth floor. The corridor was cool, very quiet, smelling of flowers and floorwax. And Zinzler's office was so clean I was hesitant to sit down. His receptionist asked me whether I had an appointment.

By then I had given the matter some thought.

"No. I'm delivering a message."

"Yes?" And she put her hand out.

"My message is for the doctor."

"I'll have to know what it is."

"I can only tell you that my client regards it as highly confidential."

Client? she was thinking, as she looked at my army jacket, combat boots, sunglasses.

"Just a minute."

While she was out of the room, a woman and a girl of about seventeen or eighteen entered from the outside corridor, the mother looking suspicious and hateful, the girl rather stupefied, as if she'd been hit on the head. The girl also looked ill. I was

sure she was pregnant and that the doctor was going to give her
an abortion. The mother, annoyed that I was witnessing their
arrival, gave me a black look.

"Go in," the receptionist said to me, and began apologizing
to the mother and daughter for the delay.

Doctor Zinzler was waiting for me in the office. He was half
out of his chair and as soon as he saw me he frowned, knowing
that I was there on false pretenses.

"You have a message for me?"

"It's more of a question."

"Yes," he said, and hurried me with a movement of his hand.

"This friend of mine was wondering whether you'd take care
of his girlfriend."

He was an old man and he had an old man's terrible stare.

"She's pregnant."

His stare made me keep talking.

"She doesn't want to be pregnant. She's looking for an,
um—"

I didn't want to say the word, but in any case I didn't have to.

He said, "Who sent you here?"

If I said Mrs. Mamalujian it might get back to her, and she'd
die if she knew it was me.

"My friend."

"What's his name?"

"You wouldn't know him."

He had already started heading for the door. That was my
signal to leave. He said, "You came to the wrong place."

But I knew it wasn't the wrong place. I knew that was his
business. But he didn't like my looks.

"How much does it cost?"

"I'm very busy," he said, taking my arm and steering me out.

"These friends of mine are pretty desperate."

He said, "Maybe they should have thought about the conse-
quence of what they were doing."

I pushed his arm away and was about to hit him when I heard
a gasp—either the mother or the daughter. And if I decked him
there were witnesses. I now saw that they were wealthy. So was
Zinzler. But I wasn't. That was why he said it was the wrong
place. I had planned on raising the money, whatever it cost; but
it wasn't a question of that. You had to look wealthy. I was not

humiliated. I was angry. And my only satisfaction was that in the split second in which I had raised my fist to hit him he might have feared for his life. Going downstairs I regretted that I hadn't said to him, *I'm coming back to kick your ass.*

On the Greyhound Bus to Boston I considered how much I hated that doctor, and I began to dislike Mrs. Mamalujian. When she put her glass out someone poured gin into it. When she approached a door, someone opened it. When she stared at something in a glass case they took it out and showed her. If she had gone to the doctor he would have done what she wanted. These things cost money. I had no money, and it seemed as though, having none, I did not exist. What annoyed me was that I had not thought much about this before, and I had been happy.

9.

Going back to the pool was like going home. I slept in Medford, but I didn't live there. My life was a system of secrets. My mother said, "How was the Cape?" and I said "Fine," remembering that I had said I was going to the Cape for the weekend. How could I say I was going to New York City with a fifty-year-old woman in order to find an abortionist? They did not know me at home anymore. They knew me better here at the pool, but even so my life was hidden.

I ate at the pool. I kept spare clothes in the lifeguard room. I took my showers in the changing room. I did most of my reading at the pool—all these fucken women writers, Muzzaroll said, seeing Evelyn Waugh, Caryl Chessman and Rainer Maria Rilke. Muzzaroll was proud that he had never read a book by a woman. "Joyce Cary!" he screamed one day. Another fucken woman.

I also got my messages at the pool.

Mrs. Mamalujian called me the day after I returned from New York.

"How about dinner tonight?"

"I don't think so," I said. "I'm not very hungry."

"That's got nothing to do with it."

The trouble with being rich was in thinking that food had nothing to do with hunger. *Lunch is a figure of speech* she had said not long ago.

"I've got a nice place in mind," she said. "Whale steaks!"

I was determined not to go. I had a clear memory of two of them.

I said, "I'm pretty busy"—to remind her that she was not busy at all—and, "I've got some things on my mind"—to remind her that her head was empty. But she just laughed and hung up.

One of the things on my mind was Lucy. I had not called her, because I was afraid to tell her that I had failed. And why should I see Mrs. Mamalujian if I hadn't seen Lucy?

She left me a note one lunchtime saying *I must see you. Love, L.* and I had the thought that the problem was solved and that she was eager to tell me so. Sometimes, these supposed pregnancies were just a scare—that was what people said. It was nerves. You worried about being pregnant because you missed your period and you went on missing it because you went on worrying. You weren't pregnant. You were just worried.

I met her after work. She was glad to see me but she was still very pale.

I said, "How are you?"

"I feel okay," she said.

I thought that meant she wasn't pregnant anymore.

"Is everything all right?"

"No," she said, and my heart collapsed: we were still stuck.

She said, "What about New York—what happened?"

"Not much," I said, and she knew it meant *nothing*.

She nibbled her lip and I knew she was fretting.

The jukebox in the Harvard Gardens was playing "Get a Job" and almost drowning out what Lucy was trying to say.

"I'm afraid," she said. "I don't know what to do."

"What do you want me to do?"

"Just help me." She put her hand on mine. "Want to go back to my room?"

I had no sexual urge at all. I didn't want it, I didn't dare, I had lost interest. It seemed to me that after all these years I was beginning to understand what a sin was.

I said, "It's money, you know. If you're rich you can have anything." I thought of my failure in New York—it had all been rejection. "If you don't have money in America you're out of luck."

"You talk as though it's better in other countries," Lucy said.

"You could get an abortion in another country. In Russia, for example, where they don't believe in God. You'd just go to the hospital and that would be it."

Lucy had started to cry.

"My mother keeps calling me and asking me to go home for a visit. But I don't want to. I'm afraid she'll ask me questions—or she might guess."

"I'll go with you," I said, before I could restrain myself. I was sorry the moment I said it. Then I had to go to the toilet. I gave her my wallet and said, "Take some money out and pay for the beer, will you? I'll be right back."

She was sobbing at the table when I sat down again.

"Oh my God. Oh, my God."

"Please, Lucy. People are looking at you."

But she wasn't sad—she was angry. She said fiercely through her tears, "You've been lying to me. You're nineteen. You're just a stupid kid." And she flung my driver's license down.

And I could tell that her mother felt the same way. Mrs. Cutler—that was Lucy's name—was a very nervous woman, about fifty. It interested me how she could be the same age as Mrs. Mamalujian and yet be totally different—as different from Mrs. Mamalujian as a man is from a woman. She wasn't angry that her daughter had brought a young kid in an army jacket down to dinner; she was crestfallen. There was a look of collapse in her eyes; she was nervous and wore an apron. None of this Mrs. Mamalujian chatter and assurance—no makeup, no big hats. Mrs. Mamalujian had an irritating laugh and an original face. She defied you to think about her age, and then you couldn't imagine it. Mrs. Cutler was apologetic and shapeless, and she looked like an old woman.

She said, "Was it a good trip down?"

We had taken the bus to Plymouth and then caught a local bus to Manomet, and walked the rest of the way, to the house above the cove. We had sat in gloomy silence the whole way. I read Camus' *The Stranger*. Now and then I glanced at Lucy and thought: This is what marriage must be like. It was like being unhealthy. You just sat there with the other person and you had to be very careful.

"It was nice," I said. "I like the South Shore. The North Shore is all snobs."

Mrs. Cutler said, "We used to have ever such a lovely house on the cliff when Lucy's father was alive. But we had to sell it. I couldn't keep it up."

Lucy didn't say anything—but it was a disapproving silence.

"You must be famished. I'll bet you could tear a herring."

"I'd like to show Andy the beach before we eat," Lucy said.

We walked down the road, which was warm crumbling tar on this late-August day. Tall grass, weeds with blue flowers, and small thorn bushes lined the road and had a lovely dusty smell. A car rattled past and the man at the wheel waved.

"You know him?"

"I know everybody here," Lucy said glumly.

She took a sudden step into the grass, and I saw she was on a path. I followed her down the cliff to the beach.

"It's pretty."

"It's awful. It's dull," she said. "Can you imagine what it's like to grow up in a little town like this?"

Waves smashed noisily against the rocks. The rocks were rounded and black and looked like tumbled cannonballs.

"That was Mr. Philpotts," she said, pointing up at the road. "Now he's going to tell the whole town that he saw me and you going down to the beach."

"What's wrong with that?"

"He'll describe you," she said.

"I don't care."

"That's the trouble with you," she said, and walked away from the rocks to where the beach was smoother with sand and pebbles.

"We found a whale here once. A little one. At first we thought it was a mattress, or one of those tractor tires that wash up out of nowhere. It was so strange. It was right here"—she kicked a

[172]

groove into the beach with her brown loafer—"and its mouth
gaped open. It was lying on its side like a big fat flounder. When
we jumped on its side the eye bulged."

"How did you know it was a whale?"

"Because it wasn't a shark."

I was thinking: People always complained about them, but
their little towns seemed wonderful to me.

"What are we going to do?" Lucy said, without any warning.

Just that question caused my sick feeling to return. It was like
a hole in my stomach.

"Don't worry," I said. "I'll think of something."

"My mother doesn't suspect anything."

"That's good," I said.

"It makes me feel horrible."

I wanted to start walking fast and keep walking down the
beach alone, to Plymouth, to Duxbury, back to Boston and
beyond.

"I'm so afraid," she said.

She touched me and I felt a panic, but I didn't want her to
know how frightened I was, or that I didn't want to touch her.
So I took her hand and I kissed her and I made myself even more
panicky than before.

"It's a nice beach," I said. "Funny there aren't more people
around. Especially at this time of year. I wonder if they need a
lifeguard?"

Lucy was looking down.

"What happened to the whale?"

"One day it was there, the next day it was gone. The tide took
it away."

That was perfect—the dead stinking thing with its jelly-eye
just floated off and left the beach clean. I prayed for that easy
solution for us.

Lucy had started to cry. Was she thinking of the whale?

"We'd better go back," I said. "Your mother will be wondering where we are."

She blew her nose and then looked up at me with hatred. She
said, "Why did you lie to me? You're nineteen years old. You
don't know anything. Tuck that shirt in. Don't you know any
better?"

We walked back to the house, not saying anything. I wanted

to go—just leave on the next bus. But I felt guilty and I didn't want them to know it, so I stayed. I talked, because Lucy didn't say anything. In my nervousness I told them the whole plot of *The Stranger*—and it seemed silly and pointless when it was reduced to a few sentences.

Mrs. Cutler said, "These French books can be very interesting."

I knew she was bored and frightened by me, and I hated Lucy for not saying anything. I tried to get her to talk, because I thought if she kept quiet she might begin to cry.

Mrs. Cutler said, "Won't you have some apple pie?"

"I'd love some," I said, and then I had another piece to please her.

"You have a good appetite," she said. "That's a good sign. Lucy's hardly eaten anything."

Lucy looked up, and at first I thought her expression was angry. But then I saw she was sick. She got up from the table and hurried out of the room. I heard her tramping down the hall.

Mrs. Cutler said, "Lucy tells me you're a lifeguard. You must be a very good swimmer."

"It's a pool, so there's not much swimming involved. The kids push each other under. That's the real problem."

"I've always loved the water. I can't imagine what it would be like to live in Ohio, say, and never see the ocean."

I thought I heard Lucy throwing up several rooms away.

"The dangerous part of a pool is the deep end," I said. "People go in over their heads. You have to watch them like a hawk."

It all seemed innocent and easy to me, and I wanted it that way, and wondered why I hadn't been satisfied with it. I hadn't watched them like a hawk. I had read books in the lifeguard chair and hardly looked up except to see what time it was or what Muzzaroll was doing. I hated myself for searching for more than I should have and for complicating my life and ruining Lucy's. And what about Mrs. Mamalujian? I said that I was a lifeguard but that obvious thing was the most untrue thing about me.

When Lucy came back to the table her face was chalky, and it seemed much whiter because she had put on lipstick.

She said, "I think Andre wants to go."

"No," I said. "I want to help with the dishes."

They said they wouldn't let me, but I insisted and snatched up dishes and silverware. I resented doing it, and I wanted to go, but I was unable to bring myself to say it. I stacked the plates by the sink, and looked for a dishcloth and they kept saying, "Don't bother."

"You could sit down and read the paper," Mrs. Cutler said.

That horrified me—being a sort of husband or father, sitting in a wing chair, reading the *Globe* under the lamp, while the women clanked the dishes and whispered. I wanted to go.

"You've missed the last bus," Mrs. Cutler said.

"That's all right," I said.

"You can stay here. Lucy, make the bed in the spare room."

"No, no," I said, because I saw myself in a box upstairs all night, and then more of this at breakfast tomorrow. "I've got a friend in Plymouth. He's expecting me to stay."

Lucy looked sharply at me.

"I'll just put these dishes away and then I'll shove off."

"I wish we could drive you," Mrs. Cutler said. "We used to have a car. We used to have a lot of things."

I hated the way she said that, and I wanted to leave before she said anything more. But she offered me a coffee and I couldn't refuse.

Mrs. Cutler sat there looking bleary-eyed. How much worse she would have looked if she had known what was happening here.

Lucy said, "Go to bed, Mother. You know you never stay up this late."

"We've got company, Lucy." Then she yawned. She still wore her apron. There was a stack of knitting next to her chair—ropes of wool and a half-made sweater. "But I can't keep my eyes open."

When she stood up I realized that I would soon be alone with Lucy, and I was nervous again. The hole opened in my stomach and weakened me.

"I have to go, too," I said. "Thanks a million for the dinner, Mrs. Cutler."

"Come again," Mrs. Cutler said.

Lucy went as far as the front gate and said, "What's this about a friend? You didn't mention any friend."

"I forgot to."

"I'm frightened," she said. "You don't seem to realize that."

"I realize it," I said. Why couldn't the tide come up and take me away?

"What are you going to do about it?" she said in a low desperate voice.

I had no answer, so I hugged her and kissed her and told her again not to worry. Then I said I would have to get going or I'd be late, because it was a long walk to Plymouth. I let go of her and ran into the darkness and down the road.

But I turned back and took the narrow path to the beach. I could see the edge of beach from the froth on the breaking waves. I went to the far end, where they had found the washed-up whale. I crouched on the sand and lay down. It was a clear moony night, and the sand was still warm, but after a few hours the air turned cold and the sand became damp. But I had nowhere else to go. I had been lying. I didn't have a friend.

I shivered all night, and in the morning Lucy was standing over me.

She said, "You're nineteen. Why did I ever believe you? You're sleeping on the beach!"

I was startled and too cold to think of anything.

"That's what nineteen-year-olds do. They sleep on the beach. They're brainless."

Lying on the damp sand had made my muscles ache. I stood up and almost tipped over.

Lucy said in a hard voice, "I'm going to need some money. Three hundred dollars. You'd better find it, sonny."

It was like a challenge. She was a different person from the one I had fallen in love with as I knelt in her closet on Pinckney Street. It was hard to remember how we had laughed or made love. She didn't trust me anymore. She was like an enemy. I was afraid of her.

I said, "Don't worry—I'll get the money." I knew where I could.

Then there was no more to say. We walked heavily through the sand to the cliff. That little conversation about money took away the rest of our love.

10.

On Labor Day, the end of summer, Kennedy was back in Boston campaigning—marching in a parade, shaking hands, being bright. He was a living reminder that I had nothing. I did not wish him ill, but it was impossible to see his smile and not wish to see it wiped off his public face. But I disliked him most because I was certain that he would be elected. Nixon had a sloping and snoopy-looking face and shifty eyes. Very few people liked or trusted him. I wanted this unpopular man to be president, so that he would be opposed and mocked. A charming and glamorous person like Kennedy could get away with murder.

But I could not have gone to the parade even if I'd wanted to. It was the last day the pool was open, but because it was the middle of the week there was a foul-up in Accounting and we were paid for two weeks. At lunchtime we cashed our checks at the Harvard Gardens. I had one hundred and seventy-two dollars, including last week's money, which I had been intending to deposit.

Larry said, "Look at this wad," and showed me a roll of bills.

"Mine's bigger," I said. "That's not spinach. That's cash." I sandwiched the thick stack of bills into Baudelaire, because I didn't have a pocket big enough.

"Fantabulous," Muzzaroll said, and grinned and blinked at the money pressed into my copy of *The Flowers of Evil*.

Muzzaroll wore flappy trousers and black spades and sunglasses. A pack of cigarettes was folded and tucked into the short sleeve of his red *Lifeguard* T-shirt. He had a yellow Sicilian face and hairy ears. He shook his legs and strutted and said, "I'm hep."

" 'I'm hep,' the fuckstick says. Vinny, you are such a loser. Parent and I have real money—big bucks. You've got shit and you know it."

"I've got nine inches, so I don't need money," Muzzaroll said.

We were walking down Memorial Drive toward the pool, feeling happy.

"Let's lock the pool up and buy some beer and get drunk, because as from today I'm unemployed," Muzzaroll said.

"You deserve to be unemployed. You're a fucking banana-man."

"And you take it up the ass," Muzzaroll said in a friendly way.

"You wish you could," Larry said. "Instead of playing pocket-pool."

"See this nickel? I could make a phone call right now and be in the sack in about fifteen minutes. I got a broad in Orient Heights begging me for it. Sometimes I have to put my hand over her mouth I get her screaming so much."

"You put your hand over her mouth because she's got bad breath. I know her. I put the boots to her."

"You wish," Muzzaroll said. "She wouldn't go near yous."

Because he was speaking to both Larry and me he carefully made a plural of *you*.

"She's a dog," Larry said. "She's got a lopsided face, like someone sat on it, and one tit's bigger than the other. A real bow-wow."

"She's beautiful," Muzzaroll said, and put a cigarette into his mouth. "Give me a match, shit-for-brains."

"Your face and my ass," Larry said, and punched him on the arm.

Muzzaroll stuck a finger up and said, "Rotate on this."

They only talked like that when they were feeling pleased. It sounded terrible, but it was very casual. The more obscene and abusive they were the friendlier it was. I knew I would miss them.

"Parent's thinking about his dick. Don't worry, kid—give it a year or so. If it doesn't grow you can turn queer."

"And you can go down on him," Muzzaroll said.

"You wish you could."

"Fantabulous. There's a package store. I'm going to snag some beer."

All this odd hilarity was because the pool was closing, and we knew we probably wouldn't be seeing each other again. There was very little malice in them. When they were afraid or uncertain they were polite, but being foulmouthed was a form of intimacy—it showed how far they could go.

I was thinking about Lucy—how I had seen her only once lately, to give her the three hundred dollars I had borrowed from Mrs. Mamalujian. I had sworn that I would never see Mrs.

Mamalujian again; but I had gone back and asked her for the money. My only consolation was that she had so much money she wouldn't miss it. But I planned to pay it all back, fifty at a time, until my debt was cleared, probably next year.

Meanwhile, I wanted to forget the mess I had made of the summer, and I tried to stop myself thinking about Lucy.

At four o'clock we blew the siren we used for suspected drownings and emergencies. The kids complained as we cleared the pool. But this was the only fun we could look forward to: the last hour of the last day.

I walked to the edge of the pool. Every evening on closing the pool I looked into the ripply water and expected to see a dark body on the bottom—a shadowy thing that had lain there dead all day as swimmers splashed back and forth above it. There was nothing, but it was always my fear.

Now we had the place to ourselves. We opened the case of beer and set up the canvas deck chairs. And as the traffic roared past the fence we pretended that we were millionaires and that this was our private pool. The sun was still high over Cambridge, across the river. We stretched out and we drank beer and listened to Arnie Ginzburg's rock and roll show.

"I'm going bollocky, I don't even care," Muzzaroll said, and pulled off his bathing suit. His penis looked like a fat little otter. "They can't fire me!"

Larry threw an inner tube into the pool and then sat in it, drinking beer and bobbing in the deep end. "They can't fire any of us. We don't work here anymore." He swigged the beer. "Hey, Muzza, what are you doing this winter?"

"I don't know. Maybe work for the state. Maybe shovel snow. My brother-in-law's got a car wash. He's looking for a manager. What about you?"

Larry said, "I was just thinking. I worked in a bakery last winter. It sucked. What about you, Parent?"

"College," I said, looking up from *The Flowers of Evil*.

They didn't reply just then, but after a while Larry said, "You got the right idea. Get an education."

"One thing's for shit-sure," Muzzaroll said, "I ain't going in no fucking army."

"Anyway they don't take faggots," Larry said.

Muzzaroll laughed. "Know what we should do? Send out for

pizzas. And just stay here until it gets dark. Then get some ginch."

He phoned The Leaning Tower of Pizza and asked them to deliver three jumbo pizzas. While we waited for them, two girls walked by the fence on their way along the riverside path.

Larry said, "Hey, girls. Come here, want to swim? This is our pool. We rented it for the day."

"Sure you did," one girl said. She was laughing, but she hesitated because the pool looked so odd and still.

Muzzaroll was sitting in the inner tube now, with a can of beer in his hand, and wearing a baseball hat.

"He's an animal," Larry said.

"Did you guys break in?"

"She thinks we broke in! Hey, we rented it, no kidding. Ask him. He goes to college. He wouldn't lie to you. Tell them, Andre."

"Seriously, it's ours for the day," I said. "You're welcome to join us. It's all paid for."

"The fat one's yours," Larry whispered, and in a louder voice, "We just sent out for pizza. Want a slice?"

The girls were giggling and looking interested, and then as I looked at them—they were both pretty, neither one was fat—Larry said something that sent a chill through me.

"Andy—there's your girlfriend."

I looked up, expecting to see Lucy and saw Mrs. Mamalujian getting out of a yellow taxi.

"So long, deadass," Larry said. "When you come back you're going to find me and the Bananaman planking these broads in the locker room."

He could see that Mrs. Mamalujian was beckoning to me. I didn't want her to come in, so I put my clothes on and hurried out.

She said, "I just happened to be passing. Want a drink?"

She had had a few already. It was the way she stood there and the sulky way she talked.

"No, thanks," I said.

"One drink, Andrew. It's a holiday. And I want a word with you, too. Is that too much to ask?" She had this pompous and offended way of speaking when she was half-drunk, and then after a few drinks she would slobber or weep.

Behind me, Larry and Muzzaroll were making the two girls laugh. The pool was empty, and the sun was going down. They had beer and pizza. I wanted to stay with them and have a laugh. But I had no choice, and Mrs. Mamalujian knew it. She opened the taxi door and I got in.

"Most of the bars are closed today," she said.

"There's probably one open on Charles Street," I said. I didn't want to go too far from here. I would talk to her for a while to humor her and then hustle back to the pool.

The bar was called The Library, which annoyed me, because there were only crappy books on the bookshelves—books for decoration. I ordered orange juice and Mrs. Mamalujian a double gin.

"I'll bet you're proud of yourself," she said.

"Is there anything wrong?"

" 'Is there anything wrong?' he asks." She might have been speaking to the waitress as she put our drinks down. She said, "You used me."

She was wearing a big floppy-brimmed hat and sunglasses with yellow lenses. Her head looked like a wilted daisy and when she tried to look at me her hat wobbled. She was drunker than I had thought.

"You toyed with my feelings," she said.

"What are you talking about?" I said. "I leveled with you."

"What a clown. You kept your clothes on all night in New York. Sleeping in your clothes is batty. You said you were afraid of fires in hotels. But I know better."

"I am afraid of fires," I said, but I saw myself full length on the bed in my army jacket and combat boots. The thought made me cringe.

"You can't treat me that way, Andre. No one does that to me and gets away with it."

"I didn't do anything," I said lamely.

"Right!" she said—too loud, and when people looked around she showed them the lipstick on her teeth.

"I've been very straight with you. I haven't lied. What are you accusing me of?"

I whispered so that she would whisper back.

"I just got through telling you," she said, shouting to defy me. My mother always said *I just got through telling you that,* and

I wondered whether I would forgive Mrs. Mamalujian for saying it.

"I'll never forgive you for it," she said.

That was another one I hated. What was going on?

A squeak, just like the lurch of a rusty hinge, seemed to come out of her hat as she bowed her head. It came again, the beginning of a sob.

"I left my husband for you," she said. "And you don't care."

I said, "Look, I have to get back to work."

"You're not going anywhere," she said, suddenly angry. "You're not running out on me."

"I have work to do," I said, thinking of Larry and Muzzaroll probably frolicking with those girls, lucky dogs, while I sat here with this crazy old woman. And I knew it was my own fault.

"You never call me."

"I called you last week."

"Because you needed money. That's the only time I hear from you. When you need something."

"That's not true," I said. But it was partly true. After refusing all her lavish gifts I had weakened and asked her for three hundred dollars. I had been desperate. "Anyway, I'll pay you back."

"You bet you will," she said, in a way that made me dislike her. People were puzzling. They contained these other people, who were strangers. I was surprised to hear that voice. It was like Lucy saying to me on the beach at Manomet *You'd better find it, sonny.* Whose voices were these?

Mrs. Mamalujian ordered another double gin.

"You think I'm drunk," she said.

I denied it.

"You're a liar," she said. "Look at the pansy with his orange juice."

I started to get up.

She said, "You're not leaving."

"Yes, I am."

"You're not going anywhere until I get my money," she said.

I could only think of the doctor in New York who had said *You've come to the wrong place*, because I had no money. He had sent me away, and now I felt humiliated again. Mrs. Mamalujian had a mocking smile on her face, and her expression was a taunting one that said, *I've got you.*

"You're staying with me," she said.

It was the only hold she had on me—the money. But I had a hundred and seventy-odd dollars. I took it out and counted it onto the table, and pushed it over. "Plus a buck in change."

"No," she said, and put her hand over her mouth.

"Don't move—I'll be right back," I said. "I'm going to get the rest of it." And before she could speak I ran out of the bar and down Charles Street towards the pool.

The four of them were at the far end, near the diving board. Muzzaroll was holding his hairy belly and demonstrating a dive. Larry saw me and trotted over to me.

"See what you're missing? They're nurses. It's action. That pretty one is all over me."

"I need some money," I said.

"Smile, Andy. It's not the end of the world." He had pizza sauce on his cheeks.

"I need a hundred a quarter. I'll pay you back."

"I'm good for fifty."

"What about Vinny?"

"He's good for fifty. I'll steal it out of his wallet."

He got the money quickly and pushed it through the fence, apologizing for not giving me more. But he said that he too had to settle a debt.

"Thanks," I said.

"What are friends for?"

That was perfect, and made me calm; and now I remembered where I could get the rest.

I wondered whether the place would be open. But I need not have worried. It was Labor Day, a holiday on which there were always terrible car crashes. And as the nurse said, they always needed blood. I saw Loretta, and when she smiled I rolled up my sleeve and stuck my arm out.

I had only been gone a half an hour.

Mrs. Mamalujian burst into tears when she saw me enter The Library, and she began to snatch at my hand as I counted the money onto the table. But I kept counting—Larry's fifty, Muzzaroll's fifty, and the twenty-five I had been paid for my pint of B-negative.

"That's three hundred dollars," I said. I felt weak from the loss of blood and the running back and forth.

"You completely misunderstood me."

"Why did you say you wanted the money back?"

"You know I didn't mean that!"

Yet it was too late. She was balling up the bills, and that was how I left her, crumpling the money like wastepaper. I wanted to stop her. I wanted to take it. But it wasn't mine.

I couldn't face the pool after that. I sat on a bench by the river until darkness fell at about eight o'clock; and when I couldn't stand to see another happy hand-holding couple strolling past me I stood up and started writing in my head, the beginning of a poem, *Drunk on the drooping street, watching your sad ass retreat* but couldn't go any further. On the bus home, reading Baudelaire I decided that the word that described my feeling for Lucy was *spleen*.

I had not avoided her. I worried; but because I felt so ignorant I did not want to think too hard about her. The day after Labor Day and then the whole week before I left for Amherst I called Miss Murphy's and left notes at Pinckney Street. I was sure she had gone away. She hadn't asked where the money had come from. She didn't care. And I felt it had been that money that had ruined our love.

She called the day before I left home. My mother answered and handing me the receiver she said sourly, "It's some girl."

That was how little she knew. In her eyes I had spent the summer getting fresh air at the MDC pool, and had saved some money, but not enough.

She was listening, so I could not say what I wanted to Lucy, nor could I ask any leading questions. But Lucy seemed rather detached, too. She had registered at Boston University, she said. She had found a place to live on Newbury Street. She had agreed to stuff envelopes for the presidential campaign. And she finished by saying, "I've been out all day buying books."

I had worried about her! I had sat on the bus and for the thousandth time that summer gone back and forth to Boston on the shuddering thing, looking at the poster that said *For regularity take a lemon in water every day for thirty days*. But she was all right: she had a new room, she was buying books and starting classes. And I was heading for Amherst in my army surplus clothes. I was short of money, doomed to a part-time job, and had to look for a place to live. Another summer had come and gone, and I hadn't written anything except some bitter poems.

"I'm leaving tomorrow," I said.

"What time?"

"I don't know." I didn't want to see her.

"How are you going?"

"Bus."

After I hung up I was annoyed that I hadn't said anything to her, and when my mother said, "What do you mean you can't find your pen? It didn't just walk away!" I screamed at her.

"What's got into you?" she said.

"I wish I weren't going back to school."

"Where do you wish you were going?" she said, and her tone was that smug stumping one, as if I didn't have an answer.

"California," I said. "Or Africa."

"With your attitude you'll never go anywhere."

You don't know me, Ma, I thought. My secrets were safe.

There was only one bus to Amherst, and I was early because I had a duffel bag full of old clothes and a suitcase stuffed full of books. It was a hot Friday in mid-September and I had dragged all this luggage from Medford, bumping people on the bus. I saw other college students with suitcases, and looking happy and hopeful. I wanted to tell them I was a communist and watch their faces harden. But I didn't believe it anymore. Maybe it was better to say nothing and just go away. But was there any point in going if no one missed you?

I got a shock when I saw Lucy standing by herself, staring at me near the ticket window, like a ghost that's turned into a person.

"Do you have a minute?" she said.

She had always seemed pale, and I had found it attractive. But today she seemed plumper, her face a bit fuller and a little blotchy from overdoing it—pink hot-spots on her face and arms. She was wearing a yellow dress. Her sunglasses had white frames—new ones.

I realized that I was afraid of her as I was afraid of Mrs. Mamalujian.

"I'm really glad to see you," I said.

We found an Irish-looking bar in Park Square. What a summer it had been for going into bars! The television was on—

Kennedy making a speech: more promises, more rhetoric. His campaign was all promises about starting over again, doing good in the world, lots of work to do. But he was not going to roll up his sleeves and dig in—we were. He would be sailing off Hyannisport and the rest of us were going to backward countries to show them how to raise chickens.

"He looks so smug," Lucy said.

"I thought you were stuffing envelopes for him."

"No. I'm doing that for the Young Republicans. What's wrong?"

"Becoming a Republican is like becoming a protestant."

"I am a protestant," she said.

"I mean, it's not like believing in something. It's like putting on a hat."

"You think you have all the answers, don't you?" she said, and she sounded so much like Mrs. Mamalujian that I began talking fast to change the subject.

"Kennedy's going to be the next president," I said. "Nothing bad ever happens to him. He lives a charmed life. We're going to be stuck with him for eight years."

"So you're a Republican, too."

"I'm an anarchist," I said.

"God, you say some stupid things," she said, and sighed.

A man next to her said to the bartender, "Did you just fart?" The bartender said no.

"It must have been me," the man said, and frowned and raised his glass.

"Let's sit over there," I said.

Kennedy was saying *We will go forward* like a man reciting blank verse.

In the booth, Lucy said, "I owe you some money."

"That's okay," I said, but I was also thinking how much I would like to have three hundred dollars. It was hard for me to brush it aside: that was a motorcycle. "I don't want it. Hey, are you feeling all right?"

We both knew what that was a euphemism for.

She said, "I'm fine."

She wasn't pregnant, that was for sure, or it would have shown.

"I want to repay you," she said.

She seemed very tense. Was it what I had said about Republicans and protestants? She was a different person from the one who had walked along Pinckney Street with me last July—even different from the person who had shown me where the whale had washed up at Manomet. She was like someone I had known a long time ago that I was still forgetting.

"I really do want to give it back," she said. "Don't you want it?"

It was dark in the bar but she didn't take her sunglasses off.

I tried not to be tempted by the thought of her giving me the money back. But I was.

I said, "I don't care," and hated myself for not having the guts to say no.

Lucy said, "You're just going to get on the bus and ride away, as if nothing's happened. Just turn your back on everything and everyone. Just vanish."

I said nothing; I glared at her, because that was exactly what I wanted to do, and that she had nailed me down like that left me nothing more to say.

"You probably have a girlfriend in Amherst."

"No," I said. "I don't even have a place to live."

"Know what I think?" she said—and her voice was nastier than I had ever known it, not her voice at all—"I think you're going to be all right. Better than all right. I can see it. You're going to be a success. I don't know what it will be, but it's going to happen."

It was the opposite of what I thought, and hearing her say that was like mockery.

She said, "And I know you want the money back."

I shook my head, but it was too vague a way of refusing, and she could tell that I was weakening.

She took her glasses off and wiped them with a napkin. She was either smiling or else on the verge of tears—it was that same look, an expression of hers that I now knew well. She put the glasses back on and faced me.

"Someone gave me a phone number," she said. "I called, and a man answered. He sounded grumpy, the way old people do. But he said he'd do it. I was to meet him in a certain bar in Brockton. I borrowed my aunt's car and drove there. He was fifty or more and looked like a tramp. He wore old clothes. He hadn't shaved. As soon as I saw him I wanted to go home and forget it. But I knew I couldn't—it would be worse at home. He asked to see the money. But he wouldn't leave the bar. He kept saying, 'Just one more,' and trying to get me to drink. I actually had one I was so nervous. And then, when I had just about given up hope, he said, 'Let's go.' We went in his car. I think he had been waiting for it to get dark. It was all back roads. I lost track of where we were and I thought *What if he kills me?* He slowed down in the darkness and turned into a dirt road—so small I hadn't seen it. I really felt lost but I was too frightened to cry. He stopped the car in front of a derelict house. I could see the broken windows in the headlights. He lit a candle inside. It was one of those places where kids go to start fires and smoke and scribble on the walls. There was a mattress on the floor and we had to be careful where we stepped because of the broken glass. He took my money and then said—"

There were tears running from beneath her sunglasses.

"Lucy, please," I said.

When she saw that I wanted her to stop she set her face at me and continued.

" 'Take your skirt off,' he said. And then he began swearing at me and pushed his pants down and just forced himself into me. I hated him too much to cry. He smelled, and I knew he was drunk. *Now he's going to kill me*, I thought. But he didn't. He fussed around and took some metal tools out of a paper bag. He had had that bag in the bar. I had wondered what was in it. His tools. Then he did it, flicking one of them into me. He told me that it would take about six or eight hours to work. He drove me back to my car."

"That's horrible," I said. I thought she had finished. I didn't know what to do, but I wanted to go. It was far worse than I had imagined. I turned away. On the television above the bar a man was kneeling next to a small child who was hugging a cloth doll, and he was saying *Has anyone told you that you're a very brave little girl?*

In her dull determined voice, Lucy said, "As I was driving home I got a pain, like a knife in my side. I almost crashed the car, but I kept driving until the pain was unbearable. I pulled into a Jenney station and the man pumping gas pointed out back. I went into the ladies' room and had it in the toilet. I thought I was going to bleed to death. I couldn't move for about an hour. The man wanted to call the police, but I wouldn't let him. When I got home my mother said, 'You look pale—are you all right?' And I said, 'I'm fine. I—' "

It was only then that she started to sob, and she did so in a subdued and suffering way that made me want to die for having caused it. Then she saw me watching her, and she sneered.

"That's your three hundred dollars."

I wanted the bus to crash and for me to be burned alive—or else to keep going, past Amherst and Pittsfield and out of the state. Was it enough to leave home?

I was still reading Baudelaire, the opposite pages this time, in French. *Anywhere out of this world,* and a poem about his lover—naked except for her jewels, wearing makeup. Gleaming buttocks. Moorish slave. Like a captive tiger. In front of a fire with its flamboyant sigh. She was black, and she yearned for him.

Keep going, I thought. Anywhere out of this world. I didn't want anyone to know me. I didn't deserve to be missed. But home was too big and too hard to get away from. Every state would tell me I was a failure. How could I leave? Home was the whole country.

THREE

AFRICAN GIRLS

1.

The barefoot student was being led towards my office from the clump of blue gums, where he had been hiding. But why was he smiling like that? When he came closer I could see his wild eyes did not match his crooked mouth. It was a ganja-smoker's smile—Willy Msemba, at the hemp again. Rain was beaded on his black face.

Like an executioner, Deputy Mambo jerked the boy along. Mambo's mud-smeared shoes flapped beside Msemba's bare feet.

"Headmaster." Mambo always sounded sarcastic when he said that word. He knocked and pushed open my office door in one motion.

I told them to come in, but they were already in—water and footprints and clods of mud. Whole raindrops were caught and trembled unbroken in the springs of their hair. Not many of the students had hair, not even the girls. It was a head-shaving country, because of the lice.

Willy smiled at his toes. His feet had shed what looked like smashed cake. He was shivering in his wet shirt, and still smiling.

"I found this boy smoking."

Smoking always meant smoking ganja.

The wind shook the blue gums—shreds of stringy bark and pale fluttery leaves. It was gray cold April in Nyasaland, one of the months of blowing fog. The fog drizzled down and was so dense the country seemed tiny. It reddened the earth and made the roofs rattle.

Just then, Miss Natwick dived out of her room across the

schoolyard. She was one of those small, stiff-legged women who when they hurry look as if they are going to tip over. She was a part-timer, and one of her subjects was needlework, but, even so, she could not understand why she had not been put in charge of the school after Mr. Likoni left. Another reason was that she was a white Rhodesian.

No sooner had she entered my office than Mr. Nyirongo passed by the window on the veranda. Instead of entering, or continuing on his way, he paused and began gaping at us, his tongue swelling between his lips. He was clearly interested in the sight: Willy Msemba dripping on my office floor, and on either side of him Deputy Mambo and Miss Natwick.

I was pacing behind my desk. I had only been headmaster a short time and I was still self-conscious. I hated being observed handing out punishment. I knew I was an inept disciplinarian but I hoped that the students would see me as a fair and just headmaster and not take advantage of me. It was simple logic: if they liked me they'd behave. That was the American way. My predecessor, Mr. Likoni, used the British method. He bent wrongdoers over a chair and flogged them.

"This boy is doing it every lunch break," Deputy Mambo said. "Just sitting in the trees and smoking his ganja. I think some very severe punishment is called for."

In Deputy Mambo's lapel was a gleaming button with a big black face on it—Doctor Hastings Kamuzu Banda. This scowling Banda would be head of the government after independence in July, when Nyasaland became Malawi. It was not a happy face, not even a sane one, and I sometimes felt that Africans in the country wore the button to frighten non–party members or foreigners like me.

Perhaps Mambo saw me glance at the button. He said, "Doctor Banda wants firm discipline in Malawi."

"This is still Nyasaland," I said.

But we both knew that it was nothing. Nearly all the white settlers had left, and only the British governor general still hung on—he had been delegated to hand the place over to Banda.

"I'd like to hear Willy's side of the story," I said, because I felt that Mambo was pressuring me.

"They all smoke," Miss Natwick said. "Heavens, where do they get the money from? They're supposed to be so poor!"

To her, smoking meant just that. She did not know what ganja was. It would have thrown her if she had.

"I think he steals it," Deputy Mambo said. "I hope the head-master does not approve of stealing."

All this time Willy Msemba was smiling his crooked smile.

"What have you got to say for yourself?"

He looked at me and, though he knew me, in his drugged condition it was as though he was seeing me after a very long time. He seemed surprised: What was his old friend doing here! His eyes were loose and sort of drowned-looking.

"Allo, Mister Andy!" he said in a gurgly voice.

Miss Natwick went *pah* hearing him use my first name—and not even Andre but Andy.

"Mr. Parent," she said, in a correcting way, talking to him. "At Salisbury Academy we always said, 'Headmaster, Sir!' "

"I see him Farraday night," Msemba said to Miss Natwick, and gave her the same strange grin.

"What's this about smoking under the trees?"

But he ignored me. He was deaf and still smiling, his eyes rolling and his head wobbling. Now he turned to Miss Natwick.

"He go jig-jig."

"Listen to me," I said.

"Mister Andy!"

"I regard this as a serious infraction of the rules."

"Oh, yes, this guy like to dance too much!" the student said to the room at large.

"I won't tolerate smoking at this school."

"What is this imbecile talking about?"

"Ask him how he came by the money," Deputy Mambo said.

Msemba said, "He twist and shout!" He stamped mud off his feet. He cried, "Beetriss!"

"I don't understand a bloody word of this."

He was saying *Beatles* but I decided not to translate.

Mr. Nyirongo frowned through the window and turned his swollen tongue on me and stared with sad eyes, Miss Natwick was squinting. Deputy Mambo had loosened his grip on Msemba.

For the fact was, I was now at the center of attention, not Msemba. I was twenty-three. I had been headmaster only two months, since Likoni left, and these people had wanted my job—

still wanted it. They claimed I was not doing well, was not mature, dressed sloppily—was an American. And yet they could not deny that the school ran as smoothly as ever, and was certainly cleaner than it had ever been under Likoni. And I had plans.

"Everybody like this guy," Msemba said. "Especially the girls!"

Rubber mouth, I thought. His lips were the texture and color of an inner tube, and they were still flapping.

"For punishment," I said, trying to shut him up, "make ten bricks."

"And especially—"

"Twenty bricks! Now get back to your classroom. And what about you teachers?"

No one was listening to me. Msemba took several odd sliding dance steps, and then he began to stamp, as if he were killing roaches.

"Like this one," he was saying.

"Get him out of here," I said to Deputy Mambo.

"He is being insolent," Miss Natwick said. "The bloody cheek!"

Msemba nodded, seeming to agree. He said, "Dancing with African girls."

"Take him away," I said.

"African girls!" Msemba said.

He had the African inability to pronounce the word *Africa*. It came out sounding like "Uffaleekan."

Deputy Mambo said, "What is this boy saying?"

"Even my sister!"

"That's a euphemism," I said.

"Every day!"

"That's a lie," I said. "Now off you go."

Deputy Mambo's face had gone blacker, but it was creased with little whitish lines—his eyes tiny, his mouth clamped shut, his nostrils huge and horselike in fury. He wrenched Msemba's arm and hustled him out of my office, taking his anger with me out on the boy.

Mr. Nyirongo chewed his tongue a moment longer and then moved away, his chin at the level of the high windowsill.

"Monday mornings at the Academy after prayers," Miss Natwick said, "one would read off their names. The offenders would line up in front of the entire assembly. The headmaster took out his birch, and one by one he bent them over a chair and thrashed them. 'Thank you!' 'Next!' They passed out sometimes. Some were sick where they stood." Her teeth were dull yellow bones. "Salisbury."

"Likoni tried that. It didn't work."

"Because he didn't hit them hard enough."

"This isn't Rhodesia, Miss Natwick."

"That's pretty bloody obvious." And she left.

Threshed, possed out, bleddy: it was an amazing accent.

After school that day, and long after the students had gone home—their smell of soap and dirt and a stillness that was like a sound lingered in the empty classrooms—I saw Willy Msemba making bricks. He was no longer smiling. The effects of the weed had worn off and left him groggy and dazed.

"Easy punishment," Deputy Mambo said. "More like playing."

Where had he come from? But he often popped up. He had the envious person's habit of creeping out of nowhere, and he was critical in an envious way too.

I decided not to hear him.

We watched together. Msemba had trampled a hole full of wet clay that he had dug and soaked. He then softened it with his feet, and mixed it with straw, and crammed it into brick-sized boxes, and tipped it out on the ground to dry. He was nearly done. His legs were muddy to his knees, and there was clay from his fingertips to his elbows. That was the point, really—that and our necessity for the bricks: a new latrine.

"He should have had a hundred bricks," Deputy Mambo said. "He should have been beaten with a stick."

But he was staring at me like a preacher, and I knew what he was thinking: African girls.

So now I was in the doghouse, not Msemba. I had been made headmaster after Mr. Likoni was appointed minister of education in the new government that was coming in three months. The promotion was not a comment on Likoni's ability. He was a drunkard who had once taken a course at Aberystwyth in Wales. He had hung his certificate on the wall. There were no more than a dozen university graduates in the country. It was very easy to rise. I was a good example of that.

I had been in Nyasaland seven months as a Peace Corps Volunteer. I was too far in the bush, on too bad a road, to get many visitors. There were angry stray dogs near the mud houses. Quail ducked into the grass. Owls sat on the road all night. We had greeny-black land crabs that looked like small monsters. We had hyenas—they tipped over my barrels. I used to see the hyenas loping off in their doggy seesawing way when I returned to the house after midnight. We had snakes. The hill behind the school was a huge rock that I had once thought of climbing; but now the idea tired me. We had thirty different kinds of birds but no one knew their names. *Mbalame,* people called them, and it was the same word for plane. My house was high enough so that I could see Mount Mlanje, the whole plateau, in the distance—blue and flat-topped, with dark green tea planted beneath it. There were no other Americans at the school. That suited me, because I regarded myself as something of a loner, and rather a romantic figure, in my squashed hat and wrinkled suit and stained suede shoes.

It was screechy and silent, old-fashioned Africa, smelling of woodsmoke and wet earth. And strangest of all to me these spring months: it was cold.

I was in charge. But a headmaster at twenty-three was unusual, even in this unusual country. Some of my boy students were twenty, and many looked older than me. The girls were younger, but some of them had given birth and had small children. That was their secret. They pretended to be schoolgirls and I pretended not to know about their kids. There were 156 students. They were all skinny and popeyed and barefoot.

Willy Msemba was one of the rare ones—virtually the only delinquent, but a cheerful one. And he was intelligent. He read Mickey Spillane. He wrote me an essay which began, "My name is Msemba. I'm a cop. I was in Chikwawa. I saw a broad—pointed breasts, fat face, ironed hair, a real doll. But she was tough. I had to kick her before she would volunteer the information I needed—"

The other students were well-behaved and in general the discipline was so good I never really believed that we would get our *chimbuzi*. That was the point of the brickmaking. We needed a new latrine. The fence around the ditch was broken, and the ditch itself was nearly full; and it stank. It made you think that these people were grubby and hopeless. I knew that was not true and I wanted to prove it with a new *chimbuzi*. I envisioned a big solid symmetrical thing with this year scratched on it, *1964*, and when people asked what I had done for these Africans in their year of independence I could say that I had gotten them a brick shithouse.

The earth around us was clayey enough for good bricks but we didn't have enough discipline problems to guarantee a steady supply. I gave them five bricks for lateness, ten for not doing homework, fifteen for fighting, fifteen for littering (chewing and spitting sugarcane on school premises), and so forth. It was supposed to be twenty-five bricks for smoking hemp, but Willy Msemba had been on the verge of revelations, and so far my private life had remained secret. He was buzzing, and I had to get him out of there. I had not wanted to antagonize the boy. He knew too much.

I thought—as punishment—brickmaking was a good idea. It was dirty and useful. Yet I was criticized for being too soft. I was friendly towards the students. Deputy Mambo and Mr. Nyirongo spread the word that I was afraid of the students. Miss Natwick said that the trouble with Americans was that they were so bloody diffident. That was the most painful kind of criticism, because I was not quite sure what she meant and I hated looking up one of Miss Natwick's words in the dictionary (*Lacking in confidence; timid*).

I kept on. It was better to be whispered about for being a weak headmaster than for that other thing, that I had tried to keep secret. And I knew that the students liked me. I spoke the language, Chinyanja, and I had learned all the proverbs in *Nzeru Za Kale* ("Wisdom of the Old Folks")—"He who cries for rain also cries for mud"—that sort of thing. I quoted them in morning assembly. "If your face is ugly, learn to sing." I was the first American any of them had ever seen. For some I was their first white man. Being an American—and I was friendly—gave me power over the students, and the school ran well.

It was a new school—a compound of four squat cement buildings with tin roofs that clattered so loudly when it rained that we had to stop teaching until the rain eased. There were verandas on the classroom blocks and in the center a trampled space where we held morning assembly. Outside my office door was a foot of railway track that I banged with an iron rod at five minutes to eight.

Morning assembly was a prayer, a song, and a pep-talk. There was as yet no national anthem. We sang *Mbuye Dalitsani Africa*, "God Watch Over Africa," a sort of Pan-African hymn with the lugubrious plodding melody of a funeral dirge. Likoni used to read from the Bible—usually the Psalms. I avoided the Psalms but I liked Jonah, Ecclesiastes and Ezekiel—especially I liked declaiming about the valley of bones. I also read from Aesop's Fables, and well-known speeches from Shakespeare, and memorable poems. I made appropriate comments. I read announcements and I called the roll. On these cold mornings the wind fluttered the blue gums and made the tin roofs moan and snatched at the children's clothes as they stood shivering. When they heard their names they answered "Heah" or "Sah."

A new road connected the school to the lower road which, once used for logging—it led through a forest—ended at the township of Kanjedza. I had built the school road. Building it had made my reputation. In old Likoni's time it had been a narrow path through chest-high thorn bushes and scrub. I wanted the path widened. "Big cars will pay calls on us," Deputy Mambo said. But it wasn't that—I didn't want cars. I merely imagined a long sweeping road that would dignify the school and the hill.

For the road I asked the Public Works Department to send us some workmen.

"I can send some men, but you will have to pay them," the works manager told me over the phone. His tiny distorted voice came out of a heavy old-fashioned receiver.

"Why can't you pay them?"

"PWD is in suspension," he said. "The British have left."

"Who's in charge?"

"That is the question."

Independence was not until July and at the moment there was no one in the department to okay an order. Men still showed up every morning, but there was nothing for them to do; and although they were on the payroll they received no money.

I had a budget. I had allotted sixty pounds for the road, which seemed plenty—over a hundred dollars.

"Send me six men."

The men arrived on bicycles. They stared at the students until assembly ended, and then they hacked at some bushes and bullied a big tree. Afterwards they slept under it. They said they wanted more money and when I refused to give it to them they pushed their bicycles down the narrow path and pedaled away.

Fifty-four pounds remained. Mr. Nyirongo said that the headman of a nearby village would supply the men to clear the road, but that he wanted a bribe.

"It's just bushes," I said. "If the students weren't so sleepy they could trample a new road."

Everyone said that the students had worms, which was why they were so languid.

But I had an idea. I went to the bank in Zimba and changed the remaining fifty-four pounds into "tickeys"—small gray threepence coins. I returned to the school with canvas money bags hanging on my bike. I had almost four and a half thousand tickeys. At the end of the next day's assembly I shocked the students by declaring a holiday.

But before I dismissed them I said, "Watch me."

I went to the path with my bags of coins and walked the length of it, flinging tickeys left and right, the width of the road I wanted.

Like locusts, the students descended hungrily, tearing at the bushes, and by the middle of the afternoon the land was cleared. A little tidying made it into the road I wanted. That was my first significant accomplishment as a young headmaster.

I was popular also for my special homework policy. Because the students lived in mud huts with no electric lights, I made a rule that all homework was to be done at school, before the kids set off for home. And they had homework on weekends, but none on Friday afternoons. This meant that we teachers had no weekend papers to mark.

The school was called Chamba Secondary, after the hill just behind it. The word signified Indian hemp and it was also a frenzied and futile dance. Everyone who was told what it meant said, "Very appropriate!" But I regarded that as unkind. Give them a chance, I said; and I also thought: Give me a chance.

2.

But the main reason I made sure we had no papers to mark on weekends was that I was busy those days with my own affairs. I wrote the school rules and I fitted them to my life. That odd boy Willy Msemba had been right when he twisted his face at me and said, "African girls!"

It was my secret life—my real life. The Peace Corps knew nothing about it. I had always lived two lives, but in Africa this second one became fuller and freer. I sometimes thought that it was the best reason for having gone there, especially then, just before independence, when no one was in charge.

It had started in the most innocent way, my first week in Nyasaland. I was in Zimba, the one-street town. I had pedaled through the rain to mail some letters. (It thrilled me to write letters from Africa. I was the hero of those letters. But it was so hard to be truthful and not take liberties.) On Saturdays the post office closed at noon, and so afterwards I killed time in the small market—squatting women selling misshapen and dusty vegetables. I ate lunch at the Zimba Coffee Shop. The place was owned by two Greek brothers and was run by a yellow-haired Greek woman. She sold me a cheese sandwich, a curry puff they called a *samosa*, and a cup of strong coffee. She watched me eat, and she gave me the familiar attention of the white people there, as if she were a distant relation.

That made me uncomfortable. I walked into the rain. There was not much else in the town—five Indian shops, all selling identical merchandise, canned goods and cloth; a car-repair shop and gas station, a branch of Grindlay's Bank, a fish and chip shop, a bakery, and The Nyasaland Trading Company. None were run by Africans. Two old women were the sales clerks in The Nyasaland Trading Company. This was a general store in a low wooden building. It stocked colonial merchandise—jars of jam, stationery, clothes, last month's London newspapers, books, ink, shoes, oil lamps, rubber boots. When I walked in, one of the women was wiping a feather duster (and they sold those too) against a contraption they called a radiogram—a large varnished cabinet with a yellow plastic window.

"It's a wireless, and it also plays gramophone records," the woman had told me on my first visit, and I had gone away mumbling the words.

Most of the white settlers had left the country for good. The shelves were becoming very dusty. Africans did not buy Birds Custard, Bovril, Swan Vestas, Dundee Thick-Cut Marmalade, Fenwick's Gumboots, Hacks Honey Lemons, Gentleman's Relish, Nairn's Capital Oatcakes, tins of Bath Olivers or Battley's Pickled Walnuts.

I browsed in the Nyasaland Trading Company until the rain stopped, bought a Penguin paperback—a novel set in the tropics by a writer I admired, S. Prasad—and then I started back to Chamba on my bike, bracing myself for the three-mile journey, which was mostly uphill.

Passing another shop, I saw a mass of small bottles and cartons in the window, and it was my first indication of the Nyasalanders' liking for patent medicine—DeWitt's Worm Syrup, Philipps' Gripe Water, Goodmorning Lung Tonic, Iron Tonic, Liver Elixir, Red Syrup ("For Strength"), Kidney and Bladder Pills by Baxter, Fam-Lax, Day-Glo, X-Pell, Reg-U-Letts, and Letrax ("Expells Roundworms, Hookworms, Whip-Worms and Threadworms"). There were skin lighteners—TV Beautybox Day and Night Skin Lightening Pack, Dear Heart Skin Brightener and Glo-Tone. And hair straighteners—Hairstrate, and Glyco Superstrate. This shop had customers inside, but reading these labels I thought: Where am I?

Farther up the road, at the edge of town, there were African men lingering outside a shopfront. There was music at the door, a harmonious howling. Later I realized that this was my first taste of the Beatles: in a back street, in Zimba, a small town in Nyasaland, in Central Africa. It was not a shop. I went nearer. It was noisy, there were African girls at the windows, and young men in sunglasses watched me from the veranda. A sign above them was clumsily lettered BEAUTIFUL BAMBOO BAR.

Did someone wave to me? I thought I saw an African girl beckon, but she had vanished when I looked again. Anyway, I went in. It seemed dark inside. The few lights made the interior indistinct and had the effect of making the place seem darker and more shadowy. It was one room and it smelled dankly of piss and dirt, like a crawlspace. It was damp, smoke blew through one window, the mirror was streaked with green and red paint, and on the walls were shelves of beer—small plump bottles of Lion and Castle Lager.

The bartender wore a T-shirt and a tweed vest and ragged shorts and plastic sandals. He approached me nervously.

I said, *"Moni. Muli bwanji, achimwene?"*

Hello brother: it was the friendliest greeting.

He was too astonished to reply at once. Then he said, "You are speaking."

"Yes, brother."

"Oh, thank you, father," he said.

"What is your name, brother?"

"My name is Wilson."

They all had names like that—Wilson, Millson, Edison, Redison; and Henderson and Johnston.

"Thank you, Wilson."

"And what is your name, father?"

"Please stop calling me father."

"What is your name, sir?"

"Please, brother."

"Yes, *achimwene*"—and he almost choked on the word—"what is your name?"

"My name is Andy."

"Oh, thank you, Mr. Undie," he said.

He told me that I was the first *mzungu* ever to go into the Beautiful Bamboo Bar. That cheered me up. Wasn't that the point of my being in Africa?

Nearby, there were five or six girls sitting at wooden tables. The first thing I noticed about them was that they had no hair—or very little, no more than fuzz. But their shaven heads seemed to emphasize the shapeliness of their bodies. They wore dresses, but even among the shadows in the bar I could tell they were naked underneath. They were barefoot, but that seemed strangely appropriate to their having no hair on their heads.

I sat at a table with two of them and drank a beer, and I talked to them in their own language. They asked me where I had learned it.

"Would you believe Syracuse University?" And I added, "Upstate New York. United States."

They laughed, because everywhere outside Nyasaland sounded magical. And yet I knew that Nyasaland was the only place that I wanted to be.

"American," one girl said, trying the word out.

It seemed that they were working casually in the Bamboo. They had come from distant villages. They believed Zimba was the big city; they had attached themselves to this bar. They lived out back. The jukebox was playing *Shimmy Shimmy Koko Bop,* and an African girl was doing a flat-footed African dance.

Her name was Rosie. She said her favorite singer was Chubby Checker. She also liked Elvis, Del Shannon and The Orlons.

"Who are the Orlons?"

"Wah-Watusi," Rosie said.

"Oh, them."

"And Spokes Mashiani," she said. "South African."

That was the kind of conversation—names of singers, names of songs, and how much can you drink, and have you ever seen a lion? And *Shimmy shimmy koko bop.*

Finally, Rosie said, "You're the teacher up at Chamba?"

I said yes, and turned to the door. It had gone dark outside.

"The big house with the flowers in front," she said.

Shimmy shimmy bop.

"It used to belong to Mr. Campbell. He went back to England."

"They all went back to England," Rosie said.

The other girl said wistfully, "They just left us." She sounded like an abandoned child.

I said, "But I'm not leaving."

"That's good," Rosie said.

I said, "Come and visit me someday."

"Yes," she said, and put her hand over her face and giggled behind it.

I took a breath and said, "What about now, sister?"

She made a sound, her tongue against her teeth, that was stronger than yes.

We left, walking side by side. I pushed my bike because I could not carry her on my crossbar uphill. She said that no one minded her leaving: the Bamboo was not very busy.

"No money for European beer—just for African beer." She meant the porridgey stuff the market women sold in old oil cans.

In the pitch-black forest I took her hand. It was hard and heavy, tough fingers and a palm the texture of an old boot. But I hung on to it.

At home I sat her down and poured her a glass of gin. She sipped it, making faces. She was barefoot, and I could see that her feet were rough and cracked like her hands. Her green dress was both fancy and ragged, and the strip of lace at her collar was torn.

I made a fire in the fireplace, burning eucalyptus logs, and we sat in front of it on the sofa Mr. Campbell had left. But Rosie was restless. She sniffed around the room.

"Books," she said.

She looked at the pictures—of Scotland, from calendars. Of cats, of dogs. I asked if she liked them. She said no. She kept prowling.

"Table." She smoothed it with her hand. "Flowers. Looking glass. Curtains. Carpet. Knife and fork. Tomato sauce. Mustard."

Next to the cluster of sticky bottles on the table—they too were Campbell's—we had dinner, served by Captain. Captain was my cook: he also had been left by Campbell. He was too nervous to disguise his leering, and he spoke to Rosie in a language I did not know, perhaps Yao or Tonga. I caught the word "American."

She ate hungrily and with a lot of noise, wetting her fingers on the food and then wiping her lips with the back of her hand. I learned then that the frantic manners of the poor are their way of not wasting a crumb. Eating made her perspire, too, and sitting across from her at the table I was aroused and wanted to make love to her.

After the kitchen was silent—Captain gone—I took her leathery hand and, saying nothing, led her into the bedroom. She stepped out of her dress and folded it neatly on a chair. Then she sat on the bed and tipped onto her back and lifted her legs. I knelt before her and started, and a moment later she shrieked,

"Mwamuna wanga!" ("My man!"). As soon as I had finished she wanted me again. We made love three times in the same sort of sandwichlike way. It had been over a month of abstinence for me. She fell asleep and snored all night. In the morning I took her back to town—downhill, on the crossbar of my bike.

"Do you want money?"

She just laughed.

"I want a beer," she said.

It was nine o'clock in the morning, but the Beautiful Bamboo was open. I bought a Castle Lager for Rosie from the sleepy-eyed bartender and a glass of sugary tea for myself. We sat in the empty bar, saying nothing, listening to the bell at the Catholic mission being rung. It sounded stern, like a school bell.

That was Sunday. I spent the rest of the day writing letters, and Rosie appeared in some of these letters. Letters were all I had. I lived for them—writing them, receiving them. Nyasaland was a country with no writing. And I was always touched by the wornout way the envelopes looked—so battered and resolute, having reached me from so far.

I kept writing until the sun set behind Chamba Hill. I was happy. I often found memory sexier than actual experience, and anticipating a woman was always an erotic pleasure. All day I had been preparing myself for my return to the Beautiful Bamboo. I went after dinner, my bicycle lamp shaking in the dark on the bad road.

"Rosie is not here," another girl said, and she stayed to talk. Her name was Grace.

Between us we drank eleven bottles of beer and when my eyes refused to focus I knew I had had enough. I stood up clumsily and headed for the door. On the veranda I paused and felt a hand close over my fingers. I thought it was Rosie, because it was cracked and large and had weight but no grip, like a kind of dog's paw. It was Grace.

"I come with you."

I couldn't speak. I was moving forward. I tripped on the edge of the open sewer and staggered.

"Sorry!" she cried.

I turned back and tried to set my eyes on her. She was a blur. And yet I did not feel drunk. I was small and sober inside a big drunken body.

"I love you, mister," she said.

She insisted on pushing my bike. I was grateful to her for that. I walked behind her, catching my toes on the ruts, and feeling unsteady in the darkness. At Chamba we did not talk. We went to bed like an old married couple and were immediately asleep. But in a dark morning hour I woke up and felt her damp skin against mine, and I snuggled against her. She helped me and then almost killed my desire as she chafed me with her rough hands. She muttered and sighed in pleasure, a kind of laughter, and then she went snufflingly to sleep.

Her smell kept me awake for a while. She had the same odor as my students—soap, dirt, skin, sweat. It was a human smell—a rank sort of dead-and-alive odor. It was dusty and undefinable, like mushrooms.

She was gone in the morning. She had vanished, leaving a dent and a smell on the sheet that was about the size of her body.

Captain said, "She told me 'sorry'—she is seeing her sister today," and he put a plate of eggs in front of me.

He was a small, bucktoothed man who had been a cook in the King's African Rifles. He could make scones, he could make mint sauce and gravy, he baked bread. He spoke little English but he knew words like "roast" and "joint" and "pudding." He spoke army Swahili, though we stuck to Chinyanja. He was a Yao from Fort Johnson, and a muslim. Now that he had seen me with African girls he seemed to regard me in a different light. He became friendlier, slightly more talkative and familiar, but at the same time protective.

"Next time I can take the girl back to town on your bicycle—if you say yes."

He used the slang word for bicycle: *njinga*, which was the sound of a bicycle bell.

"Yes," I said. "Next time."

He knew something that I had only just realized, that there would be many more times. I was happy, but that Monday morning, walking down the road I had built, towards the school, I itched. Before morning assembly I found dark flecks clinging to my pubic hair. I pinched one out and took it to the science block to examine it under a microscope. I saw that a crab louse is aptly named.

There were other customers in Mulji's Cash Chemist in Maravi that afternoon, so I whispered *lice*.

"Crab lice or body lice?" Mulji said out loud, and everyone heard: *Grab lice or bhodee lice?*

The powder he sold me killed them all. I combed out the dead nits, spent a busy week at the school, and on Friday I was back at the Beautiful Bamboo.

That had been my first week in the country, and that was how it was every subsequent week. Friday, Saturday, and Sunday nights I picked up African girls at the Bamboo and took them back to Chamba. I returned them to town in the morning, or else Captain did, carrying them on the crossbar of my bike. There were about twenty different girls at the Bamboo. They were not jealous. They never asked for money. I think they simply wanted the experience of sleeping with an American. And I wanted them.

We danced in a jumping, shaking way, to the Beatles and Elvis and Major Lance and Little Millie and "The Wah-Watusi." A song I hated was "How Do You Do It" sung by Jerry and the Pacemakers, but they played it all the time. I developed a taste for the woozy penny-whistle music they said was South African.

Being dancing partners was part of their function at the Bamboo. And yet they were neither customers nor workers. They hinted that they were runaways. They hung around. There was always food for them, and always beer. I never saw money change hands.

On Fridays I was impatient. I had a few beers and went home early, with an African girl. They were interested in my house, but not particularly impressed. I liked the place. I lived alone. I had three bedrooms and a fireplace and all of Campbell's old *Spectators.* I liked sitting on the veranda and looking at Mlanje Plateau—the great slab of rock rising out of the dark-green tea estates. I had a flower garden, and Campbell's herbaceous borders, and my own pigeon loft. Some days, Captain put a cloth over his head and slaughtered a pair of pigeons, cutting their throats according to muslim custom, and made them into pigeon curry.

Captain also did the shopping, leaving me free on Saturdays. That was the day I stayed late at the Bamboo. I did not leave until well after midnight. I never left alone. Often I reached home as dawn was breaking. I would be pushing my bike uphill.

That was lovely. The sky would lift and lighten, and night seemed to dissolve and grow rosier as I reached the top of the road and left the forest. The birds would be screeching and the cocks crowing. There was always mist in the air and the grass was soaked.

I walked to the center of my sloping lawn as the sun appeared at the edge of the far-off plateau. The African girl was behind me, parking the bike under the pigeon loft, and the jingling woke and fluttered the birds.

And then on the lawn I unzipped and pissed into the sunrise, a whole night's beer, rocking back on my heels and feeling wonderful the morning chill, the pink dawn, the dampness, and the tootling birds.

The African girl walked in front of me and laughed at what I was doing. She left footprints in the dewy grass—dark feet showing in silver. She stood there—the bursting sunrise behind her thin skirt dazzling between her legs.

3.

That was how it was for five months; and then Likoni left and I took his place, and for the next two months it was even better. As headmaster, I made the rules. And that was the situation— frenetic, happy, I lost count of the nights and girls—when Willy Msemba was brought into my office and given bricks to make.

It had all been a secret activity. It was what Africans them- selves did on weekends. The Peace Corps office didn't know anything, but so what? To me it seemed almost virtuous— making love to African girls. What was the point in being in Africa if I didn't do that? Promiscuous was not the word for it. My activity was different, it was explosive. During the week it was nothing, and then it was a frenzy—three girls a weekend. It overstimulated me, and those days I could not sleep; but by Monday I was calm again.

I was young, I felt it was temporary, I had just had my twenty-third birthday. That day I copied Milton's poem about turning twenty-three into my notebook. It contained a line that gave me a pang: *Time, the subtle thief of youth* . . . I was changing fast. I mistook maturing for aging and was desperate to use all the time I had. I could not have done more. It made me extremely tired.

Once I went to sleep while teaching a class. It was night school. I taught it Tuesday and Thursday evenings. It surprised me: I had never heard of anyone going to sleep while talking. I had been telling my English class the story of *Animal Farm*. They were too dim to read it themselves.

"The pigs began to quarrel," I said.

The Tilly lamp fizzed on my desk.

"They accused each other of trying to waw . . . aw . . ."

And then I went to sleep. My hand still supported my head and the warm buzz of the lamp kept me under.

When I woke up, no one spoke; no one giggled. They were mostly older people, very polite, and they liked me. Falling asleep while teaching made me seem eccentric and harmless. And of course half of them slept through the lesson, too. I became popular. Tell us about cowboys, they said. Tell us about guns. Do you have a horse? Have you flown in a plane? Did you ever meet Elvis? Are you rich? Are you a Christian? What language do Negroes talk? Can Superman really fly? Not one of them believed the world was round, but all believed in witches. They felt they had been swindled by the British. I had arrived in the country at the perfect time: they were ready to be Americans. I could only encourage them.

The African girls at the Beautiful Bamboo had the same attitude as my students. They were not merely susceptible to Americans, they were infatuated. Having overcome their fear of whites, they realized that we found them desirable, and they liked themselves better. Some of them had stopped wearing torn dresses, and now wore printed T-shirts and blue jeans. One shaven-headed barefoot girl wore a floppy sweatshirt printed with the head of Beethoven.

Some were very young—fourteen or fifteen; and none was older than twenty. They were sturdy, hard-fleshed and slim—in

Nyasaland no African was fat. At least I had not seen one. Their hands were so calloused they could hold hot pots without noticing; they walked miles barefoot; and they could pop bottle caps off with their teeth.

They had one thing in common: they were unmarriageable. They had disgraced themselves in various ways, and had been kicked out of their villages. A few were rebels and had run away, but most had had children or abortions or been involved in intrigues. A few had committed petty crimes. At least one was a witch—or so the others said. None could expect to marry an African man. They had no status, they had no dowry.

It took months for me to discover these things, but when I did I understood why they were amazed that we chased them and took them home and made love to them. We desired them! They had been rejected by their families and their villages, and we romanced them.

I was single-minded, but it was not much trouble. I had everything I wanted: unlimited and guiltless sex. And because this was Africa and they were black it was not only a pleasure, it was also an act of political commitment. I pondered the fact that I was in Nyasaland, in Central Africa; and then I smiled, knowing there was nowhere else I wished to be. Sometimes I thought: I'll never leave.

All that sex could have driven me mad, but I think it made me judicious. It concentrated my mind during the week and it kept me from pawing the students. I felt it was my duty to discourage such practices, though Deputy Mambo and Mr. Nyirongo did it all the time—fucking the little girl students in the grim, scolding way that they had learned from the missionaries.

I was occasionally tempted. After night school one evening a big goon named Eddyson—a part-time janitor—knocked at the window of my house. Usually he found me wild pigeons for my loft, but tonight he brought me a slender girl. She was smiling nervously and wringing her hands.

"Thanks, brother," I said.

The three of us stood on the shadowy veranda.

"Take her, Mr. Anderea."

Her name was Emmy. She had big dark eyes and a thin pretty face, and she reminded me of a warm reptile. She would wrap herself around me and laugh with her tongue out. I knew such girls, younger than she—I took her to be fifteen. It was not her age. She was a student. I couldn't.

I sent them away. I didn't want Eddyson pimping for me and I knew there had to be a clear line between my two lives.

They crashed away, trampled the herbaceous border and cut through the hibiscus hedge, Eddyson explaining that I was probably too tired and Emmy meekly agreeing. Later he told me he had her himself on the way home, tipped her onto her back, just like that, under a tree. "And I got mud on my knees!"

It was not hard to lead two lives and to keep them separate when they were both so satisfying. One was sex, the other work.

There were no more mentions at school of the Msemba incident, but the silence was so deliberate it was like an accusation. They had had a hint from Msemba of my secret life and I imagined they were reminded of it every time they saw his twenty stacked bricks. And were probably reminded of my failure, too. We would never get the new *chimbuzi* at this rate.

I endured a week of silence, feeling defensive but fairly happy; and then had a visit from the Peace Corps. My conscience was usually clear but authority made me feel guilty. I was in my office adding up the attendance register and heard a vehicle on my road—the tickey road. That was a rare enough sight, but it was more unusual even than that—the Peace Corps jeep, with Ed Wently at the wheel. I heard chairs being scraped and teachers calling their classes to order. Kids were springing from their desks and standing up to see who the visitors were. It was their road, too.

Someone else was with Wently on the front seat. I guessed it was an agency man or a poverty tourist—why else would anyone come here?—but when the jeep drew up to my office I saw that it was a fellow about my age, with the look of a volunteer. It was the ready-for-anything look: willing but a little wary.

"Got a new recruit for you, Parent."

His name was Rockwell, he was nervous, and I knew at once it would be a mistake to call him Rocky. He was round-shouldered and a little pale and sly-looking. He did not smile. But like a lot of humorless and unsmiling people he had a startling laugh. It was sudden and terrible, not really a laugh at all.

"We don't actually need a new teacher, Ed."

"You can find room for him. What do you say?"

That was the Peace Corps attitude—make room, double up, hustle, look good, compromise, and keep smiling: very old-fashioned. Be full of pep! The Peace Corps showed up without notice and you were supposed to jump; and then you wouldn't see them for months. They were in Washington, being congratulated on their good work. Or they were at embassy parties in Blantyre.

Ed Wently disliked me. He was a jock, a member of the Blantyre Club rugby team. The club did not have any African members.

"They don't play rugby," Wently had said.

I wanted to make an issue of it and force him to resign from the club, but I could not get any volunteers to agree with me. My feeling was partly political and partly a desire to be a nuisance. And then I stopped caring. I lived my own life. I believed that I was on my own, in my wrinkled suit and squashed hat; in my house, with my cook, and my pigeon loft, the only *mzungu* for miles around.

That was why I was so dismayed when Wently told me to make room for Rockwell.

"We don't have a spare house."

"You've got three bedrooms, Andy!"

I thought: Shit. And there was something in Rockwell's expression that told me he was none too keen on living with me. He had hardly said a word. He had only laughed and that had alarmed me.

"You've got a Peace Corps house," Wently said. "You have to be flexible."

That was always the possibility in bush posts—that once you got used to them the circumstances changed, and you had to adjust again. And because we never had advance warning, every visit was a surprise.

I liked the country, I enjoyed being headmaster, I loved the African girls. But the thought of being in the Peace Corps discouraged me. I hated this jock, Wently, bringing up the Peace Corps—they offered no support, they only imposed on me, and they took all the credit.

"What can you teach?"

Rockwell said, "I was doing a little chemistry and math at my last place."

"Where was that?"

"Sierra Leone. I asked for a transfer."

Probably bush fever: a crazy—a freak.

I said, "We're trying to build a *chimbuzi*. You can get going on that. And you can help Mr. Nyirongo with Form Three math."

"What's a *chimbuzi*?"

"You'll have to start learning the language," I said. "It's a shithouse."

Rockwell then pronounced a strange sentence.

"I've always been very excited about sanitary facilities."

We stared at him.

"That's what I couldn't stand about Sierra Leone."

I could not think of anything to say.

"The restrooms," he said.

"The restrooms?"

Even Wently was baffled.

Rockwell said, "Yeah. People went to the bathroom in the street."

I reminded myself to write that down.

"No one does that in Nyasaland," Wently said, and put his arm around Rockwell's shoulder, the way jocks hug each other. "You're going to love it here, Ward."

So his name was Ward Rockwell. But from that moment I thought of him as Weird Rockwell.

"Bodily hygiene is so important," Rockwell was saying as he went down the road.

It was a bad start. And things did not improve. He did not speak the language. That was crucial. Without noticing it I had been using it constantly. I gave him my grammar book and taught him the greetings, but he showed no aptitude.

I asked him whether he spoke any foreign languages.

"A little Tex-Mex," he said.

"Is that like pig Latin?"

"Are you serious?" he said.

He pronounced it *sirius*, like the constellation. That was the California in him. He had been raised in Houston but after UCLA he had stayed in Los Angeles. He said *contimpree peeners* when I mentioned (to irritate him) that I liked the look of rotting flesh in the work of Ivan Albright. His birth sign was *Jiminie*.

It was bad enough that he spoke no Chinyanja. It did not help that his English was peculiar. *Innerteenmint*, he said and *hoorible*.

"Hey, that cook. When I tell him to inner, I want him to inner."

It took me awhile to work that one out.

"The cook's name is Captain. He doesn't speak English."

"Everyone spoke English in Sierra Leone, even the servants."

I thought of three rejoinders to this. But we were in the bush. An ill-judged remark could cause weeks of miffed silence. I decided not to risk it just then.

"But my cook in Kenema was minilly deficient," he said, and made his first and only joke in the year I knew him. "Kenema was an enema."

He had the California way of saying *hamburgers*, heavy on the *ham* and swallowing the *burgers*.

He was pudgy and lumpish and he had the heavy person's curse: terrible feet. They were visibly twisted and made him totter. "I've got wicked arches," he explained. "I have to wear cookies in my shoes." He made the word sound like *shees*.

The word *hygiene* made him show his teeth, and he said it constantly. It occurred to me that all his talk about cleanliness was just a way of talking about filth; and his bowels were his favorite subject. He was preoccupied rather than obsessed, and not disgusting enough to be truly interesting. But his cast of mind made him an untiring latrine-builder.

Only a few days after he arrived there was progress. He staked out the footings and started digging the runoffs, and near the clay pit was a rising stack of new bricks. I showed him my design for the *chimbuzi* but he said it was not ambitious enough. He took me around the site and showed me how he was going to enlarge it. I helped him measure the new dimensions. He talked about his bowels as he worked on the latrine, like a gourmet cook rejoicing in his hearty appetite.

Captain did not like him. He asked me if the new *bwana* was a *Yehudi*. I hated having to answer but the answer was no in any case.

Rockwell could only speak to Captain through me. "Tell him I hate hard-boiled eggs," "Tell him not to inner my room," "Tell him—"

"Look," I said. "Captain works for me. Don't keep giving him orders. If you don't like it here, find another place."

"It's okay here," Rockwell said. "But I sometimes wonder if that guy washes."

"He's a muslim. He washes more often than you do."

"Yeah," he said doubtfully.

"Five times a day."

This impressed Rockwell. "Bodily hygiene is real important."

He washed his own floor, he scrubbed his own clothes, he disinfected the bathroom every day, he hung a container of chemicals in the cistern that turned the toilet water blue. Sometimes he did not talk to me for several days, and then he would talk nonstop, often incomprehensibly, about a mail-order business he wanted to start in California. And he talked about our *chimbuzi*. He took that very seriously. He dug test holes, drainage ditches, and laid some of the foundation stones. "It's the basics and the insides that really count. It's like your body. You've got to be clean inside, get all the poisons out—"

A parcel was delivered in a Land-Rover from the Nyasaland Trading Company. It weighed ten pounds and even well-wrapped its odor made my eyes sting.

Rockwell was delighted when I gave it to him.

"It's urinal candy," he said. "For our new sanitary facility."

He was very methodical, which made him heavy going in conversation, because he talked the way he worked. His political conservatism seemed like another aspect of his toilet-talk, and he had stories to support his theories. One revolting one was about some Africans in Sierra Leone who refused to flush toilet paper down the hopper.

"See? You can't teach these people anything."

"Not true. The Peace Corps brought oral sex to Nyasaland."

"That turns my stomach," he said, and looked genuinely wretched. "Think of the germs."

But I had wanted to upset him. The only way I could live in the same house was to disagree with everything he said. It was a way of doing battle. I discovered that doing that, disagreeing on principle, meant I was wrong a great deal of the time and often made a fool of myself.

Rockwell did not usually answer back. If I hurt his feelings he sulked. He wouldn't fight. He said, "Words! Words!" and ran to his room. But after his silences he opened up: bodily hygiene, what happens to food in your intestines, the new sanitary facility—and sometimes it was Africa and the Peace Corps.

"When I go back I'm going to write a book. I'm going to call it *The Big Lie.*"

"I thought you were going to start a mail-order business."

"The mail-order business will give me the free time to write," he said. "By the way, I notice you write. Always whacking away at your typewriter. What is it?"

It was my other secret; but so dark was the riddle of writing that even though I did it every day I was afraid to think about my ambition, and never said a word to anyone else about it. Rockwell had heard me typing, that was all. It was a source of pride to me that no one in the world had ever seen me write a word of fiction.

"Letters home," I said. "Anyway, what kind of mail-order business?"

"You promise you won't steal my ideas?"

"I promise. That's a performatory utterance, you know."

"Words." He was grinning. "Words are neat."

This was late one night in front of the fire. The fire always gave him frightening features, and his eagerness tonight combined with the jumping flames on his face made him seem much crazier than usual.

"Do you know how on labels it says, 'Keep in a cool dry place'? All sorts of bottles say it—alcohol, shoe polish, you name it, thousands of them. But what is a cool dry place? Most people don't really have one. So that's going to be one of my main items."

This was insane, and his friendliness only made it worse. What was he talking about? I decided not to alarm him by asking, but simply said it was a tremendous idea.

"Think so? I do too! I figure it'll be a kind of really neat box. Sort of lid, lined inside, little chambers"—he was shaping and hacking with his hands—"and on the outside it'll say *The Cool Dry Place*."

"Sounds terrific," I said, and wondered whether he would guess what I really thought if I excused myself and went to bed. I said mail order had great possibilities.

"But Ward Rockwell's going to have thousands of stock items. Ever notice how bottles of polish and stuff like that has directions saying, 'Wipe with a clean soft cloth'? And you can never find one when you need it?"

"You're going to sell them."

"Right. In a little see-through pouch. I'm going to call it *The*

Clean Soft Cloth." He looked very pleased with himself. He said, "In the same line I'm going to have that other essential product. Guess what?"

"Can't guess," I said. I could have but I knew it would be a mistake.

"*The Damp Rag.* Ever see the label that advises you to apply whatever it is with a damp rag? I'm going to sell them. In hermetically sealed envelopes, pre-dampened rags. See, the thing about rags"—his voice was cracking—"rags are filthy. But my rags—"

I wanted him to stop. He went on. He told me of his elaborate system of shelves for directions that said "Keep out of the reach of children" and his specially engineered coin for "Pry up with a coin."

At last I went to bed. I assumed that his nutty ideas were a result of fatigue and isolation. He was tiring himself in the building of the *chimbuzi*. I decided to break a vow I had made and introduce him to the Beautiful Bamboo. He was a slow steady drinker, and beer made him even more monotonous. When he was drunk he was solemn. He sat in the noise and music, ignoring the girls. He drank and sweated and sulked. And then he went home, putting one foot ahead of the other.

"Guess what I hate about that place."

"Tell me."

"You can't talk there," he said. It was very dark on the road. "The thing is, Andy, I feel I can really talk to you."

That alarmed me. I said, "You know, those girls are friendly. All you have to do is say the word and they'd go home with you."

He made an exasperated noise and then said, "The word is germs."

I had arranged for Gladys to meet me at the house, because I wanted to keep my secret safe from Rockwell. But his attitude affected me. It was more than disapproval—it was horror. I could not perform. It was his fault. Gladys just laughed and squeezed the useless thing. It seemed to me the worst fate on earth to be impotent.

The next night was a Monday. Rockwell had worked all day on the latrine—I could tell by his glazed eyes. I hoped that he would go to his room and calm himself by polishing something, but instead he joined me in front of the fire. I had wanted to sit there and brood about my impotence.

"Words," he said. "Words like 'bored housewife.' That turns me on."

He had been thinking.

"Words are real funny. Words can be neat. 'Semi-naked bored housewife.' "

What was he doing in Central Africa? He should never have gone so far from home. This country was having a bad effect on him—the distance, the isolation. He was probably a very ordinary person, but being here was turning him into someone else. Yet I did not pity him. I resented him. I thought: What if I stay impotent?

He took the poker and hit the fire and grinned.

"People say 'I've got to drive out to the airport' or 'He misses his kids' or 'It needs a new cartridge.' It's all words. People never said those things before. Someday we won't say 'It has to heat up before it'll work.' It'll just start. I mean, 'heat up' is very physical."

He was talking to the fire in a slow droning way.

"We'll be moving into advanced electronics. 'Heat up' is like sex. We'll stop having machines like that. They'll be cool and clean instead. And very small."

Saying that, he made his eyes small. Then I tried not to look at him. I wanted him to talk about hygiene. Why didn't he?

"Words like 'bottle.' Bottle's really strange. The more you say it."

I thought: Bottle is not strange. You are.

" 'He's not ready for that kind of commitment.' A few years ago you'd never hear anyone say that."

Out of the corner of my eye I could see that he was smiling at the fire.

"Or 'My eyes are my best feature.' People never used to say that. They do now."

I said, "I don't think men say it."

"I mean women," he said. "See, I figured it out. I was putting in some pipe today and thinking—there's man words and there's woman words."

"What are woman words?"

" 'I'm going to cry my eyes out.' "

He said it quickly and looked very pleased with himself. And then he spoke again.

" 'I haven't got a thing to wear.' "

He was droning but I knew he was animated, and I had never seen him so absorbed, even on the subject of his bowels. I wanted to stop him. I wanted to say: *Ward, Africa is outside the window. Look at it.*

"Hey," and he poked the fire a little too roughly, "a few years ago you'd never have heard anyone say, 'Her semi-nude body was found in a shallow grave.' "

That smile. And he did not need me to encourage him.

"You wouldn't have read, 'Clad in only her torn underwear she was floating facedown in a ditch.' "

"No," I said.

"There was evidence of sexual assault," he said. "Her bruised and partly clothed body was found by a jogger."

He was still smiling.

4.

That same week I moved into a tiny two-room house in Kanjedza. They called it a township. It was one step up from a slum, literally so, because it was on a hillside, and lower down at the foot of the hill was a slum of mud huts called Chiggamoola. Kanjedza was a settlement of about a hundred concrete sheds— tin roofs, no running water, outside *chimbuzis*, no trees. Paths eroded by rain to gullies. Smoky fires. Mad scabby dogs. I always carried a stick because of the dogs. In the African locations the dogs barked only at whites.

I had a neighbor, Harry Gombo. I complained that the houses were damp.

"At least they are not mud houses," Harry said.

He was embarrassed by crumbly mud walls and thatched

roofs. "He is mudding his house," he said of a poor man he disliked. He often used the word "primitive." He never saw that the virtue of a mud house was that it was disposable. It was abandoned after two or three years. Yet these cement huts in Kanjedza would go on rotting and stinking forever.

But I was happy there. I saw my move as brave and stylish. I was the only *mzungu* in the area. It was a bit like being an explorer. Look at this white kid in the middle of an African township. The other thing was that these townships were regarded as very dangerous—but I knew better. My rent was five pounds a month. Captain had one room, I had the other. He said he had lived in worse places, but I gave him more money nonetheless: Hardship Allowance. I had simply moved out and left Ward Rockwell my house at Chamba Hill. I wanted to live in an African way.

The roads through the township were so steep and rutted I could not ride my bike. When it rained the roads were sluices. Some of the huts had been undermined by rushing rainwater and were tipped and slumped into deep ditches. Others were cracked from having subsided. Weeds grew in the tin roofs. There were chimneys but there was smoke everywhere—and furious dogs and skinny chickens.

It was a peculiar mess of a place. Harry Gombo said Africans were not used to this sort of hut. They cooked inside and scorched the walls and sometimes set them on fire. They pissed against their walls. They did not plant anything—the ground was pitched too sharply and was too stony. They had chopped down all the trees and used them for firewood. Their goats had eaten the rest of the greenery—the bushes, the grass. The chickens pecked at rubble, the dogs fought over old corncobs. There was always a rubber tire smoking beside the road. It never caught fire, it never went out, it always stank.

To keep warm in this cold season the Africans built fires in buckets. Sometimes they asphyxiated themselves. None of the huts were painted. Each one was ugly and uncomfortable and had a nasty smell. Just behind, where there should have been a garden or a bougainvillaea, was a latrine in a shed—the *chim*.

Captain hated it here, I knew, but he did not complain. It was most of all a blow to his pride. It was also harder for him to cook properly in such poor conditions—no more scones, no more meat pies, no breadmaking, no slowly roasted joints. He was used to the electric stove at Chamba; the oven; the refrigerator. Here we had a screened-in box—"the meat-safe." I urged him to cook African food, which was easy enough. He finally relented and then every meal was the same—a lump of steamed dough served with a dish of thick stew. You broke off a piece of dough, rolled it into a dumpling, made a deep thumbprint in it and pushed it through the stew. When it was very wet you ate it. I drank tea, I drank beer, and like the Africans I varied my diet with cookies and hard candy: biscuits and boiled sweets, the British legacy. Captain brought home finger bananas and sour oranges from the market. I killed the taste with black cigarettes which cost a penny each—a tickey for a box of three.

This was my home—at last, an African hut.

The girls I brought to it were not so intimidated as they had been by my house on Chamba Hill. One of the girls was a neighbor. Her name was Abby. She worked at the Rainbow Cinema, taking tickets. She was nineteen, she had two children, she was long-legged and pretty—and strangest of all, she was a runner on the Zimba town track team.

She said she was a very fast runner. "I do not know why!"

It was a mystery to her why she was able to run the two-twenty in less than 33.2 seconds. She was not interested in distance running; she was a sprinter. She was that way in bed, too: very frantic and then it was all over.

More than anything Abby wanted to run in Rhodesia. Rhodesia seemed distant and glamorous. She was sure she could win the women's two-twenty in Nyasaland and be sent to Salisbury to compete.

Nyasaland had these prodigies—the natural athlete (a mother of two); the math genius (barefoot village boy); the long-distance traveler (the young man who walked two thousand miles to Nairobi "for an education"). One of my students, a tiny Tonga with a swollen face, was brilliant on the penny-whistle; and another, a ball boy at the Blantyre Sports Club, was an inspired tennis player. But these exceptional people were seldom taken seriously, and indeed most of them saw themselves as clowns. They would do little more with their gifts than be messengers or hawkers, and they would all die young.

Harry Gombo was a book salesman. He wore a cowboy hat,

which contrasted oddly with his buck teeth and his pin-striped suit. He liked the singer Jim Reeves. He wondered whether I had met the man. Harry sang "This World Is Not My Home (I'm Just A-Passing Through)." He wrote long abusive letters to his district manager in Salisbury.

"I have sent another fizzing rocket to the bwana."

He wanted a company car.

He said he was glad to have an American for a neighbor. He admired me for romancing Abby, the track star. He worried about her and her two children. He said I could be their daddy. He sang the Jim Reeves song, "That Dear Old Daddy of Mine."

Abby brought her two children over to my house when she worked late at the Rainbow. That did not help. It changed my mood when I came with her and had to step over their little sleeping forms—so still on the floor, like mealy-sacks—in order to get into bed with Abby. She roused them and sent them to sleep in the narrow hallway between the two rooms. They picked up their ragged blankets and tottered sleepily away, and they were soon asleep again. But that took away all my ardor.

One night I took Rosie home, and the next morning I saw that she had a bulging belly.

"Are you pregnant, sister?"

She said yes with that click of her teeth.

"Whose is it?"

She said, "Yours!" and laughed in a taunting way.

She kept it up and my blood ran cold. I was so worried that I started to do calculations. It was hopeless, because I could not remember when I had made love to her—all the times. But I said it was impossible and I tried to seem very certain.

"Get on me," she said. She rolled onto her back and lifted her legs. Foreplay was unknown in that country.

I could not perform. The mention of her baby, the size of her belly, and the sun streaming through the window all killed my desire. I had been genuinely afraid by the easy mocking way she had said, "Yours!"

I suggested that instead of making love we have a cup of tea. She said okay and hopped out of bed. Captain made us breakfast and while he was out of the room I asked her how many months?

"Three or four," she said.

I screamed, "I haven't touched you for six months!"

"Don't make noise," she said and squinted at me.

"I am not the father."

She said, "I was just joking."

"Black humor."

She said she had no idea who the father was, but when the baby was born she would go to the Chiperoni Blanket Factory and compare the child's features with the men in the rag room, and then she would know.

Captain took her into town on the bike and that night I brought home a different girl. I always saw Abby on Sundays, because there was only one evening show. These days she never stayed late. Her coach had told her to drink a lot of milk and to sleep well. She was training for the race that would get her to Rhodesia.

I asked her why—though she was in training—she let me make love to her.

"Because I am so close to you," she said.

This seemed very tender.

"My house is just this side. It's easy."

The township was a mess—it smelled, it was muddy, it was noisy, and at night it was so dark that if you weren't careful you would fall into a ditch. All these were characteristics of the country. But there was no crime. The Africans in Kanjedza were too poor to get very drunk, and they worked too hard to stay up at night raising hell. There was cooperation—people helped each other, minded each other's children, cooked for each other, did their washing together at the standpipe: clothes in the morning, dishes at night. They were village courtesies, and though it seemed an unlikely place to find them practiced, the Africans saw nothing unusual in it. The township was not a mess to them. They said they were proud of their cement huts and tin roofs. But they were city Africans and rather lonely.

In spite of the bleakness and the outward dirtiness of the huts, the broken and smeared windows, the ragged curtains and splintered doors and the way they put boulders on the roof to hold the tin down—in spite of this, when the African girls emerged from the huts they were fresh-faced and clean, in starched blouses and pleated skirts. All day they lurked looking frumpish in sarongs and old coats and rubber sandals; but when they went into town they were dressed up and unrecognizable. They wore pretty dresses and the men wore neckties and jackets.

Harry Gombo wore a three-piece suit and carried a carved walking stick. He usually wore a felt hat, too.

"Do you like my sombrero?" he said.

We were on our way to the Kanjedza shop everyone called the canteen.

"We call that a porkpie hat," I said. "You're a snappy dresser, Harry."

He told me that he had grown up in the low-lying town of Port Herald and had never worn more than a pair of shorts until he was eighteen.

"And then I went about in a little singlet."

"What's a singlet?" I said, taking out my small notebook.

"A vest."

He meant an undershirt.

He said, "But you Americans have everything."

"There were a lot of things I didn't have."

He said he was surprised, but he believed me. And when I didn't say anything more, he asked, "What things?"

I thought awhile. I wanted to be truthful.

He said, "A gun?"

"No, I had a gun."

"What, then?"

"Sex, mainly."

He said, "I poked my first girl when I was eight or nine." He was smoothing his silk tie as we approached the canteen. Then he sat on the bench in front, but very carefully, to keep the creases in his trousers. "When did you start?"

"Too late—later than I wanted," I said. "When you have to wait a long time for things you never get enough."

"Sex is like eating."

"America's a very hungry country, Harry."

"I had a white woman once. She was big and fat. I loved her. But she was transferred. Her husband was in the Forestry Commission." He smiled gently and said, "Doris."

"What are we doing here?"

He stood up and tapped his walking stick on the veranda of the canteen.

"Cuff links," he said.

African girls were what I needed. Just after I left Harry I saw Abby hurrying to her house.

I said, "Want to visit me, sister?"

If they said yes it meant everything. I sometimes said, "Want to go upstairs?" This was regarded as a great joke, because the houses all had one story. But that upstairs business was also unambiguous.

Abby said, "Okay."

As soon as we finished making love she said she had to go quickly—she was late for running practice.

"Why did you come with me then?"

"Because you wanted me."

I walked with her to the track and on my way home a barefoot girl beckoned me from beside the Lalji Kurji Building. I was curious. She said, "Do it to me here," and leaned backwards against the fence, bowlegged.

"I can't."

She laughed because I was ridiculous. Didn't I see it was the only way? She said she lived in a small hut in Chiggamoola with her mother. She demanded that I begin. She said, "Put it in."

"My feet hurt. I've got wicked arches. I have to wear cookies in my shoes."

She was still laughing.

"That's why I can't do it standing up."

One Friday, feeling eager, I asked a girl named Gloria to come home with me. She said she couldn't leave without her friend, a skinny girl no more than fourteen. The girl was in conversation with a sinister-looking man in sunglasses—one of the black miners who worked in South Africa and who often showed up at the Bamboo.

"I have bought this girl a bottle of beer," he said, when I took the little girl's arm. "I can't let her go just like that."

He meant that for this two-shilling bottle of Castle Lager the skinny girl was his.

I said, "You should be ashamed of yourself, brother."

The young girl wore greasy makeup—skin lightener, mascara, and lipstick. Her face was a popeyed mask. But she had no shape. Her yellow dress hung straight down like a school uniform. She bent over like a boy to buckle her plastic sandal and I saw she was wearing school bloomers.

"What's your name, sister?"

She said something that sounded like "Boopy."

"You'd better come with us," I said, and put my arm around Gloria. I could feel her dark sinuous body beneath the loose dress. She was still damp from dancing and touching her excited me—it was like holding a snake against me.

Back at Kanjedza I locked Captain into his room, gave Boopy some blankets, and showed her where to sleep in the hallway. I made love in my room to Gloria and later woke her again. She said she was too tired. She said that she wanted to sleep—a sort of apologetic complaint.

"Take my friend."

"No!" I said. I was shocked, and I waited for her to react.

But all I heard were snores from Gloria, and her snoring made me wakeful. I lay wide-eyed in the darkness of my room, breathing in little sips.

The young girl Boopy snuffled and swallowed when I woke her, and then she giggled a little and held me. Caressing her, I was running my fingers over all her bones. She was very thin but she had large bush-baby eyes. She was a child in my arms, but as soon as I took her on the floor she snorted and sighed, and she moved like a woman who knew what she wanted.

None of my students lived here in the township—they were too poor even for this place. A few lived in the slum, Chiggamoola, but I never saw them. And so I had more freedom than I had ever had at my house up at Chamba.

I sometimes visited Rockwell at the house. It was not friendship, though I felt friendlier now that I saw less of him. It was curiosity, and a suspicion in my mind that one day he might hang himself. I liked to think that I might interrupt him and prevent it.

He had refused to hire a cook. He said, "They don't wash their hands. They don't boil the water. It's dirty."

"That's Nyasaland. That's the world. That's the norm, Ward."

"America's clean."

"America's unusual."

He lived on peanut butter sandwiches. "Hey, it's good. They grow peanuts here." His lips were always bluish. "Kool-Aid," he explained.

The Africans told me that Rockwell was *wopusa,* which meant crazy and cruel, as well as stupid; and he was cheap, refusing to hire anyone to cook his food or tend his garden. I said that Americans did not have servants, but I knew that Africans resented whites who lived alone and separate, and who didn't offer them work. I didn't like ratting on Rockwell, but I could see that living by himself, so far from Africans, he was becoming even stranger. What did he know about Africans?

I asked him this question.

He said, "I'll tell you. You very seldom see a bald one."

He had a way of nodding that was almost as alarming as the things he said.

"I've been thinking about bald people a lot recently. Ever notice how bald men often have cuts and scabs and wounds on their heads? You always see a Band-Aid up there. Now why is that?"

I said, "I'm not sure, Ward."

"I am just so grateful to you for handing over your *chimbuzi* to me. *Chimbuzi,* huh? Learning the language, huh?"

"It's coming right along, Ward."

"But I get scared," he said. "When I finish it I'll have nothing else to do."

That fear made him go slowly. The *chimbuzi* was much bigger than I had envisaged—great beehive stacks of bricks were accumulating and from what he had so far built I could see that he had made an elaborate design.

"Look familiar?" he asked me one day.

I said, "In a way."

"I based it on The Alamo. See the way the wings shoot out?"

What kept me from reporting him to Ed Wently was the fact that he got on so well with Miss Natwick. When he had reached the end of his tether, she would tell me. They sat together in the staff room every recess, drinking tea and eating dry cookies. After Deputy Mambo and Mr. Nyirongo left the room, Miss Natwick said, "You can't teach these people anything."

"That's just what I was going to say."

"I'll shepherd those lambs who've cast their idols well away," Miss Natwick said, seeming to quote a hymn. After a moment, her face hardened and she added, "And if they haven't, bugger them."

Miss Natwick would then offer Rockwell a Kitkat or a choco-late finger from her handbag and they would be there until Deputy Mambo returned for another cup of tea.

Sometimes the school seemed hopeless—not simply the shambles Miss Natwick said it was, but chaos. It was always on the verge of flying apart. But it held. I thought: This is Africa. This is the world. It is not chaos but only disorder. Dirt is the norm. Bad water is the norm. Filthy toilets are typical. Stinks are natural, and all dogs are wild. If you walk barefoot hook-worms bore into the balls of your feet. Stretch out your arm and mosquitoes inject sleeping sickness into it. Sit still for a moment and fleas leap onto your body. Embrace your lover and you get lice. Because this is the world. America is very unusual.

I went to Abby's race at the track in Zimba. She had trained and slept well and drunk milk. But it did her no good. She came fifth in the two-twenty. She said she was through with running—it was too much for a woman with kids. She was better off, she said, collecting tickets at the Rainbow Cinema and fooling with me.

That was another day, and that night another night.

5.

The best way to teach English, I felt, was to get in there and start them talking. I asked questions, I had them chant the answers, I made them compete, and when I ran out of prize candy I gave them cough drops from Mulji's, which they liked just as much. Miss Natwick complained that the students said "What?" in-stead of "Pardon?" and she objected to their saying "You're welcome."

People complained that things happened too slowly in Africa, but my experience so far was that everything moved too quickly—it was a time of rapid change, and the change inspired hope and confidence. In a matter of months the students had taken on American accents. They said, "I wanna" and "I gudda" and "I'm tryanna" and "I dunno" and "Whatcha doin" and "Whaa?" The popular songs helped. I heard a little girl named Msonko sing, "Put your sweet lips a little closer to the phone—"

Miss Natwick wrote to the minister of education. She got no reply. There was no minister of education. There wouldn't be one until July.

"No one's in charge," she said. "They've just shut up shop."

"Flew the coop is more like it."

"Blimy, the way you Yanks talk."

"Suspended animation," I said. "Politically."

"Ward Rockwell is very well-spoken though," she said. "But you're as bad as the students."

"Your needlework class is waiting, Miss Natwick."

I was in charge! I was headmaster!

Of course the students overdid the lingo; but it was also a political act. They had been taught by the British to say "Pardon" and "chaps" and "My singlet is very tatty." They had learned expressions like "It's jolly hard" and "He's a cheeky devil" and "Pull your socks up"—and they didn't wear any. The country was about to become independent, and so learning to talk American was a way of getting even with the British.

They didn't hate the British. They hardly knew them. They were somewhat beaten and bewildered, and they felt their country was a flop—they knew they were in the bush—and so they blamed their confusion on the British. When they were angry, which was usually when they were drunk, they could be very self-pitying and abusive. But the antagonism did not go very deep.

It was simple, I knew. Like many other Africans they were very lonely. The end of colonialism meant that they had woken up and found the world very large. Being poor was only part of it. They felt small and weak. And every day they were reminded of this by big strong Americans. It had probably been a good thing that the British ignored them. We took them seriously, but the gulf between us seemed to make them very sad. They did not know what to do or where to go.

And then it occurred to me that we were tempting them.

"I want to go to the United States," Deputy Mambo said. "I want to go to Kansas City."

Kansas City was always mentioned in songs.

"And Pasadena."

That was a new one on me.

"Mr. Rockwell is from Pasadena. He says there are no Africans there. That's why I want to go."

Willy Msemba wanted to go to New York. It was the setting of *My Gun Is Quick.* He wanted to meet a "tomato."

It made them more lonely when we said we were leaving next year and that they would be running the school.

"I want to go to your country," Deputy Mambo said.

I did not believe he was serious. It was temptation—a moment of envy and fantasy. I could not imagine why anyone would want to leave Africa. Was it because they had no novelty in their lives? It was the curse of being poor—monotony. And so they were attracted by anything new. Language was one such novelty: the American way. They had started saying "Lemme see" and "I wanna do it" and—frequently—"I gudda get outa here," meaning Nyasaland.

They were eager to learn. I was still an English teacher, although I had taken over all the headmaster's duties. But being headmaster was no burden. I had discovered early in my life that promotion made life easier. It was simpler to be a headmaster than a teacher, better to be a teacher than a student, and the hardest job of all was the janitor's. Eddyson Chimanga, the pigeon man, had the longest hours, the heaviest work, and the worst pay. Teaching English was a sort of penance I performed.

The American way of speaking was picked up by the girls at the Beautiful Bamboo, too. All of them now spoke English fairly well, and most of them were better at it than my students—a bigger working vocabulary, full of exotic items. Faak. Saak. Beech. Sheet. Bustud. Demmit. Deets. Breek. Us whole. Shoo ting. It was not only the Peace Corps Volunteers who took them home; it was also their listening to popular songs in a concentrated way. *I wanna hold your hand,* they said. And, *Whuddle I do when you've gone and left me.*

In a short time—just months—the American language had spread widely and taken hold.

If you don't like it, an African girl said to me one night at the Bamboo, and she showed me her drunken face, *shove it up.*

I laughed. Perhaps this was what it was like to have children and watch them grow. They were learning.

Lemme get this thing off. It was Margaret, a thin Angoni girl, struggling with her dress and doing a little two-step as she danced out of it.

It always excited and amazed me to see how women's clothes looked so small and shriveled when they took them off. A man's made a bulky mound, but a woman's were no more than a tiny heap, and insubstantial, like a shucked-off snakeskin.

Hey, cut it out! she said. *Not so fast! Gimme a chance!*

I suspected that the students too spoke that way and for the same reason—because they liked us. They wanted to imitate us. They were lonely. They really did want to get out of the country. It made our jobs as teachers easier, and it enlivened every weekend for me.

It was very pleasant to be liked. To be conspicuous and liked was the best of it. I felt special. I was young and far from home: I belonged here. It was the easiest place in the world to be. All week I was headmaster, and then on weekends I walked into the Bamboo with a buzz of excitement, thinking: *Whatever I want . . .*

I still spent Friday night with one, and Saturday night with another, and Sunday with a third.

Rockwell said he had heard that some volunteers were picking up girls in town and taking them home.

"How can people do that?"

I said, "Are you saying that we're just exploiting them? That we're not giving anything back?"

"That's the opposite of what I mean," he said. "They're exploiting us. All we do is give."

He meant his latrine.

"All they do is take."

I said, "We're not doing much for them. This is an experience for us. They're not getting much in return."

"They love it," he said.

He was partly right, which was always his most annoying characteristic.

"You probably take African girls home with you."

I said nothing. I concealed everything from him—everything I did. And I concealed it from everyone else. It was important, it was my strength, that no one knew anything about my secret life; that way they did not know me at all.

" 'This is an experience for us,' " Rockwell said. "You sound so grateful."

"I am grateful. Ward, we could be in Vietnam."

"I'm four-F on account of my feet, so speak for yourself," he said. "Listen, they've got incurable diseases. Hookworm, eye-worm, bilharzia, malaria, sleeping sickness."

"You don't get those from screwing, Ward."

"They've got the clap. We had a movie about it in training."

"Oh, dry up."

"You're going to get the crud."

Everyone said that. *He got a dose in Rhodesia*. But this was not that kind of place. It was innocent, it was new. We were still children, all of us. That was perhaps why it seemed such an odd experience, at times a kind of frenzy, and to an outsider like Rockwell it must have looked like insanity. It had become such a habit that I hated to be alone.

Sex was an expression of friendship: in Africa it was like hold-ing hands. There were times when I felt uncomfortably that it was exploitation, but then I thought: How could it be? It was friendly and fun. There was no coercion. It was offered willingly.

"You like me?" Boopy said.

"I like you, sister."

"You buy me beer?"

"I buy you two beers, sister."

"You take me home?"

"I take you home right now, sister."

"That is better," she said, and pinched me with her skinny fingers. "Okay."

They never asked for money. It seemed to be the easiest thing in the world, and now that I had moved out of my house in Chamba and was living in the African township of Kanjedza I felt I was practically on equal terms with the girls.

Equality itself was a new thing. But I also tried to please them. I was gallant and attentive. I was very grateful. In Nyasaland these were novelties, which was why I was such a success. I was not imposing a system on them, I was simply attaching myself to their system and trying to treat them fairly. These African girls had been kicked out of their villages. I was far from home, too.

I used to imagine that I had attained a kind of maturity, and

I knew I was very lucky. I thought: This is the right time, this is the right place, and I know it. It is all happening now. I was headmaster; I had a little responsibility, and a little power. And there was something about teaching English and hearing it spoken back to me that was very satisfying. Everything seemed to be working perfectly.

My weeks were full. After the busy weekend I went seriously about my duties at the school. I woke early and cycled up to Chamba through the dripping steepness of pines that had been planted by Her Majesty's Forestry Commission. I conducted morning assembly and taught my classes and answered memos. If someone forgot to do something, I did it. The *chimbuzi* was rising. If I asked anyone to do anything the answer was yes. They always said yes. The students said yes. The people at Kanjedza said yes. The African girls said "okay" and that meant everything.

One Tuesday at the end of May I was teaching my English class and felt a tickling at the end of my penis. The lesson was gerunds and participles. I sat down behind my desk, still talking, and covertly touched myself. Was my underwear too tight?

"And gerunds include words like touching, tickling and rubbing. But the word order is very important. It's a verbal noun. Take 'itching.' 'The itching was driving him crazy.' What's the subject of that sentence? Miss Malinki?"

I stood up, wrote the sentence on the blackboard, and was stung again. But when I sat behind my desk to touch it I only made it worse. But touching also gave me little moments of relief.

" 'Squeezing' is a gerund, too. Not 'They were squeezing the banana'—that's a verb. But 'Squeezing is something that often produces pain.' "

And I squeezed. It was agony. My penis was limp and overheated, and pinching it made it raw.

"Excuse me."

I hurried to the *chim.* It had walls but no roof yet, though it really had begun to look like The Alamo. And because all the pipes were in it was usable. Rockwell was nowhere in sight, and I assumed he was taking his math class.

I swayed and pissed razor blades, but the pain didn't go.

There was ground glass still streaming out of my bladder. Pinching my penis brought tears to my eyes and yet I felt it would relieve the itch.

"Anything wrong, Andy?"

That startled me. Rockwell was above me, laying brick, his head and shoulders above the end wall.

"Of course not," I said. Had he seen the flame colored rosette at the tip of my dick?

"I think this is coming along real good, if I do say so myself."

He disappeared, and I heard his boots on the rungs of the ladder. I tried to leave, but he met me at the door and began gesturing with his trowel.

"Notice how I staggered the joists and reinforced the supports? That's for added strength. And what do you think about the returns on those corners?"

He wanted to talk. He propped himself against the door, blocking my way, and drew my attention to the hardwood beams.

"They look great," I said. My penis was on fire.

"I figured a traditional design was best. Something you could adapt. You're probably wondering why I didn't make it look like an African hut, with mock-mud walls and a thatched roof."

I had been wondering—and what was the point of making a traditional American design, the primitive Spanish look of Fort Alamo? But I wanted to scratch myself.

"I'm not wondering, Ward. Excuse me."

He didn't hear. Bores are always deaf.

"See, the point is they never had sanitary facilities before. *Chimbuzi*, as I understand it, just means latrine—well, we're just talking about a trench."

"It's beautiful."

"I'm not asking you how it looks," he said, somewhat offended. "I'm also talking about strength and durability."

"It's the best *chimbuzi* in Nyasaland."

"Don't put me on."

I wanted to claw the itch out of my penis.

I said, "Ward, it's a shithouse. It's a great shithouse, but it's still a shithouse. Don't get carried away. Did you join the Peace Corps to build shithouses?"

He set his face at me. I frowned at him. I was perspiring; my penis throbbed.

"You're a very moody guy," he said.

"I have to get back to my class!"

But he was deaf.

"Hey, if I can say after two years in Africa that I managed to accomplish one thing—and even if that one thing is a sanitary facility, I'll be very proud. Now you're probably saying to yourself, 'Hey—' "

I was saying to myself: I once thought that. It was as though in his wordy way he was satirizing me. And God I was in pain.

"Later!" I said, and ran into my office. I slammed the door and massaged my penis, trying to ease it. But the tickle, which had become an itch, was now a fiery agony.

The pain was inside. It was enclosed, it was not visible, it was within me. It did not occupy a large space. It did not need to. It hurt like a sliver of blue flame. And as the hours passed it was like something molten, a hot pellet was forming in a vein of fire, and when I tried to soothe it I succeeded only in enlarging it and extruding it through the length of my penis. The pain was intense. I could not think of anything else.

I went back to my classroom and told them to start an essay, using as many gerunds as possible; and then I sat in my office and suffered.

The other effect, just as bad, was that it deadened my penis. And it was worse than dead—it was desecrated, mocked and humiliated. It was useless—impossible to erect, forever limp, and unimaginably painful to piss with. It could not function, and I hated myself for the euphonious phrase that it was neither a hose nor a horn. When the throbbing pain subsided it felt like a hot noodle. I imagined that it had turned black. I expected it to drop off. I tried to keep myself from clawing it, and yet— sitting there in my office—it felt as insignificant as a piece of string.

I was reminded of how important I regarded it. It was essential to me. Now it was inflamed and unusable, and I knew that something had gone seriously wrong. I was depressed. I canceled my afternoon class so that I could sit in my office and worry.

I wanted to peek at it, I kept having urges to look. Rockwell was still bricking in the latrine, so I went behind the filing cabinets and unzipped and took the sore thing in my hands. It was soft and swollen and looked mangled, like a half-cooked sausage.

"Mr. Parent?"

Miss Natwick had toppled in, flourishing a copybook.

"I think we have a plagiarist in the Fifth Form."

"Just checking the paintwork here," I said.

My surprise made me pretend to be very serious, and she immediately became suspicious.

"The paintwork?" she said in an incredulous way.

She stepped beside me as I finished stuffing the sore thing into my fly. I hitched up my trousers. I hated my penis. To divert Miss Natwick I knelt and began looking at the wall with regretful scrutiny.

"There's nothing wrong with the paintwork," she said, in a way that suggested that there was something wrong with me.

"It's raw, it's been scorched, it's all coming apart. If you scratch it the whole thing will collapse. I just noticed it this morning. It's like an infection—"

What was I talking about?

I think Miss Natwick knew. She narrowed her eyes at me and made pitying lips. She seemed disgusted when she left.

Then I looked again. I was leaking.

6.

Growing up, I had been taught to regard sickness and disease as something I had brought on myself. I was to blame for whatever illness I had. A weakness in me had made me give in to the ailment. I had a cold because I had gone out without a hat, or had gotten my feet wet. I had a toothache because I ate candy and didn't brush regularly. It was a terrible equation, because whenever I was sick I was made to feel guilty.

Now I had the clap. This was the ultimate penalty and it was peculiarly appropriate. The very organ I had misused was now blazing with infection. It was like being struck dumb for telling a lie, or blinded for staring at something forbidden. The clap was not merely a disease—it was a judgment on me.

That was what I had been taught. But I resisted it. I knew better than to think that this was a moral fault. It was a physical ailment, not a blot on my soul. It was germs. You killed them and then you were cured. I told myself that it was simply an inconvenience. And yet the guilt remained.

There was a practical side to the guilt. If the Peace Corps found out I could be sent home. It was not only that I was a blunderer, I was also a health hazard. But I was too far from the capital to see the Peace Corps doctor that day. I would not have seen him in any case. I didn't want it on my record. It had to be concealed: another secret.

The small hospital in the town of Zimba was called The Queen Elizabeth. I had taken a student there for stitches once: Emergency Outpatient. It had been a five-hour wait for him.

I went there late that same afternoon, grimly cycling. Ahead of me on the pewlike benches of Emergency Outpatient were twenty wounded and ailing Africans. On one bench alone, there was a sniveling child in a bloodstained shirt, a man with a slashed neck, another with a swollen bandaged foot, a woman with yellow liquid leaking from her bulging eye, a small whimpering girl clutching her head, and a young man with smashed toes—he had probably hit them with an ax. There was a stink of infection and rags—and the pain was audible in the gasps and sighs. I did not feel so ill here. I sat, determined not to touch my aching penis.

When she spotted me, the nurse at the table in front beckoned me forward and told me I had come to the wrong place. She did not say so, but I knew that it was because I was white. It was unheard-of for a *mzungu* to come here.

"I have to see the doctor."

"What is wrong, bwana?"

"It is my leg, sister," I said in her language.

She smiled at that—perhaps she guessed I was lying?—and said, "Mr. Nunka will see you when he is free."

"These other people were here before me."

"They can wait."

"They're sick."

She wagged her head. "They are used to waiting."

It was unfair, and yet I seized the chance to cut ahead of them. A seam of pain ran from my throat to my penis.

"Room Three," the nurse said.

On the way down the corridor, it began to throb again. I tried to wring its neck, and tears sprang to my eyes.

Mr. Nunka was washing his hands in Room Three. His back was turned to me. Drying his hands, he glanced at the slip of paper the nurse had given me and he said, "Injury to leg."

I was closing the door to the room as he turned to face me.

"Doctor," I said.

"I am not a doctor," he said. "I am a medical assistant. Livingstone Nunka is my name. Go on."

"It's not my leg," I said. Not a doctor—did he know anything? "There's something wrong with my penis. I mean, inside it."

"Any discharge?"

I nodded. "Sort of greeny-yellow."

"There is pain when you pass water?"

"Yes."

"Chinsonono."

I glanced around, thinking he was calling the orderly. But he smiled and repeated the word, and I knew he was describing my condition.

"Gonorrhea."

"Are you sure?"

"It must be," he said. "Have you been going about with African girls?"

"Yes. Now and then."

He threw his handtowel into a laundry basket and opened a cabinet over the sink.

"When did you last have contact?"

"Sunday."

"Excuse me for asking these questions. And before then?"

"Saturday."

"Any other times?"

"Friday."

He smiled and removed a large jar of tablets from the cabinet. "She is probably a carrier."

"They," I said, and cleared my throat. "It wasn't the same girl."

Now he looked directly at me, but he was no longer smiling.

"Three girls," I said.

"African girls."

He spoke very gently. He said *chinsonono* was very common, and he tipped some of the white tablets from the jar onto a square of paper and counted them.

"How do you know it's not syphilis?"

"It might be, but syphilis is much rarer. Anyway, these will cure syphilis too. And any other infections you have." He was printing on the label. "Don't worry. The symptoms will clear up in a few days. It will be gone in week."

"I've heard of gonorrhea being incurable."

"Not in Nyasaland."

"I was thinking of Vietnam."

"That is a different story."

"Don't you think you should examine me?"

"It is not necessary," he said. "But take all the tablets. Don't stop taking them just because the symptoms go away. You must finish the course. And it's a good idea not to drink alcohol or milk." He plunged a hypodermic into a small bottle. "Roll up your sleeve, please."

"What for?"

"If I give you an injection of penicillin it will get started a little quicker," and he stabbed my shoulder.

When he was done I said, "How much do I owe you?"

"Nothing. It is free. This is Emergency Outpatient—no charge."

"I'd like to give you something." I was embarrassed: he had made it so easy for me. Already I felt better. I wanted him to ask for a bribe.

"You can come by and help me someday."

"I wouldn't know what to do!"

"Just orderly work. We are so understaffed."

"I don't have any training."

"I don't have much myself," Mr. Nunka said. "But you can be useful."

The leak stopped the next day, and then the itching. But it was still sore. It felt useless—not dead but battered and limp. The thought of sex made it limper. It had lost its personality and so had I. No dick, no drinking—it was strange. At school I thought:

[241]

I have no secrets, I am exactly what I seem. One whole side of my existence had vanished. I was surprised that people treated me the same. I felt bored and simple and rather unfunny. Jokes annoyed me. But I was grateful to be cured.

On the following Saturday, conscious that I was repaying a debt, I went to The Queen Elizabeth and asked for Mr. Nunka.

"You are better," he said.

He had confidence in his medicine. And I was thankful that he did not browbeat me. The Peace Corps doctor would have given me a lecture and made me feel guilty. He would have taken the view that I had caught the clap because I had done something I shouldn't have. But that was not true—I had done nothing wrong. I had merely been unlucky.

But this African so-called savage was enlightened. He didn't make moral judgments. I had picked up a germ and he had killed it—a simple matter. I was glad to be dealing with Africans. I was so reassured by his attitude I thought I might never go home.

The cure left me feeling as I had some years before, when I had gone to confession: purer, cleaner, in a state of grace. I was healthy again. Today was Saturday but I had no plans to go to the Beautiful Bamboo.

"I came here to help you."

"Put this on," Mr. Nunka said, and gave me an orderly's green smock. It was stiff with starch.

I imagined assisting at operations, handing him a scalpel, holding a tray of instruments. He would pass me a newborn baby and I would lay the infant in a cradle and whisper to the mother *It's a boy.*

Mr. Nunka led me down a dirty corridor that smelled of disinfectant and we entered a crowded ward.

"The volunteers don't come here anymore," he said. "We used to have plenty of Europeans who worked as hospital visitors."

"Why don't they come?"

"They left the country," he said. "They were frightened of what would happen at Independence."

"But nothing has happened."

"We are not independent yet," Mr. Nunka said.

Did that mean anything?

Most of the whites had gone, though. That was why The Nyasaland Trading Company was so empty and the reason the Blantyre Sports Club was closing. The tea was not being picked, the ministries were closed.

"They used to wash the patients," Mr. Nunka said.

There were forty-seven males, old and young, in the ward, but only thirty beds. The ones without beds slept on the floor. I mentioned this to Mr. Nunka. He said, "They are used to it."

"They look sick," I said.

"They need baths," Mr. Nunka said.

He brought me a big enamel basin and a bar of yellow soap. He explained that it would take two of us to do this—one to prop the patient up, the other to scrub. We took off their pajamas and went at it, sloshing their heads first, then their arms, their torso, and lower, the disgusting rest. The first few made me retch, but then someone turned on the radio, and it played The Drifters' song "Saturday Night at the Movies," and I thought of Abby at the Rainbow Cinema. We washed a few more men, and after a while it was like scrubbing furniture.

The old African men simply lay there and groaned while we soaped them. Several of them were full of tubes and catheters and it required a certain amount of care to wash them. One of the sickest, and hardest to wash, was a man called Goodall. While we were doing him I thought: Maybe Abby gave me the clap? But then the radio played a new song, Elvis's "Return to Sender," and I forgot about Abby. We couldn't scrub Goodall. We dabbed him carefully, cleaning him like an antique. He stank, and his skin was like a lizard's, rather cold and slippery, with white flakes and scales. But I had the impression that he was enjoying his bath—he smiled faintly as he felt the warm water on him—and his pleasure took away my nausea.

"All these tubes," I said.

"Strictures have formed in his urethra," Mr. Nunka said, and he whispered, "He has been a martyr to gonorrhea for sixty years."

When we came to the last bed and washed the old man in it and the one underneath I had a view of the Outpatient Clinic. I was scrubbing a foot—I had the battered thing under my arm—and I saw a familiar figure walking up the gravel path— Gloria, heading for Emergency. She wore her red dress and a red turban, very stylish for the hospital; but she looked rather gray and gloomy.

I simply watched her as I did the foot. I knew she would have a long wait—there was the usual crowd of desperate people waiting to be seen.

"What about a cup of tea?" Mr. Nunka said, when we had finished.

I did not have the tea habit, and this tea was the color of the bathwater in the basin, a resemblance that turned my stomach. But the Staff Room was adjacent to the clinic, and I sat there and read an old issue of *The Central African Examiner* so that I could watch Gloria. She was on a bench near the wall of health posters. Perhaps she was reading *Toby Toothbrush says, "Use me every day!"* or *In Case of Burns*—first aid in pictures.

"Busy day."

"Every day is busy," Mr. Nunka said.

"Goodall seems a nice guy."

"That old man is an institution. He is a chief of the Sena people, on the Lower River."

"He seems to be in terrible pain."

"He is used to it."

Mr. Nunka pushed out his lips like a fish and sucked his tea noisily. How could he, in a such a smelly place? But it seemed he did not notice.

He said, "I want a packet of biscuits, and then I must do some bandages. I will find you here."

I waited until I saw Gloria stand up, hearing her name being called. She was treated by someone I could not see, behind a curtain. After she had gone, clutching her bottle of tablets, I discovered why she had come. It said so on the medical record that was flung into the tray for filing. Her name was given as Lundazi Gloria. She had gonorrhea.

This aroused me—not the disease, but the fact that she was being cured. So was I! As far as I knew, we were the only two people in the country who were being treated for the clap. It made me amorous. In a week we would be completely cured; we would be safe. For the first time in a week I tasted desire, and with it came a renewed feeling of mingled optimism and secrecy. But I did not follow her. There was always time.

Mr. Nunka returned and we washed more patients; bandaged

some burns and emptied Goodall's bottles. It was cold in the men's ward, which dulled the smell somewhat but caused the men to bury themselves in their ragged blankets. A light rain spattered the windows.

At the end of the day, Mr. Nunka said, "It was very good of you to help us here. I hope we will not see you again."

He meant *I think*—they often confused the English words when there was only one word in Chinyanja.

"Why not?"

"We don't have money to pay you."

That did it. I said, "I'll be back tomorrow."

The next day I worked alone, washing the old men again. I realized that I would have to wash them a few more times before they were completely clean. But I was making a visible difference. They were so dirty that one or two baths were not enough to get the grime off.

Goodall said, "Be careful, father. Don't hurt me."

I kept at it and when I finished the old chief was clean, perhaps for the first time in years. His skin was shining. He smiled. But the bath had tired him; he lay back on his raised pillows and went to sleep.

The men were so silent and inert and uncomplaining it really was like washing furniture. There were stitched-up legs and snakebites and thick plaster casts and wounds being drained. I took care to wash around the obstructions. I had spent the day alone here, and when the rain started at five, and I switched on the feeble orange lights—three bulbs in the ceiling—I slopped an old African's skinny arm in my basin. A big fly was buzzing and bonking against a window, trying to get out. It stank of sickness here, and now the daylight was gone. It was damp and cold. I was happy.

During the week at Chamba Hill Secondary School, I was fully alert and got more done than I ever had. I had never felt so rested. I had had nothing to drink, I hadn't brought any girls home over the weekend; I had spoken only to Captain. He told me he believed there were monsters in the Shire River. One he described resembled a whale-sized snake that could wrap itself around the ferry and sink it. Instead of setting him straight, I encouraged him, and he described more monsters. I listened and felt virtuous, which was also a sense of physical well-being.

I was cured of the clap and living one life. Still, I thought of Gloria, taking her penicillin.

The following Saturday after lunch I went back to the hospital.

Mr. Nunka said, "You are on your own again today, father. The other orderly has returned to his village for the weekend."

I didn't mind. I filled the basin and put on my green smock and went to the men's ward. It was harder and slower alone, because I had to prop them on pillows before I could scrub them. But I managed.

When I came to Goodall's bed I saw that he was not in it. Instead, there was a sullen man who had been on the floor. He was very ugly, which had the effect of making him look strong.

"Where is the old man?"

"They took him away."

He did not sound sorry: he was glad now to have a bed. But he saw I did not understand.

He said very plainly, "He died yesterday."

I stood holding the dripping rag.

"Wash me," the African said, and sat up.

"Wash yourself."

"I am sick," he said in a harsh complaining voice.

"Sorry, father." I was ashamed of myself for ever having felt virtuous. I handed the man my wet rag.

I did not go home immediately. I stayed and washed the patients, but I did it badly—I could not see the point of doing it well or being thorough. They didn't notice, nor did Mr. Nunka. I had wet the men, that was all. And then I saw in my reaction to Goodall's death that I had been doing this for myself, not for them. And a bath didn't save anyone from death.

That night I went to the Beautiful Bamboo. I drank beer and waited, watching Gloria dance.

"Come home with me," I said at midnight.

She did not say anything about having had the clap. Mr. Nunka had told me to use a rubber. "African girls," he had said. But a rubber was superfluous. I was certain that we were both cured.

Gloria said, "I love you," in English.

It did not mean anything. They were just the words to a song. Yet I felt very tender towards her, and held her closely, feeling like a survivor, still too terrified by the close call to feel relieved about being alive.

7.

Out of superstition, and because I had been ill and disappointed, I only saw Gloria now.

She said, "I can be your wife."

It didn't mean much: your wife, your woman. It was the same word, like month and moon, or man and husband, and even the words for marry and copulate were close—*kwata* and *kwatana*—because both meant joining.

"Kapena," I said. Maybe.

Like the other girls she lived behind the Beautiful Bamboo; all the disgraced girls, the rebels and runaways, in one hut. She sometimes stopped by my house in Kanjedza, but not before sending a small child ahead.

"The woman in the red dress wants to visit you."

I always said yes, though during the week this was inconvenient. I had my teaching to do, my copybooks to mark, and lessons to prepare. I had my headmaster's paperwork—junior staff salaries, supplies and allowances, letters to parents, memos to teachers. I had files to read and the attendance book to keep. One day, when the country had a government and an Education Ministry a school inspector might visit Chamba Hill.

Miss Natwick saw me dealing with the papers. She said, "Bumf!"

I had never heard the word before. She saw I was bewildered.

"Bum fodder," she explained, in her Rhodesian snarl.

She took delight in seeing how I had to stay late at the school. I was always in my office, even after sundown, working through the files by the light of the sizzling Tilly lamp.

I was not the only person there, however. Rockwell was often straddling the *chimbuzi,* and laboring, as I cycled back to Kanjedza. These days he would not let anyone near it, not even to use it. We reopened the trench near the blue gums. He had taken over the entire construction of the *chim.*

"Do it yourself," he said. "That's the only way to get something done right."

"I thought you were almost done."

"I had seepage in my urinals," he said. "I've got to lick these urinals."

Late one afternoon, when the whole school had emptied, I found him climbing the scaffold to resume the work his teaching had interrupted.

I walked over to watch him. He ignored me at first, and then he accused me of trying to undermine him by giving him an extra math class.

"It was Form Four—full of wise guys. I thought they'd be helping you make bricks."

"Hah! Your big mistake! Thought you could punish them by forcing them to make bricks. You thought you'd get a good latrine."

He smiled at me, and I thought how seldom it was in life that a smile was a sign of pleasure. Rockwell's was always something else.

"But because it was punishment they made bad bricks. Anyone could have told you that. What did I do with them?"

He was now sitting on the half-made roof. At his most obnoxious he always asked questions, and waited until I was exasperated, and then answered them.

"I threw every single darn one of them away."

Even his laugh was not a laugh.

I said, "Where did all these bricks come from then?"

"Punishment's no good," he said, taking his time. "You've got to motivate people properly and do things right. Then they take a pride in their work."

"How are you motivating people, Rockwell?"

"There's only one motivation—"

He started to smile, but he abandoned it when I shouted.

"You're paying them!"

"It's not much," he said, enjoying my anger. "But look at the result." He patted the top of the Alamo wall. "Now, see, there's a good-quality brick."

I was against paying anything to anybody. One of the satisfactions I took in the country was that money did not matter. The African girls never asked for it. Mr. Nunka had cured me for nothing. There were no school fees. And what was I earning? Fifty dollars a month.

"No more paying."

"You're so arrogant." He pronounced it *eeragant* and it didn't sound so bad.

"I'm the headmaster here, Ward. I can get you transferred. I'll call Ed Wently. You'll be back in Sierra Leone, watching people go to the bathroom in the street."

He was silent: the prospect clearly worried him.

"Doing wee-wee and poo-poo on the sidewalk."

"Cut it out, Parent!"

"Anyway, where are you getting the money?"

"It's charity. My church sent it." He had nails in his mouth. As he talked he removed a nail and pounded it into a roof shingle. "The Tenth Street Tabernacle in Rosemead."

It was the first time he had mentioned his church; but I should have known.

"They've got a Faith Fund—Pageant for People Overseas. They collect money from a variety night—Show for Souls. They dole it out, so that we can spread the word of the Lord Jesus, and"—and drew out a nail and slammed it into a shingle—"have Bible study in distant lands."

"This isn't Bible study."

He stared down at me.

"It's a latrine," I said.

"Still, it's in a distant land," he said, and blinked furiously.

"What if your church knew you were hiring Africans to build a shithouse?"

"All the Africans are doing is making the bricks," he said, and then in a lordly way. "I'm building the structure itself."

"Playing God with your *chimbuzi*. You should tell them."

"I think they'd be glad the money was going to a good cause."

"Shall I tell them?"

He saw that I was angry. He said he wouldn't pay out any more money from the Faith Fund. But I knew he was nearly done with the thing and probably didn't need any more bricks.

"I'm done for the day," he said.

He made his way down the ladder, and I saw that his chin had an odd pinkness, as of a burn—it looked bald and scalded.

"Did you hurt yourself? Your chin looks red."

"Nah. Just an experiment." He put his hand on his chin. "Leave me alone. I'm sick. I've got mucus in my stool."

I worked late every day and then bicycled two miles downhill through the dripping pine forest, to Kanjedza. The little boy was usually there.

"The woman in the red dress wants to visit you."

She had immense patience. It was African patience. It had something to do with having plenty of time. It was not indifference, but it was close—the mood of someone who lived in a country where not much ever happened. It was also a kind of watchfulness, like the poise of a bird on a branch. She could sit in a roosting way all day, waiting, doing nothing. Miss Natwick said they behaved that way because Africans were bloody lazy. The Peace Corps told us that Africans had parasites and as a result were very sleepy—the germs, worms, ticks, and amoebas all slowed them down.

But in Gloria's case it might have been something else. She said she was in love with me.

One night she said, "I am visiting my father. He is sick."

"Where is your village?"

"Will you let me show you?"

I could not say no. In that way she got me to agree to go with her.

We took the bus from Zimba to Blantyre and left from there on an old black steam train. It was slow-moving and it stopped at every station. On some hills the engine gasped and went silent, and the whole train rolled backwards, unable to make it to the top. Then the fireman shoveled and stoked until he had built up enough steam for the train to go up and over.

At noon we arrived at the hot flat town of Balaka. There were baobab trees, fat and gray, like misshapen elephants. There was no shade. The rest of the country was cold and drizzly, but this low-lying town was stricken with sun. The main street was a narrow track of pale dust.

"Where are you going, Mister Undie?"

She had started calling me that.

"Back to the station for a timetable."

It was an old habit. I never arrived in a place without thinking that very soon, perhaps sooner than I thought, I would want to leave. I always needed an escape route, no matter how contented I was. The timetable was chalked on the station wall. I copied it into my notebook.

We found a bar and sat in its shadows eating chicken and rice out of tin bowls. People stared at us—the white man, the African girl. I wore my rumpled suit, and Gloria her red dress and high heels.

Her village was nearby—walking distance. She took off her shoes for the hike.

When we were alone on the road I realized I had nothing to say to her. But she did not notice. Silence was another aspect of her patience.

Suddenly she stopped, knelt down and put her shoes on. I soon saw why. There were mud huts ahead, the grass roofs showing through the stunted trees. The entrance to the village was through a pair of fat baobabs—a sort of gateway. The huts were rounded and brown, like a certain kind of bread, and cracked in the same way, walls like crusts. There were about a dozen chubby huts. Naked dirty boys followed us. She knew them: Winston, Snowdon, Blair, Baldwin, and her small brothers Redson and Walton.

Some women yodeled when they saw us. It was the usual gleeful greeting in Nyasaland. Then they began chattering with Gloria in a language I did not understand.

I was pushed onto a stool and served a meal—porridge and stew. It made no difference that I had already eaten. Food was friendship here. Gloria seemed absorbed by the women, and then she brought me a bottle of beer, and some dry cookies, and at last a basin of water. I washed my hands.

"They want you to rest." She was speaking for the women behind her. "I must go and see my father."

They were so eager for me to rest, I agreed, to please them. They brought me to an empty hut, and I lay on the string bed. The walls were dry mud and the floor smooth earth and the air heavy with dust. Dirt flakes sifted down from the thatch. Just lying there made my breathing difficult and I began to wheeze.

I sneaked out and saw why they had wanted me to have a nap: the whole village was asleep—no one stirred. It was the hottest hour of the day, two o'clock.

The sun was a force. It pressed on my eyes, it lay upon me,

and I had to struggle against it in order to walk. I left the sleeping village and followed a path. Yet when I had gone too far I saw that it was not a path, but a furrow in a field. The furrow grew shallower, and then was gone, and I was lost. I came to another path, another furrow. It led to a field of broken-down corn shucks, and before I had gone twenty feet a shadow beneath me came alive—a long black snake, as thick as a garden hose. It scraped on the corn shucks as it slid past my feet. A superstition in Nyasaland said that a person had to turn back if a snake crossed his path. I did so, and went in the opposite direction. Five steps later I saw another snake—much bigger than the last one, and blacker. I imagined that there were nests of black mambas beneath all these corn shucks. It was the most poisonous snake in the country.

I was in a wide, snake-infested field. I picked up a stick and beat the shucks ahead of me in order to frighten the snakes. I had a dread of stepping on the creatures. After almost two hours of this I came to the road of pale dust. It was growing dark when I found my way back to Gloria's village.

"My father wants to see you," she said. "His name is Maxwell."

No one asked where I had been.

Maxwell lay in a cot, in the largest hut in the village. He looked much sicker even than any of the men I had bathed at The Queen Elizabeth, and I was sure he was dying. It was a bare room. There was no medicine near him, only a glass of water and a Bible.

I watched him for a moment. Perhaps he was dead already?

His voice came gasping out of the stillness.

"Are you saved?"

I said I didn't know.

"Then you aren't saved," he said. "You would know if you were."

There was a long silence, during which I realized that he had spoken to me in English.

Finally, I said, "I thought you wanted to talk."

"If you're not saved I have nothing to say to you."

Gloria was waiting for me outside. She seemed stupid and eager. She took my hand and led me away. She did not mention her father.

She said, "Tonight I will come to your hut. It will be easy. You are sleeping with my two small brothers."

I was shocked. First the father's *Are you saved?* and then the daughter's plan to make love in the same room where her two brothers were sleeping, the little naked boys, Redson and Walton.

Seeing that I was hesitant she said, "You were once such a dog that you took me and that little girl home with you and you screwed both of us."

That was true, but it seemed a long time ago. And I hated to be reminded of it. I believed that I had changed a bit, but when I was forced to think about it I saw that I had not changed at all.

I said, "What if the kids wake up? Do you want them to see us?"

"They never wake up."

"I can't screw in the same room with children, sister."

"They are used to it."

"And your father would hate it if he knew. You didn't tell me he's a religious man."

"He is so foolish. These village people are primitive"—she said "primitive" in English—"They don't know anything."

"I am a guest, so I have to behave myself."

"You are my guest, so you have to do what I say."

I had always thought she was submissive. What was this? I said, "What do you want, sister?"

"Jig-jig."

"Sorry. Not with your brothers near us."

They didn't sleep in beds. They had mats, which seemed to me much worse. The mats were beside the bed and under it. We would be screwing on top of them.

"We can do it somewhere else," she said.

I thought of the snakes I had seen that afternoon.

"Here," she said. "My man."

We were standing beside a dead tree in the darkness, whispering.

"There are snakes on the ground here."

"We will screw standing up," she said. "Come near. Near."

The word was *pafoopee*—an easy word to say lewdly.

I said no, but she insisted, and she got me started with her rough hand. She leaned against the tree and held the hem of her dress. Then she balanced herself on an upraised root and we went at it like a couple of monkeys. When we were done I remembered that her father was dying in a hut on the other side of the village. She wanted me again. *Pafoopee,* she said.

All night I heard the two children snoring beneath my bed. I was wakeful, fearing that Gloria would come in. But she stayed away.

She gave me a basin of water and a chunk of soap the next morning. No matter how thoroughly I washed I still felt filthy afterwards. Africans always looked clean. It was their secret. How did they manage to keep clean in mud huts? I was very grubby, and having washed only my hands and face, the rest of my body itched. I didn't shave, and I was too unsure of the water to brush my teeth with it.

But Gloria looked even worse than me. Her dress was dirty, and what was this dancing dress doing here? The buttons down the back were undone, and I could see the row of knucklebones on her spine. By the second day, which was Sunday, she looked very slovenly, and the other women and girls seemed embarrassed by her. She was cranky, her feet were dirty, her dress was torn.

She was oblivious of this. She said the other women got on her nerves. In the town of Zimba she was known as one of the stylish girls from the Beautiful Bamboo; but in this little village she looked whorish and silly.

The women were quiet and rather shy. They were solicitous towards me, urging me to stay in the shade and eat. They brought me African beer. It was sour, almost rancid, but I was flattered to be treated in a traditional way.

Gloria said something which I was sure was, "He doesn't drink that crap."

She told me to give one of her brothers some money to buy a bottle of Castle Lager in Balaka. I didn't want it, but rather than make a scene I gave in.

"These people are stupid."

I thought what a horrible person she was and regretted that I had come. But I was ashamed of myself too, for the more I thought about her the more convinced I was that she was like me. Had I made her that way? It was not that she was Americanized. She wasn't that, by far. It was that she was a scold and a slob and very stupid.

"The old man wants to see you again."

He lay in the darkness.

"I have been thinking about you," he said.

That mattered to me and moved me. He was a wise man. Perhaps what I had sought in his daughter he would offer me. I imagined folk stories and proverbs, and memories of the settlers. He was over seventy, which meant he had been born in the nineteenth century. I looked upon his sunken face, this man from another age. He had been thinking about me.

"Yes, you are lost," he said. It seemed to me that he was chuckling. "You are damned."

I thought: That's what everyone says.

The mail train left Balaka at midnight. We boarded it, and I stretched out on the wooden slatted seat, inhaling coal smoke from the chimney. The insects shrieked at the open windows, from the black woods. Gloria was also sleeping. At one point she woke me up crying, "Help!" She said it was not a nightmare but a song. I woke at dawn, as we drew into Blantyre. My back ached; but I was glad, the sun was up, the air was cool.

But when we walked to the bus depot I knew that something had changed between us. I had seen her village. She had been ashamed of it, ashamed of her father and the "primitive" people. She was distant with me now, as if I might make fun of her. I had seen her secret. She thought I knew too much.

She said, "Bye-bye."

She never showed any affection in public, but then Africans in Nyasaland seldom did.

She was going back to her life and I to mine.

Rockwell was waiting in my office. He wanted the key to the tool shed.

I saw that his whole face was swollen. It was the same pinky bareness that his chin had been, but it was an entire mask of it.

He gave me one of his hacking laughs that meant *Watch out!* and told me that he had plucked some whiskers out of his chin and that had given him an idea. He wondered if he could do more. Over the weekend he had had nothing to do ("Because you took the key to the tool shed with you, Parent, thanks a million") and had plucked all the hairs out of his upper lip, the mustache area. He had used a pair of tweezers. He said it hurt at first.

"Then I thought what the heck. I started again yesterday and did my whole face. Hey, what if it doesn't grow back?"

8.

The African girls never talked about politics. There had been no mention of it in Gloria's village. The British had gone, a black government was coming—everyone knew that. But for now no one was in charge. It was not anarchy, it was peace. People walked in the road there were so few cars, and poor people put on their best clothes and went to get drunk, men in ties, women in dresses. Strangers talked to each other: "Hello, father," "Hello, sister." Everything was very simple. All the African girls seemed like one girl, uncomplicated and enthusiastic and pretty. I was probably no more than a white person to them, but a sympathetic one, and an American. I spoke the language, I knew how to make them laugh.

One said, "I love you because you dance with us."

We were dancing to "Mrs. Brown You've Got a Lovely Daughter."

Then the political talk was talk of independence. It was a kind of nervousness that trembled through the country—or at least through Zimba, and the Beautiful Bamboo Bar, and Chamba Hill Secondary School. It was like the expectation of a parade, the way people get to their feet and fidget just before they hear the band. The day was only two weeks off.

After morning assembly one day I had a visit from Deputy Mambo. He was wearing a red shirt, flapping shorts, and knee socks. He carried a stick. He also wore new shoes. Africans wearing new shoes always made me wary. They looked as though they wanted to kick something.

"I must speak to you," he said, and then added slyly, "Head-master."

"Come in, brother. Who are you supposed to be?"

"I am a Youth Leaguer," he said. "I am organizing our students for the independence celebration."

He did not seem to recognize me. It was as though he was peering dimly out of his uniform, sort of hiding behind it.

"What does that badge say?"

It was a stiff embroidered disk pinned under his Doctor Banda button.

"Chamba Youth League."

Chamba had a Youth League?

"No one told me anything about it."

"I am telling you. We are arranging the independence. There will be flags, fireworks, demonstrations, and what-not."

"What are the students supposed to do?"

"March," he said.

"What if they're busy?"

"They cannot be busy."

This was a very different Deputy Mambo. I wanted to kick him out of my office. But it was not my independence celebration. I could not complain that no one had told me about the Chamba Youth League. It had probably begun on some weekend, when I had been attending to other things.

That same afternoon two soldiers arrived in a Land-Rover. They wore khaki uniforms and polished combat boots. I took them for Germans. They said they were Israelis. Yonny was about my age; the other one, Moosh, was a fat, older man. Deputy Mambo had sent them. They showed me a letter authorizing their visit.

I said, "Mambo teaches Third Form geography—rainfall, our friends the trees, and what is a volcano. No one gave him permission to invite the Israeli army to the school. Know what I mean?"

"You can check," Moosh said, and turned his back on me.

I called Ed Wently from the post office in Zimba after school, but while I was describing Mambo the Youth Leaguer and his Israelis, Wently said, "Play ball," and hung up.

I had never minded when Miss Natwick had implied I was incompetent as headmaster, and it had pleased me to see Rockwell take the latrine seriously. But Mambo in his red shirt I found disconcerting. It seemed he had a secret life, too. And the Israeli soldiers at what I considered my school irritated me. Apparently I could not get rid of them.

Yonny tried to be friendly in a bullying soldierly manner. I said I didn't like soldiers marching around the school. He turned this into an antisemitic remark and said, "No one likes Israelis." Yonny lisped. I had an irrational feeling that people who lisped usually told the truth. Moosh was grumpy. One day he surprised me by saying that he liked to dance. This slob liked to dance? But he showed me a few steps and for those seconds he was a different person, and very light on his feet. I complimented him and in return he criticized me for being friendly towards the students—too easy on them, he said.

It was not long before they began criticizing Rockwell, too. They said they could not understand why he spent all that time shingling the building.

Rockwell said, "Because I want to have it finished by Independence."

They wanted to know what the thing was.

"Sanitary facilities. Rest rooms."

"It's a latrine," I said.

"You Americans," Yonny said, showing me his tongue when he lisped the word.

Moosh said that this latrine was too good for Africans. "They can be happy with a hole in the ground."

"Ever hear of cholera?" Rockwell said, and I admired the fight in him. "Africa's number one killer?"

Yonny said, "Human life means nothing here."

After school, the Israelis drilled the students, showed them how to march in step and twirl banners, and they screamed at them unmercifully. I heard the drums beating from the cleared piece of ground they called the football pitch.

I asked a Fourth Former named Malenga what he thought of the Israelis. He used a word that he had once applied to Americans, that meant "skilled in everything" (nkhabvu).

"Give me an example."

Just today, Malenga said, the younger one Yonny had taught several of the boys how to get free of an enemy interrogator. While you were standing, facing each other, you looked him straight in the eyes and without blinking or moving your head you kicked him furiously and broke his shinbone.

"They're tough guys," Malenga said.

I hated Deputy Mambo for arranging the visit of these soldiers. But now I saw Rockwell in a new light. I had thought of him as crazy and possibly dangerous, but in contrast to the Israelis Rockwell seemed a man of principle and good sense. He had his eccentricities, this toiletmaker from Pasadena, but beneath it all he had a humane mission. I had been too hard on him. While I had spent my weekends at the Bamboo Rockwell had put in extra hours on the latrine.

He had just about finished the roof. On rainy days he worked inside, painting and tinkering.

"I think I've got these urinals licked," he said, and then in a whisper, "Hey, what about these Israelites? Are you going to let them push you around?"

"Wently told me to play ball."

"I got the name of the Israeli ambassador," Rockwell said.

"Are you going to report the soldiers?"

"No. The name spooked me." Rockwell was still whispering. "Ambassador Shohat. Get it?"

I said no.

He said, "Sometimes names are messages. Like Lorne Greene, like Faye Dunaway, like that Scotch guy that runs the Nyasaland Trading Company, Dalgliesh."

I said, "Ward, please—"

"See, Lorne Greene is really 'lawn green.' And Faye Dunaway—'fading away'. Huh? You have to really think to get the message."

"What about Dalgliesh?"

"Dog leash," Rockwell whispered. "And that guy Shohat is 'shoe hat.' In other words, head to toe. It kind of worries me."

After revising my opinion of Rockwell, here he was again, getting weird. But I blamed the Israelis for this.

I was putting in extra time as headmaster, to prove that I was still in charge. I stopped seeing Gloria and went back to taking the Bamboo girls home at weekends. On weekdays I started at seven, unlocked the buildings, met the teachers at seven-thirty, and then banged the piece of railway track to call the students to assembly.

In the last week of June, Deputy Mambo came into my office, this time without knocking. It was one of his red-shirt days— shorts, knee socks, badges. How could he wear that cruel face of Doctor Banda and not expect to scare me?

"I have a request, Mr. Headmaster, sir," he said. He was always slavishly polite when he was being hostile. "About morning assembly. In addition to stories and what-not I suggest we sing a song for Kamuzu."

The man on his badge—Hastings Kamuzu Banda.

"Which song?" I said.

" 'Everything Belongs.' "

I had never heard it. "How does it go?"

Deputy Mambo folded his arms across his Youth League shirt and put his head back and yelled the song in Chinyanja:

> Everything belongs to Kamuzu Banda
> All the trees
> Belong to Kamuzu Banda
> All the huts
> Belong to Kamuzu Banda
> All the cows
> Belong to Kamuzu Banda
> All the roads . . .

"I get the idea, brother." It was tuneful but ridiculous. "But I don't think there's much point in the students singing that, do you?"

He did not reply. He moved his lips over his teeth and pressed them together, and he glared at me. I wondered whether the brown spots on the whites of his eyes meant he had a vitamin deficiency.

I had not had any strong feelings about Mambo until he showed up in his red shirt and announced that he was a member of the Chamba Youth League. I could not forgive him for those two Israelis. I could hear them, even now, shrieking orders on the football pitch.

I said, "The songs we sing are boring, but at least they're harmless."

"We want 'Everything Belongs.' "

"And Banda—who is he?"

It was just an expression—a rhetorical question. I knew who Banda was. But Deputy Mambo answered me.

"He is our Ngwazi."

It meant conquerer.

"And Chirombo."

It meant "great beast."

"Our messiah."

"Give me a break," I said.

He was still staring at me with his brown-flecked eyes.

"Founder and Father of the Malawi Congress Party. Life President of our Motherland, Malawi."

"Look, brother—"

"I am not your brother. I do not drink beers. I do not osculate with town girls wearing tight dresses and ironing their hair."

I glared at him. I hated this, and yet I had been expecting it for months.

"As long as I am headmaster of Chamba Hill Secondary School we will not sing the 'Everything Belongs' song. Is that clear?"

On the last day of June I was visited by a man who said he was from the Ministry of Education. He was English, and very pleasant. He said he liked the look of the school. No one ever praised the place, and I was grateful to this stranger.

"I didn't realize Nyasaland had a Ministry of Education."

"It doesn't," he said. "I'm with the Malawi Ministry of Education."

Hearing that gave me a late-afternoon feeling of something coming to an end.

"We're just getting sorted out," he said. "We're appointing headmasters to schools."

"Chamba has one," I said, meaning myself.

"Right you are," he said, and consulted a file. "His name is Winston Mambo and he's to take over immediately."

I made a little grunt of complaint.

"Can't make much difference to you, old boy," he said. "You'll be gone in a matter of months."

"How do you know?"

He smiled and said, "You're a bird of passage."

All the way home I kept thinking of that expression.

* * *

Mambo moved into the office and I found a cubbyhole in the science block. He fired Miss Natwick, he gave the Israelis lockers in the Staff Room—I had denied them that—and he allowed them to join us for morning coffee. He started a Youth League branch for the Fifth Form and organized the lower forms into troops of Young Pioneers. The schoolyard was thick with red shirts.

His first morning assembly was typical of the ones that followed: a Bible reading, a passage from a speech by Doctor Banda, the song "Everything Belongs to Kamuzu Banda," and a pep-talk.

"He's not even the official president yet," Rockwell said. "This is still a British colony."

It wasn't, but what Rockwell said was partly true.

It was a much stranger situation than that. It was nothing, it was an interval, between the British leaving and the Africans taking over. But it was a short interval—a moment briefer than an eyeblink in the history of the country. For the whole of my time in the place so far no one had been in charge. The Africans were hopeful and they felt free. There was no government. Everything worked. Everyone belonged.

But now I felt it was the end of the day and we all faced a long night.

Mambo said, "We will run the school the African way. According to our ancient traditions."

"Reading the Bible, dressing up in red shirts, singing about Kamuzu, following Israelis around the football pitch. The African way!"

"The Israelis are our friends."

I did not argue. I was glad to be relieved of the tedium of the headmaster's duties—doing the register, keeping track of supplies, balancing the timetable. But with Mambo in charge the school almost immediately took on a preachy political tone, and Mambo—whom I knew to be a creep—became annoyingly pious. I saw that he had become headmaster not because he liked the school particularly but because he wanted something more. He was ambitious. This was his way of moving on.

"We will have special independence celebrations at Chamba Hill Secondary," he said. "Parades, demonstrations, cakes, and a bonfire. The minister will come and plant a tree in front of the *chimbuzi*."

This was at the first staff meeting.

"Wait a minute," Rockwell said.

"I have the minister's reply. Mr. Likoni is delighted to accept this invitation from his former school. I have budgeted for a small blue-gum tree to plant."

"I built that latrine," Rockwell said. "That's all my work. I know you started it and provided some bricks, but I had to tear it down and start again from scratch. So it's all mine."

"We want to give thanks for its completion," Mambo said.

"Then write to the Tenth Street Tabernacle and mention the Faith Fund of the Pageant for People Overseas."

Mambo was scowling at him with speckled eyes, and showing his full set of teeth. He had the appearance of an old-fashioned mechanical bank, the same meaningless mouth and cast-iron features.

"It is our new school latrine. It must be inaugurated."

"I already inaugurated it," Rockwell said.

"It must be done properly," Mambo said.

"There's only one way to inaugurate a latrine—and I did it, fella."

Rockwell was not on hand the day Mr. Likoni arrived in his ministerial car. He used the road that had been trampled and cleared by students searching for tickeys. Not many months before, Mr. Likoni had begged to use my bicycle. Now he was in a new Mercedes. He had a driver. He wore a pin-striped suit and new shoes. He cut a red ribbon and planted a slender blue gum in front of the *chimbuzi*. He did not speak to me. He praised Chamba Hill Secondary and he praised Mr. Mambo. He led the students in the "Everything Belongs" song.

That night I found Rockwell at the Beautiful Bamboo. It was his form of rebellion, he said. He had been there since noon. Thinking, he said. But he looked as though he had been crying.

"What about?"

"Words," he said. "I could never ask a girl her box number, could you?"

To prevent him from plunging in on that subject, I said, "You missed a memorable occasion. Imagine making a ceremony out of opening a public toilet! The minister cut the ribbon and made a speech. That guy used to borrow my bike."

"I wish I had a woman," Rockwell said.

I turned and stared at the African girls seated at the tables, and dancing, and leaning against the wall, all of them watching us.

"Funnily enough, I don't think of them as women," he said. He looked puzzled and alarmed. He said, "I'd rather get drunk."

There were tears in his eyes.

"I had a girlfriend. That was before I joined the Peace Corps. It didn't work out. If I was kissing her in her house and the phone rang, she always answered it, and she always talked about an hour."

He said nothing for a long while. The jukebox played Chuck Berry singing "Maybelline," and then Elvis's "Return to Sender" and then "Knockin' On My Front Door" by the El Dorados. The ideal woman of rock and roll songs was a *crazy little mama.*

"If I met someone who didn't answer the phone at times like that I'd marry her." He put his head in his hands, and started to sob. But he was saying something.

"What is it, Ward?"

He raised his red eye to me and said, "God, that was a beautiful toilet. I was going to have some more urinal candy shipped over. Some great flavor."

After that, we drank without speaking, until at last he burped and said, "It's time to go home."

I looked at my watch.

"I mean the States," he said. "Stop in Paris first." *Peeris.*

"I don't care if I ever go back," I said. I realized that I meant it. I felt strangely solitary saying it. A moment later someone pinched me with a hard hand and put a friendly arm around me. It was an African girl. *Crazy little mama.*

"Hello, sister."

"Hey, man," she said.

9.

On a cold drizzly afternoon in July—Malawi's independence day—I rode my bicycle into town. I could hear music coming from the stadium, and howling crowd-voices, and applause. But the celebrations had nothing to do with me. I was just a foreign teacher; Mambo was headmaster. I hated seeing my students doing their Israeli marching, and I hated the Youth League in their red shirts. But most of all I sensed that this little phase was ending, and I was sorry, because I had liked living in a place that was neither a colony nor a republic. It had been nothing with a name, and very pleasant: it had resembled my own mood. In this special interval I had been able to pursue my secret life.

The natural place for me that day was the Beautiful Bamboo. I realized then that a bar is a safe neutral place, where I had a right to be. And the fact that there were African girls in the bar made it friendlier. More than that—it was where I belonged. Looking around, I saw that at one time or another I had slept with every girl I could see.

They were draped over the chairs and leaning on the bar and staring out the window at the rain. It was too wet and cold to go to the stadium, and anyway, the main independence celebration was in the capital. It was taking place at the moment. The radio was on. I could hear the band playing "Everything Belongs to Kamuzu Banda."

"This rain is very strong," I said in Chinyanja. The word I used for rain, *mpemera*, was very precise. It meant the sweeping rain driven into the veranda by the wind.

"Sure is," a girl said, and another said, "Yah."

How long had they been replying this way?

The Beautiful Bamboo had never looked dingier. It was filled with hairy smells and the droning odor of wet shoes and muddy boots and sodden clothes. The shadowy darkness seemed to make it stinkier, and the noise didn't help—the shouting African men, none I knew, and the radio competing with the jukebox, playing "Downtown" by a British singer.

And over the radio came the sounds of the Malawi Police

Band. Until today there had been no Malawi Police—who needed them? But the band was playing so that students all over the country could do their Israeli marching. In the Zimba stadium Mr. Mambo was standing under his headmaster's umbrella, taking credit for his goose-stepping students as he had for Rockwell's *chimbuzi.*

Rosie was heavily pregnant. She went back and forth with a tray. I bought a bottle of beer and sat alone, near the radio, to drink it. I bought another bottle. Twelve was my limit. I had a long way to go.

The Chiffons were singing, "He's So Fine."

"What these stupid colonialist people did not understand," Doctor Banda shrieked, "was that we Malawians want to be free! That is why I came from London. They called me! I heeded the call. *Kwacha,* they said—"

His words were drowned by a group called The Shangri-Las singing "Leader of the Pack." I could no longer hear the independence celebration clearly on the radio, only its crackle. An orange light glowed in the large plastic dial. I could feel the warm radio tubes on my face. It was not like a radio at all but rather like a device for heating a room.

Rosie came over with her tray. Her dress was tight against the ball of her big belly.

I said, *"Kwacha."* Dawn: it was the slogan.

She said, "Hey, ya wanna beer?"

I said yes, and it frothed when she opened it.

Was that squawk Doctor Banda's nagging voice on the radio? Americans said he was a charismatic leader. I never saw that. I suspected that he was insane. That freed me. What he said made no sense. But he was their problem.

It was then, in the noise of the Bamboo, that I was certain the interval was over. It had been an instant, no more than a tick or two of time. How rare it had been, how unexpected. I had seen it all. I was where I wanted to be, and I'd had everything I wished. I was still like a man on an island, among African girls. They were willing, unsuspicious, careless, and pretty. They did not attach the slightest importance to sex. It was too brief to be called pleasure, but it was fun. I felt very lucky.

The drunker I became the luckier I felt. I was braced against the bar feeling nothing but gratitude; and I was glad I was twenty-three. I felt, living in the far-flung world, I had every-thing.

One of my luckiest instincts lay in being able to tell when I was happy—at the time, not afterwards. Most people don't realize until long afterwards that they have passed through a period of happiness. Their enjoyment takes the form of reminiscence, and it is always tinged with regret that they had not known at the time how happy they were. But I knew, and my memory (of bad times too) was detailed and intense.

So I made the most of those hours and days. I knew when a moment was rare. This was one, and there had been many in the months that preceded it. It warmed me like sunlight. But as I sat in the bar that day I felt the shadows lengthening, I sensed the light fading.

I thought: It was bad before under the British, and it will be bad in the future with a greedy government; but it's perfect now.

Jim Reeves was singing, "This World Is Not My Home."

Grace climbed onto the barstool next to me.

"Give me one beer, father," she said.

The radio was still going, the dial was lit; a howl of *Kwacha!* came from the cloth on the loudspeaker.

"*Kwacha,*" I said, giving Grace the beer.

"Rubbish," she said. "Where have you been keeping, Mister Handy?"

"Here and there." There was too much to tell: my VD, the hospital work; Gloria and her village; changes at the school—Mambo, his Israelis, the latrine ceremony, all that. "But I'm back now."

She was drinking—slurping. She scratched her dark forearm slowly, a sound like sandpaper.

"You are still living on Kanjedza side?"

"Yes, sister." I sipped my beer and became abstracted, think-ing of a story about a waiting room. But in this waiting room no one is what he or she seems. The man with the little girl is not her father—he is a child molester.

"You are still having that smart house?" Grace said.

"Sure. Come over and see it." And I thought: The married couple are actually saying goodbye—she is going to meet her lover, he's off to visit his mistress. The cowboy is a homo.

"First I want to dance here."

"We can dance, and then you can come over to my house," I said. The little boy has a fatal disease, and one of them—probably the nun—has a hand grenade. But it was an impossible story to write—too static. No action. "We can go upstairs."

Grace laughed in her throat—a kind of gulping.

"That's a very pretty dress," I said.

"Seven pounds at the Indian shop," she said. "And shoes. Three pounds."

That meant expensive, stylish, smart. She was boasting.

"So what about it?" I asked.

She stared at me.

I thought: A story about coincidences—enormous ones. A man goes out to buy some cigarettes for his wife and is hit by a car. At the same moment she electrocutes herself with her hair dryer in the bathroom. Upstairs their infant daughter sleeps soundly, not knowing she is an orphan. No, forget it.

"Let's go, sister."

"Not just yet," she said, and laughed again. Unwelcome laughter was so irritating. She kept it up.

Could I ever get used to that laugh? Another story. A divorce. It was the way she laughed, your honor.

"First you give me money," Grace said.

This sobered me. I considered what she had said and found that I was very shocked.

I thought of a story in which the most innocent and dependable person one could think of demands suddenly: First you give me money.

I said to Grace, "Maybe I'll ask someone else—another girl," and glanced around.

"She will want money."

Why had I not guessed this would happen?

The radio was going, Banda at the stadium leading a hymn, "Bringing in the Sheaves."

Just about then—because the hymn continued in my dream—I fell asleep where I sat, with my head on my arms.

"Sorry," Grace said, waking me with her hard fingers stabbing me in my spine.

Night had fallen while I slept. The Independence Celebrations were over. African girls sat quietly at the tables in the Beautiful Bamboo. They watched the door, but no one entered.

A few of them muttered as I left with Grace—and I was limping, still waking up.

We went back to my house in the darkness, saying nothing, listening to the trees drip as we walked. Captain had left a small tin oil-lamp burning in my room, and in this feeble light Grace undressed. She hung her blouse and skirt on the back of a chair; she folded the rag she called her cardigan. She stood her shoes side by side against the wall.

There were so many ways that a woman got into bed—all the postures that meant *I'm joining you,* and the slow, reluctant movements a woman made when she was simply tired, the way she lay down flat, with no sideways motion, as though she were alone.

But I was still awake, and shortly I was on Grace. Her eyes were open, but her body seemed asleep.

"Are you finished yet?" she said.

And then I could not continue. I rolled over and looked at the ceiling. Even in this cold season, Captain had draped the bed with a mosquito net. It looked mockingly like a bridal veil.

"Do you want to stay?"

"It will cost more."

I was thinking about Africa. What an excellent place it was in the dark, and how lucky I was to be out of America and out of Vietnam. I could go on living, and from here in Central Africa I had a good vantage point on both those places; I could begin to write something that was my own. I considered the word *nocturnes.* There was no writing here at all, and *nocturnes* was a word that had to be written—no one ever said it, which was why it was still so beautiful. I had tried to write a story about these African girls, but it kept coming out funny. I did not know that its comedy was its truth. I needed to write, because so much had happened to me to make me feel lonely, and writing about these past events was the best way of being free of their power. The thought stirred me and made me want to live a long time.

That took seconds.

Grace slammed the door hard and woke the dogs, and people started calling out, and cocks crowed, as light appeared in slashes between my curtains—another day. Though something had ended in Africa I was still smiling. I wanted to go on remembering this.

FOUR

BUSH-BABY

1.

No one looks more like a displaced person than an Indian in an overcoat. My friend, S. Prasad, the writer, was waiting for me behind the glass doors at Victoria Air Terminal. His winter clothes, and his thick meerschaum pipe, and the way he glowered—his complexion was more gray than brown this December day—made him seem forbidding. But I knew better. He was an unusual alien: he knew everything about England, he had an Oxford degree, owned his own house, and had published half a shelf of books. He had won five literary prizes. "I don't want to hear about prizes," he sometimes said, making his famous face of disgust. He had lived here since he was eighteen. Still, he called himself an exile. He said he didn't belong—he looked it in his winter coat. Seeing me, he frowned with satisfaction.

He told me about his being an exile as we crossed London in the back of a taxi on the way to his house. I was listening, but I was also rejoicing in the weather.

In Uganda, where I now lived, the sun's dazzle filled the sky, so most days there was no sky. After that dangerous and squandered-looking sunlight, England this wet day looked like a city underground. It was cold, it gleamed, it was black, it seemed indestructible. But this was only a holiday interval for me. I was tired of spending hot drunken Christmases in Africa. This time I would do it right—stay here, sing carols, tramp through the snowy streets; then back to the jungle.

"I have no home," Prasad was saying, biting his pipestem. "You Americans are so lucky—you can always go home. But how can I go back to that ridiculous little island? Exile is a real word for me, you know. These chaps—"

We were at a red light and men in bowler hats and black suits, like a crowd of morticians, were crossing the road in front of our taxi.

"—these chaps have no idea. They have pensions and families and houses and, good God, they have children. They're secure. They're doing very nicely—probably putting a few pence away. What is that bespectacled son of a bitch looking at?"

It was a skinny-faced Indian in a pin-striped suit, waiting for the light to change and glancing at S. Prasad as we drove off.

"Pakistanis. They're everywhere," Prasad said. "Can you blame the English for complaining? They're no better than your bow-and-arrow men."

I said nothing, because I knew he was only half serious, and he was at his best when he was allowed to range freely. He was an intensely private and usually silent man, which was why when he stepped out and began to speak he could be startling. Also, he tested his opinions on perfect strangers. *I hate music* was one of the first things he ever said to me. He never repeated it, and so I assumed he probably did not mean it. Now he was talking about Pakistanis and Islam and Mr. Jinnah.

I was transfixed by the people—the pretty girls in short skirts, the purposeful way they walked, the curve of their thighs, and all the hurrying people, so different from the shufflers in Wandegeya.

Prasad saw that I was interested, but before I could speak he said, "London does not swing for me." And he smiled. "It might for you, Andre."

We crossed a bridge over the Thames and we seemed to be traveling outdoors for the length of it. I got a glimpse of the river and the pale winter light: white sky, black buildings. Then darkness again on the far side, and the taxi buried us in south London.

"I should move from here," Prasad said, as the taxi slowed on a narrow street of bulgey brown brick houses. "I've put this little place on its feet. It's time to go."

The house looked freshly painted—bright trim, a new gate, a garden in which the slender trees still flew tiny white tags from the nursery.

"You ring the bell," Prasad said, pocketing his latchkey. "Sarah likes a little drama."

His wife appeared a moment later, and threw her arms around me, and exclaimed, "Andy!"

"I've been thinking of a small flat in an area that is uncompromisingly fashionable," Prasad was saying behind me. I could tell he was biting on his pipe. "Haven't I, darling? Oh, do go in!"

I had been an admirer of Prasad's writing for about four years when we met by chance in Africa. He said he was passing through; he was restlessly working on a book that he carried from hotel to hotel. He read some things of mine and said, "Promise me one thing. That you will write about this place."

He meant Africa. I promised I would. And so we became friends. When he and Sarah left Africa he urged me to spend Christmas with them in London. Christmas was a long holiday in Uganda, where I was teaching—three weeks of rain and stifling heat, and nothing to do but drink. And there was nothing to keep me there—I had no family. So I gladly went to London. I was grateful for Prasad's invitation.

"You've never been here before!" he shouted in his friendly way. "Sarah—it's Andy's first day in London!"

He laughed very hard and asked me how old I was—although he knew. And then he became grave and motioned with his pipe.

"You saw Nyasaland and Tanganyika before you saw England," he said. "You think it's nothing, but that simple fact will probably affect you the whole of your writing life."

From the other room, Sarah said, "Nyasaland and Tanganyika have new names, you know."

"But who can pronounce them, darling?" And he laughed. "They're jolly hard—but I'll bet Andy can!"

Then he took off his jacket and tie and put on his pajamas. He wore a purple bathrobe with velvet lapels and carpet slippers. It was eleven o'clock in the morning. He said he had work to do.

He saw that I was puzzled.

"I dress for dinner," he said. And he laughed. "I dress for dinner!"

The next morning when I came downstairs for breakfast I saw Prasad sorting Christmas cards. He took a letter from another pile and handed it to me. It had a bright Ghanaian stamp on it.

Prasad said nothing, he was still sorting the Christmas cards; but I knew he was watching me as I read it. I had been expecting this letter from Francesca.

Over breakfast he said, "Sarah, Andy got a letter this morning—from the Gold Coast! Imagine." He turned to me. "Are you going to pay them a visit, the old Gold Coasters?"

"I was thinking about it."

"But European handwriting," he said, and he squeezed his features in intense thought, and making this face he said, "French? Italian? It had a certain—"

"Italian," I said.

He saw everything.

"Ah," he said. "I wish I had your energy, Andy."

He changed into a different pair of pajamas before he went to his study, and passing me on the way he said, "All this travel, all these tickets. I imagine you're very well paid out there. The salaries are so grand. You probably have a pension plan. But what about your writing?"

"I'm going to write some articles for a newspaper in Boston," I said. "That'll pay my way."

"That's it," Prasad said. He looked pleased at the news that I was paying my way. "You're full of ideas, Andy. You have such a gift for these things."

"It means I'll have to go back via Ghana."

"The Gold Coast," Prasad said. "But you have a friend there."

He said *friend* as though he were saying *woman:* he knew.

"And then maybe Nigeria."

"More bongo drums," he said.

"Then Uganda."

"The bow-and-arrow men."

To change the subject, I said, "Are you working on anything?"

"A story," he said. "Want to hear the opening?"

This was unlike him—he never spoke about his work. I said I would be delighted to hear it.

He said, *"John Smithers was buggering Simon Panga-Matoke when the telephone rang. He withdrew, and with tainted tumescent penis entered his study. He picked up the receiver. It was the Director of the Ugandan Space Program.*" Prasad stared at me. "You like it?"

I shook my head slowly, not wanting to speak.

"I don't know how you stand it, Andy," he said. "Now remember your promise."

Sarah asked me to call him for lunch when I returned from a walk that morning.

Prasad's study was in total darkness, but when I opened the door I saw him lying on a sofa, still in his pajamas, smoking a cigarette.

"I finished my book," he said. "I have nothing to do. The book almost killed me, man. I'm like a bird with a broken wing."

My problem was that I had no name for him. He was known as S. Prasad. His first name was Suraj—no one called him that. (His hotel and restaurant reservations often appeared in the name "Sir Arch Prasad," which pleased him.) I was beyond calling him Mr. Prasad. Sarah called him "Raj." It suited him, particularly when he was wearing his purple bathrobe and his Indian slippers. I did not know what anyone else called him. I had never met any of his friends. But that second day at lunch I said, "I'd like to take you both out to lunch tomorrow."

"You go with Raj," Sarah said. "I have work to do."

"What do you say, Raj?"

It was the first time I had used this intimate name.

He smiled, and I felt we had advanced in our friendship, yet I was still conscious of our being master and student.

"Lunch is a delightful idea," he said. "And I can drop off my proofs afterward."

He went to his study—to work, he said. But now I knew he was smoking in the darkness, lying on the sofa, like a man grieving.

In the evening we watched television. I found the programs fascinating and intelligent, and I watched them hungrily, like a dog watching his meat being dumped into a bowl. Prasad hated them.

"You think that man is smiling? That man is not smiling. That is not a smile. That man is a politician. He is very crooked."

That was a documentary on the BBC. Then there was a discussion. The chairman made a joke and the studio audience laughed.

Prasad's lips were curled in disgust and pity. "Poor Malcolm," he said. He turned to me. "Promise me you'll never go on a program like that, Andy."

Sarah snickered as I solemnly promised never to appear on the panel of *The World This Week*.

But Sarah wasn't mocking me. She found Prasad endlessly amusing and unexpected. She was English, exactly his age, and such a good companion to this new friend of mine that I did not dare find her attractive.

She stood at the door the next day as if seeing two boys off to school, or an outing—she fussed and hurried us and said, "Now remember not to leave your umbrella on the tube, Raj."

He didn't kiss her. Perhaps he saw that I noticed.

"I hate displays of affection," he said.

On our way to the station he stopped at a newsagent's bulletin board and peered closely at the various cards that were pinned to it. *French Lessons. Theatrical Wardrobe. Very Strict Games Mistress Will Not Spare the Rod. For a Good Time Ring Doreen. Young Model Seeks Work. Dancing Lessons. Dusky Islander Seeks Driving Position.*

"This is a little lesson in English euphemism," he said. But he kept his eyes on the cards. "I wonder if there's anything here for you." He did not move his head, and yet I knew he was watching me in the reflection from the glass. "No, I suppose not."

In the train he explained that the cards were put up by prostitutes. It was very straightforward. You called them and made an appointment. The price was agreed over the phone. And then you paid them a visit. Prasad saw that his explanation, even in his disgusted voice, had given me a thrill.

"Sex is everywhere in this country," he said. "It's the new mood. It's on everyone's mind. It's all people think about. It has become a kind of obsession."

He was biting his pipe. The passengers on the train were wearing heavy coats and scarves and hats, and their thick-soled shoes were scuffed and wet, and their faces were very white. Over their heads pink-faced women were shown in fancy underwear ads, and with red lips advertising lipstick, and in sunshine modeling bathing suits.

"Let them carry on," Prasad said. "I don't want to suppress it. I want everyone to be completely satisfied and then to stop. Let them get it over with. Let them burn."

He looked around this Northern Line train and went on, "I want that urge to burn itself out. And then I want to hear no more about it."

We went to Wheeler's Restaurant. We both ordered sole.

"Shall we have a carafe of the house wine?" Prasad said in a discouraged voice. "Oh, let's have a classic wine. You have a job, you have a few pence—didn't you say you're on expenses? And this way we'll remember it. People say, 'I drink plonk.' But why? Surely life's too short for that. Let's have a classic, one of the great wines, perhaps a white burgundy."

We had a bottle of Montrachet 1957. Eight pounds, ten shillings.

"Taste that," Prasad said, urging me to drink. "You're going to remember that."

After lunch Prasad took me to his publisher, where he intended to drop off the corrected proofs of his book. I knew nothing about it other than it was his hotel novel, the one he had carried around East Africa, on his search for the perfect place to write it.

Howletts Ltd., Prasad's publisher, occupied a small gray building of misshapen brickwork near the British Museum. The British Museum was to be our second stop—Prasad wanted to show me the manuscripts in the glass cases: "Johnny Keats, Jimmy Joyce, Sammy Johnson—even a bit of Shakey. They've got them all."

But there was a problem with the proofs, or perhaps it was the foreign rights. Whatever—it meant that Prasad would be detained.

"Oh, God," he said, in real misery. "I've let you down. And after that lovely lunch."

He said he would be busy all afternoon, but perhaps I could find my own way to the BM? It was just over the road. He would see me later at home.

"Don't be depressed," he said.

"I'm not depressed," I said, though I felt a little drunk from the wine and might have been looking rather frog-eyed. "I'll find the way."

"You're so resourceful," he said. He gave me his latchkey for the front door, in case I happened to come home late.

As I was leaving Howlett's a blonde girl was also leaving, and I held the door open for her. She was very pretty, about my age, and was dressed like a Cossack in the fashion that was then in vogue—a fur hat, a long dark coat, and high boots. I sized her up quickly and then asked her directions to the British Museum.

"I'm going right past it," she said. "Follow me."

It was her way of conveying that she was interested in me, too. She could so easily have given me directions.

Her name was Rosamond. She worked at Howlett's as an editor. But it was a small firm; she also did typing, publicity, and ran errands.

Hoping to impress her, I said that I had been to her offices with one of Howlett's writers, and I told her who it was.

"Roger thinks he's a genius," Rosamond said, hinting in her tone that she didn't agree.

"Who is Roger?"

"Roger Howlett. He's sort of the owner."

She had long hair which she swung back and forth as she walked, and her stride was brisk and Cossack-like, her sleeves thrashing and her boots clumping. People stared at her and I drew closer to her side.

"Everyone's afraid of Prasad. He's frightfully direct sometimes, and he has a beastly temper." She smiled as though remembering an incident. "What are you doing at the BM?"

"Just killing time."

She thought this was funny, but she tried to hide her reaction—probably for fear I'd be offended.

Then we were at the gates of the British Museum.

"Want to have a drink sometime?"

She shrugged and said, "My friends and I usually go to that pub after work." She pointed across the street.

"Let's meet there at six o'clock."

"All right," she said.

Inside I thought: If I hadn't had that bottle of wine for lunch I wouldn't have spoken to her, and when I thought of Rosamond's face I remembered Prasad saying *Let's have a classic.* I might marry her, I thought—my whole life changed by a bottle of white burgundy.

I was at the Museum Tavern when it opened at five-thirty, and so I saw her enter with her friends—a young woman named Philippa wearing a fur coat and a thin-faced, damp-haired young man named Ronnie.

After we had told each other our names, they asked me what I was doing in London. I mentioned Uganda, my university job there, and S. Prasad. They seemed uninterested in what I said, and so I knew they were impressed: it was the English way—pride and shyness and obliquity. Most of my colleagues were English, after all. They supposed I was an American among Africans.

Finally Philippa said that she would quite like to go to Africa.

Rosamond said that Africa had never interested her but that she would do anything to go to Hong Kong. I thought that this was her English way of pinching me, but affectionately.

Ronnie said, "You think Africa's all elephants and lions and naked savages, but actually the animals are all in game parks and the Africans are hideously respectable. They're always quoting the Bible, and they're desperate for knighthoods."

He said this with great certainty, but it was similar to what Rosamond had said and for the same reason—he was trying to provoke me.

When I smiled at him, he said, "They all wear ties and waistcoats and striped trousers. I've seen them on telly. And those cities are fantastically suburban. Andrew here probably lives in a very boring flat, or the sort of dreary maisonette you might find in a market town in the midlands."

I smiled again and said, "I guess I do."

"You see!" Ronnie laughed hard and squeezed my leg, but the pressure lingered a fraction too long, and I knew he was a homosexual.

He was the sort of boisterous, unhappy, abusive, eager-to-be-loved Englishman who always went too far in order to be the center of attention. We had them in Uganda; the Staff Club was full of them. "You'll be here next month, won't you?"

I said no.

"What a shame," he said. "We're going to have a huge demo in Grosvenor Square in front of the American Embassy. We're planning to break things."

"I'll be in Africa."

"How dull," Ronnie said, and then he turned to Rosamond. "Africa's just like Surrey."

"On the other hand, hyenas get into my trash can about once

a week. I found a snake in my kitchen last year. And last month I found a bush-baby hanging on to my window."

"What's a bush-baby?" Rosamond said. All this time she had been listening very intently to Ronnie hectoring me.

"It's a ball of fur with big round eyes—a monkey," I said. "I've only seen them at night. It's about the size of a big tomcat. The first thing you notice is its dark eyes, and once you see them you know it won't do you any harm—you want it to stay. I was just going to bed and I heard it scratching on the window bars. It was holding on with its little monkey-hands and sort of sitting on the sill as though it wanted to come in and get into bed with me. It wasn't startled to see a human being. It just looked at me with those lovely pleading eyes."

"That's sweet," Philippa said.

Rosamond looked happy, and was about to speak when Ronnie began to laugh in a mirthless and hostile way.

"Do you know there's no cure for rabies?" he said. "If one of these sultry-eyed little creatures bites you, you froth at the mouth and die the most horrible and painful death through dehydration." He smirked and went on, "It's all in that boring book with the delightful pictures of fetuses that we published last month. God, is that the time? Michael's going to scream the house down. What a pleasure to me you are, Andre. Were you named after Andre Gide, by any chance? I hope the answer's yes!"

"Michael's his boyfriend," Rosamond said, after Ronnie had gone. "He took him to the Christmas party last week. No one was the least bit shocked."

Philippa said, "I must go. It's late closing at Selfridges. I have shopping to do. 'Bye, Ros. Lovely to meet you, Andrew."

All that time I had wanted to be alone with Rosamond, and now I was content. I hoped to sit there drinking with her for a few more hours, and to get drunk, and take her home and make love to her. I saw it as something like climbing four flights of stairs, and an event taking place on each landing, drinking on one landing, arriving at her place on the second landing, and the third and fourth a bit far off at the moment to be clearly described. But I felt we were already one flight up that long climb.

We talked about African politics, and English weather, and American money. Meanwhile I was looking at her pale skin, and the way the heat of the pub had reddened her cheeks and dampened her small ringlets of hair against her forehead and neck.

She said there was a play she wanted to see sometime. I said, "We could go together," and she quickly agreed. I said, "We should go out to eat—"

I loved saying "we" and watching her eyes brighten. I hadn't touched her.

"Have another drink," I said.

She smiled and shook her head. "Do you know what I'd really like?"

Then we were outside, swaying, hugging each other in order to stay upright. I thought: If I'm this drunk so is she.

Yellow light lay in spattered puddles on the black street, and pelting raindrops were dazzled by the headlights of oncoming cars. We walked through the rain and London seemed more than ever like a city underground. This wet sloppy weather looked dramatic to me. The rain and my drunkenness made me feel romantic and reckless. In the back of the taxi I took Rosamond in my arms and kissed her, and slid my hand under her huge coat, and groped for her. She didn't resist; she squirmed and helped me a little—moved closer to me and touched my hair. Before we reached her street she had made it clear with her hands and her tongue that I could make love to her. Nowhere I had ever been had seemed a better place for kissing a stranger than a London taxi.

In the dark hours of the following morning she said, "Are you surprised I slept with you so quickly? I'm not usually such an easy lay. But when you told me that story about the bush-baby I trusted you somehow. I knew you wouldn't hurt me. And I knew you wouldn't turn me down."

Bless that bush-baby, I thought, and I remembered Africa.

I told her I had to go but that I wanted to see her again— tomorrow. *Today,* she said, and kissed me. I put on my clothes and walked into the street. I was not afraid to be in this empty London street at four in the morning. I walked along and when a taxi approached I hailed it, and went back to Prasad's across the river.

Prasad was in his purple bathrobe and Indian slippers, sitting at his empty desk in his study, with an unlit pipe in his fingers. He said he had insomnia.

"I'm waiting for the birds to start chuntering," he said. "Are you all right, Andy? Of course you are!" He sniffed and smiled—he'd had a whiff of Rosamond. "You young chaps!"

I felt I had arrived in London at last.

2.

Within a week I began to have habits and haunts in this city: I invented routines and kept to them as a way of dealing with strange places and lengths of time.

I slept late, and after lunch Prasad and I went for walks. We visited bookstores, we went to an uneventful séance at the Brixton Spiritualist Church, we went to museums. He was my guide. He was a solitary man. He knew everyone, but he had no close friends. His loneliness had made him intensely observant, as though this studious scrutiny were a remedy for being lonely. He knew the most obscure details of the paintings in the museums. He would lunge at the pictures, pointing out brushstrokes. "It's a tiny smear. Now step back. It's a person—is it a child? Back farther. It's a man. Look at the hat!"

I could only think how many afternoons he had spent looking at these pictures on his own and discovering these secrets. I liked him, I was grateful for his friendship, and I admired his writing; but his isolation frightened me. I wanted my life to be different.

He grew quieter as these afternoons wore on, and at the end of the day he always asked, "Are you meeting your friend?"

"Yes," I said. "At that pub I told you about. Why don't you come along?"

"I hate pubs," he said, and he made his sour face. It was his look of disgust, as when he talked about sex, or meat, or bad books, or music.

"She'd love to meet you," I said, although that was not true.

"I am quite happy," he said. And he looked happy: declining, refusing, withdrawing—such actions gave him pleasure. He sometimes smiled when he said no. "I don't want to know any new people."

That was the way it went. I spent my days with Prasad and my nights with Rosamond, one life turning within the other, and both spinning within me. I always met Rosamond at the Museum Tavern and we always drank too much and always took a taxi back to her flat in Victoria. Before dawn I got up groggily and wandered the streets until I found a taxi to take me across the river. I never saw her building in daylight, and probably would not have recognized it if I had. We always spoke of going to movies or plays, but we never went.

We made love recklessly, like strangers—mishearing every cry. Rosamond groaned and sighed and fought back; and when I relented she encouraged me, startling me with certain words. This prim blonde English girl with her interesting job and her dainty way of drinking, would take off her pretty dress and pretend to be a whore. Plunging blindly on in the darkness of her room, I was almost convinced. She loved it when I told her she was hungrier than any whore that I had ever known.

Afterwards, when we lay panting for breath, I thought of Prasad. "This sex thing is important to you," he had said. "You young chaps. All that libido." And once in a matter-of-fact voice he said, "I've got a very low and unreliable charge."

It was a week before I realized that Rosamond had what she called flatmates—there were three other young women in this large apartment, and each had her own bedroom. One of them was Philippa. We returned one night to find Philippa in the kitchen with a young man. I felt we had interrupted them in something very tender.

"Andrew, I'd like you to meet my fiancé."

The formal word surprised me and made me feel faintly indecent.

His name was Jeremy. He was in advertising. He said, "You Americans have some super ideas," and seemed very nice and a bit shy.

Philippa said, "Howlett's could do with some good advertising ideas. Roger thinks book promotion is vulgar."

"Michael says he'll never be a really first-rate publisher because he's too much of a gentleman."

This conversation continued for a while, and I listened and

said nothing. But I was thinking: They are living in the world, generating ideas, publishing books, making money, thinking up advertising slogans, working from day to day and solving problems. Nothing they did or said had anything to do with me. I pretended I had a job, I said I was a writer; but really I was simply living in Africa, waiting for something to happen to me.

Rosamond said, "Andy lives in Africa."

It was as though she were explaining why I was so silent.

I had run away, but I had run so far it was interesting.

Jeremy said, "There's an enormous future for tourism there. Especially in Kenya."

Was there? I lived not far away and I did not know that.

Rosamond said, "Andy's a writer."

Hearing her say that made me think that she was proud of me, and I felt a pang of love for her.

"We were just making cocoa," Philippa said. "Would you like some? We've made masses—I used all the milk, I'm afraid."

Rosamond and I were pleasantly drunk and wanted the feeling to last. We said no to the cocoa, and locked ourselves in her bedroom. We undressed each other impatiently.

"The better you know someone the less you're interested in their clothes," I said, and unhooked her black bra.

"You're drunk," Rosamond said, in a drunken way, and pulled me to the floor, and wrapped her legs around me.

"They're going to get married after Christmas," she said after we made love. We were stuck together, still on the floor. "In a beautiful little church in the Cotswolds. They never go out. They're saving all their money for a deposit on a flat."

It seemed such a pleasure to be married. I thought of Prasad and his wife in their house in south London. Sarah fussed over him and poked fun at him. But she also helped him. She read his proofs, she cooked, she ran the house. They seemed very close, as though they had formed their own intimate little society. That was the reason he seldom went out, and it was why they did not mind my staying away these nights with Rosamond: Raj and Sarah had a private life to which I could not be admitted. It seemed to me that nothing was more exclusive or unknowable than a happy marriage. It was the rarest friendship in the world, I felt.

"It would be nice to be married," I said.

Rosamond said nothing and then she giggled in the darkness and said, "What are you saying to me?"

"Would you like to get married?"

"I don't know," she said. She tossed her hair. "I've never given it any thought."

But when we made love again shortly afterwards she whimpered and began to cry. Her face was wet with tears. She said, "I'm happy," and held me close to her. She hugged me. She said, "I won't let you go. I'm going to keep you prisoner."

When I struggled to get free, she laughed, and became aroused once more.

I was haggard when I arrived back at Prasad's that early morning: I clucked, seeing my face in the hall mirror.

Prasad opened his study door and said, "I think you like this girl."

He was in his pajamas. The man never slept.

"She's very nice," I said, and heard her saying through clenched teeth *Bite me—I'm a whore.* I had to repeat to myself, Yes, she is very nice.

"Where do her people live?"

"Her, um, people live in a place called Walton."

"Oh, God," Prasad said. He made his disgusted face, but it was worse than usual. "Walton-on-Thames."

"You know the place?"

"My heart sinks at the thought of places like that."

I knew where she lived, because that very morning, before I left her apartment, she asked whether I would go home with her for Christmas dinner. I had asked her where.

"It's one of these nightmare places," Prasad said. "England's full of them."

"He's just being silly," Sarah said, later that day. "It's lovely. It's on the river. You'll have a wonderful time. Much better than our dull old vegetarian Christmas."

"We will celebrate in our usual style," Prasad said. "Very quietly, I'm afraid. My bingeing days are over."

Then he laughed, and so did Sarah. I envied them the way they had each other.

Christmas morning was dry and bright, the blue sky mirrored on the upper windows of old buildings, and the city was very still, as on the day after a great event. There were few people about, no buses, hardly any traffic, and every shop was shut. Near the station, which was closed, there were pools of vomit on the curb, still fresh, like messes of spilled soup. A peaceful silence lay over the city, and the occasional burst of church bells made this silence more emphatic.

This sunlight and emptiness was perfect for our meeting: Rosamond was waiting in her long cossack coat and fur hat on the steps of Waterloo Station. It was as though we were the only people awake this morning—we had a purpose in the deserted city. Christmas itself made me feel innocently happy, and I kissed Rosamond with such energy and hope that she shrieked. And I gave her a present, a silk scarf from Liberty's with the date of the New Year on it, *1968.*

"I'm going to wear it," she said, and tied it loosely around her neck. "It's beautiful."

I saw her glance at herself as we passed a shop window in the station. She looked pleased as she turned away.

After we boarded the train, she gave me a present—a leather wallet. I said it was just what I needed, and I showed her my old one to prove it. Then we sat holding hands, saying nothing, traveling in the empty rattling train that smelled of stale smoke and the mingled odors of last night's homeward-bound partygoers—perfume, cigarettes, beer, whiskey, fried food. There were shreds of gift wrapping and twisted ribbon among the trampled newspapers. I began to feel sad when I thought about our presents: they were the sort of gifts that people exchanged when they did not know each other well. Sitting there silently—but wanting to speak—I felt Rosamond was a stranger, and I was apprehensive about meeting her family.

It was not a long trip—much less than the hour she said it would take. England seemed such a small place, in spite of many names. It was all names, and they were impressive, but they were signs on stations, no more than that; a brief stop, no one got on or off, we moved on. The distances were slight and the places disappointing. In Africa for hundreds of miles there were hills and valleys and forests, and nothing had a name.

Walton was just small houses and roofs. Where was the river? I felt cheated by these London names. There was no green at Bethnal Green—only a street and traffic; and Shepherd's Bush was a dangerous intersection. The slum at Elephant and Castle was the worst cheat of all.

"You must be Andrew," Rosamond's father said. He said nothing more. He did not shake my hand. He did not tell me that his name was James Graves—I had to ask Rosamond that. I had been feeling cheery, but this English obliqueness sobered me by making me attentive.

We got into his small car and drove, but not far, to a house I first took to be large until I realized that it was half the building, semidetached, though it too had a name, *Rosedene*. It was two textures, stucco and brick, with a tile roof, and it lay behind thick hedges. In its small and fussy front yard there were four dusty rosebushes and a birdbath and rectangular patches of grass that looked like upturned scrubbing brushes. Everything was a tight fit—the railway line, the station, the street, Mr. Graves's car, this house, and even the guests, seated close together in the parlor drinking Christmas sherry. The sun streamed through the windows and warmed the Christmas tree and released a fragrance of pine.

Mr. Graves wore a thick suit and heavy shoes, and his wife an apron—she was just doing the roast potatoes, she said. There was Rosamond's younger sister, who was also pretty; her name was Janey and she had a ringing laugh that made Mr. Fry, who sat next to her, squint in an exaggerated way. Dave and Jill shared a big chair—she sat on the arm. Dave was a red-faced man in a yellowish suit, and Jill a plump woman who, under the pretense of restraining her husband, actually encouraged him.

"So this is the Yank we've been hearing about," Dave said.

"Don't be beastly," Jill said, and laughed as she pushed his head.

This made Dave smile. "They say everything in America is bigger than over here. Cheers, James"—Mr. Graves had refilled the tiny glass of sherry—"Happy Christmas. God bless." He took a sip. "That right?"

His eyes were on me in an aggressive stare. Did he want me to answer him?

"Oh, Dave, don't start," Jill said, and laughed affectionately.

Mr. Fry said, "I've got a cousin who went out there. Canada. Toronto, I think. They usually send a Christmas card."

"A big Christmas card," Dave said. "Bigger than ours."

"I don't come from Canada."

Rosamond said, "Andrew's from Boston."

"They're more English than the English," Mr. Graves said.

Now they were all staring at me, waiting for me to speak again.

"How are you getting on here?" Mr. Fry asked.

Before I could answer, Rosamond's mother spoke up. She was twisting her apron in her hands. "People criticize us, but this is ever such a small place, and we're not as wealthy as we used to be."

I did not know whether this woman was talking about herself or England, but it hardly seemed to matter. Still she clutched her apron.

"Oh, do leave Andrew alone," Rosamond said. "You're just putting him off."

I loved the way she chewed the word *orf.*

"If I don't see to the roast potatoes," her mother said, and she left the hot room without finishing her sentence.

"Because of the blacks," Dave said with force in his voice, his cheeks tightening. "That's why they criticize us. Your friend knows a bit about that, I reckon, Ros." He created a silence in the room with his confidence. He said again, "Blacks."

I could not hear the word without seeing dark dumb blunt things, like stumps in a burned forest.

Mr. Graves cleared his throat and began to speak. I was relieved to think that he would lighten the atmosphere. He smiled, but I realized that his smile was only to give an edge to his sarcasm when he said, "But do we get a word of thanks? Not a bit of it. I tell you, my heart goes out to those Rhodesians."

"Andrew works in Uganda," Rosamond said, as a sort of protest.

"He would, wouldn't he?" Dave said, which made Jill laugh.

Janey was looking at me eagerly and smiling, the fascinated younger sister, with her lovely eyes and her large young lips.

Mr. Graves said, "That's just what I mean, Ros. Now the Americans are going to Africa and saying what a bad job we did of it. Well"—and he glanced at me—"see how they like it."

"I'm sorry to have to say this," Mr. Fry said, not sounding sorry at all, "but the Americans are welcome to them. They can have every damn one of them."

"And not only in Africa," Dave said. "There's a few round our way I'd like to send over."

"My mother used to say, 'American men cry a great deal, and they never take their hats off when they go inside," Mr. Fry said. "She often went to the pictures, my mum." And he smiled.

The conversation turned and turned, like a merry-go-round that I was trying to get on, but each time I made an attempt it speeded up. I saw that I would fall if I just leaped aboard, and so I did nothing and felt foolish.

Dave was telling a confused story. It took awhile for me to realize that it was a joke, about a black man at a bus stop who was asked how long he had been here. He said, "Five years." The Englishman replied, "That's a long time to wait, even for a Number Eleven bus." Dave compounded the malice of the joke by swearing it was true.

Mr. Graves said, "Drink up, everyone. I can hear Dickie calling us."

Rosamond's mother was called Dickie?

"That's the spirit," Mr. Fry said, seeing me smiling, "don't take this mob seriously."

I nodded and smiled again realizing that the name Dickie had made me smile, and then I wondered whether Mr. Fry was being sarcastic.

"I've always wanted to visit America," Jill said, as we filed into the dining room. "See the Statue of Liberty. See Niagara Falls. Do they really have cowboys out there?"

"That's the question my African students always ask," I said.

She did not hear me. She was handing me a Christmas cracker and yanking at the same time. There were a series of pops and shouts. Then the reading of the mottoes, and everyone put on a paper hat.

"Poor Andy," Rosamond said. "I'll pull your cracker."

"I'll bet you will," Dave said, and Jill shrieked.

And then I put on my paper dunce cap.

We sat close together around a small sunlit table of steaming vegetables. Mr. Graves straightened his paper hat and talked about Rhodesia. "Those are our own people," he said. Mr. Fry was next to me, not eating but mashing food onto the tines of his fork and making a lump of it like an African daubing a wall. On my other side, Rosamond sulked in embarrassed silence, hearing her father use the expression "our kith and kin in Rhodesia." Her mother—what was your name if people called

you Dickie?—looked tired and tearful. Perhaps she was drunk.
She said we mustn't miss the Queen's Christmas message on
television.

"That went down very well," Mr. Fry said, arranging his knife
and fork parallel on his empty plate.

"Talkative, isn't he?" Dave said to Rosamond, and when I
looked up I saw everyone staring at me again and laughing
loudly—much too loudly, when I said nothing.

The Christmas pudding was doused with brandy and lighted.
A blue flame flickered around it for a few seconds. I was given
a crumbling wedge. I ate a forkful of it, and tried another, but
when I bit down I cracked a tooth and began to choke. Then I
took a small smeared coin out of my mouth.

"Andrew's got the sixpence," Rosamond's mother said.

"That's lucky," Mr. Fry said.

"I guess I'll need it to pay my dentist," I said.

No one laughed.

We went into the parlor again to have coffee and to watch the
Queen on television. The Queen looked very white and nervous,
and she was sitting in a room just like this parlor, rather cluttered and fussily arranged, with framed family pictures, doilies,
porcelain knickknacks, footstools, and frilly lampshades.

Mr. Graves awkwardly proposed a toast and then everyone
except Dave and Jill went for a walk to the river, which was as
still as a pond and black, with black leafless trees on both banks.
Before we had finished our walk, a wreath of fog gathered on the
water, and then night fell—the early darkness of an English
winter.

"Will Andrew stay for tea?" Rosamond's mother asked her,
although I was standing next to her.

I hated the way the question was put, and so I pretended to
be deaf. Rosamond made an excuse and said we'd have to go
back to London right away.

On the train she said, "I'm really sorry," and nothing more.
Now I was grateful for her silence. She took my hand. I felt
miserable. There seemed something final in the pressure of her
hand on mine.

"I was expecting you somewhat later than this," Prasad said,
when I returned to his house, and then he looked closely at me.
"Oh, God, what happened?"

I told him of my Christmas visit.

"Pay no attention to them," he said. "They're inferior people. Did they have one of these depressing houses, and a monkey wagon in the driveway? You should have nothing to do with them. Just walk away. Don't be sad, don't be angry. These people are only dangerous to themselves."

He was making stabbing gestures with his pipestem. He wore his pajamas, his bathrobe, his slippers—and the socks I had given him for Christmas.

"And the girl—you must leave her, Andy," he said. "Forget her. Forget the family. They're nightmare people. The house. The opinions. Do you want that? Do you want that nonsense and a little monkey wagon?"

"I don't know what to do," I finally said.

Sarah was looking sadly at me and thinking *Poor Andy*.

"Just"—and then Prasad raised his hands, like a priest at the consecration, giving his words weight—"leave her."

"I don't want to hurt her."

"She'll be very relieved."

After Sarah had gone to bed, Prasad took me into his study and opened a filing cabinet. He showed me some of his notebooks, his novels written in longhand. He was a man of great assurance and decisiveness, and so I was surprised—even shocked—to see his handwriting, the hesitations, the blotches and balloons and crossings out. Whole pages were disfigured, and many were recopied three or four times. And then I realized I hardly knew him.

"You want to be a writer, Andy. But you see?" He opened another notebook—words blacked out, scribbles, his fine handwriting deteriorating into a scrawl. "It's terrible, man. But if you're serious you have a lot of work ahead of you."

He was gone when I woke up the next day. Sarah said he was lunching in Kensington. I watched for him, and I was standing at the window when his taxi drew up. There was someone else inside.

"Cyril Connolly," he said. "We shared a taxi. You know him?"

"*The Unquiet Grave* is a masterpiece," I said.

Prasad winced, as he always did when he didn't agree with something I said.

"He saw you at the window. He asked who you were."

"What did you tell him?"

"'That's Andre Parent. An American writer,' Prasad said.
"'He's going to the Gold Coast.'"

"What did he say?"

"That he knew your work," Prasad said, a smile rising on his lips.

"What work?"

"Exactly. You haven't a moment to lose."

3.

The main street of Accra was scattered with squashed branches
and trash, and some of its potholes were large enough to hold
three children, just their dark heads showing above the street as
they played in the yellow mud of the hole. I felt sick to my
stomach, queasy in this humidity and heat after the cold air of
London. Africa now seemed to represent ill-health and failure.

Francesca was driving. She steered around a pothole that
would almost have swallowed her little Fiat. "They always say
they are going to fix them, but they never do. It's always lies."

She drove badly, making me sicker. We were shopping. We
tried to buy beer for New Year's Eve—tomorrow. There was
none to be had in the entire city. But why were we buying it
today? Why hadn't she thought of this before? She had known
a month ago that I was coming.

"They are always out of it! You can't buy coffee! You can't buy
lipstick! Did you get the makeup I asked you to buy at Boots?"

"It's in my bag."

"And they always smile stupidly and say 'Don't worry.'"

The cynic habitually says *always* and *never,* but after only three
months in the country had she any right to be cynical?

Francesca was tough. That was surprising first of all because
she was tiny and looked helpless. But she was solitary and self-
reliant, and she had the melancholy of the Italian woman who

faced life alone—no husband, no children, no church. They left Italy and made their lives elsewhere. In her independence and her anger she seemed to me extraordinary. But I was uncomfortable with her—because she was older than me, she wouldn't say how much older; and because her melancholy could turn from thoughtful pessimism to bleak sadness. I knew when: sadness gave her bad posture.

She had gone first to London, where she had learned English, and then she visited Boston, where we had bumped into each other on a bus to Amherst. We had exhausted each other one weekend, making love, and then she was gone. We stayed in touch by letter. She was in Paris, then back in Sicily, among people she hated. My being in Africa gave her an idea. After a while she turned up in Ghana, teaching at the university, English, of all things. But it was not very demanding work. It was a place much like my own—middle-aged students doing high school work.

"These are the laziest students I have ever taught. They never do any studying. It's always, 'I forget to read the book!' "

When a person with an accent imitates the accent of another person, the satire usually collapses into self-parody. And I had found that most people who tried to imitate the way Africans talked were racists. It took me a little while to realize that when Francesca criticized Ghana or the Africans she did not regard it as racism. She felt it was the opposite—proof that she was truly broadminded. Perhaps she was. She certainly seemed confident. It took confidence to laugh and mimic and lose your temper in Africa, but it was tiring for me to watch and listen.

"Africans are really hopeless," she said.

"I need to meet some Ghanaians," I said. "That's why I came here."

"I thought you came to see me."

"Right. But I have to pay my way. I'm writing an article."

"What is it about?"

"Ghana after Nkrumah," I said—and she still had a questioning smirk on her face, so I continued, "What now?—Who's in charge?—What next?—Are we at a crossroads? On the one hand *this,* on the other hand *that.* It's a thumbsucker."

She laughed—she liked hearing new expressions in English. And laughter turned her into a new person—she made a loud approving noise and her small body became supple. She had short black hair and golden skin. She loved the color green—dresses, scarves, even underwear—and because she was short she always wore interesting shoes—high heels and basketwork things with built-up soles.

"I can introduce you to some Africans," she said, and drove on.

She lived in a hot little apartment in a building that was faced with plaster that had turned from yellow to gray in the damp heat. So many of the buildings in Accra looked brittle and moldy, like stale bread, and the streets too were crumbled like old cake. The sky was heavy with the dull gleam of stifling clouds, and even at night the air was clammy and unbreathable.

That first night, when we couldn't buy any beer, we sat surrounded by packing crates and tea chests—she said that she hadn't had time to unpack properly and anyway found them convenient for storing her things. They were like cupboards, she said. They gave the room the cluttered and stacked-up look of an attic or a storeroom. Her ceiling fan was no more than a whirring distraction. It made the calendar rattle against the wall, but it did not cool me.

Francesca wore a Ghanaian cloth wraparound, which slipped loose as she leaned over and spooned some sinister-looking stew into my plate. I looked down and saw lurid vegetables in greasy gravy. There was bread but it was hard and dusty, and the butter tasted of soap.

"This food is disgusting," Francesca said. "My cook is good for nothing."

I said nothing. It was obvious the food was bad. In any case I had no appetite. The coastal heat affected me like a sickness.

When I said I wasn't hungry, Francesca squawked for the cook. He entered in a stiff and almost ceremonial way to remove the plates.

Francesca plopped her spoon into her plate, as the cook made a little bow.

"You want pooding, muddum?"

"No, no, no, no, no." And she waved him away.

Silently the table was cleared, and I saw that it was not a table, but another packing crate.

"Why don't *you* cook, if he's so bad?"

"I hate cooking," she said.

Then it was clear to me why she treated him so rudely. It was one bad cook blaming another.

"I just like eating," she said.

The cook was padding back and forth, one room away. We sat restlessly, and her sentence still hung in the air. The ceiling fan went *ark-ark*. Someone else's radio penetrated our wall, and there were children's shouts from the street, and laboring cars and choking dogs. The kitchen door clattered: the cook was gone.

"I'm still hungry," Francesca said.

"I'm not surprised."

But she was smiling.

"Now I'm going to eat you."

She switched the light off, but the yellow light from the street brightened the room and gave the packing cases crooked shadows. Francesca was standing before me.

"I like these Ghanaian dresses," she said. "So easy to take off."

She unknotted it and it slipped to the floor. She was naked. Her body was lighted by the streetlamps and stripes lay across her curves like contours—the shadows of the window bars showing on her skin. She dropped to her knees. I looked up at the ceiling. *Ark-ark*—the fan had a froggy voice; and later with the bed creaking it was like a jungle racket.

I woke up the next morning feeling ill. The humid heat was a weight that squeezed my eyes. It was a sense of oppression, like a memory of suffocation, and I sweated as though running a temperature. Francesca said it was a normal day in Accra. A normal day was like a fever.

I foresaw a week of this fever and this food.

"Why don't we take a trip?" I said. "We could drive somewhere up-country in your car."

I had a feeling that if we went north it would be cooler, and I hated this broken-down city.

Francesca was frowning—her way of showing me she was thinking.

"We don't have any plans for New Year's. There's hardly any food in the cupboard. And there's nothing to drink."

"You are criticizing me," she said peevishly.

I denied it and said I was sorry, but so feebly she knew I was lying.

"And it might be fun to take a trip."

Now I regretted leaving London so suddenly, and I missed Prasad and Rosamond and the black gleaming streets.

"We could go to Kumasi," Francesca said. "There's a hotel where no one ever stays. It's very green in Kumasi and a bit cooler. But what about those Africans you wanted to meet?"

"Where are they?"

"One lives in the next block of flats," Francesca said. "He works for the government. He might have some stories for you. His name is Kofi. Everyone is named Kofi or Kwame. We can see him before we go."

I was so eager to leave I immediately packed my bag, and began hurrying Francesca. But this made her dawdle all the more. At last she said there wasn't time to see Kofi, and he was so boring what was the point?

"I have to see him," I said.

He was a man in his late twenties, with the sort of protruding teeth that gave him an amiable expression. He laughed each time he spoke, and everything he said was a compliment. "You are so young. You are so handsome. When Francesca told me you were a professor I imagined an old man. But not a smartly dressed young lad—"

Was this what Francesca meant by boring? I found it worse than that. I wanted to tell him to shut up. I said, "What ministry are you with?"

"Ministry of Works." He smiled. "It is all bribery and corruption. That is the African way. It is hopeless."

"The roads are in rough shape in Accra."

He laughed very hard in a mirthless way.

"In Accra they are good! You should see the rest of the country!" His laugh went *ark-ark-ark* like Francesca's fan. "The minister steals money and gives it to his wives. He has four wives. He has a house in London. He is a devil." He laughed again.

"You don't sound angry."

"Why be angry? Life is short. We say 'Be happy—don't worry.' You are in Africa, my young friend. Have a drink. It is New Year's Eve."

He took a bottle of beer from a crate on the floor and opened it. He splashed some beer on the threshold. "That is a libation," he said. "For the gods."

"Which gods?"

"All of them."

He filled three glasses.

All this time Francesca was sighing—a sort of audible boredom. We drank a little and Kofi emptied the last of the bottle of beer into my glass. It was very bad for the host to drink the last of the beer, he said.

"I thought they were out of beer in Accra. How did you get it?"

"Bribery and corruption," he said. *Ark-ark*. "I will get you some crates. As many as you want. Leave it to me, my friend."

There was a murmur in the next room. Kofi yapped in his own language, a sort of crow-squawk, and a woman appeared. She was about fifteen years old, and wrapped in a pink cloth; she was pregnant and perspiring.

"This is my lady wife, Mr. Endro," Kofi said. "She doesn't speak English. Just a simple village girl."

She was barefoot, and breathless from the heat. She dabbed her face.

"When is the baby due?"

"One month or so," Kofi said. "It will be our first child. You can be godparents. Or uncle and auntie."

Francesca sighed again, but Kofi did not seem to mind. He was flattering, obtuse, full of promises and compliments. He never sat down. He walked up and down, laughing in his croaky way, urging us to drink more. He was much cheerier than the rather solemn-looking Ugandans I was used to. But he was repetitious, and I wondered whether he were drunk. He was scathing about the Ghana government. "They are like vultures," he said. "There will be another coup, oh sure," and he told me—laughing the whole time—how Nkrumah had misgoverned the country.

"I'd like to meet someone in the government," I said.

"Sure. The minister? The perm sec? The deputy minister? I can arrange it for you. Have another cup of beer, please."

Everything seemed so easy. An hour with a politician or civil servant was just what I needed. I could see someone at the American Embassy ("A western diplomatic source told me"), and talk to people at the market in Accra, or other friends of Francesca's; and I would have my article about Ghana, which would be my air fare for this month of travel.

"Any of them," I said. "All of them. I just want to ask a few questions. Listen, are you sure you can fix it up?"

"Leave it to me. I can fix it up." He seemed to be trying out my words, making them his own. "When you come back from Kumasi give me a tinkle and I will fix it up."

He uttered two crow-squawks at his wife, who stopped dabbing at her perspiring face and tramped heavily out of the room. She returned with two bottles of beer.

"I've had enough," I said, and snatched my glass off the table.

"This is a present," he said. "You take them with you. Happy New Year. African custom."

"We don't want it," Francesca said, bluntly, snapping her jaws at him.

"But the young man wants the beer," Kofi said, winking at me.

Francesca was annoyed, and it showed. But Kofi seemed not to notice, or perhaps he didn't care.

"You are welcome here," Kofi said. "We respect teachers in Ghana. They are like gods to us. We are thirsty for education."

On the road to Kumasi, I said, "You weren't very polite to him."

"Kofi? He is like an Italian," Francesca said. "He thinks only of himself."

"If he gets me an interview with the minister I'll forgive him for anything."

After a long silence Francesca said, "Sometimes you say such stupid things."

I was driving the Fiat now. The little car strained on the rising roads—but the road was better than I had expected. Contrary to what Kofi had said, as soon as we left Accra the road had improved. We entered a higher and more wooded region. But the foliage was messy and cluttered, a disorderly forest of broken and hanging trees and dense bamboo. The birds were frenzied, and every hundred yards or so there was a dead dog in the road, some of them plump and bleeding, but most of them old and as stiff as mats. The roadside huts matched the trees and had similarly shaggy roofs. What houses I could see—the more solid buildings—were stained and cracked.

I compared what I saw here with what I knew in Uganda and Malawi. My Africans seemed more sensible and quieter, and the woods and forests more orderly, the roads in better repair. I could put that in the article.

I was so intent on thinking of the article and driving the car that I did not speak for a long time, and then I started talking, and as I did—asking questions and answering them myself—I realized that Francesca had not said a word for half an hour. Her face was averted.

"Are you sulking?"

"No," she said. "But I wish I hadn't taken you to see Kofi."

"Why? Because he ignored you?"

"He didn't ignore me," she said quickly. "But did you see how he treated his wife?" She mimicked someone spitting. "They're all like that."

I drove on. Ramshackle forest. Goats. Men on bikes. Mammy wagons.

She said, "I didn't realize until I saw you two together how much I disliked him."

"And how much you like me?" I said, intending to tease her.

"I do like you, Andre. You know that. Sometimes I think the feeling is stronger than liking you." She frowned and turned away.

I put my hand on her knee. "You know I love you."

"Don't joke about it," she said. "It's bad for me to like you so much." She faced me and said crossly, "I want more than this!"

"So do I." I meant it, and I said it with such force that she turned to me again and touched my face tenderly and let me kiss her hand. She snuggled closer and let my fingers drift between her thighs.

"This is the bush."

"I like the bush," I said.

The shaggy roadside woods were a preparation for shaggy Kumasi. It was a green town with sloping streets and small shops and municipal buildings plastered with red dust. Its trees were shapeless, like gigantic weeds on long stalks, though there were prettier ones, like tall feathers. We arrived as it was growing dark, and found the Royal Hotel where we registered as man and wife. There was no beer available at the hotel, so we drank the bottles that Kofi had given us.

The hotel smelled of dampness and dead insects. The wood squares of the parquet floors had worked loose. We ate mutton and boiled vegetables in the empty dining room.

The waiter said in a reproachful way, "It is New Year's Eve. The people are all at the parties in the bars and nightclubs."

We heard the shouts and the music from down the street.

"What shall we do?"

Francesca said, "Come upstairs and I'll show you."

I had never known her so amorous. We did not leave the bedroom until after midnight. Drunken men were staggering and singing in the street. We went back to the room and made love again, and then slept until noon.

That day we drove to the palace. I said, "It doesn't look like a palace." We went to the museum. It was shut. So was the market. Without people, the streets and shops looked dirty and ugly.

In bed that night Francesca said, "I thought Africa would be darker. More dangerous and mysterious. Sometimes I want to leave—just go away before I start to hate them."

She held me tightly. I wondered what it would be like to travel with her. When she was amorous she was like a child. I liked that—having a lover, a daughter, a wife: one woman. And I liked the thought that she was strong, that I could depend on her.

"Happy New Year," I said. That I was with her on this day— surely that was significant? "We'll have to get used to saying nineteen sixty-eight."

Francesca hugged me and said, "I'm happy, Andre."

It was just dawn the next morning when I sat up, thinking I wanted to take a piss. I felt a familiar itch—a thread of irritation—inside my penis. I squeezed it, holding it like a toothpaste tube, and a gob of thick yellowish fluid collected on its tip. I rolled over and cursed.

Francesca threw her arm around me.

"Don't," I said, and shrugged. "I have some kind of infection."

We found a Ghanaian doctor in Kumasi. He sat me down and put on plastic gloves and examined me. He asked me some simple questions.

"It is gonorrhea," he said. "Don't worry"—he was writing a prescription—"this will clear it up. Are you married?"

"No," I said.

Francesca had waited in the car. I got in and said, "He says I've got VD."

She crossed her legs, but said nothing.

"I know where I got it," I said, trying to control my voice. "What I want to know is where did you get it?"

She began to cry. And then I knew, and I saw him clearly, his buck teeth, his bulging eyes. I remembered all his promises, and how she had said nothing.

I put the car into gear—it was such a little car. We tottered towards the coast.

"Where are we going?" she asked.

"Nowhere," I said.

4.

"You must drink," the African man next to me said. We were on the flight from Accra to Lagos. Bottles of beer were being handed out to the passengers. "You must have one or two."

The doctor in Kumasi had told me not to—alcohol reduced the effectiveness of the penicillin.

"I can't," I said. I still itched.

"Can't *drink?*" He grinned at me in contempt, showing all his front teeth.

"I'm an alcoholic," I said. "If I have one drink I'll want to have another. And then I'll get drunk and totally screwed up."

"Yes! Yes!" he said eagerly, laughing hard, and pushing a bottle at me. "Go on!"

"And then I'll vomit," I said.

He was wearing a new suit. His hand went to his lapels, which he smoothed, as he laughed again, but in a discouraged way. "I understand," he said.

He was an economist. Feeling I had nothing to write about Ghana, I pressed him for his views on Nigeria—he was a lecturer at the University of Ibadan. He was very precise in his figures, and mocking in his manner. When he told me how Nigeria financed its industrial projects he spoke in a voice that was both gloating and complaining.

"You want to know the terms of reference of this little exercise?" he said. He drank and wiped his mouth. "The company pays over the odds in order to establish itself. The minister concerned takes a twenty-percent cut—and he sends this money to London or New York. The company has an exclusive license, so it pushes its prices up. When the minister sees the profits he demands his share. That's how it goes on. The companies and the politicians are conspiring against the people." He smiled at this. "Neocolonialism is not just an empty term. It has an actual meaning. No matter how much money this country makes it will always be poor. Nothing will change. In financial terms we were better off under the British."

"But in political terms Nigeria is freer, isn't it?"

He laughed at this. "We have had two military coups!"

"I thought Nigeria was more unified now."

"There is going to be a war here," he said, dropping his voice. "In the east—Ibo land. Don't go there. It's not political, and it's not about money. The Ibos are fighting for the most important thing—their lives."

"How do you know this?"

"I am an Ibo," he said. "And what do you do?"

"I'm a teacher," I said. "In Uganda."

"Are you on holiday?"

It was always foolish to mention writing or journalism in Africa, so I said, "Sort of. I'm also seeing a friend."

"I thought all the foreigners left after the last coup."

"My friend is a Nigerian," I said.

"God help you!" he said, and he laughed so loudly that several people turned to stare at him.

And then the plane was descending, streaking past mud huts and junked cars and the scrappy rooftops of small shacks.

The economist hurried out of the plane. I thought: *He's not real.* The next day, talking to other Nigerians—editors, a re-

porter, a publisher's representative—and a U.S. Embassy official, I had the same thought, that they were not real either. They
were acting. Their actual lives were hidden from me, but for my
benefit they had cast themselves in the colorful role of writers
or businessmen or teachers or tribesmen. In each public person
was a smaller stranger person who bore no resemblance at all
to the one I saw, and I was always on the point of demanding
Who are you? or *Who do you think you are?* when I remembered,
with a little shock, who I was.

I had not seen Femi for a year. I had never thought I would see
her again. I did not want to startle her and so, instead of calling
her, I called her brother George. This was after I saw the editors
and officials, for the sake of my article.

George appeared at my hotel. He was so black and smooth he
seemed to be wearing a second skin: he was like someone else
within that slippery skin—but who?

"Come, we will have a drink!" He was hearty, expansive,
energetic. He would not look me in the eye. We went to a noisy
club five streets away. That was the strangeness of Lagos. From
a fine, expensive hotel it was a short walk to a dangerous slum.
There were prostitutes in the club—tall skinny girls in tight
skirts, wearing orange and blonde wigs.

George shouted for two beers, and when they were brought
and we touched glasses his eyes met mine and he lost his smile.
"I am very sorry for what happened," he said.

I could see this was going to be an impossible conversation.
His mood was somber and apologetic, but the place was noisy—
brass band, people dancing and flailing their arms, old women
shrieking. I had to ask him to repeat that sentence, and the
second time, shouting it so that I would hear it, he sounded
insincere. But I knew he was not.

"The family is very ashamed!" he yelled.

"Let's not talk about it."

"We found the boy! We beat him! We took some money!"

"I can't hear you," I said, shaking my head. But I could, and
I didn't want to.

"Why are you not drinking your beer?"

"I'm sick!" The symptoms were gone but I was still taking the
penicillin.

George smiled: he didn't understand. He went on shouting.

I pretended I couldn't hear him through the music and the noise, and at last he gave up.

Eventually he said, "Femi wants to see you."

It was what I wanted to hear. I stood up, and George followed me outside.

As soon as we had left the noise of the club and were in the street, George changed. The apologies were over. He laughed at the heavy traffic and the horns. He told me he was planning to study engineering in Kaduna. He talked about his own life. And he seemed relieved to be talking about something other than Femi—that talk was lost and forgotten in the twanging music and the shadows of the club. He was no longer hearty. He looked depleted; he was quiet. After all that effort he had nothing more to say.

George had given me Femi's address without telling me where it was. The taxi driver snorted when I told him, and he drove for an hour, never leaving the same ruined road. It was midday, and we went slowly in a line of contending cars, past low buildings and daubed signs. Did it look familiar to me because the whole of Lagos looked chaotically the same? It was an ugly place. Its noise and heat seemed like other aspects of the same disorder. That—the ruin—was real. Everything else was unreal. It was not a city, the money was worthless, the food was bad, the air stank, the poorest people were extravagantly dressed in bandannas and bright robes, with turbans and sashes and crisply folded togas.

It was the way Femi was clothed. Her turban matched her gownlike dress, the purple and white cloth shot through with gold thread; and there was something Egyptian in her bearing, the way she held herself, all that cloth wrapped neatly on her head, and even in her features, slanted and slightly hooded eyes and full lips and rising cheekbones—pharaonic. She was like a black cat wrapped in gold cloth.

That was how she looked when she shoved aside the rag that hung in place of a door. A chicken ran out from behind her, its head down, clucking madly.

Her village—if it was a village—was near the airport. It was part of the continuous ruin by the roadside. The planes roared low overhead, landing, taking off, leaving a smell of diesel fuel in the hot air. Gray soap bubbles and gobs of toothpaste ran in a trickle of wastewater through a furrow in the dirt and gurgled into a ditch—a lovely sound that made me look at the nauseating thing. Femi's hut was made of paper and planks and flattened oil cans. But she was a beauty.

We didn't kiss—we shook hands: her mother was there. Her mother did not speak English, and so she was especially attentive. She was also dressed in a lovely gown, with a shawl and a drooping headdress. She watched us closely while we were standing in the dusty hut, but as soon as we sat down on opposite sides of the room she seemed to lose interest and she drifted away.

"So, where are you coming from? George said London. I said hah!"

"I was in London for Christmas."

"Sometimes even Nigerians go to London for Christmas," Femi said. She had heavy lidded eyes that became absolutely unseeing when she was scornful. "I think it is a bloody waste of time."

"Where would you go."

She looked up, becoming interested again. "Maybe to Ikeja."

She was from Ikeja.

"Or maybe to Uganda."

I had hoped she wouldn't say that.

"Everyone misses you," I said.

"The people are very primitive, but it is a pretty place," she said. "I remember the bush. The people are so backward there. That is why they are friendly. Bush people—"

A plane went overhead, perhaps taking off, perhaps landing. It drowned the rest of her words. She finished her sentence with a shrug.

"You like it better here?"

"Cities are better," she said. "I don't like it here. But this is my mother's house. I came here after the surgery and just stayed."

I almost asked *What surgery?* until it struck me what the euphemism stood for.

She stared at me. She was theatrically dressed, as for an opera or a pageant of some sort, something unreal; but the things she said were factual. They cut deep and made me remember.

"How is your life?" she asked.

"Moving right along," I said. "And yours?"

"Not so bad. I'm still weak," she said. "I thought I would never stop bleeding. They said to me that sometimes people die of it. That's what they told me afterwards."

Her lids grew heavier and made her haughty again and more pharaonic as she raised her head.

Her mother reappeared. She had a skull-like simian face, the color of shoe leather and just as dry and full of creases. She entered laughing softly and set a bottle of orange soda onto a plate. She produced two glass tumblers from a cloth, and wiped them with the cloth, and poured the orange soda into them, taking her time and laughing, not hearing anything but watching with wet reddened eyes.

"Why didn't they tell me before? That people die of it?" Femi said.

The mother had distracted me from what Femi had been saying, and so I asked a simple question and then regretted it as soon as Femi answered.

"Because they can't stop the bleeding," Femi said. "And I lost so much blood I was fainting all the time. I took iron tablets. I am still anemic."

"God, those planes are noisy," I said, as another roared past, making the flimsy walls of the hut vibrate.

"And my family was ashamed of me," Femi was saying.

"But that's over now. You can finish your studies."

Femi looked away. She wasn't listening to me. She said, "When I left this place to be with you in Uganda they were so happy. It was such an adventure. They were proud of me. George was boasting about me." She frowned and said, "And me, I was happy as well."

I said quickly, "It wasn't my fault."

"And when I came back so soon they were just sulking like hell." She touched her turban, steadying it with a long red fingernail and said, "I did not think I would come back. It is horrible to go back when you don't want to."

"I didn't want it, Femi."

"It was very hard," she said. "And then it was worse. I mean, then I had to go to the village."

"Which village?"

"Where they do these things. Where they cut you. Where the old woman was living. She was big and fat. She cut me. That is why I was bleeding."

As she said *bleeding* another plane went over. It became a drone and a dog barked crazily, choking on its barks. The air in Femi's hut smelled of dampness and heat and of the ditchwater with the toothpaste and soap scum that stood bubbling beside the hut.

"You didn't have to go to the village," I said.

"But I wanted to finish my studies."

"Did you start in September?"

She half closed her eyes. It meant no. "I was still bleeding then."

I hated this conversation. It was like visiting—not a hospital but a leprosarium or a village of sick people. There was a pathetic stink of neglect in the air.

But what else could she say? This incident was all that linked us now. She had visited me in Uganda, and after a month with me she said she was pregnant—two months pregnant, the doctor said. At first I had said, *That's impossible.* But I was wrong. She had another life, and so she had returned to it, and I had tried to forget about her.

I had visited her out of friendship, but I did not want to hear this.

"And the boy didn't give me enough money, so my father paid for it."

"I would have given you the money."

"Why should you? It was not your problem."

That was true.

"It was the other boy."

She was twenty-one, but we were all boys to her. It had made me feel like a boy but it had turned me into a man—and it had turned her into a woman. Yet she wasn't bitter. Her manner was still dismissive and haughty.

"The other boy was getting married. He was from Onitsha, an Ibo. And these days he is fearing about the fighting. There is trouble in the eastern region. It is all shit. I want to go away. Are you angry?"

I shook my head: no.

"White people look angry much of the time," she said.

"I'm not angry, honey."

"But I made you sad," she said. As she changed position on the chair her gown shifted and the purple and gold tumbled over her knees. "I was sad. And I was sick, too."

There were dogs and children bawling outside, as though competing or quarreling, the mutts and the kids, and with this racket was a jangling of tin plates.

"Maybe you can come to Uganda sometime for a visit," I said.

She smiled, but it was a sad smile, and she made a noise that sounded like no.

"I think you will be happy in the future time," she said. Her face twisted like a little girl's, frowning, and she looked funny and glum, not wanting to be pitied.

When she made that face I was reminded of how I had loved her, how she had seemed solid and patient and tender; and how I had hated to see her go. The worst of it was that she had blamed herself for it all, and that she had been brokenhearted, facing her family.

"You'll be happy, too," I said.

"I never will be," she said. "But I can try."

Her mother put her head through the ragged curtains and chattered at us, urging us to drink the orange soda.

"She thinks I am stupid. When you go she will criticize me."

"Then I won't go," I said.

"You must go," she said flatly. "I don't care about this old woman, my mother. She wants me to be someone's wife and have children and get beaten by my husband."

And then I began to ache, and to wish that I could take her back with me. But it was too late. We had had our chance and had made a mess of it.

"They all say, 'Where is your beautiful Nubian?' "

"Those stupid people," Femi said, and she laughed. She was pleased. "What is a Nubian?"

"It is a tall black woman with a lovely long neck, from the Sudan."

"The bush!" she said, and made a dismissive click with her bright teeth.

"Have you got a girl now?"

"No," I said. "No one."

"You can find one," she said. "If you have trouble I will find one for you." And she laughed again at the absurdity of it. "A nice village girl who will cook your meals and be very quiet. One that is a bit primitive and obedient."

"Like you?"

"Oh, no!" And she laughed again. "I am a modern girl. I like the fast life—music and dancing. I like reading books, too. I listen to the wireless. I use lipstick."

"I want one like you."

"That is nice," she said, nodding her head and then elevating it in pride, becoming a Nubian. "That is a nice thing to say." She smiled at me. "I am glad you said that, because when you leave I am going to be sad again."

"Don't you have a friend?"

She closed her eyes briefly: no. "That stupid boy got married in Enugu, and he is afraid to come here because there is going to be a war." She sighed and said, "I would like to go away in a plane"—one had just gone overhead—"but I think I never will. I can forget the other thing, because it is in the past. But I get afraid when I don't know what is coming."

I was glad when her mother returned and pressed me to eat, because the rest was ritual. I ate—steamed yams and stew, while the mother and daughter served me, saying nothing. They brought me a basin of water; I washed my hands; I said I had to go—I had an appointment at the Ministry of Information, for my article, that didn't include any of this.

Femi walked with me to the road. Dressed in her robes, she seemed especially tall and stately, with her fine turban and the bangles on her wrists, and her haughty eyes. The wrecked huts were all around us, and the mangy dogs and dirty children, and the tin shacks and the planes overhead screeching so loudly that when at last we kissed she exclaimed and her words were lost. I could not hear her, but she was laughing, and I wished I knew why.

5.

At dusk in Kampala, in the district of Wandegeya where I lived, all the bats—thousands of the mouselike things—flew squealing from the tall trees by the swamp and darkened the sky. That was how night fell every day in bat valley.

From my taxi I saw them rising like shreds of soot, little fluttering smuts. I had just arrived back from Lagos, after that long Christmas trip. I looked up and saw the bats, and stared at them. The sight was not threatening. It was something that occurred every day in Wandegeya. So I knew where I was. It wasn't horrible—I was home.

My apartment smelled of my parrot, Hamid, the plastery odor of his droppings. The bird made a bubbly growl when he saw me, and I let him out of his cage and smoothed his gray feathers and stroked his beak. He flapped around the room for a while, and then settled down, gnawing the spines of my books. There was plenty of food in his bowl, and his cage was clean, so I knew that Jackson had been feeding him.

I was restless, and yet I had no desire. I was still infected, still taking penicillin. I saw there were cockroaches in the pantry—dozens of them, from the food that Jackson had left. A moldy loaf of bread and an open bag of flour were covered with roaches. I wondered whether I should fire him. He had a habit when he was in a hurry of sweeping garbage into a kitchen drawer and forgetting about it. That drawer was the origin of our roaches.

I walked down to the Young Hok Grocery and the Chinese owner sold me some roach spray. After a satisfying hour of killing cockroaches and sweeping them up I unpacked my bag, made a stack of dirty laundry and looked over the books I had bought in London, Frantz Fanon's *The Wretched of the Earth*, Conrad's *The Secret Sharer,* and an old copy of *Tarzan of the Apes.*

Reading *Tarzan* and drinking gin I dozed on the sofa and then dragged myself to bed. It was not until I woke the next morning that I reflected on what had happened to me over the previous three weeks: staying with Prasad, my affair with Rosamond, catching the clap from Francesca, and seeing Femi again. I lay in bed turning it over in my mind, wincing when I remembered mentioning marriage to Rosamond, angry at the thought of Francesca introducing me to her venereal Ghanaian, and depressed at the thought of Femi wearing her finery in her dusty hut, and *I am still bleeding.* A week here, a few days there, an afternoon, a long night: it had all been hectic, but I could not help thinking that it had been a failure. It was as though I had been to a party—a great whirl; and I had come home alone.

I stayed in bed, enjoying my loneliness, pitying myself in my solitude, and savoring the thought that I was in debt and would have to work hard to write three articles to pay for the trip. It was a week's work: it didn't worry me. My anxiety lay in all I was hiding—concealing Francesca and the gonorrhea behind an essay on Ghanaian politics, and never letting on that in between my visits to Nigerian ministries I had seen Femi looking stately in her slum. And I would write something about England without mentioning Rosamond or S. Prasad. I hated conniving at what was unreal, and yet the concealment also fascinated me. I was not sure whether these different women and the odd and inconvenient events of their lives were more important and truer to the world than any of the stuff I wrote. Anyway, I suppressed it and kept it as my secret, and so it was like a parallel history in private. I sometimes suspected that it was vastly more important than anything that I had made public, but that it accumulated far too fast for me to make sense of it. Much better for the moment to write these articles and to continue my novel about Yung Hok, the Chinese grocer, another solitary man.

I was happiest in this divided mood when I was speaking another language. Jackson came in and said, *"Habari gani, bwana?"*

And I replied in Swahili. That other unreal self was let loose to be a bwana and jabber about his trip. I crouched inside him and looked around at the world.

I went to my office at nine. Veronica, the Muchiga secretary, brought me a cup of coffee and asked me if I would please dictate a letter to her.

"I want to take the examination, Mr. Anderea. I must improve my speed."

I dictated a letter to the prime minister of Uganda, objecting to the practice of female circumcision in the eastern region.

"You are very rude, Mr. Anderea," Veronica said, as she scribbled the shorthand notations. She then typed it on the letterhead where I was named, *Andrew Parent, B.A., Acting Director, Adult Studies Institute.*

"We Bachiga have no female circumcision," Veronica said, watching me make corrections in her typing.

"No, but you have your delightful Urine Ceremony."

She gave me an earthy smile. It was she who had described the ceremony to me—the new bride putting her naked bottom on the hands of all her husband's brothers and pissing, to seal the bond.

"I think you also have funny customs," she said.

"Really, Veronica?"

"Europeans like to have toilets inside their houses," she said. "I think it is very unclean."

"I agree."

She went away, giggling at her audacity, and I swiveled my chair around, so that I could look out the window.

In the big splintered tree on the lawn outside my office there were gray herons nesting—I saw the mother heron shoving food down the open beaks of her fledglings. Beneath the tree the gardener was whacking clumps of weed with a sickle. He wore incredible rags that had once been trousers, and an overcoat from the King's African Rifles, and a torn hat. He was perspiring and wiping his face with a brown rag. His bare feet were as big and as cracked as a pair of shoes.

Sitting in the shade of the hedge were the students who had stayed for the holidays—classes had not yet begun. I recognized Francis Omolo, a purplish man from West Nile, who had all his bottom teeth knocked out, according to the custom of his tribe; Mr. Kato, the schoolteacher from Trans-Nzoia, on the Kenya border; Chango Muwenga, who wore a Mao button; and an undersized man named Mgubi who lived on the other side of the Mountains of the Moon, among the pygmies of Bundibugyo. They stayed here, because it was too far to go home. They had books, but they sat on them. The grass was damp.

At the edge of the lawn were bamboos and weaver birds madly shrieking in their nests. I could hear the bicycle bells and car horns and the buses changing gear beyond the hedge; and I could just see the white minarets of the Ismaili mosque on a distant hill. Looking out this window I tried to call up the sight of the cold gleaming streets of London, but it wouldn't come. I could only see Rosamond, her fur hat and long coat, and I felt vaguely disatisfied that we had parted so coldly. Yet I could not imagine her here—or Francesca either. I could not imagine this place, or myself, any different. Africa was what it was—permanently unformed. It was clay that never hardened. It was much better for someone far away to think about it and picture it than for that person to come here and be disappointed by the broken streets and the noise and its incompleteness. And what would they make of the bats? The name was enough. I envied people who had never seen Africa.

I scribbled a memo, *Books set in Africa by writers who had never been there. Tarzan, Henderson the Rain King, The Unbearable Bassington and* . . . Veronica interrupted me with another cup of coffee, and I briefly felt happy, understanding that I was having difficulty writing my novel about the Africa of the Chinese grocer because it was an Africa that had never been described before. How could I make that unexpected man believable? How could I make this real—the sunlight flooding my office and fading my books and yellowing the stack of curled-up letters on my shelves? "Acting Director" was right. I was just a caretaker, helping this place along, keeping it dusted. No one expected very much, because this was Africa. None of us was under any pressure at all. We could never succeed, nor could we fail. I had a job here, though I didn't belong. I felt like Yung Hok, the Chinese grocer.

As I stirred my coffee, the bursar rang. He said, "Have you been away?"

I said no, just to see whether he would challenge me—after all, I had been away almost a month. He laughed—three quacks.

His name was Mr. Wangoosa. He was a member of one of those churches who believe you are either saved or damned. He was saved; I was damned—he had made that plain enough to me the first time we had met, so I felt no need to be polite to him. He had already consigned my soul to Hell.

He asked me for the list of new students.

I said I didn't have the list, and thought: What new students?

"I reckon you have masses in the pipeline," he said.

That was the current expression for being busy. I said, yes, though I did not have anything at all in the pipeline.

I went home for lunch after that, walking slowly in the sunshine and cutting through the heat. Jackson had fried some bananas and made a curry.

He said in Swahili, "I told the cook upstairs about your safari in Europe and what you said about West Africa—that it is no good. He was very excited to hear it."

"Good," I said. I was eating, and he was hovering over me. "Do you know there are cockroaches in the kitchen?" I didn't know the word for roaches—I used the all-purpose word for insects, *doodoos.*

"I will kill them completely," he said, making a murderous swipe with his very large hand. "What food do you want to eat for dinner?"

"No dinner tonight, Jackson."

"Please give me some money," he said. "Twenty shillings."

He had broken teeth and bloodshot eyes and a torn shirt and long skinny arms. He crushed the twenty shilling note in his hands and touched it to his forehead.

"That woman Miss Rashida came looking for you," he said. "I told her you were on safari in Europe. She will come back."

He left and I lay on the sofa, thinking about Rashida, and how complete this life was: a job, a house, a salary, and friends—even a girlfriend. When I was away I had forgotten it all; and if I had stayed away I might never have remembered that I had a real life here.

There was an Extra Mural class in the afternoon, one that had nothing to do with the Adult Studies Institute. This class had been organized by my predecessor, another acting director. It was called English for Diplomats. The students were all embassy personnel in Kampala—a Greek, a Rwandan, an Egyptian, two Chinese, and the Italian ambassador. It was regarded as a coup to have an ambassador in the class, and as long as he attended we kept it going.

The Chinese were from the People's Republic, Mr. Chen and Mr. Sung. They wore Mao suits and they hardly spoke a word of English. Mr. Solferini the Italian was a dapper and very courtly man who had lived in Somalia for twenty years. His English was poor but he was rich in gestures. He urged me to go to Somalia. It was a good place for hunting. Mogadishu, he said, and kissed his fingertips. Leopards, wild pigs, rabbits, birds. The rest of the class listened and watched. They were very shy.

Usually we practiced speaking lines of a dialogue that I wrote on the blackboard. Today it was about borrowing money.

"I waant to bowrow zum mooney frem yo, plis," Mr. Solferini said.

"Da iss da seko tie dis wik you ha as-kid me dat," Mr. Chen said.

"I nid eet forr an aimairgency," Mr. Solferini said.

"Emergency," I said.

"Hay-mergency," he said.

The rest of the diplomats listened with apprehension, fearful that I would ask them to speak. But everyone took a turn: that was the routine. They did so, stammering, trying to keep their dignity.

After the class Mr. Chen and Mr. Sung lingered and presented me a copy of Volume One of *The Selected Works of Mao Tse-Tung* and a recent issue of *China Reconstructs,* with a portrait of Mao on the cover.

"Maybe you can teach me to speak Chinese," I said.

They laughed nervously at this.

"I would like to go to China," I said.

"China, yes!" They had no idea what I was saying.

When I spoke again they looked panicky, and bowed, and hurried away.

It seemed I was always talking to people who hardly knew English. But I did not mind, and I was often glad of it, because I was able to preserve the monologue in my mind, and remember it. In London, speaking English all the time had tired me and made me lose track of time. It was another world. I had not been real there; and I had just passed through Ghana, and listened in Lagos.

I was happier here. Even the most exotic sights here—the bats, the herons, the Nubians with their teeth knocked out, the Dinkas' foreheads, which were bumpy with ornamental scars, or the muslim women in their black silk shrouds—were so familiar to me I found them restful. The Ugandan soldiers, always red-eyed and drunk, seemed to me odder and more dangerous. But they kept to their camps and their roadblocks in the bush.

The phone rang. It was the librarian, asking whether I had initialed the acquisition file. I said I was dealing with it. I liked being able to say that meaningless sentence and for the librarian not to care. He was an English homosexual who lived in an apartment block that adjoined mine. He called his African lover his house boy. Like me he was real when he was home.

All day I had been thinking about my articles—one about England, one about Ghana, one about Nigeria. If I had a good thought I could simply embroider upon it. I felt the excitement of having an idea that I had not set down—it was still fluid and provisional, ink that had not yet dried, like my life. I liked living in this temporary way.

When the office was empty and Veronica had gone home I started my England article on her typewriter, and filled a page. Then I put it away. Night had fallen, the bats had flown. Africa smelled differently at night—it was less dusty, and had the damp fragrance of flowers. But it was noisier at night—the screech of insects, the car horns, the shouts. *Rafeekee,* someone cried, calling his friend.

Rashida was waiting for me at my apartment, sitting on the steps, with her elbows on her knees.

She said, "Your cook said you had come back."

She spoke in Swahili. She was shy because I had been away, and she always spoke Swahili when she was nervous.

I said, "You look very pretty, *habibi.*"

She was about seventeen and small, with a funny malicious face and skinny legs. Her lipstick made her look like a tough woman but when it wore off at the end of an evening she looked like a child. Today she was wearing a red dress and high heels and a yellow shawl. Her cheap jewelry jangled and she looked lovely to me. She had large brown eyes and long lashes. She was proud of her Hamitic nose and thin face.

"Are you hungry?"

"I ate some bananas."

"What about a drink?"

We were still speaking Swahili, but she replied in English, "No beer. I don't want," as though to impress Allah with her indignation.

We went inside and Hamid began to squawk, imitating the squeaky door. Rashida called to him—*kasuku*, parrot.

"How long were you waiting for me?"

She shrugged—didn't know, didn't care.

"I want to go dancing," she said, and then coyly, "No jig-jig."

"First jig-jig, then dancing."

She just laughed and twisted her shawl tighter.

I poured her a glass of orange squash, and opened a bottle of beer for myself. Rashida drank in silence, and I distractedly examined the label of the beer bottle, the script of *Indian Pale Ale* and the emblem of a bell, from the brewery on Lake Victoria. I drank that one and another, glad that I had taken the last of my penicillin at breakfast.

Rashida was playing with the parrot, saying *Kasuku, kasuku.*

"Come here," I said, and switched off the light.

She got up shyly and sat beside me on the sofa. The curtains were open and the glimmer from outside was enough light. I hugged Rashida and ran my hands over her and kissed her. She primly kept her hands in her lap, and her knees together, and when I made a move to lift her dress she resisted. I laughed and kissed her again, and was aroused. It was the first time since Ghana that I had had any desire.

"Let's jig-jig, then we'll go to a nightclub," I said, and slipped my hand under her dress.

"You are a monkey," she said.

"Yes. I am a monkey."

"Tell me you love me."

"I love you," I said, and I thought: I am not real—this is playing, this is fun.

"I love you, *habibi.*" She kissed me, and then licked my face. She stood up and giggled and took her dress off, and folded it carefully on the sofa so that it wouldn't wrinkle. She was wearing a red slip, edged with lace that I had given her, and a pair of red shoes that were scuffed from all her walking. She yawned, twisting her slender body inside the flimsy slip, and I reached out for her. She dodged my hands and hurried into the bedroom on her clacking shoes.

Not then but later as she was leaving the bedroom to go to the toilet, she opened the door and paused and looked back at me. In the light from the hall she looked lovely—delicate and black, like a kitten, on her tiptoes. She said in English, "I am coming just now"—to reassure me that she wasn't running away—and I felt my desire for her returning in me, and thought: I am happy.

We made love again, and she was like a cat, biting my neck, clawing my back, and thrashing, weeping in her orgasm, until finally she shuddered and lay still.

"I am not finished," I said.

"What do you want?" she said calmly.

I told her.

"Do you love me?"

"I love you, *habibi.*"

She smiled and pushed me down tenderly.

After that, we went dancing at the Gardenia, until I was too tired to move. I dropped her at her house—just a hut near the Indian beauty parlor where she worked.

"I have no money," she whispered.

I gave her some, pretending to be drunker than I was. And this isn't real either, I thought.

The days passed. I went to my office and dictated letters to Veronica. I wrote my articles. She typed them. Mr. Wangoosa asked me about students and plans. "Everything's in the pipeline," I said. Nothing was in the pipeline, but each day had its events.

The parrot woke me with its squawks when Jackson uncovered its cage. Then I had breakfast—tea and papaya, and now and then Jackson fried me an egg. I read the *Uganda Argus* in my office, and at eleven went to the Senior Common Room for a coffee with the other faculty members. Back to my office, to sit and look at the herons, until lunchtime, usually at The Hindoo Lodge, with Neogy and Desai. If we had a curry we always went to the panwallah afterwards, and I walked home with a wedge of *pan* in my mouth, and spitting betel juice along Kampala Road. After a nap I went to the office again and answered the phone. "I'm dealing with it." "I'm studying the file." "It's in the pipeline." And then teatime flowed into sundowner time at the Staff Club, and I drank beer—often with Rashida—until I was drunk. *I love you, habibi,* we said.

Saturdays were simpler. I shopped at Yung Hok's, and then had a curry in town and drank all afternoon, until Rashida finished work. Then we danced and made love and slept until noon on Sunday, when the London papers went on sale at Shah's. One Sunday I read about the demonstrations in London and saw pictures of the angry students. I understood their anger, but I hated the unanimity of the mob. Rashida was fascinated by their heavy coats and hats, their beards and scarves. That Sunday, like all the rest, we spent the afternoon in the Botanical Gardens, and we finished the day in bed.

The bush-baby returned. It scratched on the screen and seemed to plead for food. I gave it fruit—soft melons and drooping bananas—and it was always eager for more. It clung to the window. I went on feeding it, but I never let it in. What would it do inside my room?

Rashida had no name for it except *nyama,* which meant meat or animal and was interchangeable. She was *nyama,* and so was I.

I kept my office hours; clocked in, clocked out, and drank, and made love to Rashida. I wrote my Yung Hok novel in my office, because there was no other work to do until the students came back. I could not imagine being happier. Kampala was a lovely place, of yellow-plaster shops under leafy trees; a small town scattered across seven rounded hills.

I read *Robinson Crusoe,* and felt it was like my life. I read *Tarzan* and felt the same. I read *Victory* and *The Secret Sharer.* I was the hero of every book I read.

I did not envy anyone, or want anyone else's life. I had everything I wanted. I could only imagine someone envying me. But I felt I was unlike anyone else on earth—not better, but different—and that, having just realized that, I had just begun to live. So my whole life was ahead of me. I was twenty-six years old.

Rashida laughed when I asked her about her plans for next week: the future hardly existed for her. Her laughter was genuine. It was absurd to contemplate the future. Her fatalism absolved me, and it took away all her questions.

But she was particular about her appearance—very conscious of her shoes and her dress. Her hair was always done—the other girls at work experimented on her. She mocked me for wearing sneakers with a suit, or a T-shirt with a sports jacket.

"You dress like an African in the bush," she would say, looking scornful.

Only appearances mattered. It was so easy to forget how much people cared about fashions in Uganda. If you wore the wrong clothes you were conspicuous. But this also made life simple. I had to remind myself that I was no more than a white man to anyone here—most of all to the other whites. So I kept all my secrets. I had a disguise that no one in Africa could crack: a white face.

One of those nights when Rashida laughed at my mismatched clothes we went to see *Thunderball,* a James Bond movie, at the Majestic. Rashida loved James Bond, and was thrilled by the fires and explosions and speeding cars in the movie. Afterwards we drifted to the Gardenia, and danced among the prostitutes and drunken men. Later, walking down Kampala Road I heard an inhuman shriek—like a monkey that had caught fire. It was an Indian boy being cornered by an angry African, Rashida said—*"Muhindi."* But she herself must have been part Indian—one of those in-between people in East Africa to whom no rules applied except the code of Islam. For a woman this meant obedience and prayers and no alcohol, though I never saw her pray.

The Indian's shrieks seemed to excite her. She hurried me to my apartment and took off her dress. She kissed me, and struggled, encouraging me. She had an eager way of touching me all over with her fingertips, and when she was most passionate I could feel the frantic bones beneath her flesh.

"Do you love me?"

"Yes. I love you."

And then she gasped, and devoured me.

"I do not want to go home," she said, afterwards. She was breathing hard, her eyes were bright.

There were two single beds, pushed together. We lay in the one nearer the window, where I always saw the bush-baby.

"I want to sleep here."

With that, she began to snore softly. She smelled of her hut, its dirt floor and its dog; of perfume and sweat and hairspray.

I woke to pandemonium—screams and alarms, car alarms, burglar alarms, a riot of bells and beeps. At first I felt I had caused it all, but I could not get out of bed to find out. The room seemed to twist in the darkness, the walls were brightly streaked from the lights flashing outside—what strange emergency was this, or was it a nightmare? I thought the room was going to fall on me. The gray ceiling whitened and seemed to ripple and bend towards me.

It was not a dream. It was an earth tremor, and it set off every alarm in the city. I lay there after the minute or so of the earth's movement and my room's twistings. I sweated and listened to the sirens. It had all passed, but I was afraid when I thought of it and how we might have died like that. I stayed awake, scarcely able to breathe. Rashida did not stir. It was Sunday. She slept until noon.

6.

There was no word in Swahili for it, or if there was no one knew it. We all spoke it badly there—it wasn't anyone's native language, and it was hardly a language at all, more like three hundred everyday words. "Earthquake" was not one of them.

But it did not need a name: everyone had felt it. The next day everyone was talking about it. One of the minarets of the Ismaili mosque had fallen down, and cracks had appeared in the parliament building, and on the stone porch of the Aga Khan School. The lights had short-circuited on the antenna at Wireless Hill. The statue of George V had been jogged off its plinth, and at the National and Grindlay's Bank a large mirror had shattered.

It was otherwise pretty harmless. Kampala was not a fragile town. So it was a thrill, and our pleasure of having lived through an extraordinary event resulted in a whole friendly day of perfect strangers talking to one another. "I thought it was thieves." "I thought I was drunk." "Did you see the mosque?"

Rashida had slept through it. She laughed at my attempts to describe it, because there was no word for it. I said the earth shook, and I tried to show her how it felt.

She said, "You are dancing," and laughed.

Her laughter annoyed me. It was not just the silliness of it, nor my feeling like a buffoon for doing a charade of an earthquake because I didn't know the word for it, nor my irritation that she had slept through it all. The fact was that she didn't care. Even if I had been able to make her understand she would not have cared and would probably have laughed. Her fatalism would have turned it into one of those things she always accepted.

For me it had been a nightmare. If I laughed I did so out of blind paralytic fear—my giggle like a death rattle. I might have died in that narrow bed with this snoring teenager beside me. It was not how I wanted to go—crushed and buried by the cinderblocks of Semakokiro House, the staff quarters, at the age of twenty-six. The memory of it frightened me. I had not known that cement walls could bend without breaking. I kept imagining bricks falling on my face.

Rashida said, "It was the wind."

For a moment I wanted to hit her for being so stupid. And then I saw how foolish it would be to hit her. An instant later I lost all interest in her. She was still laughing at me. I took her home to her hut.

I needed someone to share my fear with. But that evening there was no one on the streets. They were afraid of another quake. Most of the Africans felt it was a judgment—felt this not because they were ignorant savages from the bush but because they were Christians of a fairly forbidding type. The white expatriates did not have a better explanation.

I cruised in my car until the bats flew off, and then went back to Rashida's.

"She has gone out," a woman said from the depths of the hut.

Rashida always called this brown, serious woman "auntie," and I had surprised her in her old faded wraparound.

"Did she go alone?"

"No. With an Indian."

I was not jealous. I was cross with myself for having sworn that I was not going to see her tonight and then as a last resort dropping by, assuming she would be waiting. Why should she wait for me? I knew there was an Indian she liked—because he had a car and he took her dancing. He gave her lengths of printed cotton cloth from his shop, which she had made into dresses. Did he know I gave her fancy underwear?

It was very dark in Wandegeya, and it was quieter now that the bats had taken off. It was too late to go to the movies, too early to go home. I could have gone to the Hindoo Lodge but tonight I did not want to eat dinner alone. I saw some Africans peering through the back window of a shop, hanging on to the shutters and the bars, where inside an Indian family was watching *I Love Lucy*.

In this nighttime neighborhood anyone with electricity was conspicuous. You saw them through their windows because it was too hot for them to close their shutters. And when your eyes became accustomed to the darkness you could see the Africans by the roadside, standing or sitting, waiting for buses, roasting ears of corn, stirring peanut stew, staring back at you.

I hated driving at night, because of these wandering Africans on the road, and the cyclists and the dogs. Big dumb cows browsed by the roadside too. I sat in my car in the black night near Rashida's hut, not thinking of her, but only of the earth tremor and the way my ceiling had twisted and seemed to fall, and all those burglar alarms that had made my heart pound.

When there was nowhere to go and nothing to do in Kampala there was always the Staff Club. It was just a room in an old building that stood on its own under a drooping gum tree. It had been chosen for its isolation, because of the noise. There was music—a phonograph beside the bar. And there were always shouts, but friendly ones. The members felt happy and heroic for being misfits.

I saw some bright drunken faces under the lights, through the open windows. Three cars were parked in the long grass. As soon as I shut my engine off I heard the voices—not angry, just loud and boozy, someone contradicting someone else.

It was Crowbridge, shouting, but he stopped when I entered.

"Look who's here, our American friend, Bwana Parent," Crowbridge said.

"So you all survived the earthquake," I said.

There was a silence. Crowbridge said, "We're not talking about that. We're sick of hearing about it. If you want to talk about it you can bugger off right now, bwana."

"You're interrupting something, Andy," Potter said.

Crowbridge went on with his story.

I knew it was about a man named Hassett, who had left

Uganda at Independence, because Crowbridge said—he was speaking to Potter—"You remember his hangovers? He said if he could sleep till noon he'd be all right, but if someone woke him at eleven he'd suffer all day. Anyway, that bitch from Kololo we used to call the Marchioness of Gush was after him something chronic. She rang him up at half-past ten one morning. He had really tied one on the night before. He was still half full of alcohol. He got to the phone somehow and shouted into it, 'I do not take personal calls at my residence before noon, now please get off the line!' Bangs down the receiver."

Mungai and Okello laughed, thinking the story was over, but Crowbridge took no notice of them.

"A few days later he was going past the post office. You know how he was—the way all drunks are—different every hour of the day. At five o'clock he was positively friendly. There's the Marchioness up ahead with her two daughters, and they're all tits and teeth. Hassett says, 'Why hello there. I didn't realize that you had such a lovely family. Give me a ring sometime—I'm usually at home in the morning.'"

This time no one laughed. Potter yawned into his hand. Mungai and Okello looked apprehensive. Crowbridge went on drinking. He didn't seem to mind that his story had fallen flat. They were always telling stories about people who weren't there. As soon as you left they talked about you—what you had just said, or the way you looked, or how much you had drunk.

An African named Kwasanja was at the far end of the bar with Godby's wife—Godby nowhere in sight—talking to her in an aggrieved way.

"I didn't mind it when they called me black," he said. "But when they called me colored I hated it. I said to my landlady, 'What do you mean *colored?* What color, eh?' She did not know what to say. She was just some bloody working-class woman."

Godby's wife said without any feeling, "I'm a bloody working-class woman." Then she turned to me and said, "You haven't paid your bar bill."

She did not like me much. A year before, sitting together at the Staff Club—we were alone—I said, "Let's lock up this place and go to my house for a drink." She knew what I meant. But when I made love to her she howled, "Graham! Graham! Graham!" and I stopped, withdrew, couldn't go on. She punched me and began to cry with frustration, but what could I do?

Graham was her husband, a junior lecturer in the Geography Department.

Her name was Alma. She always wore big loose dresses, even though she was rather small. She chain-smoked, sitting hunched at the bar holding her cigarette like a monkey clutching a nut. I liked her indifference to things, the way she simply came along when I said, "Let's go." I had been shocked to hear her say her husband's name—surprised when she raised her voice. She sometimes brought her little baby to the Staff Club, and he sat drooling in a stroller while she drank. She had a degree in mathematics but was refused a job in the Math Department because the head of it, an old-timer named Tarpey, said he didn't want a bloody woman on the staff. So Alma did the bar accounts, adding up the chits we signed.

"It's about time you settled your bill."

"I've been away," I said. "England, actually."

"I don't believe you," she said. "You're not due for leave for another year."

"I wasn't on leave. I was on vacation."

"What a waste of money," Alma said. "You could've gone to Mombasa."

"Where's that poppsie of yours, Andrew?" Crowbridge said.

"I don't have a poppsie."

"That Nubian," he said.

"She's not a fucking Nubian," I said.

Potter said, "I think the really attractive ones are the Batoro. Fort Portal is full of crumpet."

"And Kabale as well," Kwasanja said. He was from Kabale.

They began one of the standard Staff Club discussions: which African women were the prettiest.

"Who's barman?" I said. "I'd like a beer."

Crowbridge stepped behind the bar and took a bottle of Indian Pale Ale out of the vibrating refrigerator.

"And a double gin for me," Okello said.

Pouring the second tot, Crowbridge held the almost empty bottle up for all to see, showing us that there was less than a tot swilling at the bottom.

"Barman's tot," he said, and added it to his glass.

"We should have real music," Potter said. "We should have food. We could do sandwiches. We could do a five-bob lunch."

"Bring it up at the next meeting," Alma said.

"I am buying you one bottle of beer," Okello said, moving to the stool next to Alma's and placing the bottle in front of her.

"Thanks very much, but you're not getting anything from me," Alma said. She was pleased with herself and sucked smoke out of her pinched cigarette.

Did she remember howling *Graham! Graham!* Poor Godby, everyone fucked his wife, while he was home looking after their baby. I had the impression that after all this drinking and screwing, the Godbys would go back to England and live a quiet little life in a place like Walton-on-Thames, as though nothing had happened.

People lived in a wild and reckless way here, but they seldom got hurt. Africa had a reputation for danger, but the worst of it was the boredom, the long nights, the yearning for something else, the stories I had heard before. Yet there was always Mombasa.

Crowbridge said, "I have to go. Who wants to be barman? Potter?"

"I will do it," Okello said, as Potter shrugged.

"Mind you sign the chits," Crowbridge said. "Don't make a pig's breakfast of it." And he left. I had not realized how drunk he was until I heard him start his car, and grind his gears, and go humping and bumping through the grass.

"You were in Nyasaland, Andrew, weren't you?" asked Potter, and without waiting for a reply, went on, "There's masses of patchouli there. The department needs some." He was in the Botany Department. "Know anyone there who'd send me some?"

I tried to think of someone. There was not a soul. I did not write to anyone there, I could hardly remember their names. The Americans were gone. The Africans I knew could barely write. I had left them all behind. I seemed to be going from world to world.

"There must be someone," I said, knowing there wasn't.

Kwasanja was singing to a record,

> *Malaika*
> *Nakupenda malaika*
> *Namini fa nyenye . . .*

Then he signed his chits and left—another drunken car, bumping through the grass.

Okello poured himself a drink from the newly opened bottle of gin. In the same motion he raised the bottle to his mouth and took a long swig, his Adam's apple pounding.

"Christ on a bike!" Potter cried.

"Barman's tot," Okello said, wiping his mouth with the back of his hand.

"You're signing for that, Festus!"

It was the first time I had ever heard Okello's Christian name.

Mungai said, "When I was in London they did worse things than that."

"This club is losing money," Potter said. "Ask Alma. She does the books. Is it funny, Alma?"

"I wouldn't know," she said. "I'm going home."

"And me, I am going," Okello said, following her through the door, to the darkness and damp grass.

Mungai said, "Over Christmas she wanted me to poke her. We went to Wireless Hill in my car. I tried, but I couldn't!"

"That's no way to talk about Alma Godby," Potter said. "You'd better be careful, mate."

"I am drunk," Mungai said. He was smiling, perhaps thinking of Alma in his car on Wireless Hill.

"That's no bloody excuse."

"I am going home," Mungai said, and staggered out.

"The bastard didn't sign his last chit," Potter said.

The song *Malaika* stopped. There was silence.

" 'Over Christmas she wanted me to poke her,' " Potter said angrily, mimicking Mungai. "What's wrong with these people?"

He began tidying the bar, putting bottles away, banging them down. I did not share his anger. I too had tried to poke Alma Godby.

"How did you know Okello's name is Festus?"

"He was a student of mine," Potter said. "They're all former students. Kwasanja read economics and did a degree in political science at LSE. Mungai was one of Peter's students. He's a bright chap. He drinks too much and he talks too much, but then," he smiled, "so do we all."

I took another beer out of the refrigerator, and opened it, and signed for it.

Potter was absorbed in the *Argus*. I tried to imagine what sort of students Okello and Kwasanja had been. Probably very hard-working and optimistic, preparing themselves for Uganda's independence and following the advice of their young teachers, Crowbridge and Potter. Now they were all drunks, taking turns with Alma Godby.

"Quiet tonight," Potter said, looking up from the paper.

"Where is everyone?"

"There's a jazz night in town," he said. "At that bar near the museum."

"What's a jazz night?"

"Loud music and cheap wine," Potter said. "Gramophone records. Waste of time, if you ask me."

He began filling his pipe, pushing tobacco in with his thumb. Then he paused, stared into space for a minute, and smiled.

"This is much cozier," he said.

He arranged his things on the bar counter, his tobacco and pipe, his matches, his knife, his tamper, newspaper, glass of gin, bottle of tonic; he was like a man working at a desk, becoming very orderly, the way some drunks in the club did.

I said nothing, only watched, remembering the earth tremor.

"Oh, yes. Festus was a very bright chap," he said. "Years ago."

He wanted to reminisce. He wasn't even thirty-five, and he was looking backwards.

I said, "Which bar near the museum?"

"Waste of time," he said. "Have a drink, Andy."

"I've got one, thanks."

I don't want to spend another night in this place, I thought.

Potter said, "Did you see Festus following Alma out the door?" He smacked his lips. "I can see him driving his hand smartly up her jumper."

Nor did I want to ponder that.

"I think I'll go down to the jazz club," I said.

Potter frowned. "I might as well go with you."

We went together in my car. The bar didn't have a name, but it was easy to spot—all the cars, all the music and noise. It was Dixieland music, and the bar looked like a little roadhouse anywhere in the world. We parked under a thorn tree and pushed through the crowd on the veranda—they were all talking about the earth tremor, what it had felt like, what they had thought it was. They had the tipsy hysteria of survivors, congratulating themselves that they were still alive.

At the bar Potter said, "Can't even get a bloody drink."

I saw a very pretty blonde, about twenty or so, talking to a big bald man on a settee against a wall. The man got up and went into the other room. I said to myself, Oh well.

I went over and sat down next to the blonde. She smiled at me, but more in surprise than in welcome.

"Hello," I said, and just saying that single word convinced me that I was drunk. "How about that earthquake—amazing huh?"

She sighed. She said with feeling, "It frightened me rigid. Everyone thinks it was so funny. I hated it."

I wanted her to say more—it was what I wanted to hear. To encourage her I said, "Hey, I was scared shitless."

"You're an American," she said.

"How did you know that?"

She smiled again, and then laughed softly.

I said, "Are you with anyone tonight?"

"Yes. He's just gone to the loo."

I said, "Then listen carefully. Meet me on the steps of the library at six-thirty tomorrow. Okay?"

She nodded, because the big bald man was approaching with a look of alertness on his face and that same tension was visible on his scalp, too. I excused myself and ducked out, amazed at my boldness.

On the way back, Potter said, "What did I tell you? Waste of time."

7.

I saw her through a break in the hedge, and I lingered because I was so relieved. She was sitting on the low steps of the library, smoking a cigarette. She did not have the thoughtful and vexed expression of a person waiting for a stranger, but rather she looked contented, with light on her face, the last bright sunshine before the sun dropped beneath the trees. In that moment before we met I had the irrational thought that we knew each other and were friends. Of course it wasn't true. It was a good feeling though—happiness and flickering hope. She was smiling.

She stood up and stamped on her cigarette when she saw me crossing the road. With the sun in her hair and in her summer dress she was very pretty. She was nearly as tall as me. She looked confident, and it was only when she spoke that I realized she was shy—but shy in an English way, watchful and formal and a little hesitant.

"Shall we get a drink somewhere?" I had asked her, trying not to stare at her.

And she was saying, Oh, yes—That's fine—Wherever you say.

I said, "What about the Veranda?"

It was a bar that adjoined the Speke Hotel.

"Isn't that expensive?" she said, and smiled again.

I was touched, because it wasn't expensive at all, but just another bar in a town that was full of them.

"You're a student," I said. Students were always thinking about money and economizing in bewildering ways.

"Yes. I'm getting a Dip Ed."

"And what are you going to do with it?"

"Go into the bush and teach," she said, with such eager independence that I felt excluded and already a bit abandoned.

At the Veranda we found a table under the trees, which had strings of lights in their branches. They were flame trees, and a blossom plopped on the table as soon as we sat down.

"Maybe I should wear it in my hair," she said, and picked it up and fixed it over her ear. She looked exotic.

Then she glanced into her compact mirror and frowned. "God, I look stupid!" She clawed it out of her hair.

The waiter brought us our drinks. She sipped hers and seemed detached and appreciative. I guzzled mine out of nervousness and said, "I didn't think you'd be there."

"I didn't think I would either," she said. "I'm fussy about being picked up."

"You must be. I mean"—I was still guzzling—"you let me pick you up."

"I had other plans but they fell through," she said.

There was not the trace of a smile on her lips.

"Really?" I said. "That bald guy? Was he busy?"

"He's actually very nice. He's an anthropologist, studying the Bwamba. He's frightfully het up about their circumcision ceremonies."

"So you were going to meet him, were you?"

She laughed and said, "Don't listen to me. I didn't have any other plans. I went to the dentist today and had a tooth pulled. To tell you the truth I didn't think I was going to make it to the library. But I'm glad I did." She took another sip of her drink. "I feel better already."

"I was glad to see you."

"You mean that, don't you?" She touched my hand, but casually, as though in a reflex, like touching wood for luck.

She inhaled the fragrance of the flowers around us and said how happy she was to be here.

"In this bar?"

"In Africa."

"Why is it that people in Africa are always talking about being in Africa?" I said. She did not reply, so I went on, "It might be nice to live somewhere else, in order to talk about something else."

"I came here to teach," she said. It sounded like a reproach, but it was the strength of her conviction that made it seem so. "I wouldn't want to be anywhere else."

I knew exactly how she felt: it was the way I had felt in Nyasaland, my first year.

She loved being in Africa. Very well, so did I. And so I chattered and boasted, trying to impress her, because I wanted to see her again. I was the acting director of the Institute, I said. I ran the place, I had eighty students and five part-time lecturers. I didn't tell her that everyone else had quit and gone home, that I was the only person left to do the job and as soon as a qualified African applied I would be replaced. I told her that we had regional centers all over Uganda and that I would shortly be setting off to visit them.

"I'd love that kind of job," she said. "One that involved traveling up-country."

"You're welcome to come along."

"You don't need my help," she said.

She was very firm—I admired her for it. But I was also wondering how it was possible to tempt her.

I could see that she had a definite objective—being in Africa, teaching in the bush, being independent. She was a free spirit, and she knew what she wanted. I could not be part of her plans. My job was here, in Kampala. And I had no other plans.

I was careful in my questions. I did not want to be disappointed by any of her replies. She said she was a Londoner; she had gone to Oxford; she liked Wordsworth and D. H. Lawrence; she was a socialist, her father worked for the Water Board, she had acted in various plays—Rosalind in *As You Like It* in a student production. This was just chat; I did not want to go any deeper and discover that she had a lover.

"Please let me pay my share," she said, when the waiter brought us the bill.

She meant it—it was another example of her insistence on being independent. I was impressed but a little uneasy—I wasn't used to women paying their way.

I said, "Do you want to see the best view in Kampala?"

She seemed puzzled but said yes, and I drove her to Wireless Hill. We parked on the edge of the summit and looked out at all the lights. This hill was a place for furtive lovers who had cars—there were two other cars parked nearby, and people embracing on the front seats of them. The lights were scattered in the bowl of the town, and behind the mosque and the cathedral and the illuminated mansions and monuments was the impenetrable blackness of the Ugandan forest on one side, and Lake Victoria in the distance, under a warm and pockmarked moon.

I kissed her, and we embraced innocently for a while, just holding on, as though consoling each other. I wanted more but I didn't know what to say.

Finally I said, "I really like you."

"You hardly know me."

"I know enough."

Then she relented. "I'm glad you like me," she said. "I like you too."

As she said it I saw that the car parked next to mine was Graham Godby's old Austin. Inside, Alma Godby's head was jammed against the rear window. An African with her, smiling with effort, his eyes popping, I saw very clearly was Festus Okello. They looked as though they were beating time to music with their wagging heads. But I knew better, and just as Alma's head seemed to flatten against the glass and slip down, I turned away.

It was embarrassing because it was predictable, the Kampala custom of getting laid on Wireless Hill. It was always adulterous expatriates, and I saw there was something selfish and routine about it. I had parked there many times in just that way—because this was where you took the person you couldn't take home; it was more secret than a borrowed apartment or the little hotel in Bombo that we called the knocking-shop. This was where an adulterer took someone to be safe from his mistress. It was one of the darker and more desperate places. I had once found that thrilling, but when I saw Alma and Festus in that trembling car I became flustered. It seemed to me a bad beginning for us.

I said, "I like you so much that"—thinking fast—"I don't want to sleep with you."

She was silent. Then she snorted. "What a strange thing to say. God, you're funny!"

"I mean, I'm happy being with you," I said, hurriedly. "I mean, for now. I mean, don't get me wrong. I'm very interested in sex."

She was looking out of the front window and smiling at the lights.

"That's very reassuring."

She had an English person's devastating knack for balancing a statement between irony and sincerity.

"Sometime we must try it," she said. "But it might help if you knew my name."

Her name was Jennifer—Jenny; though she didn't tell me until the next day. It was her way of teasing me and also of making me wait. This time I waited for her, at the swimming pool. She said she swam most days.

"Don't you?"

"I can't do it here," I said. "It gives me the creeps to stand around in my bathing suit while Africans hang on the fence watching. Look at them."

There were five ragged Africans clinging to the chainlink
fence that surrounded the pool, and others lay on the grass,
looking in. They were there all day, watching the expatriates in
the swimming pool, wearing small tight bathing suits, splashing
or sunning themselves. The nakedness fascinated the Africans,
and the idea of people lying in the sun was such a novelty that
the Africans simply gaped, wondering why they didn't move.
Whites in the sun had the torsion and muscularity of snakes, and
like snakes the most they did was blink.

I avoided the place usually, though this voyeurism seemed an
appropriate African response to whites in Uganda who stared at
bare-breasted tribeswomen or Karamojong warriors who never
bothered to conceal their thick floppy cocks.

"I give African kids swimming lessons," Jenny said. "I've
taught some of the students to swim."

"I wouldn't swim here. I'd hate Africans staring at me."

"That's just silly. That's snobbery."

It was our first disagreement. She was intelligent, logical, and
articulate; but I also felt she was wrong.

"You probably dislike swimming."

"I used to be a lifeguard."

That night I took her to the Hindoo Lodge. Jenny liked the
place—vegetarian food served at communal tables. The waiters
were Brahmins, though they wore grubby pajamas. I saw my
friends Neogy and Desai and I introduced Jenny. They smiled
from a nearby table and watched her eat. It was the only orthodox restaurant in town—water in brass jars, a washroom in back,
no knives or forks. Jenny made no fuss, though she had a little
difficulty managing the rice with her fingers.

"Those men are staring at me," she said.

"Because you're eating with your left hand."

"So what?"

"You're suppose to eat with your right hand, and make love
with your left."

"Tell them I'm ambidextrous," she said.

After that we often ate out—at the Sikh's, at the Grand Hôtel
and the Greek's, at Fatty's and the Chez Joseph. I introduced her
to spending Sunday afternoons strolling at the Botanical Gardens among milling Indians, and usually we had tea afterwards

[336]

at the Lake Victoria Hotel. I was very happy, except when Jenny said how much she was looking forward to finishing her diploma course and her posting up-country. She spoke enthusiastically of the isolation of teaching school in the bush, in places like Gulu or Arua, or even more distant towns like Pakwach and Kitgum and Moroto, haunts of naked cattle rustlers with flopping dongs.

I did not want her to go, but I never said so. I said that I might visit her. In the meantime we could spend our time together, if she happened to be free.

"I happen to be free," she said.

"I have to visit some listening groups," I said. "Would you like to come along?"

"What's a listening group?"

"We used to have tutors all over the country, but the government cut our budget. So I organized groups in outlying villages and gave each group a radio. We broadcast lessons to them over Radio Uganda—English, political science, African history, whatever. Every few months I visit the groups to see whether any problems have arisen."

"Where do you go?"

"Everywhere."

The morning Jenny and I left Kampala was one of the happiest in my life. It was sunny, and we raced under a blue sky, going west towards Kabale, past the rivers and the swamps that were choked with feathery papyrus, and the smoky villages that lay under scarred baobab trees, and the plains of Ankole where there were giraffes and gazelles. We stopped in Mbarara for lunch at the little hotel. As we ate, a Land-Rover drew up—some tourists and guides in safari clothes, hacking jackets and broad-brimmed hats and big boots; they were hunters, and very excited to be in this apparent wilderness. After lunch we sped off again towards Kigezi District, where the road twisted around the low hills and volcanoes.

I had never traveled these roads with another person. I had always gone alone. It was wonderful to be with this woman. We talked about books we liked. We took turns quoting poetry we had memorized. She recited Wordsworth and T. S. Eliot; I did Baudelaire and Robert Frost. We chanted "Ozymandias." We sang folk songs, and when it grew dark in the winding roads of Kisoro, we sang Christmas carols.

It came upon the midnight clear
That glorious song of old . . .

We arrived at the government rest house at ten o'clock after a twelve-hour drive, and took turns in the bathroom. The dining room was empty. The African waiter brought us steamed bananas and stew, and bottles of Primus Beer smuggled from the Congo—the border was nearer than Kampala. The insects were loud. We sat on the veranda, where it was cool enough to wear a sweater. I could see the lamplights in the huts through the trees and could smell the smoke of the cooking fires.

"God, I love this place."

"I'm glad to hear you say that," Jenny said.

I loved the smell of woodsmoke, the clayey odor of the dirt road, the racket of insects, the sound of a jangling bike and its feeble bell, the fragrance of the jacaranda after rain, and the way the giraffes loped when they hurried, the great hot distances of the day and even the simpler evocative smells of the rest house, the varnish and floor wax and cooking bananas.

"Maybe we should turn in," I said. "We have to drive again tomorrow."

In our room there were two single beds. Jenny had thrown some clothes on one, and I had done the same with the other—so we had each staked a claim.

But after I turned the light out I said, "Can I get into bed with you?"

She was silent. Was she asleep so soon?

"I promise to behave myself," I said. "I just want to snuggle next to you."

"Okay," she said. I could tell from the way she said it that she was smiling.

Her skin felt damp and warm in her cotton nightgown. She was perspiring slightly. She went to sleep and began to breathe softly in a dreamy way. I could not sleep. My heart was pounding. I was awake, with wide-open eyes.

I touched her, and this woke her. She drew away.

She said, "You promised not to."

As I kissed her and lifted her legs and parted them she said "No," but the sound she made when I entered her was a sigh like a yes.

* * *

I saw my class, and then we set off. It seemed an empty land.
There were few people in between the towns—no villages, only
animals. We drove in the darkness of the high forest and then
broke through to the plains. In one place there was a herd of
elephants. We tried to count them, but got to sixty and lost
count, distracted by the crested cranes and the wildebeest
nearer the road. We said nothing about last night.

"Did you know a wildebeest is a gnu?" Jenny said.

She also knew Grant's gazelle from Thomson's gazelle, and
the names of the various thorn trees. She told me that elephants
grieved when one in a herd died—they actually mourned and
trumpeted and sometimes tried to bury the carcass.

We continued north to my listening group at Katwe, where
there was a salt lake, and to Lake Edward, which was full of
hippos, some up to their nostrils in water and others grazing
and snorting and shitting—whirring the lumps with their tails,
like shit hitting a fan. We went past the copper mine and the
deserted railway station at Kilembe, and we entered the region
of tea estates—still there were no people, only the lovely dense
tea bushes. It was sundown when we reached Fort Portal. We
stayed at The Mountains of the Moon Hotel and made love
again.

We crossed the mountains on a narrow road through the Ituri
Forest. It was shadowy and damp in the forest and we were
pestered by pygmies when we stopped to rest. These people
were smaller than the ferns and they hid and threw stones at the
car when we refused to take their picture. When I blew the car
horn they vanished, thinking I was going to drive into them. I
was glad to have Jenny with me, in this forest. I realized that
I could carry on for a long time—as long as we were together
I had no reason to go back. We slept in each other's arms in a
narrow bed at Bundibugyo, and a few days later we drove north
to Gulu, where she had asked to go. The road turned from mud
to sand, zebras watched us change a tire, and we were stopped
at a roadblock by toothless Acholi soldiers with shiny faces and
wicked-looking rifles. They asked for bribes; I paid up—and
Jenny was chastened by the casual menace of those men. Gulu
was hot, and its only sound was that of locusts howling. The thin
trees were penetrated by the sun, so there was no shade. Hawks

hovered over grass fires, occasionally dropping on mice and snakes that were put to flight by the flames.

It was only ten days of travel, but at the end of it we knew each other well—so well that when we arrived back in Kampala I kissed her and said, "I love you."

I had always felt that love was a word that had been worn smooth by overuse, and yet she seemed slightly shocked when I said it.

8.

She did not say that she loved me. Instead she used fond and oblique expressions that tantalized me. If she had been American I would have known what she meant—if she had been African it would have been much plainer to me. But she was English, and the language could be as maddening and ungraspable as smoke. I meant a lot to her, she said. She was as happy as she had ever been with anyone, she said. The trip had been tremendous fun, she said. She had been desolated by having to come back to town, she said. She would miss me enormously . . .

I wanted more. There was no more. She was going away. Within a few weeks she passed her exams and had her diploma. She delightedly told me that she had been posted to a bush school in the highlands of Kenya. Wasn't it absolutely super?

I said yes, because she seemed so pleased. But I was sick at the thought of it.

"How could the Ugandan Ministry of Education send you to Kenya?"

"I was sent by the British Ministry of Overseas Development," she said. "It's a three-year scheme."

It was the first I had heard of it. She was part of a high-powered economic aid program; but she had never mentioned it. It was partly that she never boasted and seldom talked about herself; and also that I had done most of the talking.

"I know the white highlands," I said, and she winced. But that was how they were known even with Jomo Kenyatta as president. "It could have been worse, I guess. They might have sent you to Zanzibar."

"I'd love to go to Zanzibar," she said.

I found her enthusiasm very discouraging and wanted to say *What about me?*

"What if you got married?" I asked. "What would the ministry say?"

"It's just for single people—couples aren't as flexible. Anyway, I have no plans."

Before she left we spent four days at Lake Nabugabo, where there was no bilharzia, and so we could swim. We lived like castaways in a cozy hut, cooking our meals on a wood fire and drawing water from a well. I paddled her in a dugout canoe to the leper colony on the island—we had brought them sheets to be made into bandages. We gathered wild flowers and pressed them into Jenny's book. We made love. And driving back to Kampala she said it had all been tremendous fun.

She cried when she left for Nairobi. She took the overnight train. On the platform there were Indians, Africans, British, refugees, Greeks from the Congo, Belgians from Rwanda, people going only as far as Tororo or Jinja, or nine miles down the line; other people leaving for good, with everything they owned, and their servants watching them like orphans. Everyone was saying goodbye differently.

"Don't be sad, honey."

"I'm not sad," she said. "I'm so excited to be starting I can't control myself."

"I'll miss you."

"I'll miss you, too"—but would she have said that if I hadn't prodded her?

"I'll write to you."

She said, "I'm terrible about answering letters."

I hated that.

"Can I visit you?"

"It's so far!" she said, but in a surprised way, as though the thought had not occurred to her that I might want to visit her.

The whistle blew. A bell was rung on the platform. It was a steam train—noisy, drawing attention to itself, and it gathered speed slowly. No other vehicle on earth seemed to depart so reluctantly or with such self-importance.

I walked beside it, feeling forlorn, and when the train finally left it took a part of me with it. I felt physically incomplete, as if I'd suffered a stroke—part of my body wasn't working. For the first time in my life I understood why lovers always talked about their heart. It seemed the most fragile part of me, and I could feel it squeezing below my throat.

I went back to my squawking parrot and sat among the books he had gnawed, feeling a paralyzing sadness.

I had always loved being alone, and so departures—no matter whose—left me feeling free, even happy. Parting from someone allowed me to go back to my life—my real life, which was always interesting to me because it was hidden. This secret life was usually peaceful and in my control. It was not a refuge or a hole I crawled into to be still and silent. It was an active thing with noisy habits, and it contained the engine of my writing.

It had been a succession of departures in my life that had made me feel bold—sometimes like a pilgrim and sometimes like an adventurer. I took pleasure in seeing myself as wolfish and slightly disgraceful. I had loved being with Rosamond in London, but I had felt liberated in going away; and the same with Francesca in Accra and Femi in Lagos. In Kampala I had always regarded the prospect of a night with Rashida as exciting, but the next morning I had never wanted her to stay longer, and those afternoons at the Botanical Gardens could be very long. I liked sleeping alone. It was only alone that I had good dreams. Sleeping with a woman often gave me nightmares. I never tried to explain it. It was only that in my life so far I had been happiest when I was alone and had elbow room. I liked to wake up in that same solitude.

But from the moment Jenny left, I missed her. Her train pulled out and I went home like a cripple. I saw Rashida on my way through Wandegeya. She was just leaving the Modern Beauty Hair Salon where she worked, and I recognized her white smock and pulled up next to her.

"Hello *habibi.* Are you a nurse?"

"Yes, *bwana,*" she said, without a missing a beat. "I have some *dawa* under here"—and she touched her smock. "It is good medicine. It will make you feel strong."

That was the relationship: corny jokes. I felt friendly towards her but nothing more. She was a person I had once known.

I was too confused to write to Jenny, and when I did my letter was incoherent. It was an attempt to hide my jealousy, my sadness, my loneliness and fear. I simply said I missed her. And I told her how when I was writing it there was a scratching on the window above the bed. I had looked up and seen the big lemur eyes of the bush-baby. He seemed to be appealing to be let in. I gave him a piece of banana, keeping him outside. He seemed sorrowful. I wanted to take him into my arms, and I became tearful as I watched him. That story was true.

Love did not seem the right word to explain how I felt. I was physically sick, I felt weak. I missed Jenny, but I also missed myself—I missed that other person I had been when I was with her. I had not been a tease or a manipulator or a baboon wagging his prong at her. I had wanted to please her. She had made me kind and generous, she had made me patient. I liked myself better behaving that way, and because she had left I had lapsed back into being the other person. No, it was not love but rather a kind of grief—I missed her and this other self. She was the daylight that had showed me my secrets, and most of them weren't worth keeping.

I never lost this grief, but along with it I was also angry that she had left me. Then the anger passed and self-pity replaced it. I sat in my room listening to the mutters of my parrot. In my office I went through the motions of working; and I hardly spoke, because all my sorrow was in my voice.

People said, "Are you all right?"

They knew I wasn't.

When I said I was fine they knew I was lying, because of the sadness in my protest. I was sure that they talked about me all the time in the Staff Club.

They were too hearty with me. They made a great effort to be friendly. Their effort made me feel worse.

Crowbridge said, "Are you leaving?"

I shook my head. "What gave you that idea?"

"Someone mentioned the University of Papua–New Guinea the other day and you went all quiet."

People in Uganda were always looking for a new place to go, permanent and pensionable jobs in the tropics—warm disorderly countries which offered good terms of service. This university in Port Moresby was the current one.

"I'm not going anywhere," I said.

"Excellent," Crowbridge said. "There's a good chap."

He bought me a drink. I drank slowly, sadly; I didn't have the energy to get drunk. I simply grew sadder.

"How's your Nubian?" Crowbridge said.

Then I felt much worse, and I left without saying anything, knowing that I had made myself conspicuous and pitiful.

At home I managed to make myself drunk and wrote a fifteen-page letter to Jenny, gasping as I scribbled and finally collapsing over it. When I read it the next morning I tore it up. It was a harangue. It contained phrases from a book I had been reading, Kafka's *Letters to Milena*—morbid love letters. My own would have frightened her.

It would have been convenient, I thought, if we'd had a mutual friend to tell her about me: Andy loves you—He's really suffering—He's in terrible shape—He's quite a good writer, you know—And he's director of the Institute—only twenty-six!—But God, we're worried about him—He's never been like this—We hardly recognize him—He hasn't been the same since you left.

I could not say such things myself. I didn't want to excite her pity. I wanted her to love me in return and for us to talk about the future.

In my loneliness, feeling abandoned, I made plans for both of us—marrying Jenny, having children, getting a job in Hong Kong or Singapore. I wanted to get away from Africa, which now made me feel like a failure—and Africa was my rival for Jenny's love. I also resented her, because she had destroyed my love of solitude, invaded my secret life; she had made me need her.

I wrote her friendly letters and suppressed my fear. If she rejected me I knew I would leave. I applied—just to be sure I had an alternative—for a job in Kuala Lumpur and one in Oulu, at the University of Northern Finland.

Three weeks went by. My impatience affected me like a fever.

I felt ill, I stayed in bed, and the bush-baby appeared at the window like a mocking demon. One night I went to the Staff Club, not because I wanted to but because I knew that if I didn't I would become the subject of further gossip. I found the energy to get drunk, and when I went home I burst into tears. I realized that I was moved by the thought of myself alone, drunken and blubbering. I had never wallowed like that before—and my pleasure in the pathetic melodrama horrified me.

One day I thought of killing myself, but when I went through step by step—the locked door, the note, the rope, the noose, the kicked-over chair—I laughed and embraced life and felt vitalized by the thought that I would never kill myself.

I might kill Jenny, though. I'd never leave her, I'll never stop loving her. But I might kill her.

When she wrote at last, four weeks after she left Kampala, I felt worse, not better.

It was a postcard, a picture of a goofy Kikuyu man with varnished-looking skin and dents in his face. He was carrying a leather shield and a curio-shop spear. The message said, *Dear Andy, Some settling in problems (no water!) but the girls are sweet and the other teachers very helpful. I have my own house and inherited the previous tenant's cook. Very hectic at the moment, term starts Mon., but I'll write again when I get a chance! Love, Jenny.*

Three things bothered me about the note—that it was short and breezy, that it made no reference to the six letters I had written, that it did not invite my affection. I hated exclamation marks. She was fine, she was happy; and knowing that made me miserable.

I could not call her. The phone lines to Kenya were always out of order, and when they worked you heard a faint deep-in-a-well whisper that made you feel lonelier, because you had to shout at the voice that was always saying *Talk louder. I can't hear you.*

How could I shout the things I wanted to say? How could I stand to get a mouse-whisper in reply?

When Friday came I was restless. I went to sleep drunk and woke up at four o'clock in the morning on Saturday, wondering what to do. I saw I had no choice: there was only one thing. I dressed in the dark and got into my car and drove away, out of Kampala. The streets were empty. The forest outside town was black, but

as dawn broke I saw Africans washing near their huts and waiting for buses and heading for the cane fields. I had breakfast at
Tororo and then crossed the border. The immigration official
on the Kenya side yawned at me—both a greeting and a growl—
as he stamped my passport. At midmorning in Western Kenya
five African boys with dust-whitened faces jumped out at me
from the elephant grass at the shoulder of the dirt road. They
had just been circumcised and become men: they showed it by
howling at me and shaking painted shields. Farther along there
were baboons sitting on the road grimacing at me with doglike
teeth. The road went on and on, past tea and wheat and corn
and cactuses and stony hills and mud huts. The mileposts told
me I was nearing Nairobi. The sun was going down over Mu-
thaiga as I turned north on a narrower road. Just before seven
o'clock my headlights illuminated the sign UMOJA GIRLS SCHOOL.
It had been a twelve-hour drive, but I wasn't tired. I was excited—more than that, my nerves were electrified.

I turned into the driveway, between thick hedges, and went
slowly. There were heavy red blossoms on the bushes and big
brown petals flattened in the dark wheeltracks.

Two girls in green school uniforms stepped aside to let me
pass. But I stopped.

"Where is Miss Bramley's house, please?"

"That side," one said, and the girl next to her muffled a
giggle.

Only then, hearing that sound behind the girl's hand, did I
have doubts. They rose in my throat and made me queasy. What
if this was all a huge mistake? I had not warned Jenny I was
coming. She might be with a man—or out of town for the weekend. Maybe she had gone to the coast. I knew nothing about her
life. Everything that had seemed right to me before, and for the
whole of the long drive, now became uncertain. I felt awkward,
even fearful, after I spoke to those African girls. I almost went
away then, but I forced myself to go on.

Her house was behind another hedge. Every building here
was hidden by foliage. Her lights were on. I did not go all the
way. I switched the engine off and eased the door shut, and
walked to her window.

She was with an African man. I watched. I could not hear
anything. She stood facing him—he was simply staring, listen-

ing. She was smiling. Was he her lover? It didn't matter, I told myself. It just showed me how little I knew her.

I wanted to leave. I was trembling. I couldn't interrupt—didn't want to. It wasn't right. I was such a blunderer. Perhaps she had written me a letter, which had arrived that morning in Kampala; but I hadn't received it because I was on the road. Perhaps the letter said, *Dear Andy, I have been putting off writing this letter, but I can't put it off any longer* . . .

It was a twelve-hour trip back to Kampala, it was almost two to Nairobi. But how could I go back right now? I had to reject the idea; I was exhausted. But I would have to go, because now I understood the brief postcard, the long silence, the girl's giggles. I was sad, but I had to knock and see her, so that I could say goodbye.

She could not speak when she answered the door. Her face seemed to swell with unspoken words. I took it to be the shock of acute embarrassment. I began to apologize.

"I couldn't call you," I said. "I thought I'd visit. Don't worry—I'm not staying. I can see that you're busy—"

I was still talking but she wasn't listening.

She smiled and said, "You're wearing *takkies!*"

I had dressed in a hurry. I wore a black suit, a T-shirt, dark glasses, and tennis sneakers—*takkies*. It was the Kenya word for them.

Behind her the African had become very still.

"I'm sorry to interrupt," I said.

Now we both looked at him.

He said, *"Mem, chakula kwisha? Wewe nataka kahawa?"*

"He's your cook!" I said, much too loudly.

"I'm afraid so," she said, and she turned to the African, *"Kwisha, asanti sana. Hapanataka kahawa. Kwaheri, John."*

"Why don't you want a coffee?"

"Because I want to be alone with you," she said.

When he left, Jenny said, "He makes fruit salad and dumps it into the bowl with yesterday's leftover fruit salad. I eat a little and he adds a little every day. The bowl is always full. It's a bottomless fruit salad. I've been eating it for more than three weeks. Surely that's not healthy? I was just explaining—oh, Andy"—and threw her arms around me—"I'm so glad to see you. I've been missing you. I can hardly believe you're here."

We went directly to bed. We made love, then dozed and woke and made love again.

In the darkness of her bedroom I said, "I love you."

"I love you, too."

"I mean I really love you," I said. "I'm in love with you."

It was a hopeless word. It didn't work. But when she hugged me, I could tell from the way she held me, from the pressure of her body, that she was happy and that she probably did love me.

She was smiling the following morning.

"Do Americans always wear *takkies* with a suit?"

I stayed until Tuesday. We walked to a nearby hotel, the Izaak Walton. It was on a trout stream, whites came up from Nairobi to fish here. We had dinner and walked back to Umoja Girls School in the dark. We drove to Meru, to look at Mount Kenya. We inhaled the jacaranda. Morning and evening we made love.

When in my life had I not looked forward to setting out in the morning and leaving, alone? But I hated the thought of leaving Jenny. I was consoled by the thought that she seemed sorry too.

She said, "Will you come back?"

"What do you think?"

Three weeks later I returned. And then she visited me, coming by plane and landing at Entebbe. We spent the weekend together—making love, talking, procrastinating, and finally hurrying to the airport so that she could catch her plane that Sunday night.

It was a winding country road and so full of people walking and riding bikes, and so crowded in places with children fooling around that it took all my concentration. It was not until after she had gone that I recalled her taking my hand and saying casually, "By the way, my period's late. I'm sure it's nothing to worry about."

9.

Popatlal Hirjee was a goldsmith. His eyes were yellowish under heavy lids. He was very fat, and his hands were so plump that the three or four rings he wore were buried by the flesh of his fingers. He sat crosslegged on cushions in his shop, like a pasha. When I picked up the gold wedding rings he had made he dropped them into a jangling set of scales and counterbalanced them, throwing weights into the opposing pan and sorting them. Then he dug a diamond out of a brooch and set it in Jenny's ring.

He never moved from his seated position, and he did all this sorting and weighing without speaking. His breathing—the heavy man's gasp—had the sound of something being scorched.

His assistant said, "We can write names in them—your name in her ring, her name in yours. And the date."

I wrote this information on a scrap of paper. Popatlal Hirjee gouged the names and the date on the inner surface of the rings. Hers said *Andre 4-Aug-68.*

"*Bariki,*" the goldsmith said. Blessings on you.

I drove one last time to Umoja in Kenya, and picked up Jenny and her two suitcases. On our way back to Kampala we stopped at Eldoret for the night. Two days later we woke in each other's arms.

"We're getting married today," I said. "I love you."

To wake up and say that seemed reckless and wonderful.

We went together to the Kampala Registry Office. The contract was read to us by an African in a three-piece suit. Our witnesses were my Indian friends, Neogy and Desai, and their extravagant signatures appeared on our marriage certificate. We gave a party at the Staff Club and before it was over we drove towards Fort Portal, stopping for our first night at Mubende at the rest house near the witch tree, and the next day at The Mountains of the Moon Hotel, where we spent a happy week.

The night we arrived back in Kampala the bush-baby appeared at the window—not looking for food, not even restless, but simply watching. He returned on successive nights, and over the next few weeks, with his large eyes staring in, my life changed.

Jenny said that Hamid would have to go. We couldn't have a parrot and a child in the same house—and how could I stand the damned bird gnawing my books and shitting on my furniture. And Jackson went too when Jenny discovered that he hid garbage in kitchen drawers; I hadn't been able to break him of the habit. We hired Mwezi—her name meant moon—a bucktoothed woman who made scones and who longed for the baby to arrive. The house was cleaned, perhaps for the first time since I had moved in.

The bush-baby watched; it asked for nothing more. It came and went, and was no longer a portent. I had my own bush-baby now. I loved waking beside her, I eagerly left work and hurried home to her. My habits changed. I seldom went to the Staff Club. Jenny was the only person I needed. We went out together—eating, drinking; sometimes we went dancing. I bought presents for her—an ivory carving, a silver buckle from Zanzibar, some kitenge cloth. We took long trips to West Nile and Kitgum to visit my student listening groups. I became very calm.

And my novel came alive. It was about Yung Hok, the Chinese grocer—the only Chinese shopkeeper in the country, the ultimate minority, a single alien family. I had once seen him as vulnerable, but now that I was married I saw that he was strong and that he was part of a family—he had a wife and children I had not noticed before. He wasn't a symbol of anything. He was himself, an unusual man. He was something new in my experience, and he made me see the country in a new way. This made him vivid, and so I was able to write about him. For my spirit and inspiration I silently thanked Jenny. I worked in the spare bedroom, delighted that Jenny was nearby. I had no reason to think about leaving Africa now. I was at last home.

At about this time I saw an item in the *Uganda Argus* entitled AMERICAN WRITER DIES. It was Jack Kerouac. He was forty-seven. Years ago he had seemed old to me. Now he seemed young—much too young to die. The item did not say how. I thought about him, and how I had read *On the Road*, and I could not remember whether I had liked it. I continued writing my own novel.

I always had lunch at home now. Mwezi usually cooked it, and after we had sent her away we made love in the afternoon and had a nap before I went back to work.

One of these afternoons, waking from the deep and sudden sleep produced by energetic sex, I looked across the pillow and saw Jenny turning away. She was murmuring, trying to stifle her sobs. The bush-baby appeared at the window—listening.

"What's wrong?"

She said, "Everything!" and began to sob out loud.

"Please tell me," I said, horrified to see her so distraught.

"Isn't it obvious?"

It was not obvious to me.

She said, "I feel miserable." Her crying was not dry breathless hysteria or panic; it was slow painful sobs like waves breaking.

What made this so awful was that I was so happy—until that moment. I had never been so happy: I had told her that many times. I told her again, and this time it made her scream.

"Of course you're happy!" she said. Her face was wet, and the fact that she was naked made her crying seem worse. I could see misery in her whole body.

I got up and handed her my bathrobe, because I couldn't bear to look.

She said, "You haven't had to quit your job. You have work, you have money. I've given up everything—even my name. I never wanted this to happen. I have nothing to do."

It surprised me. I never imagined that anyone would object to having nothing to do. Why would anyone want to work if they didn't have to? What she said baffled me so completely I did not know how to argue against it.

I said, "We take trips, don't we?"

"You do all the driving!"

"I know the roads," I said. "I know the shortcuts."

"I can learn. I've driven in Africa. I speak Swahili," she said. "I'm not stupid. I have an Oxford degree—and you made me quit my job."

She became quieter and that worried me more, because she had been sobbing in grief, and this seemed to turn to anger.

"Now I'm just like all these expatriate wives I used to pity and despise. I'm a memsahib—you made me a memsahib. I stay at home and wait for you."

I wanted to say *You're lucky,* but I didn't dare. I disliked her for making me fearful of saying it. But she was lucky, I was convinced of that. It seemed perverse of her to be so unhappy. But then didn't pregnant women get fits of depression like this and wasn't this all attributable to that? The bush-baby clinging to the window grille seemed to see it that way.

Jenny complained a bit more, then described what she hated about being a memsahib, and she said that she hated dealing with Mwezi. These were mostly irrational grievances and because of that I was able to understand them. She was being cranky.

Then she sat up and said, "I came here to teach Africans. That was the only thing I wanted. And you put a stop to it."

That was when I lost my temper.

I said, "Teaching Africans what? How to speak English. How to do math. That's ridiculous. I'm sick of doing it—sick of hearing about it. Half the students here are married and have families, and they pretend they're schoolboys. They say they want to go abroad and study. They're lying—they want to get out and never come back. They hate their lives. They want a ticket to England or America. They hate farming. They want to wear suits and neckties. Those girls you were teaching will all end up in a village pounding corn in a wooden mortar. They'll have ten kids each and a drunken husband. What is the point of teaching anything here except farming?"

"You dislike Africans, I know you do," Jenny said.

"The only friends I've had for more than four years here have been Africans—and some Indians. What you're saying is bullshit. You don't know me."

"You make remarks about them," she said. "Don't deny it. When we were in Moroto—"

"You mean, those bare-assed Karamojong? Was I supposed to pretend they weren't naked? I'm standing there with you and those men and I see four huge salamis swinging back and forth, and so I make a remark about a delicatessen."

"It was so cruel," she said. "You could have pretended you didn't see anything."

"Oh, God," I said. By now I was dressed—and I was late for work. "That's perfect. Pretend you don't see their dongs. Pretend this is a real city. Pretend they don't kill each other. Pretend they don't envy and hate you. Pretend you're not white. Pretend they're not staring at your tits. Pretend your teaching is helping the country. Pretend you're not here to have a grand old time in the bush. Pretend that in a few years there's going to be a big improvement in Uganda. Pretend the president is not a total asshole as well as a murderer, a torturer—"

I stopped, because Jenny had begun to cry again.

"You want a job? You can have mine. Then I can stay home."

"You'd hate that."

"I'd love it," I said. It was what I wanted most: to sit at home all day, working on my novel. "I'd love to sit in that room and write."

"I don't have a room!" Jenny said. "This is your house! Everything is yours. I hate it!" She was sobbing terribly and choking.

"Please don't cry," I said.

She let me hold her.

She said, "I am so unhappy."

"Maybe you're feeling lousy because of the baby," I said.

Her eyes went cold. She said, "Jesus, you don't know anything, do you? This baby is the only thing that makes me happy."

The word baby made me look up: the bush-baby had gone. At what point in our yelling back and forth had the little creature taken itself away?

"What about me?" I said. "Don't you love me?"

"I don't even know you," she said sorrowfully and wiped her tears away.

There was no conclusion—only a parting, because I had to go back to work. I felt dreadful, and I felt overwhelmed; I had no answers. Would it always be this way?

I worked on my novel, and I was surprised that I was able to continue it. It went as smoothly as ever. It was a relief and a consolation. My hero, Yung Hok, ran his grocery store and made plans; he too had a private life. But Mrs. Yung Hok, who up to now had been enigmatic, took on a life of her own and became a character. She was a very discontented person and had violent fits of anger, and sometimes when she screamed at her husband he went silent and his neck seemed to shorten, and he squinted like a small boy being nagged by his mother.

10.

I had married a pretty girl who turned into a dissatisfied woman very quickly. But it was not over. Another woman began to emerge in her. Jenny changed again, she became bigger and blanker and rather slow. Her shape altered, she was quieter, she slept more, she developed a passion for pineapple juice. She was a different person altogether, with different thoughts. She was softer, slower, a bit weepy. She was heavy, she was earthbound. The change fascinated me—and it released me from my terror of being accused by her of having subverted her life. Now she had another life, too.

We always went shopping at the market on Saturday mornings. One sunny Saturday, we were driving down Kampala Road, and had just passed the twittering bats, when we saw an Indian approaching on a motor scooter. He waved and his machine wobbled as he slowed down.

He was screaming.

"Go back, go back!"

He looked absurd, screaming on the empty street, in this sleepy part of town, with the sunshine beating on the trees and making green shadows, and all those twittering bats.

"They'll kill you!"

Another car drew up behind me. The Indian looked over his shoulder and then back at us, and he screamed again. Once I had heard that same scream—when an Indian was being set upon by an African, late one night; Rashida had found it exciting. It was utter panic.

The car behind me was beeping for me to move. I looked and saw an African at the wheel, gesturing for me to move on.

Jenny said, "What's wrong with that Indian?"

His face was gray, he had flecks of spit on his lips. Now he was raving at the car behind me.

"Go back!" he screamed. "They will kill you!"

His Hindi accent made the words somehow less urgent.

I said, "What's up?"

He did not reply. He jerked his motor scooter, nearly tipping it over, and rode away—climbing the curb and speeding down a dirt path between the trees.

It was very confusing—only a matter of seconds had passed.

"Oh, shit," I said, feeling fuddled.

Jenny's mouth was gaping open. In a voice I did not recognize as hers, she said, "Look."

Far ahead, at the crest of the road, where I expected to see cars I saw people, ragged Africans, all men, a crowd of them as wide as the road. They plodded along towards us, motioning, and a moment later I heard their cries. They passed a shop and broke its windows, they passed a car and overwhelmed it, they were gesturing with sticks, they were flinging stones.

The car behind me was still beeping, and the African driver—as though he was part of this trap—was pushing his hand impatiently at me. He stuck his head out of his window and called out *Move along!*

It was the bursar, Wangoosa, a man I had never known to raise his voice. His eyes were small and his teeth huge, and he was angry that I was hesitating. And he was so close to me that I couldn't reverse my car. Nor could I go forward—the ragged African mob was coming nearer.

I tried to make a turn, to go around Wangoosa and get away. It was an awkward maneuver on such a narrow road, and as I struggled with the steering wheel, Jenny began to cry.

Then the mob was on us. The windshield was punched apart. It broke quickly into pieces so small they dropped like liquid into our laps. Jenny screamed as blood appeared on her knees and hands.

I was shouting too—protesting—but the howling of the mob was so loud I could not hear my own voice. The car had darkened because of the Africans surrounding it, blocking out the light. It was shadow and panic and the strong smell of their dirty clothes. The back window went with a splash, and a side window splintered. They were clubbing the metal of the car, hammering the roof and the doors.

The Africans' smooth babyish faces were clear in the front window. Their clothes were torn, their hair was tangled and dirty, they were sweating. They were all laughing, and now they were rocking the car, trying to tip it over. I had the impression of a great number of big dangerous hands and dirty fingers snatching at me.

Jenny was now hysterical. There was no way I could get her out of the car unless I got out first, and from the moment the first window broke I had been trying to open my door. It was impossible. The Africans pressed against it held it firmly shut.

Still I shoved at it with my shoulder, and I shouted, "Stop! My wife is inside! She's hurt—she's bleeding—"

They paid no attention to me. They were intent on smashing the car, and in their eagerness to club the roof they stood away from the door. I managed to open it wide enough to squeeze myself out, and I braced myself to be clubbed, raising my arms to ward off the blows.

There were none. The Africans stepped aside—they were grinning at the car, and still laughing. Now I saw there were many of them—we were surrounded by hundreds of Africans, all of them holding sticks and iron bars. One moved past me to hit the door with an iron bar, and he hit it so hard he lost his grip. The bar went clanging to the road.

A struggle was going on at Jenny's side of the car. I put my arms over my face to protect myself and shouldered my way through the crowd. But she was gone. The car was rocking, it was empty.

I hated the laughter most of all. The mob had turned my car into a toy they had decided to break. I felt helpless and weak, and I was desperate, because I could not see Jenny anywhere. The Africans were all around me, and I moved with them: I became part of the mob—part of their will. We were overturning my car—I was among them.

Then my arm was gripped and I was being tugged out of the mob, moving sideways into the sunlight.

"Come with me."

It was a small, beaky Indian in a gray suit. He was half my size, but I needed his strength to get me free of the Africans. He helped me nearer the sidewalk and just then I looked up and saw Jenny pass behind a door.

The little Indian rushed me through the door, then slammed it and bolted it—three bolts. Just as he slid the third bolt someone began pounding on it. I knew who it was: I had seen their hands.

But the beaky man was smiling.

"They cannot break it. The door is strong."

The hammering grew louder. Still the Indian smiled—he was smiling at the door.

"I made that door myself," he said. "In my own workshop. I know my business." He smoothed his suit. "But just to be on the safe side we will go to the roof, where it is comfortable."

He led me to the stairs and looked back at the door, which was being thumped.

"That is a political matter," he said. "That is nonsense. That is—"

And he loudly cleared his throat and spat.

On our way to the roof we passed a landing. Hearing us, an Indian woman stuck her head out of a beaded curtain and said something to the man.

"Your wife is inside. Not to worry. She is receiving treatments."

Jenny was sitting, murmuring, her skirt hitched up and her thighs painted with antiseptic. Her forearms were cut, her dress was torn. I hugged her awkwardly and she began to whimper softly.

"We're okay," I said. "Thanks to this guy."

"C. D. Patel," the man said, and straightened and put out his hand. "Carpentry, furniture, bedding. And you?"

"Andre Parent."

"Your occupation?"

"I'm a writer."

We had tea and cakes under an awning on the roof as the last of the rioters passed beneath us on the street.

"What was that all about?" Jenny asked.

"African fuss and bother," Mr. Patel said. "They attacked the British High Commission—they broke the doors down. Glass doors. And then they ran riot."

His wife clicked her tongue in disapproval.

"It is a political matter," Mr. Patel said to her, smiling.

"That was a nightmare," Jenny said.

Mr. Patel was still smiling. "It is balderdash," he said.

When he said that I was certain that I would be able to bear it, and understand it, and write about it. And in that same moment I was also certain that I would leave Africa as soon as I could.

"You must have some sweetmeats," Mr. Patel said. "My wife has prepared them. We call this *gulabjam.* Please take."

I was still listening to the last of the mob.

"They wrecked my car," I said. "What do we do now?"

"You will be able to go home soon. I will drive you in my van."

I remembered that I had seen policemen near my car, after I got out and the mob had surged around me. Why hadn't they helped me—why hadn't they stopped the attack? I was trembling with anger and was about to describe this—and all my other complaints, like Wangoosa, who had honked at me and obstructed my retreat—when Jenny suddenly stood up. She was not steady on her feet. She braced herself by gripping my shoulder.

"Oh," she said softly and touched the great curve of her abdomen.

She tried to take a step, but she hesitated as water coursed down her legs and darkened her skirt. In the next second the Indian's wife scrambled to her feet—before I could react. But I was looking at Jenny's face. She seemed at once very calm and quietly surprised, as though she had just heard something—but no ordinary sound, it was a whisper from the heavens, something pulsing in the air.

FIVE

LEAVING SIBERIA

1.

It was winter in Siberia. I had been expecting deep snow and drifts, and had already rehearsed the phone call I planned to make in Khabarovsk: how cold it was, the icicles, the blizzards. But we traveled deeper into Siberia and though it was very cold, the snow was thin and disappointing. For miles at times there was nothing to see but slender peeling birches under a heavy sky—as if all the snow still lay packed in the low-hanging clouds, and was about to fall on me.

I was traveling westward from Japan and had been thinking about that phone call since Hokkaido, where I had tried three times to make it. It rang and went on ringing—the ring that makes you see the room again, but empty. It was Sunday in Japan but Saturday in London. Maybe she had gone away for the weekend?

The trouble with taking long trips was this suspense, which could be tormenting, and I hated guessing what was going on. But I had left in a hurry—I had left under a cloud. After six weeks I had called. This was in India, a miserable line, the squeezed and ghostly voice of the Indian telephone that makes you think of a séance. I heard her say faintly that everything was all right.

There were no letters waiting for me in Singapore two months later, but I was there a week and one arrived the day before I left. It was a short letter: she said she missed me. After that there was silence. I was in Vietnam, and when I knew it was impossible to call I stopped thinking about it. I kept writing my notes—it held me together, it ordered my thoughts, it helped me forget, and when I reread them I was consoled.

In Japan they said it was easy to call England. True, but no one answered. And then I had to leave. I was on a Soviet ship in the Sea of Japan—high waves and blowing slop; then in the cold brown city of Nakhodka; then on another train to Khabarovsk. Why was there so little snow in Siberia?

In those days before group tours to the Soviet Union the solitary traveler was escorted by an Intourist guide, who had a car and a driver. It was usually a large black limousine, and the driver a bad-tempered man or woman dressed like a bricklayer. The arrangement was intended to keep travelers in line—the guide a sort of jailer and nanny, of intimidating size. But I was not intimidated. I felt special. I was flattered that they thought I might be dangerous and needed to be watched. I enjoyed imagining that I was a spy. I liked having my own guide. I was very lonely.

After four months of continuous travel I suspected I was half crazy. I had forgotten why I had set out on the trip. But it no longer mattered, because I was on my way home.

That was why the phone call was so urgent. I needed to be reassured that home was still there, that they were waiting, that I was loved and expected. I had been sending letters into the dark.

In Khabarovsk, Irina said—"Is unusual"—and she implied that any unusual request was impossible. She meant the phone call.

Irina was my guide. She was from the Siberian city of Irkutsk, which she considered a cosmopolitan place. She had been posted here against her will, but she was making the best of it. She was young and very heavy, and she smelled strongly of perfume and of her hairy fox-furs. She was disappointed in me.

She said, "Where is your overcoat? Where is your scarf? And you have only these shoes?"

My coat was Japanese. It was too small. I had bought it for its rabbit fur collar. I had thin wool gloves and a ski cap lettered *Hokkaido.*

"I thought I could buy a scarf and boots in Khabarovsk."

"Is not possible to buy such things here," she said, and she laughed. That bitter laugh was the first indication I'd had that she hated being in the city where these simple necessities seemed like preposterous luxuries.

Irina was also disappointed in me because I was not interested in her. "From Scotland," she said of her thick woolen scarf. "Made in Italia," she said of her gloves. I could not understand her being so label-conscious, but I got the message. I kept my Intourist vouchers in a lovely leather pouch that I had bought in Thailand.

"Is nice," she said the first time she saw it. "Is expensive?"

"Frogskin," I said. That was true. "Very cheap."

She sighed and looked out the window of the car. I knew I had failed her. She wanted me to woo her a little, give her a present—perhaps some perfume, or a trinket; and she would let me overpower her, if it happened to be convenient. Then she would shriek a little and demand me again. Afterwards she would put on all those clothes—the two sweaters, the boots, the furs, the Scottish scarf, the Italian gloves, and having reapplied all that makeup, off she'd go. Sank you.

Instead, all I asked was the chance to make a phone call to London.

She didn't like the request. No one used telephones in the Soviet Union. They sent telegrams on thick brownish paper. The words in the message were counted twice and initialed and stamped, and reread, and examined, until it was not a message at all but simply capital letters turned into rubles.

"Is necessary?" she said doubtfully.

She meant: What was the point in going on a long trip, and visiting interesting places like Siberia, if your main aim in being in those places was to call home?

"It's urgent," I said.

"Is not easy to find telephone."

Her frown said: If all you want from me is this phone call you are wasting my time.

But I knew this was the only way I could go home, by phoning first, and I said, "There must be lots of telephones here."

"Of course," she said in that insulted tone that I associated with people in poor countries: Do you think we're savages?

"I meant for international calls."

She shrugged, using her furs, which made it a theatrical gesture. She said, "We can be able to telephone Kiev. We can be able to telephone Leningrad. We have trunk line. Trunk call."

Why was it only foreigners who used words like "trunk line" and "purchase" and "clad"? Was it because the words went out of date by the time they reached these distant countries?

I said, "What about London?"

I wanted her to say *Of course* with the same indignant certainty she had used before.

She said, "First is necessary to book the telephone."

"Yes."

"And then is necessary to telephone Moscow."

"Yes," I said, and waited for more. But she was thinking.

"And then we must make inquiry."

"I want you to do this for me, Irina, please."

"Is breakfast time," she said, "in Moscow," and squeezed her tiny watch-face between two large dimpled fingers. "We go to museum now. Famous museum."

Stuffed animals with bright glass eyes, dusty birds, dinosaur bones wired together, fossils, paintings of mustachioed men, baskets and ancient tattered aboriginal mittens, and pots and weapons that made me think: Could they cook with these? Could they kill with those? The building was overheated. Everything I saw was dead, and the way the floorboards creaked made me sad.

"Now we visit to factory."

"What about my phone call?"

"Is important factory, making poolies, weenches—"

"Irina, please."

She did not reply. She spoke in Russian to the driver. I had no idea we were going back to the hotel until we arrived there. Irina muttered and got out, but when I attempted to follow her the driver said something Russian to me in a scolding voice, and I sat back in the stuffy car.

"Is booked," Irina said, when she returned to the car. "Now we visit to factory. Then we see river. Is coming darkness soon."

"What do you mean 'booked'? Booked to London?"

"To Moscow."

"Will they connect me to London?"

"I think so. I hope so." She saw my face and smiled at me. She said gently, "Don't worry."

In the late afternoon, which was dark, I was walking up the steep riverbank to the car, and it struck me that I had gone too far. I had been away too long. What was I doing, slipping on this ice in this freezing place? The dark, the cold, and the stillness were all Siberian. I should never have come here.

Siberia seemed like death but was less final. It was more like a fatal illness, an especially anxious and even painful sort of waiting. A shallow heartbeat marked the time passing like the soft tick of a clock. It was a condition I had just begun to know: Siberia meant suspense. It was not death, but dying.

Back at the hotel I wrote my notes—about Irina and the factory, the museum, the bank, the statue in the main square, the look of the houses, the river, and the way the old men had been fishing through holes in the ice. In these notes I was expert at leaving things out. I said nothing of the phone call. There were in my travels certain simultaneous anxieties that I did not have to write down to remember. In fact, not writing them down meant that they were always passing in my mind.

Irina had said the call would come at eight. It didn't—I did not expect it to be punctual in Siberia. I was surprised when the phone rang just before eight-thirty: Moscow.

"I am calling London," I said.

"Number, please?"

I said it slowly, I repeated it, and I was so preoccupied I did not hear the operator nagging me to put the phone down until she began to shout.

The call came an hour or so later.

"Speak louder, please!"

I said, "Darling, can you hear me?"

"Yes."

It was a faint voice, the merest vibration in a sea of sound, but it was unmistakably Jenny's.

"I'm in Siberia. I've had so much trouble trying to call you— first in Japan, and now here. I had to call Moscow first"—and then not getting any response I became self-conscious and said, "Are you sure you can hear me?"

"Yes."

One-word replies usually made me talkative, but this made me uneasy as well.

"Is there anything wrong?"

"You woke me up."

"I'm sorry—I didn't know. Jenny, I'm in Siberia!"

"It's six o'clock in the morning."

It sounded distinct and complaining, but I blamed the line for distorting it.

I said, "I miss you."

There was no reply to this.

I said, "Can you still hear me?"

"Yes."

"What are you doing?"

"I was sleeping. You woke me up."

One can always tell from the pauses and the tone of voice when the other person wants to put the phone down. I felt this strongly, but it was so disturbing to me that I resisted it and kept talking.

"I'm coming home soon."

After a pause, she said, "When?"

"The end of the month."

"You said you'd be home by Christmas."

I started to explain.

"It doesn't matter," she said. But she was not letting me off. This was not sympathy or a way of excusing me. It sounded more like: *You* don't matter.

The receiver had gone cold in my hand. Another silence was loudly buzzing in my ear.

I said, "I'm so lonely here."

"It was your idea. The whole trip. I didn't want you to go."

"It's been very hard—"

But she was finishing her own thought: "It doesn't matter now."

I said, "Jenny, I'm really sorry I woke you up. I'll see you in a few weeks. I love you. Can you hear me? Darling, I love you."

"Jack misses you," she said.

Her voice was still cold. I blamed the wire, the baffled sound, the echo.

"I must go," she said. "I'm standing in the hall in my nightdress. I'll catch cold—"

"I'm in Siberia!"

My scream frightened me, but the line had gone dead.

[366]

"Thirty-four rubles," Irina said the next morning at the service desk. "You make a very long telephone call."

I pretended to be intent on counting the money.

"Everything is all right now," she said, and smiled at me. She gave me the receipt.

I said, "Yes," but I knew something was badly wrong. I did not want to think what it was. I only knew that it was very urgent that I hurry home.

No more stops, I thought. I took the Trans-Siberian that night straight through to Moscow—eight days of the twisty, jouncy train, and the cold and the birches. I spent Christmas Eve drunk with the kitchen manager in the dining car, and Christmas day at the window.

I thought of a story. A murderer is so overcome with remorse at the thought of his crime and the fact that he has not been caught, that he changes his name and takes the name of his victim. His personality begins to alter, and it softens to the point where he is very meek and timid, and at last he is himself murdered.

Why does this story happen in this macabre way? I could not answer the question, so I thought of another story, about an American in London. *He stood at the window, looking out at the street*—always the same opening sentence. I knew everything about this man, that he was my age, that he had been in Vietnam, that he was alone. Looking out the window, he saw a streetsweeper being bullied by a young man. What made this particularly awful was that the streetsweeper's son witnessed his father being humiliated. The American followed the bully through south London, and picked a fight with him and killed him. The story was the price he had to pay for doing that: a long story that I saw in vivid scenes.

I did not stop in Moscow any longer than it took to cross the city in wet snow and get a Polish visa. I boarded the next train and went straight through to the Hook of Holland, seeing everything in a blur, and reading the whole time to hold myself together.

My book was a collection of Chekhov's stories; I had started it in Russia, and now I was on the last story, "Lady With Lapdog." It was the progress of a love affair, and it appalled me with its truthfulness. I kept reading, and stopping; reading, and stopping. When I finished it I sat silently in the train, holding the paperback in my hands. I read it again. I read it four times. Each time I was drawn and stalled by the same paragraph, which began, *As he was speaking, he kept thinking that he was going to meet his mistress and not a living soul knew about it. He led a double life, one for all who were interested to see . . . and another which went on in secret.*

It was something I understood perfectly, but it was a way in which I had ceased to live. I had one life now—I had Jenny and Jack. I had no mistress. I had been happy at home, which was why I had felt secure enough to leave for such a long time on this trip: I had a home to return to. But the description in the story was such an accurate description of how I had once felt. *And by a kind of strange concatenation of circumstances, possibly quite by accident, everything that was important, interesting, essential, everything about which he was sincere and did not deceive himself, everything that made up the quintessence of his life, went on in secret . . .*

Not anymore, I thought. I had rid myself of my secrets; my life was simple now, and I shared it with my wife and son. But still the paragraph nagged at me. *He judged others by himself, did not believe what he saw, and was always of the opinion that every man's real and most interesting life went on in secret, under cover of night.*

Not mine; but crossing the Channel I became sad, and the sadness stayed with me. It was deeper than a mood—it was more like a physical condition. I could not bear to read the story anymore. I kept having nightmares that I was still in Siberia.

2.

After all that time I was very eager to see her. I also wanted to be seen. Was I the same? How did I look? I needed someone to tell me I was all right. That was one of the anxieties of coming home—the fear of someone saying *You've changed, you're different,* and looking closely at your face and frowning.

I had been married to Jenny for five years, but traveling for nine—since Africa; so the travel overlapped the marriage, and circumscribed it. It was not a routine, nothing annual or planned far in advance. It was an impulsive going-away, whenever I could. It was not an escape, but a means of concentrating my mind and being alone. It helped my writing. I found it extremely peaceful to travel. And it gave me ideas. It seemed to suit Jenny, a modern woman, whose idea of freedom was a job. She knew that to me travel was air.

Marriage made travel possible by giving me a corresponding sense of peace: I was not a searcher, looking for another home; I was a wanderer, interested in everything and always intending to return to my little family. For me, nothing was better than arriving back home. I was reassured by the solidity and the dullness, by the smells and the pictures on the wall, and by the familiar simplicities. Most of all I was reassured by the faces of the people I loved, Jenny and our son Jack.

I arrived in the dim late afternoon at Harwich, but it was night, black and blowy, when I reached London. I met some Indians in the taxi rank at Liverpool Street Station, and we agreed to share a cab to south London. We were aliens in a strange city, trying to save money. And having been so long in India it seemed more natural for me to talk to them than to the English people waiting for a taxi.

When we were under way one said, "We were just cooling our heels at that cab stand. The driver stopped for you, my friend."

"Where are you from?"

"From Broach, in Gujarat. You are knowing Gujarat?"

"Ghem cho. Magia ma chay."

"Oh, it is so incredible, Mr. Bhiku," the man said to his silent companion. "This American is speaking this difficult tongue."

"I only know six words."

"So what? You use them superbly."

They complained of the cold in London, but after Siberia it did not seem cold to me—only wet and gleaming a sulphurous yellow, like the streetlights. London in winter had often seemed to me like a city underground, in a damp dripping cavern.

"I'll get out at the next corner," I said, and gave them half of what was showing on the meter.

"And your name is?"

"Andre Parent."

"Enjoy the rest of your visit, Mr. Andre."

What was the point of correcting them? And it was partly true: I was temporary, an alien, just a visitor. A paying guest, in the English phrase.

I had deliberately gotten out of the taxi in the High Street, so that I could walk the rest of the way home, completing the journey I had started almost five months before, when I had walked to the station. I liked walking; it was like writing in longhand.

And perhaps I had another reason for walking. I didn't want to be announced by the noise of a taxi. All London taxis had a loud and peculiar shudder. I wanted my arrival to be a surprise. I had not spoken to Jenny since that phone call in Khabarovsk two weeks before.

I was very apprehensive as I pressed the bell. I felt like a stranger—worse, like an intruder.

There was a human shadow on the frosted glass of the door; and the mutter, "Who is it?"

"It's me," I said.

The door opened quickly.

"Andy!" Jenny threw her arms around me and kissed me, and all the warmth of the house and its lovely ordinary odors flowed over me through the doorway, warming my face.

Upstairs I went into Jack's tiny room. He was awake—he had heard the bell and the commotion. He peered at me in the dark and seemed shy. Why was he hesitating?

"Jackie, it's me," I said. "I'm back."

"Dad," he said—it was a gasp of relief. He raised himself up and hugged me with such strength that it seemed to me more like panic than love. And with his skinny arms around my neck I thought: I'll never go away again.

It was that lifeless period in London, between Christmas and New Year's—the holiday that is like low tide, or an endless Sunday afternoon. Empty streets, gray skies. But inactivity was just what I needed after all the motion I had endured.

Suddenly I belonged to them again. I went shopping, I began cooking dinner, and in a passionate and grateful way I performed the most humdrum chores. I washed the car, I put up shelves. I had missed Christmas, but the tree was still standing. I disposed of it and put away the decorations.

Jenny said, "You seem to have all this energy."

"I'm so glad to be back," I said.

It was New Year's Eve. We had always made a point of not celebrating, not going to a party; simply giving thanks that the old year had ended peacefully and then going to bed before midnight.

She had not replied to me. I said, "Aren't you glad? Didn't you miss me?"

We sat smoking among the ruins of the meal and two empty wine bottles.

Jenny spoke very deliberately when she was being truthful. In her measured way, choosing her words, she said, "It was so awful when you went. It was such an emptiness. I was so desperately lonely that I pretended to myself that you were dead."

She saw from my face that I was horrified and could not hide it.

"That was the only way I could manage to live from day to day."

I said, "The only way I could manage was by imagining that you missed me terribly. That you were waiting for me."

She said nothing, and I gathered from her silence that she had not been waiting. For a moment, it crossed my mind, as it had during that phone call from Siberia, that I might have died— been blown up in Vietnam, or poisoned in Burma, or frozen in Siberia—and it would have made no difference.

"Don't frown, Andy, please, I *am* glad you're back. I had forgotten what a good cook you are, and Jack is a different boy—he really missed you. He used to go all quiet, and I knew he was thinking of you."

"Bedtime," I said, looking at the clock. It was ten minutes to twelve.

We made love that night and other nights—not passionately but with a sort of insistence on my part. I kept wondering whether she would resist or refuse. She didn't resist, but neither did she take much pleasure in it. Yet that was not strange. After such a long separation we were still not used to each other.

She worked at a branch of Drummond's Bank off Ludgate

Circus. She was supervisor in the Foreign Exchange Department in a district of London where money was constantly being changed. Her pay was good—she earned more than I did—and her position was equivalent, on the bank's scale, to assistant manager. Her hours meant that we had needed a so-called mother's help. Before I had left there had been a girl in the back bedroom—Betty, from Bradford.

"What happened to Big Betty?" I asked soon after I arrived back.

"She left before Christmas. She's doing a diploma in education. She said she wants to work with handicapped children. 'Brain-damaged yoongsters' is what she called them."

"I can take Jack to school from now on. Then we'll have the house to ourselves."

"I was hoping you'd take him. We still have Mrs T. cleaning three mornings a week, so you won't have to do the dusting."

"I wouldn't mind doing the dusting!"

"You're so domestic all of a sudden."

"Yes. Because I had a feeling sometimes on that damned trip that I'd never get out alive. That I'd be in some horrible place like Afghanistan or Siberia and wouldn't be able to leave. I used to think—what if I die? What a long expensive road to travel, and all that trouble, just to die."

"You're home, Andy. Don't look so worried."

"I did nothing but worry. I got very superstitious. I was afraid you wouldn't be here when I got back."

She kissed me. She said, "It's wonderful to have you back."

I looked closely at her face and then she turned away.

After all that dislocation, and the uncertainties of travel, it was paradise to be in this quiet, terraced house in a London back street. People said it was the dreariest part of south London. I was a stranger there, but I felt at home: it was life, and I was happy. I spent the day doing small things, taking Jack to school, and then making his lunch and giving him a nap; afterwards we went for a walk, and shopped, bought food for dinner, and I cooked. In between, when I had a quiet moment, I looked over my notes. I was daunted by them—the strange handwriting, the bizarre-sounding place-names. There were four large note-books, about five hundred pages, filled with my writing. There was too much of it. I wanted to do something with it, but what?

I imagined the book, but I had never written that sort of book.
I was afraid to begin.

It was a relief to have household chores to do. They kept me
from thinking; they were brainless and tiring; they were just
what I needed. Little Jack seemed to me a perfect child, and I
knew that he was glad I was home. He had a serious face, very
pale from the English winter and perfectly smooth. He had small
beautiful hands and deep brown eyes that were so expressive I
did all I could to please him. I gave him treats, bought him
chocolate at the corner shop, and cakes at Broomfield's for tea;
I watched television with him, holding him on my lap. When he
was at school I missed him so much that sometimes I went early
to meet him, and loitered until he appeared.

"What do you want for lunch?"

"Paste sandwiches, and sausage rolls"—he had already ac-
quired a London accent—"and, Dad, can we have jelly—the
kind they have at birthday parties?"

It delighted me that I could make him happy by being with
him and offering him these simple things.

I said, "I missed you when I was away."

"But you're home now," he said, encouraging me.

"And I'm not going away again."

"That's good, because we have to go for our walks and sail my
new boat."

I had bought him a toy sailboat that we floated on the pond
at Crystal Palace. It was a large muddy park, with gardens, and
great stretches to run about in. The pond was in a glade, and
we always brought stale bread for the ducks. After these outings,
which left Jack with a pink nose and cold hands, we took the 73
bus back to Catford.

We watched television—the children's programs, *Blue Peter,
Crackerjack,* and *Doctor Who.* I thought there was nothing better
in the world than to sit with my small warm son on my lap,
watching these simple-minded programs. His laughter made me
hold him tighter. Why had I ever gone away?

All morning, when he was at school, I longed to see him. If
for some reason I had to go out I rushed back to be with him.
And he never disappointed me—he was always eager to see me.

The weekends seemed blissful—the bliss of a routine—shopping at the supermarket in Sydenham on Saturday morning,

then home for lunch, and doing odd jobs in the afternoon. Jenny always made dinner on Saturday night. We seldom went out. We talked of going skiing—some year, for sure, when Jack was older. The best part of Saturday was going to bed early and making love. On Sundays we drove into the Kent countryside or went to a museum. I carried the boy on my shoulder.

I never asked what was coming. This was what I wanted—a happy home. The anxieties I had felt in travel were in the past. In returning home I became the person I really was. Travel was another life I had left behind.

Jenny said, "How's your book coming along?"

A book had been my whole reason for that ordeal. I had not started it, but I said, "Fine."

"What do you do all day?"

"I write, I play with Jack, I smoke, I watch children's programs on television."

"Do you have a deadline for the book?"

"Sort of," I said. "The contract says 'spring '74.' "

"That's soon," she said. "Three or four months. You don't seem worried!"

The trip had almost broken me; so what would a book do? My secret was that there was no book—none that I cared to write. For the moment, I wanted nothing more than this—the little family in the little house in a corner of a dark city. I was safe.

"What happens if you don't deliver on time?" Jenny asked. "Do the publishers get their money back?"

"I spent it," I said. "But even so, I think I'll get extra time."

And I thought: What if she knew the truth—that I had not done anything, that the book was a fiction, that in an average day with his crayons Jack wrote more than I did?

She said, "It's lucky for you I've got a good job."

It was true. I also felt secure because she was working, and she was proud to be working. Her conception of labor was that it liberated you. I believed that she had it slightly wrong—that her work liberated me and gave me time. And now it seemed there was a coherence to my life. There was also a completeness. I suspected that she knew I wasn't working. Perhaps she was proud of being the breadwinner. I did not dispute it. For about a month after I returned I was happy and had no other life.

And then it ended. We were at Crystal Palace Park, late one

afternoon towards the end of January. It was a cold day, and darkening—the sky against my eyebrows. But I was keeping a promise to Jack. I had the sailboat under my arm as we entered the park by the great brick gateway.

As we walked towards the pond, Jack tugged my hand and said, "I want to see the dinosaurs."

I thought he was confusing this place with Hyde Park. The Natural History Museum and its dinosaurs were near there.

"There's no museum here," I said.

"Not the museum—the dinosaurs."

"Do you mean the zoo?"

"No! Not the zoo—the dinosaurs!"

"Listen, Jack, there aren't any dinosaurs here."

"Yes!"

It was terrible to hear him insist. He then began to sob in frustration, and ran ahead of me, along a path, towards a garden I had never seen before. And there in the garden was a large greeny-bronze stegosaurus (it said so on a sign) with a long tail and horns, seeming to claw its way past a rhododendron. In the twilight it looked half alive, like a creature that came out at night.

"There," Jack was saying. His face was white. "I told you!"

He was a lovely boy, but he had the crowing pedantry of most bright children; he was infuriated by contradiction. And he showed me more dinosaurs in the shadowy garden. I was touched, because the creatures were five times his size.

My next question simply slipped out in a kind of admiring way.

"How did you know about these things?"

"I came here with Mummy's friend."

I struggled to say, "Is Mummy's friend a woman or a man?"

He answered promptly and all at once I was freezing.

Jack had said, "What are you looking at, Dad?"

I said, "Nothing," and meant it.

He had seen a change in me that instant. I talked to him glumly, trying to decide what I should do next. I could not think. My mind was a blank. I had no plan.

The next day I took up my notebooks and began to reread them closely, and all the sadness and difficulty of my long trip came back to me. I felt sorry for myself, because I had been right in Siberia: my suspicions were confirmed. I had been fooled. I felt I was back in Siberia, and it was then that I remembered the entire telephone conversation, and all of it upset me.

The thought that I had suppressed then, and that I allowed myself to consider now, was that my call had been a great surprise to Jenny. It had been six in the morning. I never wanted this to be true, because it had been my gloomiest and most tormenting suspicion, but while we had spoken on the phone she was with someone else. He was lying on my side of the bed, waiting for her.

Perhaps it had not awakened them, but only interrupted them.
Let it ring.
No, it might be him.
So what?
He'd wonder where I was. Let me up, darling.
That was why she had been worse than noncommittal; she had been cold.
Who was it?
It was him. Don't worry. He's in Siberia.

Now I had a secret, and it was like an illness. My habit of concealment was so highly developed I was able to accommodate it. But it was painful—hiding it, living with it. The secrecy re-created the double life that I had once been used to. But it was not simple, and it was not the game I had invented as a teenager. I was thirty-two. I knew that a double life is not an alternating existence of first one then the other, like an actor changing clothes. It is both lives being felt and led simultaneously.

And so all the time I was with Jack, watching television or meeting him after school; or cooking for Jenny, or shopping, or going to the laundromat, or telling stories, or listening, or making plans, or making love—all that time, the secret twitched within me.

I believed that she too was leading two lives and that, unused to doing so, she would be careless. I could not wait for her to slip. I searched for proof.

First I looked in the house. There was her dressing table in the bedroom, full of drawers. All burglars and housebreakers go for the main bedroom and make straight for the dressing table: they know it contains everything. I sifted through and found foreign coins, hairpins, broken pens, her passport (she had not left the country in my absence), receipts for gas and electric bills, used checkbooks and jewelry. I recognized all the jewelry. So she had not been given that kind of present. I studied the check stubs—nothing there.

Her clothing was more revealing. Did the fact that she had bought quite a lot of new underwear mean something? I felt it did. But it was all I found. She seldom threw anything away. This meant her drawers and shelves were full. But it was junk, it meant nothing—it was old bus tickets, and out-of-date season tickets and timetables and broken pencils and cheap watches, and old clothes. Looking through this pitiful stuff only made me sad. I found a snapshot of her holding Jack and taped it to the wall over my desk.

Jack said, "What are you doing, Dad?"

"Cleaning out these drawers."

"Can I help you?"

"No," I said sharply, and then more gently, "No."

Leaving Siberia I had imagined a long story about a man in a road humiliated in front of his son. I remembered it now, and thought of the man's pain, and how the American who had watched it all from his window had taken his revenge.

Jack knew something and because he was unaware of what he knew it was the one subject I could not raise with him. My questions were impossible, though I often looked into his lovely clear eyes and thought: *Tell me about Mummy's friend—did he often take you to the park? Did he play with you? Where did he eat?*

Then he would know. The questions would alert him and then he would have a secret. He would have to live with that.

Where did Mummy's friend sleep?

Jack smiled at me. He knew everything and none of it was wrong.

What was his name?

I had the power to take his innocence away. Just a suggestion from me and he would be brought down. How simple and true the Bible story was, about Adam and Eve wanting to know too much.

I was tempted; but I loved the child too much to involve him in this. Instead, I developed a routine of looking through Jenny's handbag and briefcase. I usually did it twice. As soon as she came home from work she rushed to see Jack, and she usually read him a story. Then I went swiftly through her bag—keys, receipts, money, tubes of mints, scraps of paper, stamps, address book. I scrutinized these. And her briefcase held accounts-sheets, computer printouts, photocopies of exchange rates to four decimal places, financial analyses, and her *Evening Standard.*

Later in the evening, she washed her hair or had a bath. Then I looked again more carefully. I had studied every name in her address book. Nothing.

Every day I searched her bag and briefcase, and the only question in my mind was why, after all these weeks, did she keep these meaningless scraps of paper, and the foreign coins and rubber bands? Why didn't she throw away the stale tube of mints?

"I can't find my season ticket," she said one morning.

It was zipped into the side pocket of her black handbag and it was in a plastic holder, which also held two second-class Christmas postage stamps.

"Have you looked in your handbag?"

"Of course I have!"

"Let me look. I might be able to—"

"Don't you dare touch that bag," she said in so severe a way I knew she must be concealing something.

A day or so later she said she had found her season ticket. I did not ask where.

I kept searching her bag whenever I had a chance, because she had been so insistent that day that I refrain from touching it. If she said she had bought a new pair of gloves I asked where, and I checked the label in the gloves to make sure she was telling the truth. If she said she would be working late I found an excuse to call her at the office at that late hour. I looked for loose ends, for any inconsistency. There was nothing, and it seemed to me that was the most incriminating fact of all; for one or two loose ends or unexplained moments would have been natural, but none at all was very suspicious.

I studied all her receipts, no matter what they were for—a new chair, a pair of socks, a haircut. If there was a nameless telephone number on any piece of paper, I called the number. I got Jack's school, the doctor's office, and even the bank, though it was not her office. Each time I put the phone down without giving my name.

"How's your work going?" she asked. It was always the friendliest question.

My work! I had no work, except this fossicking in her handbag and searching the house for clues.

I said, "Slowly"—which was a lie. She believed me. "But my study's cold. I need a warmer room."

Doing nothing at my desk made me cold, and after a morning of it I got up and my hands and feet were numb.

She said, "Oh, yes, I borrowed the electric fire."

I had forgotten there had been one in the room.

"I was wondering where it was," I said, just to see what she would say.

She became very evasive. First she couldn't remember. Then she said she had given it to someone. I asked who. She said, no, she hadn't given it away—she had brought it to the bank. But it had broken—one of the bars had snapped. It was being repaired. A new element was being fitted.

She was a terrible liar. I almost felt sorry for her. But why was she being evasive?

Without any warning, I went to her office in the bank late one afternoon at closing time, three-thirty, and demanded to see her.

"My name is Andre Parent. I believe my wife works here?"

I had never been there before.

"Surprise, surprise," one of the older women said in a stage whisper. And still smiling—friendly and malicious in the English way—"These men who make unannounced visits to their wives at work!"

But Jenny was unperturbed. She said that she would not be through for two more hours. We agreed to meet at The Black Friar for a drink after work. When she arrived at the pub she was more relaxed and friendly than I had seen her in a long time, and she said, "We should do this more often," and kissed me.

We went home together on the train, holding hands, and while I made dinner and paid off the babysitter, Jenny said she was going to have a bath. As the spaghetti sauce bubbled on the back of the stove, I considered Jenny's bag. I would not look— not after the pleasant hours we had just spent. But when I heard the door slam and the shower running I could not resist; my habit was too strong.

And I was so used to the paraphernalia in her bag that I immediately found the note, folded in half.

I would like to say in the nicest possible way that I love you in the nicest possible way.XX

No signature, no name.

I brought it into my room to examine it under my desk lamp.

"Daddy," Jack called out. "You didn't read me a story!"

I was not looking at the note anymore, but rather at the picture of Jenny and Jack. Who the hell took that picture?

3.

Jenny came out of the bathroom in her robe, her wet hair tangled, her face pink with dampness and heat, a bit breathless from the exertion, and self-absorbed in the way that people are when they wash themselves—completely off guard.

I said, "I know you were having an affair while I was away."

She said, "It's all over."

She had been surprised into the truth.

"So there was someone."

"I don't want to talk about it."

She walked away, toweling her hair. I followed with my questions.

"Who is he? Do I know him?"

"It doesn't matter." She seemed very calm.

I had not mentioned the note I had found, or the snapshot I was sure he had taken. I had simply blurted out my accusation, and she had not denied it.

"How could you do it?" I said.

She was not apologetic. She reacted sharply. She said, "You

went away. You left me—I was all alone. You didn't even ask whether it was convenient—you just left."

"And you went to bed with this guy!"

"What did you expect me to do?" I was astonished by the way she so easily admitted it and defended herself. But it annoyed me that she was not contrite. "Did you think that after you were gone I would spend night after night alone in this house?"

"I spent night after night in crummy hotels alone."

"Perhaps you should have found someone to sleep with. I would have understood that." She said it almost tenderly, but her voice became resentful when she added, "It was winter in London, and so dark and cold it was diabolical. You were in Turkey and India. Burma. Japan. Fantastic places."

"They were awful! I was alone—I hated it."

She rounded on me. "You chose to go. 'My trip, my trip.' I got tired of hearing you talk about it. And you didn't have to go. I begged you not to."

"We needed the money."

"That's not true. I have a job."

"I had nothing to write. I had nothing to do. I couldn't face the thought of sitting around."

"I didn't want you to go, but you went. You have to accept the consequences."

"You're incredible," I said. "You couldn't wait for a couple of months, until I came back."

She said in a correcting and teacherlike tone, "Four and a half months."

"You couldn't wait!"

"Why should I? You were doing what you wanted. You weren't waiting—you were having a good time."

"It was miserable," I said. "I can't tell you how awful it was. You know that. I wrote to you almost every day—"

And now I saw her opening the letters. She stood by the front door and put her fingers under the flap of the envelope and clawed it apart. She pulled the sheet of paper flat, looked closely at the hotel letterhead—something misleading like *Grand Hotel, Amritsar*—and then glanced down and saw *missing you very much and can't wait to see you.* After that, she went off and met the man.

"And you hardly wrote to me. Now I know why."

"I told you why. It was as if you had died. I didn't want to think about you. It just made me miserable."

"Anyway you were screwing this guy, so I guess you had your hands full."

"I knew it! I knew that's all you'd care about—the sex. You can't imagine that it was anything else."

"If you have a lover what else is there?"

She was determined to make her point, for the sake of her pride. She said, "There are a lot of other things. There's friendship. You wouldn't know anything about that—you have no friends, you're too selfish. And there are practical things. One day the car wouldn't start. He started it by getting the battery charged—"

"He charges the goddamned battery and you hand him your ass," I shouted. "Where was he sleeping that night? Huh? You woke up with him and the car wouldn't start. He was sleeping in my bed!"

She had gone sullen. She squinted at me and said, "I'm not going to say another word. How dare you talk to me that way."

I wanted to hit her. It was not kindness or compassion that restrained me, but rather the thought that if I started I would not stop until I had beaten her brains out—hurt her badly, throttled her, or killed her. It was not the gentleman in me that stopped me but rather the cunning murderer, who knew what violence I was capable of.

So I didn't hit her then. We went to bed, and without warning or any preparation I rolled her over and pushed her legs apart. In silence—but daring her to resist—I entered her and bore down on her in a rapid and brutal way.

It exhausted me. She had not uttered a sound the whole time. I realized soon afterwards, as I was dropping off to sleep, that she was crying softly.

"What's wrong?"

She tried to stifle her sobs. She said nothing.

The only regret I had was that she might be feeling sorry for herself rather than for me.

In the days that followed, every moment we were together it was on my mind. In the middle of the most innocent conversation about such matters as Jack's progress at school, or the loose slates on the roof, or should we buy a new carpet for the hall, I would say, "Who is it?"

"I told you—it's over."

"Did he sleep here?"

"I don't want to talk about it."

"He took you out. He took you to the park."

"Please stop. If we go on like this you're just going to end up screaming at me."

"Crystal Palace Park—I know he did. And Greenwich, too. Don't lie—I know it."

It was Greenwich Park in the snapshot. I had studied it with a magnifying glass and seen the hill and a corner of the Observatory in the background. And I resented such a good picture of Jenny and Jack, both of them smiling and happy. I knew it was taken with an expensive camera—something about the size of the print, the clarity and color. We had a cheap camera; we had no money. His was obviously a 35mm, and he probably had a shoulder bag with lenses and filters, someone serious and at the same time very egotistical, the way I imagined all obsessed photographers to be, sticking his nose in everything, because everything belonged to him, and believing he was bestowing a great favor on my wife and child by taking their picture. He had slept with my wife and played with my child.

Look at the dinosaurs, Jack. Let me hold you up so that you can see them. Here you go—

That same day, in Rangoon or Calcutta, or some other pitiful place, I was sitting in my underwear on the edge of my bed, with a book on my knees to write on, and beginning my letter, *Darling—*

"I know he slept here," I said. "How could you let him? Sleeping in the same house with Jack! You let your son see you screwing another man. You are a bitch, and what a whore—"

But she had started to cry. That was what I wanted, to reduce her to tears. It was the only satisfaction I had: that she might be sorry and ashamed, that she might be afraid.

She said, "If you want to leave me, go on. But please don't hurt me any more than you have done. Go—"

I didn't want to go, nor did I want her to go. What I wanted was impossible. It was a wish for the whole affair to have been imaginary. I wanted it never to have happened. I wanted her, I think, to deny it. But in her sorrowful honesty and her anger and her tears, she admitted everything.

I said, "Poor little Jack."

Jenny was crying.

"He knows all about this. He has seen everything. He will always remember it."

Jenny's tears were like a further admission that this was so.

"Please leave me alone, Andy."

She knew she was weak, and that my anger gave me strength; but her weakness was my only hope. It was no good my knowing one or two distorted details. I thought: If I know more, if I know everything, it might make it easier.

"He works in the bank, I know that."

I didn't know that. It was simply the thought that only someone in the office could have passed her the note. I was sure it had been handed to her—slipped somehow—and not sent.

She was sobbing—she didn't reply.

"It's probably someone I've met."

Her eyes were red, and the flesh around them was loose and raw. They were like two wounds, still bleeding.

"As soon as I was gone you took up with him, and all those letters I wrote meant nothing—"

"I loved getting your letters," she said, and I was hurt because I wanted her to deny the other thing. "I saved all of them—even all the postcards. I have them upstairs. You don't believe me."

But I did. I had seen my letters in the back of one of her drawers, all neatly stacked. I knew everything that was in those drawers.

I said, "He slept here, you cooked for him—I'm sure Betty knew about it, too. That's probably why she left—"

Jenny's face was in her hands. Was this true? I thought: *Deny it.*

"—and I know that the day I called you from Siberia—early that morning—you were with him in bed. You had been out the night before. You hated my waking you up. That's why you were so snappy with me, even though I'm your husband. He was in the bed, on my side of the bed, waiting for you—"

She was still crying bitterly, and I thought: *Say something.*

"—And he's waiting for you now. He writes you notes. You're still seeing him!"

She said, "No—it's over!"

It was her only denial, and it was a terrible one, coming just then, because it meant that everything else I had accused her of had probably been true.

4.

It was not only the thought that someone else had made love to her—though that appalled me and wakened in me a primitive insanity: a man with a hatchet got to his feet and began to dance in my mind. There was something worse. In many ways, mine had been a dangerous trip. I remembered the bad episodes, the rickety buses on mountain roads; the poisonous food and water; hotels that were firetraps; the abusive and crazy people I had met; Vietnam.

I might have died. It had always been a persistent worry of mine that I was doomed to die in a casual accident in a dismal place, where I had no business to be. I often dreamed of train smashes, of my arms being hacked off by an angry mob, of catching fire. I always traveled as a stranger. But I reassured myself with the sentiment that my family was waiting. It was a methodical superstition, like singing to keep my spirits up, and as long as they were thinking of me I would be safe—they were keeping me alive; and if I died they would be brokenhearted.

Now I knew better. I knew that if I had died it would have made little difference. They would have been sorry in the guilty way that people are when some awful thing they desire deep down actually occurs. It might have been convenient, my death, for someone else had already taken over and totally displaced me. He had sat in my chair, written at my desk, probably used my books. He had put his feet on my Chinese stool. He had slept on my side of the bed, and made love to my wife, and played with my child. I imagined it in the simplest way. My vision was of the dining table, and a sticky spoon in the jam jar. It was there when I left; and then I died, and someone else was at the table. But the jam jar hadn't moved. It remained, with the smeared spoon in it. The pronouncement *It doesn't matter if you die* is devastating. She hadn't said that, but I knew she was thinking it.

And I saw now that my death would not have mattered. I was a fool for ever believing in my importance. I felt I didn't count. Knowing all this was like dying; not cut down with one swipe of a blade, but going slowly as the truth sank in and spread like an infection.

I had always thought the most cynical lines in literature were in the Jacobean play *The White Devil,* by John Webster, and went something like: Before your corpse is cold your wife will be screwing:

> *O man,*
> *That lie upon your death-bed and are haunted*
> *With howling wives! Ne'er trust them; they'll remarry*
> *Ere the worm pierce your winding sheet,*
> *Ere the spider make a thin curtain for your epitaph.*

It had seemed too cruel and taunting to be true.

It was true. I believed my case was worse, for I had not died but had only gone away.

She had said: *I pretended to myself that you were dead.*

She also said she had told me everything. Could that be so? I thought: There must be more. She said there was nothing.

"What's his name?"

"What good will it do if I tell you that?"

"I'll know who it is."

"It's all over," she said. "You're back. It's different now. Don't you see that I love you?"

"If you loved me you wouldn't have done that."

"I didn't realize you'd take it so hard," she said. "I hadn't guessed it would hurt you."

"It's killing me."

"I wish you wouldn't be so melodramatic," she said.

I grabbed her by the shoulders and shook her, and then pushed her against the wall, abruptly banging her head. She was shocked, but she made no sound except a sudden gasp, so I did it again. This time she was frightened and hurt, and she began to cry.

"Please—"

"Melodramatic!" But I knew that melodrama is nearly always the result of that accusation.

My instinct was brutal. I only knew the effect of my anger on her after I was violent. I wanted to hit her again. I could only prevent myself by picking up an ashtray and smashing it on the floor. I succeeded in frightening her—indeed, she was terrified. Her terror gave me no pleasure, but it did calm me, by making her passive.

From the little room upstairs came Jack's just-woken voice. "Daddy, what's that noise?"

I knew that if he had not been there I would have gone much further.

How many times after that did I tell him, "I dropped something"?

He wanted passionately to hear me say that, though he knew it was a lie. Lying made me responsible. He feared that one day he would be burdened by the truth.

It was a storm that had broken over us. In old folktales witches have the gift of being able to whistle for a wind. I saw Jenny as having this witch's gift, but the wind was still blowing, long after she wanted it to stop. We were all afraid; we all wanted it to be over.

In my jealous anger I looked for more proof and when I could not find anything I was only the more suspicious, because finding nothing at all seemed like definite proof that something was being concealed.

"Stop—you're hurting me!"

"Tell me his name!"

"Daddy—Mummy!"

We were angry voices and thuds and screams. We were the worrying couple you hear from a window late at night, their voices so loud you can't tell which window. Screaming at each other, screaming at the window so that someone might hear. At their most desperate they want everyone to hear them fight. And you think: They're ignorant, they're dangerous. We were them.

She said, "Why shouldn't I have done that?"

I said, "I wanted you to be better than me."

She said, "It's absurd that you should hate me because you find I am just the same as you."

"It's not absurd—it's logical," I said. "But you're worse!"

And in between these quarrels we sat down and ate, we watched television, we slept together. I did not hate her. We were in love, and I was dying.

Death was in all my dreams. I opened doors on familiar rooms and there was no one inside. I searched the woods for my son and saw him far-off, holding someone else's hand. And when I looked down I saw that what I had taken to be a side of raw beef in a ditch was my corpse in a grave. There were never any mourners in my dreams, there was no grief, there was no evidence that I had ever existed. I dreamed constantly of flying—soaring low over hills and keeping to their contours. When I crash-landed, exhausted by the speed, my bones broke like chair legs snapping.

I woke from such dreams as if I had not slept, my body ringing with aches. And then I could not do anything except follow the brainless routine of an angry housewife. I took Jack to school, I dusted, and did the dishes, and then I met Jack and fed him and I forced him to have a nap because I needed one. I disliked the entire day, but was not capable of anything else. When Mrs. Trevor, the charlady came, I went out alone—usually to Drummond's Bank, where I lurked, often following Jenny home, shadowing her, and then at the station hurrying to the ticket barrier and pretending that I was meeting her.

I saw nothing. She never spoke to anyone. She read her *Evening Standard* and that was that. And nothing was more dispiriting to me than to sit in a London train filled with homeward-bound commuters. They were tired and pale and rumpled; I was sure they dreamed, but they looked defeated. Being among them frightened and depressed me. Once I had felt like an alien: I was different, I had hopes and my own work, I was a bird of passage. Now I suspected that I resembled them—we were all being cheated.

I opened her mail, and I discovered that the phrase "steaming open a letter" is meaningless. There is no such process, none that serves any purpose. Steaming destroys the envelope, the ink runs, it makes a mess. It was the postman who showed me the best way.

A postage-due letter had come from the States and I had to pay twenty pence on it. The handwriting was irregular: a reader's letter, care of the publisher. They could be very kind or intensely irritating. I needed a kind one; I didn't want the other.

I hesitated with my money and said, "I wish I knew what was in it."

The postman said, "Here, got a pencil?"

He inserted the pencil point under the flap at the side—not the one that is licked, but one that is stuck down already, one of the seams of the envelope—and by rolling the pencil he separated the glued seams, and opened the triangle at the side.

The letter began, *I have never written to an author before.* I read a bit more and then handed over the twenty pence. And nearly every day a letter came for Jenny. I opened them all the postman's way, but they told me nothing. They were from Oxfam, and her college tutor, and the Labour Party.

The note I had found in her handbag I was sure had been passed to her at work. And the other week, when in my fury I had said that her lover had been someone at work she had merely sobbed. She had not denied it.

There were not many men in the bank, and I knew most of them by sight. One sat at a desk near the Enquiries window. He was about my age, early thirties, and he worked with an air of concentration, seemingly unaware of the noise and motion going on around him. He did not wear a suit like the other men in the bank. His corduroy jacket was slightly stained, but his tie was fashionably wide and bright. He looked out of place there. He reminded me of myself. The name-slot on his desk said A C SPEARMAN.

The other men in the office whose desks and name-slots I could see—Dinshaw, Roberts, Wilkie, Slee—all wore dark suits and looked dull and rather stupidly hardworking. They went home defeated, like the commuters I saw swaying on the 17:43 to Catford Bridge.

I loitered because I had nothing else to do, and I followed Spearman for a few days, as I had followed Jenny. He lived in Sydenham, which was suspiciously near, though he was on a different line. He always went to Charing Cross Station alone. There was something about his shoes—scuffed, misshapen, with worn-down heels—that convinced me he was the man. He lived on the top floor of what had once been a huge family house, now divided into flats. His name was beside one of the eight bells.

"I know who it is," I said.

Jenny had just come home. She was always at her most vulnerable then, too tired to fight; she wanted to sit quietly and have a drink. She was grateful that I had made the evening meal, and that it was ready.

She had put her briefcase down and was sitting away from the light. She was pale and looked exhausted.

She said, "Please don't."

"I'm not starting a quarrel," I said. "I'm not angry anymore. I believe you when you say it's over. I'm working on my book. It's just that I know—"

Every word was a lie.

"It's Spearman—I know it."

She sighed and said, "No, no," unwilling even to argue.

When I started to insist she put her face into her hands.

She said, "I'm glad you believe me when I say that it's over—"

There was no irony in her voice: she really did believe me.

"But it wasn't Andrew Spearman. That poor fellow. He lives in fear of being sacked. I loaned him the electric fire."

"I could ask him about you," I said. "I know where he lives."

"Andy, please. If you promise me that you won't make a scene, I'll tell you who it is."

She was speaking from the darkness on the far side of the lamp, and she remained in the shadow as she went on.

"Sometimes it's better to know the facts. The less you know, the worse it is for your imagination. I wish you had never found out."

I said, "I promise I won't make a scene. I just want to know. I agree with you about the facts. My imagination is really dreadful sometimes."

I was talking softly, but I was trembling. Didn't she know that I would have promised anything? But it was like lying my way into a building—conning someone to gain entrance. It was more than that, though, because I was smiling, I was agreeing with her, I was using my charm and putting her at ease. It was like seducing her, and with a sigh—seeing no alternative—she submitted.

"It was Terry Slee," she said. "Don't be angry, darling."

"I'm not angry at all." I thought: I'll kill the bastard.

5.

I should have known. She had not chosen a man who resembled me—she had chosen my opposite. He was older—divorced, I discovered—rather well-dressed in a conventional bankerish way (the same uniform with slightly brighter stripes). He was worldly and ambitious. I woke every morning with the sense that I was far from home. This man was a Londoner, like my wife. He was the assistant manager at the bank. He had probably hired her. She saw him every day. I found that unbearable. I hated the way she had called him Terry—so familiar. The truth didn't ease the pain. It only made it worse. I thought: There's more, there's always more.

Because she had chosen someone unlike me in every way I felt she had rejected me. I might have been able to rationalize another American, or explain a ne'er-do-well; and I had almost gotten used to the idea of Spearman and his broken shoes. But this ridiculous spiv, who had dumped his wife, so pleased with himself, his three-piece suits, his copy of the *Financial Times,* his affectation of carrying a sensationally battered briefcase—this was an insult. How could she?

And I had met him. Just before Christmas two years ago at The Black Friar. I had arrived early. They came in together breathless, laughing, pink-faced from the cold air, sharing a joke. Jenny saw me and stopped laughing.

"This is my husband."

"I've heard so much about you," he said. Not all English people shook hands; was that the day I learned it?

"I haven't heard anything about you."

"Perhaps that's just as well."

He spoke with a trace of a smile, believing that he was devastating.

Why hadn't I suspected him? It was simple: because he was such a horse's ass. I would never have guessed that Jenny would take up with someone like that.

I had been so wrong about her, so deceived, I felt justified in retracting my promise—all my promises.

"What are you thinking?" she asked me one day.

I have decided not to kill you, I thought.

When I did not reply, she said, "You never listen to a thing I say."

I had no clear intention, only a general idea of destroying him; of making him as miserable as he had made me.

Every morning at eight-thirty, Jenny went to work. I stayed at home, wondering what to do, and stupefied by the thought that she had set off to meet him. They were together all day. I often imagined them sharing a joke, as I had seen that first time. The joke was me.

Almost every evening she said, "How's your work?"

She did not dare say *Your book.*

"It's coming along."

There was no book. There wasn't even a start. A book seemed like an evasion of all this, and anyway I was incapable of writing anything. My work was my dealing with this deception, even if dealing so far meant doing nothing. It occupied the whole of my privacy and had displaced everything else in my mind.

I imagined shooting him—suddenly opening fire, as he mounted the steps to his home; not killing him, but wounding him terribly, tearing an ear off, severing a hand, disfiguring his face, crippling him. He had a flat in a house in Islington. I sometimes loitered there. I thought of breaking all his windows, or setting the house on fire; pouring paint stripper over his car. I had heard of a man being able to bear severe persecution, even torture, and then breaking down completely when his dog was stolen. Slee had a cat. I had seen the creature at his window. I devised various ways of hanging the cat.

One night in February, Jenny said that she would be home late, and would I babysit? I said, of course I would. Later that evening, doubting her, I called her at the bank on her direct line.

"This had better be important, Andy. I'm going through the Chancellor's budget proposals."

That sounded convincing, she was in the office, as she had said.

"Sorry to bother you, darling. I couldn't find the cough syrup. Jack's got a cold."

"There's some cough mixture in the upstairs bathroom—"

But I was only half-convinced. I called Slee's number in Islington.

"Hello . . . Hello," he said. "Who is this? Speak up!"

I was satisfied. I put the phone down.

But I liked hearing his puzzled and irritated voice, and so after that, whenever I had the chance, I called him.

"Hello . . . Hello . . . Bloody hell. I don't know what you—"

I was always determined to be the one to hang up first. On one occasion I played a tape of a dog barking, on another a sound-effects tape of maniacal laughter. I woke him at four o'clock in the morning, and the next time I tried his number was busy. To thwart me he left his phone off the hook. This was only ten days or so after I had discovered his name.

One Friday night Jenny called to say that she would be late.

"That's all right," I said. "I'll be waiting."

I then dialed the Islington number. It rang and rang, but I had had four gins and my drunkenness made me patient.

Strangely, after so many rings, a woman's voice came on the line. It was a timid and defensive whine, elderly and unsure of its vowels. The woman's dentures wobbled, and she gave the impression, when speaking, of sucking candy.

"Mr. Slee is not here at the moment. You'll have to ring back some other time."

"Can you tell me where he is?"

"I'm sorry, I can't. I'm just up here feeding the cat."

"You see, it's an emergency. There's been a break-in at the bank. Criminals, I'm afraid. It is absolutely vital that I get hold of Mr. Slee."

"I don't know about that," she said, audibly weakening. "Who are you anyway?"

"Officer Remington," I said, glancing at my typewriter. "I'm a police constable. Crime Squad."

"You sound like a Yank," the woman said in a blunt bewildered way.

"That is correct, madam. Federal Bureau of Investigation. This an external matter. I must ask you to keep it absolutely confidential."

"He's at Mr. Wilkie's for the weekend. I've got the number here somewhere—"

She dropped the phone with a clang, then returned, rustling paper and panting, and read me a ten-digit number.

"Can you tell me where that is?"

"Afraid not," she said, and then she protested, "You said you only wanted the number!"

"Of course. I was just curious. Thank you, madam."

After I put the phone down, Jack called out, "What are you laughing at, Daddy?"

Jenny appeared at about nine. I brought her a drink. She sat quietly, in the mute recuperating way she always did when she returned home. I left her to herself for a while, and then I sat next to her and we watched the news.

The main story was of a bomb in a milk churn in Northern Ireland—footage of a country lane, with a five-foot crater beside a hedgerow. In the background was a lovely meadow, a stone farmhouse, and farther on blue wintry hills.

"I wonder what it would be like to live in the country."

"Very boring, I imagine," Jenny said. "And it takes ages to commute. South London is bad enough."

"Doesn't Wilkie live in the country somewhere? I remember your mentioning it."

"Kent," she said. "That's different. He's on the main line."

"Where's his house, anyway?" I asked lightly.

"Sevenoaks. Don't even think of moving there. I'd never go."

Greville Lodge, Wilkie's house just outside Sevenoaks, was of gray stone and it had the odd sunken look of solitary houses in the English countryside, as if it were slipping into the soft earth. In the meadow next to it were a dozen browsing cows, and in its circular driveway four cars. It was a house party, and on this rainy afternoon the guests were inside, probably having tea and looking forward to a drink, and then dinner—the English ritual of feeding and drinking to fill the time.

I had told Jenny I was going to Folkestone.

"For my book," I said. My book was my excuse for everything. But there was no book.

I reflected on what I was doing: I was standing on the outskirts of Sevenoaks, in a narrow lane, in a light drizzle, in the early deepening dark of a February afternoon. The patter of the dripping trees was like soft applause.

My heart was racing. I was very excited, because this was the place I most wanted to be, and I was on the attack, facing the problem head-on. I also felt a wicked and irresponsible thrill at the thought that I might be crazy. I had gone to such lengths to be here, made such a mystery of it. Standing under the dripping tree, and hiding behind the hedge on this drizzly Saturday afternoon, seemed both absurd and appropriate. But I didn't need to explain my behavior to anyone, and I giggled, thinking: My craziness is my excuse. But I also saw that my insanity was my personal and unique logic for living.

I walked the nearby lanes in the dark, letting the rain fall on me. No one must see me here, I thought. I put my head down each time a car went by. I could have spent the time drinking in The Horse and Groom, which I passed three times, but then I would have risked being seen. And: If I am seen I will be recognized—they will remember me later and the photo-fit picture of a dripping American would be shown on the news.

Keep this mission secret until the moment of action, I said to myself, and I laughed at my own words.

Then it was eight or so, and I was drenched. The lights were blazing in Greville Lodge. I mounted the steps, smiling, and reminded myself not to smile.

The bell chimed inside, and the door was opened by a woman in a white blouse and black skirt.

"Telegram for Mr. Wilkie," I said. "I need his signature."

I had first taken this woman to be Wilkie's wife, but when she said softly, "Just a moment, sir. I'll tell him you're here," I realized she was a servant.

Stepping softly on the long carpet, I followed her down the hall and into the dining room. It was not until I entered this lovely house that it struck me how ugly I looked. I caught sight of my raw wet face and wild hair in the mirror.

"Something about a telegram—"

The woman twitched when she saw I was just behind her.

Wilkie stood up. He was small and angry, and his size, and the way his standing up hardly mattered, gave him a peculiar fury.

"Who are you?" he said.

The room was warm, and fragrant with food; another mirror, and bright lights and pictures. Eight of them were seated around the table—Slee at the far end. He looked almost amused. He did not recognize me. I knew he was thinking: Wilkie's got a problem. I watched him as I spoke.

"Message for a man named Slee," I said.

His face went smooth and bright with anxiety. He started to stand up. There was a twitch in his cheek.

"Sit down," I said, and drew a pistol out of my pocket.

One woman breathed hard in a pumping motion, nodding and moving her shoulders, and another screamed like a cat. The men were petrified and silent—afraid to do anything because they would reveal the extent of their fear. And the thing was a water pistol I had taken from Jack's toy box. I held it half inside my sleeve. Just an hour before, in the rain, I had pissed into it, dribbling into the small hole.

I said, "I don't want to use it, so don't make me."

Wilkie was fussing, but more carefully now. He was saying, "See here. If this is a robbery—"

"Shut up," I said.

I loved the frightened way he backed up and made his mouth square.

"This isn't a robbery," I said. "I'm Andre Parent—"

Someone whispered, "Jenny's husband."

"And that man, Slee," I said, pointing with my pistol and making him wince, "has been fucking my wife!"

"That's rubbish!" Slee said, speaking to a woman across the table, obviously his companion, possibly fiancée.

"While I was away," I said. I was dripping on the food, my sleeve over the table. I liked the suspense, the way they listened and gave me room. "This bastard came to my house. Messed around with my son, and got into bed with my wife. Yes, you did."

Wilkie was staring at Slee.

I said, "That's unprofessional, you slimy fucker."

"Please calm yourself, Mr. Parent," Wilkie said. "I can take care of this. Come to my office. We can discuss—"

"Shut up," I said.

A woman started to cry and so I skipped the rest of my speech and said, "I've got a message for you." I took a piece of paper out of my pocket.

I hated the way Slee glared at me. I guessed he was thinking, *I'll get you.*

With my coat steaming and my hair over my eyes and water dripping from my elbows I read the paper.

" 'I would like to say in the nicest possible way that I love you in the nicest possible way.' "

Slee's face hardened.

"You wrote that to my wife."

He said, "What if I did?"

Surprised by his arrogance, I menaced him with the pistol, making him squirm. I said, "Take it," and handed him the wet paper.

He took it in his fingers like a turd.

"Those are your words on that paper," I said.

He pinched the paper but said nothing.

"Eat it," I said.

"Don't be ridiculous," he said.

"I'll shoot!" I moved nearer him and my big wet sleeve trembled near his face. "Now stick it into your mouth and make it snappy."

The heavily breathing woman was whimpering, trying to contain her sobs; but they burst through her nose.

Slee put the paper on his tongue and closed his mouth on it.

"Swallow it."

He hesitated. I jerked the pistol again to startle him. His mouth moved and from the effort of it tears came to his eyes.

"If you go near my wife again, you fucker, I'll kill you."

He looked as though he was going to vomit. The others, perhaps realizing they were safe—that my quarrel was with Slee—were very quiet and attentive, except for the whimpering woman. All their worry about my intrusion had changed into a sort of resentment directed against Slee.

He stood up slowly, as I backed towards the door. It was the feeblest show of defiance.

"Sit down," I said.

I could tell his teeth were locked together.

I took a step towards him and said, "You're dead, asshole," and squirted my pistol at him. "You're history."

"My eyes!" he shrieked—the suddenness of it alarmed me. He put his hands over his face. But before he could recover and chase me I ran out of the room, I heard someone say, "Is it acid?" I slammed the dining room door so hard the wall shook and there was a series of crashes, like china plates or vases, or perhaps large framed pictures, dislodged and hitting the floor.

I fled into the rain, laughing.

6.

Sunday we went to Richmond Park and looked at the deer, and had tea in a drafty old building on the west side of the park. Jenny said, "On my way to the loo I saw a sign saying Bertrand Russell grew up here."

Jack said, "Who's Bertrand Russell?"

"A famous man, who was very clever," Jenny said.

"He was a silly shit, with a filthy mind, who hated Americans," I said.

"Daddy said 'shit,' " Jack said, trembling with excitement. His lip curled and he said, "Shit!"

On Monday, as Jenny was putting on her coat, I told her I had been to Sevenoaks. I wanted to prepare her.

"I've taken care of your friend Slee."

Leaving out the wild hair, the wet raincoat, and the water pistol filled with urine, I told her what I had done. "Made a fuss" was the expression I used. I did not say that I had ordered him to eat the message, though as I was telling her in euphemisms of the encounter I kept seeing his tears as he choked on the piece of paper, like a young child being forced to eat cold oatmeal.

"Oh, God," she said, hesitating at the door. "Oh, God. You didn't. You fool. How could you?"

For a moment I thought she had decided not to go to work. She looked sick, she looked terrified. The craziness of it came to me as I saw her face.

She said, "This had better not be as bad as you make it sound."

I knew it was worse. I had left all the bad parts out. But I was counting on their summary, and expected them to exclude the details: dripping on the table, yelling at Wilkie, saying "fucker," and squirting piss in Slee's eyes, not to mention making him chew and swallow the paper.

Just the way she slammed the door when she got home told me that it was going to be a long night. She did not say a word to me until Jack was in bed. We had taken turns reading him his current favorite, *Ant and Bee and the Rainbow,* how they created the colors. I lay in the darkness reading, and dreading what was to come.

"Are you out of your mind?" she said.

Fury had given her a different face. She had stiff unpleasant features and hateful eyes. Her skin was the color of cement. She loathed me.

"Are you crazy?" she said. "Do you realize what you've done?"

All these questions; and there were more.

"What are you playing at? Do you want to get me fired? What's your problem?"

She then told me what I had done. It was a surprisingly accurate version of my caper at Greville Lodge—conning the maid, bursting in, interrupting the dinner, snapping at Wilkie, swearing, making Slee eat the paper, frightening everyone with the gun. The gun was the worst of it: the English hatred of firearms, their horror of all weapons as instruments of intimidation.

She told it meaning to shame me, but as she spoke it all came back to me and seemed wonderful. Remembering it, I smiled.

"It was a water pistol," I said.

"He thinks you might have damaged his eyes. There were chemicals in it."

"Piss," I said.

"You're sick," she said, disgustedly.

"He deserved it. He deserved much worse than that. He was lucky."

"It wasn't only him, you know. You ruined their dinner party—you ruined their whole weekend."

"If I'd had a real gun I would have shot him," I said. I remembered the Mossberg I used to own when I was fifteen. I pictured Slee's look of terror as I threatened him with it, and the way he wilted and bled as I shot him. "I will shoot him."

"Wilkie thinks you should see a doctor. I was in his office an hour. He was so humiliated—and you can just imagine how I felt. He kept telling me that he would have gone to the police if it hadn't been for Terry—"

"Stop calling him Terry!"

"I'll call him anything I like. You should thank him. He persuaded Wilkie not to press charges."

"What charges? Making him eat a piece of paper? Is that a criminal offense? Hah! I'd love to see him in court."

I saw him saying, *Then he made me put the paper into my mouth, Your Honor,* while people in the public gallery laughed.

"You terrorized those people," Jenny said. "You broke some valuable china. Mrs. Wilkie was hysterical. Oh, God, you're pathetic. You think this is funny."

When she said that I remembered the moment of squirting Slee, and the way he had put his hands over his face, and I laughed, thinking *My eyes!*

"You're mad because I forced him to eat a piece of paper. Hey, it was his own piece of paper! It was funny. I'd do it again. I'd make him eat more."

"I'm not cross about that," she said. "I know your pride was hurt. I didn't realize you'd take it so badly." She had become very rational, but was still angry. I hated her in her logical moods, because she was intelligent, and I could only get the better of her when she lost her temper. "What I object to is your making a mess of things—ruining the weekend. And especially all that talk. You can't keep your mouth shut, can you? Now everyone in the bank knows."

It seemed to me appropriate that she should have to face them. She had wanted to hide and be blameless.

"You brought it on yourself," I said. "If you hadn't fucked the guy this would never have happened."

"I told you I was sorry," she said. "I told you that I still loved you, that I was glad you're back, and that I wanted our life to continue as normal." She had been looking at her hands; now she raised her head and looked me in the face. "But that wasn't good enough for you."

It wasn't: true. I needed the triumph of humiliating that man. Now we could continue.

I said, "We'll be all right."

"No," she said. "You've spoiled it. You've put me in a horrible position. I can't forgive you for that."

"That's right—stick up for that asshole. He didn't put me in a horrible position. Don't think about me." But sarcasm didn't help, and I could not keep myself from adding, "I'll shoot him!"

"You've made my job practically impossible," she said. The hatred in her voice hurt me, because the voice itself sounded so logical. "I have no respect for you."

She was pale, and had the thin starved look that always emerged in her when she was infuriated. But there were no tears. No matter what I said she would not lose her temper.

"You'd better find another place to sleep."

"This is my house!"

"Then find another room," she said coolly, "because I don't want you in my bed."

My study had no heat, but it had a sofa, and there I slept that night, snoring under my overcoat and still wearing my socks, like an alienated madman in a Russian novel.

The next day, waking alone in the cold room, I had the impression that I was still in Siberia, sniffing the frozen dusty air of Khabarovsk; that I was somehow marooned, and that something terrible was about to happen.

I lay there in the darkness, clutching my coat, at first frightened and depressed by these Siberian impressions, but at last reassured when I saw the glint at the window. The bright winter morning in London had cast a frosty white shine across my desk, my typewriter, my papers, and the stack of thick notebooks I had brought back from my trip.

I did not dare to open them then, but after I had dropped Jack at school I went upstairs, into the cold room, and began reading. I realized only then how much I had written down. I had written everything, and because I had done that I had forgotten it all. The notebooks surprised me in their detail: skies, food, trains, faces, smells, clothes, weather; and they were full of talk. It was exact talk, scribbled first on pieces of paper and then written faithfully as dialogue.

I turned pages, skipping until my eye lighted on the description of an Indian civil servant on the train to Simla, the dark circles under his eyes, the unsmiling mouth and brown suit. He was telling me of an incident in Bengal, where he had been an accountant; of a man who had threatened him. *"I'll charge-sheet you," I said, and I fetched the blighter a kick—*

I laughed out loud. Then I stopped, hearing the echo of the strange sound. For a moment in my reading I had been transported, and I had forgotten everything—all my worry and depression, the crisis in my marriage, my anger, my jealousy. I had seen the Indian sitting across the aisle from me in the wooden carriage, and the terraced fields on the steep slopes, and the way the train brushed the long-stemmed wild flowers that grew beside the track.

It was half a world away, and because it was so separate from me, and yet so complete, I laughed. It was a truthful glimpse of a different scene. It cheered me up. It was like looking at a brilliant picture and losing myself in it.

And I knew my own laugh. I had laughed in the grounds of Greville Lodge—that was a worrying whickering laugh. And I had laughed last night at Jenny when I remembered squirting Slee with the pistol. That had been wilder, with a victimizing howl in it. But this was like a shout of health, like a foreign word that meant "Yes!"

After I met Jack and fed him I hurried to my study again and brought out the notebooks. The room was cold until I began reading.

7.

Within a few days, stimulated by reading, I started to write. I worked from the notebooks; but it was not copying. I enlarged and clarified and invented. I thought of it as fabulating.

I had not finished reading the notebooks. I had gone through most of the first one, and had skimmed the rest, my eye always lighting on funny phrases or pieces of exact description. *The Booking Hall in Calcutta,* I read, and: *I woke near the window with coal smuts on my face then peeled a finger-banana for breakfast.*

Such completeness was a gift: I had needed a new world. I propped up the first notebook next to my machine and began typing, improving and ordering the narrative I had scribbled as I had traveled. In the past I had always written in longhand, copying and recopying, and feeling like a monk on a stool. But this was a speedy business. The first day I wrote five pages. It was like singing, or storytelling, because my heart was like a stone, and I discovered that I had to write in this particular way, breezing along, for me to feel better. It worked. For the hours that I sat at my desk I was—not happy, but supremely contented. I was engaged, making something happen: fabulating.

I was back on my trip, but it was a better trip, much odder, with nuisances and delays left out; no pain, no suspense, no wife. I was the fortunate traveler. The chance encounters I left in and buffed up a little. Cutting improved them. Now I was in Paris, and now in Italy, and on the next page Yugoslavia and Bulgaria. *That night while I slept we crossed the frontier.* And there was still so much to come, in India and Burma. It would be a long book.

On the first day, at six-thirty or so, the front door opened and shut. "It's me," I heard, and then "Mum!" as Jack ran from the back room where he had been watching television.

Hearing those voices, I was swept out of the world and I was back in Siberia. My room was cold, my fingers had gone stiff.

"I'll be right down," I called out.

I could not write another word. I doused the lights and shut the door and went downstairs.

"You look pale," Jenny said.

We kissed for Jack's sake.

"I've been working."

"How is it coming?"

"I don't know."

It was the truth. As soon as I was out of that room I could not think of anything I had written—I had no memory of it. It was gone, I had left it behind; and I was gloomy.

I did not ask Jenny about her work—didn't want to, didn't dare. We put Jack to bed, then had dinner. We took turns at cooking, at reading Jack his bedtime book. It was not kindness, but a practical effort to avoid conflict. We talked politely, like two strangers who happen to find themselves at the same table, people who begin by saying: *Is this seat taken?*

"I hate these dark afternoons," she said. "This bloody weather."

"It's been raining a lot lately."

It was the first time we had ever spoken about the weather. I almost laughed thinking of the married couple, at last alone, who talked about the rain.

But I liked the rain. One of my few pleasures in England was the bad weather. I liked the rain hitting the window like sleet, I liked the black afternoons; and it cheered me to see people blown and beaten by the wind. London always turned black in a gale, and black suited the city. The cold and wet kept me indoors and made me feel cozy. I had always found stormy weather an aid to writing. I liked seeing Jack in his red raincoat and waterproof hat and small boots, his face so warm and smooth, even in that chill, when I kissed him.

"Time for the news—don't worry about the dishes," I said. "I'll do them later."

We always watched the news these nights. A miners' strike was in progress. It filled the newspapers, it was the first item on the news, it was the main topic in all the political debates, and the subject of most speeches. It was a noisy drama, and while there was always a new angle or an overnight development, it continued—the picket lines, the shouting, the signs, it was all obstruction. It went on changing subtly, but it did not end. It was English in the way its dullness seemed to matter so much. The event was played out and every move recorded, like a cricket match or a chess game or a huge tree being chopped down with a hatchet. We were all spectators. But a strike was a stoppage: inaction. In a country where nothing much happened, people not doing something constituted drama. This was workers not working.

The news was always fat men in suits going into meetings and coming out of meetings, and you knew their opinions from their accents—educated right-wing, uneducated left-wing. They were all stubborn. The sameness of it fascinated me.

"I'll be home all day tomorrow," Jenny said.

"Is it a holiday?"

"Bank's closed. Everything closed. We're going on a three-day week."

"What's the point of that?"

"Government order. It's a way of saving coal. It's to break the miners' strike."

It did not worry me that the country was closing down for four days a week—in fact I liked the absurdity of it; but with Jenny at home I could not work. I needed to be alone. She hated me, and I could not work in an atmosphere of her loathing. The more I thought of it the less I liked the three-day week. It was a vindictive piece of trickery. What a country it was for refusing to work!

"What a stupid country."

"You could leave," she said. "No one's keeping you here."

I wanted to answer her, but when I opened my mouth to speak I began to cry. I thought of Jack asleep upstairs, and Jenny, the happy years of our marriage, and all my work. I had published six novels. They had been well-reviewed, they had sold moderately, but I had no money left. I knew that to make a living I would have to write a book a year, but I felt I was capable of that. Yet it was hard to be both praised and penniless; for a writer it seemed another kind of Siberia.

"Why don't you leave England, if you hate it so much?"

I sobbed and said, "I don't live in this country. I live upstairs in this house, like one of those crazy bastards who thinks the war is still on, hiding from everyone, and afraid—"

What was I saying? My face was messy with tears.

Jenny said, "God, you're pathetic."

That was a typical day—the excitement of writing, the appearance of Jenny, a gloomy meal, the miners' strike on the news and tears: sometimes hers, sometimes mine.

I felt she had given up on me. I was alone. But I had a cure for loneliness: this book. I would never have been able to write a novel or a story. My imagination was blunted. But my trip in these notebooks was like a first draft; I only needed to improve it, and improvement usually meant no more than leaving things out, not adding anything. I had brought the whole trip back with me—all the trains, all the talk, all the people. I did not particularly like travel books—the form had fatal insufficiencies. It was usually geography, and potted history, and a kind of lifeless boasting about how far the writer had gone and what he ate. I wanted something different, but I wasn't trying to devise a new form, I was only attempting to lift my mood. I always sat down sorrowful but as soon as I became engrossed in my notebooks I began to smile.

It was I think the effect of people talking. I had always written down what people said, their exact words. Nothing was more human than direct speech. It could be very simple, the place making it extraordinary. In the most remote part of Afghanistan, in the worst and dirtiest hotel I had ever seen, I was playing the game of Hearts with an American hippy. We had traveled overland from Istanbul, two thousand miles, and had just arrived in a settlement with three buildings. A telephone rang. The hippy yelled, "If it's for me, tell them I'm out!"

I had come across just that sort of thing in a book about the West Indies by Anthony Trollope. It was a scene, like a scene in a novel, that took place in a shoe shop in Jamaica. It was all dialogue, it was comic, and it seemed to have nothing to do with Jamaica. But it was telling, it was Jamaican, and it mattered because it was memorable.

So far my writing had saved me. That was also how I had managed my trip. I saw it in the notebooks. I had been very lonely traveling. I had missed Jenny and Jack. I had always thought of myself as a homesick traveler. But by writing, and especially by not writing about the very thing that was bothering me—not indulging myself—I was able to make something new of my experience, and I created a mood of appreciation. In writing well and giving the experience order I gained a perspective and discovered my place in it.

On the trip I was less intense than I was now, because I had been heading home to my happy family, or so I had thought. I had been wrong, and I found myself in a truer, colder, more imprisoning Siberia than the one I had left. I could not rely on anyone's help in getting me out of it. No one was waiting for me now—that was the worst of it, but it was also a spur. I saw that when I was writing I was not only changing my mood, I was actually using this solitude and loneliness and all the freezing indifference of the world to make a good thing; turning failure into its opposite, something sunny.

But Siberia remained. Siberia was the unfinished book; and Siberia was also the world around me every day when I stopped writing. Nothing depressed me so suddenly or made me doubt myself so swiftly than the question, "How's your work going?"

Then I was reminded of my secret life—the room in which I both worked and slept. I was living far from the civilized world and trying to make sense of where I was. In the past I had written out of a different anxiety: I had been mocking ghosts to show I was not afraid. It had worked.

But now I was in Siberia and I was terrified. Hiding that terror in my writing—because I was determined not to freeze—made my writing breezy and gave it strange grace notes. In the best comedy, there is clearly something wrong, but it is secret and unstated—not even implied. Comedy is the public version of a private darkness. The funnier it is the more one must speculate on how much terror lies hidden. I had just discovered that simple truth. In writing, though, I was not trying to be funny; I was just trying not to be gloomy. Sometimes I was drowning and sometimes swimming, and I was often surprised I hadn't died.

I was also taking the trip for the second time, and now I knew where to go and what to do. That was the beauty of a travel book. It was true of most other writing, too: it was a second chance. What looked like the gift of prophecy was no more than hindsight.

This time on the trip I was alone. I was an alien. I did not belong in this country and I had to face the fact that if I had died it would not have mattered. There was always someone else to take your place. There had been someone. From time to time, as fuel, I saw distinctly the scene in the warm, well-lighted room at Greville Lodge. The fearful faces. All the food. Wilkie trembling. "Eat it!" The man's wrinkled lips as he swallowed, and then "My eyes!" I laughed. But though I was ashamed I would have done it again.

I was writing for my life, I was writing to prove that I existed. It was as though I was inventing a written language, innovating a book, originating a point of view; taking deep breaths and trying to come alive.

Each day when Jenny set off for work I crept into my room and I wrote. Some days I worked by candlelight. The miners' strike caused these blackouts. I loved them—the sudden darkness, the helpless city lit by flashlights and candles; everything locked and closed, like a plague city. It was the way I felt—a big city lit by candles, only part of my mind engaged, muddling through. On the days that Jenny was home I hardly worked. I went out, and walked, and I realized what a foreigner I was, and how little I belonged. And so when I worked I worked with passion. It was like facing a blizzard and shouting into the wind. It didn't affect the wind but it made me strong.

The days lengthened. At some point the miners' strike ended, and both sides claimed victory. The light sharpened, and there was more of it. That helped. And spring came. Some evenings Jenny came home and said, "What do you do all day?" I did not say. Spring deepened and progressed. It was then I discovered the only predictable season in England. Summer was uncertain and often cold. Autumn was chilly and no sooner had the leaves changed color than they were gone. They did not fall as they did in Massachusetts. They were torn off the trees by the wind, or else soaked and splatted on the street. Winter was damp and dark; the dampness was colder than frost. But spring came on time, in overlapping phases and echoes; it was a feeling, then a suggestion of color, and a new temperature, and then it began to surge. It was like a song, with a chorus, a round perhaps, sung over and over again, growing louder and greener, becoming warmer; and the whole season came out of the ground.

I was making progress on my work. I needed the routine, and Jenny's indifference and Jack's demands were part of that same routine. I needed to make meals, I needed to wash the dishes, I needed to stop. It was necessary that I feel like a prisoner; it was crucial to my wishing to free myself. I had fitted my writing into all of this.

The trip had taken four and a half months. The book took exactly the same length of time to write. I now saw that it was a book. I had never found that an easy word to say.

On the day that I wrote the last page I left the house earlier than usual and went for a long walk before meeting Jack. I was an alien, a stranger, but this city did not frighten me anymore. The ugly brick houses did not depress me any longer. It did not matter that there were no vistas and that I could not see farther than the end of the road. I stopped dreaming about dying here and being buried in a muddy hole in Catford, beside the tracks. It had been a hard winter, but I had come through it. I was not afraid anymore. My work was done.

"How's your work coming?"

"It's a book," I said. But I was too superstitious to claim that it was all finished. "Almost done."

"I'm sure it's good," Jenny said.

She had not seen a word of it; no one had. That secrecy made me strong.

"I don't know," I said. I liked it for being a new thing, but I could not say it was good. And yet I was not worried.

8.

It did not matter to me whether the book was good or not, though I was sure it was funny, and I knew there was merit in that. I believed that comedy was the highest expression of truth. This traveling would not say everything to everyone but it had something for some people, I was sure. They were people like me. In the course of writing I had stopped seeing myself as special or different and began to think: There are many people like me. I had written the book in order to lose myself, and they would read it for the same reason, to get through their own Siberian winter.

There was one thing more that satisfied me. This was precisely the book I had in mind, the one I had set out to write. I wasn't looking for praise, only a way of ending the trip; and had done what I intended. When the book was finished the trip was over. Now I was really and truly home.

I liked looking at the stack of paper. A book was a physical thing, and writing seemed to me like one of the plastic arts. I enjoyed holding the whole ream of it and bumping it on my desk and clapping it square with my hands. It was quite a bundle. I loved weighing it and then opening it at random, and squaring it up again.

It was unlike any other book I had written. And I had made it less out of my trip than out of my misery and disillusionment. I had been dying; and this was a way of living. For every reason I could think of, this was a strange and happy book. And now that it was done I could hand it over and go on living. In the course of writing it I had other ideas—for stories, for a novel. And never once did I think of a story that went: Once there was a man who returned from a long trip to discover that his wife had taken a lover. That was my secret, and not revealing it was the source of my strength. I saw that I had lived my whole life that way, drawing energy from secrecy, and feeding my imagination on what I kept hidden.

Jenny and I entered that emotional region that is past disappointment and fury, and beyond argument. We had arrived at a kind of peaceful aridity that is probably despair. Fury is life, but this was nothing like that. We had long since stopped arguing. She had given up on me, and I had retreated to my room and my book. Because she had despaired of me she hadn't disturbed me. I had said hurtful things to her and she had replied with that utterly stupid formula, "I'll never forgive you—"

It was the end of June, and warm. London had a sweet smell of new leaves and fresh flowers. I had the time now to take long walks and in these hours I felt lucky to be an alien: I could possess the city but the city could never possess me. Once I had been gloomy about not belonging, but these days I saw that it made me free.

Completing the book—that happiness—made me feel generous and calm. And bold, too. Nothing bad could happen to me, because I had proven that I could overcome the worst.

I did not really know how things stood between Jenny and me, but I felt strong enough to endure anything she might say: that she wanted to leave me or that she disliked me. I did not blame her any longer for what had happened. It had driven me crazy but I was sane again. I was prepared to forgive, even if I could never forget—forgetting seemed to me stupid and sloppy.

It was clear to me that in the course of writing the book I had lost touch with her. I decided to be deliberate.

"Let's have lunch," I said. "I mean, up in town."

She was surprised, but tried not to show it. She said evasively, "The places near the bank are so crowded and noisy."

I suspected that she was afraid of me. I might start screaming at her in a restaurant: You traitor! You whore! I'm taking Jack away and you'll never see him again! The fury might come back. Wasn't it better to continue just as we had been doing, in a mood of desperate resignation?

I said, "We could have a picnic in Regent's Park. I'd bring sandwiches."

"It's so much trouble," she said, which was one of her ways of saying no.

"I have nothing else to do," I said. "I'll meet you at the bank."

She said, "I don't know."

She was uncertain of me. She knew I was capable of making a scene. I was the man who had conned his way into Wilkie's house and, at gunpoint—well, at least it looked like one—had made the assistant manager eat a piece of paper. I had dripped on the floor. I had been crazy. I could be crazy again.

"Are you all right?" she said.

She was asking whether I was crazy, and would I make a mess of it, and perhaps what was the point?

I said, "It'll be fun. Jack can have his lunch at school."

She looked frightened, but said yes, probably because she suspected I might become violent if she said no.

There were stares at the bank, and slightly worse than stares, people looking nervously away, pretending they were not interested: the absurd and wooden motions of people trying to act normal.

"I have an appointment to see Mrs. Parent."

"May I have your name?"

Surely they knew me? But they wanted to hear me say it. This was drama for them.

"I'm her husband."

That produced a sudden silence that was instantly filled with a buzz. I was admitted to the inner office. Slee was at his desk, concentrating intensely on a piece of paper. He was frozen in that posture, just like a squirrel on a branch when humans appear below, hoping to be invisible and sticking out a mile.

Jenny hurried down the stairs as soon as she got the message. She was nervous and wanted to be away from these people and this place. The bank had become a theater, and Jenny and I the actors. Everything we did mattered, and even her fear that I might revert and go haywire was obvious in her movements and part of the plot.

Some of the people when I glanced at them suddenly seemed to be smiling at me. When I smiled back they looked alarmed.

In the taxi, Jenny sat back and said, "It's a lovely day for a picnic."

There was mingled exhaustion and relief in her voice. It had been an ordeal, my meeting her at the bank. But I had played my part well, and she was grateful.

She smiled and said, "When it's hot in June that usually means we have a rotten summer."

"Summer's always beautiful in the States."

She glanced at me, a question on her face.

"I was hoping we could go there in July."

"Where will we get the money?"

"This book. As soon as I deliver the manuscript I'll get two and a half thousand—the last payment. It's more than enough."

She said what I felt: "It's something to look forward to."

The taxi set us down at the Inner Circle. We walked into the park and found a patch of grass near the rose garden.

"There's some significance about the rose garden in the Four Quartets, but I forget what it is. Anyway," I said, as I took the sandwiches out of my bag, "this is not the time for T. S. Eliot. Have a sandwich."

They were cheese sandwiches—dry and droopy in the heat. There were also hard-boiled eggs, and some tangerines and chocolate cookies. When I set out everything on the grass it looked mismatched, rather frugal and childish.

"What a pathetic picnic," I said.

"It looks delicious," Jenny said, and began to cry.

I started to explain that it hadn't been any trouble, and that I had more time now that I had finished my work; but she was sobbing—the odd gratitude of tears that is impossible to interrupt.

There was a formality and dignity in her tears, too, and she said, "Thank you for coming back to us."

I was too moved to speak, and afraid that if I did I might cry.

We ate in silence. The sun on the grass warmed us with its buttery light. The air stirred slightly and brought us the fragrance from the rose garden.

"I was very unfair to you," Jenny said, at last. "I hope you'll forgive me."

I had already made up my mind that I would, and though the wound still remained it was better to live with it than to pretend that it didn't exist. And anyway the wound she inflicted on me proved that we were both human.

"I'm afraid you're going to leave me," she said.

I was strong enough to be on my own now; but I was saner, as well, and I was rational enough to know how much I loved her and needed her love. When I had left Siberia I'd had no choice but to press on and finish the thing by finishing the book. I had done it in cold winds and black night, and alone. Now that I was done I had a choice. But I was back again, and crudely stated, getting back again seemed to me the object of all writing. It had been a long journey from Siberia.

"I want to be happy, the way we were before."

"I haven't made you happy," she said. "But if you give me a chance I think I could."

She kissed me and brushed my eyes with her tears.

"I missed you," she said. There were tears smearing her lips. "Oh, God, I missed you."

I cried too and felt happy as I sobbed, and even happier afterwards. Then we simply lay side by side on the grass, listening to people in the rose garden saying "Isn't it lovely and warm," and "It's absolutely smashing," and "I want an ice-lolly."

I was happy because I had her as a friend once again, and I was happy because my work was done. I saw that the only thing that mattered was that the book had been written in my way. The long trip had been described comically while I had remained trapped in a mood of great grief. And fear had been one of the components of that comedy. A person who is doomed writes best about life—appreciates it, anyway. The whole object had been to write the book. That was satisfactory, and it did not matter at all what came after—publication, reviews, sales, and promotion could only be an anticlimax. Writing the book had been a way of living with dignity.

I could not tell her any of this. There were things I could write, but I was incapable of saying them. My being inarticulate was probably the reason I had become a writer, and why I had developed such habits of secrecy.

"We'd better go," I said. "You'll be late."

"I'd like to spend the rest of the day here."

"There'll be plenty of other days."

She looked at me, smiling with her tearstained face, and she said, "Why are you being nice to me?"

I hadn't realized that I was being especially nice to her, but being happy was part of not noticing. I told her that I was happy, and she smiled. It was a gift to be happy and to know it at the time. Life could be so simple, and was happiest at its simplest. Secrecy had made me miserable, my own and hers.

When I leaned over to kiss her, I glanced beyond her and saw in the distance one of those low green hills in the park where in my dreams I took off and flew, my arms out like gull wings—not flapping but soaring over people's heads, just above the ground. I had felt the wind buffet my chest and create a kind of pressure that held me up, and then weakened and dropped me.

During the next month I was excited at the thought that we were going to the States. That for me meant going the rest of the way home. And I had an idea for more work: the novel which began with a man at the window, watching the father being humiliated in the road blow, and the son looking on—the novel would be the consequences of that little scene. It was all I wanted, time and ideas; that was all I needed to be happy. Everything was possible with her love. Through an effort of will I had written my book without being conscious of her love, which was why the book was strange and necessary. I was almost certain it would be incomprehensible to everyone except those people who somewhat resembled me. How many of them could there be?

I delivered my book and collected my money and bought tickets to the States for the three of us. Just before we left London the telephone rang. It was one of those late-evening calls when it was sure to be very important or very irritating. It was America, the sound draining out of the wire, and then *peep,* and then my editor's voice.

"I hope you're sitting down," she said.

I laughed, and said I had just had two pints of beer.

"It should be champagne," she said, "because I have some wonderful news for you."

I could not imagine what it could be, which was why I was so attentive. I wanted to tell her that I already had everything.

Then I discovered that the best happiness was unimaginable and couldn't be forced. It was like a different altitude bringing on a physical change: breathing was easier, time was altered. And years passed—mostly sunshine. Good news, good news.

SIX

TWO OF EVERYTHING

1.

The plane cut lumberingly through the winter-bright afternoon, and down below I could see the geography of my childhood—the neck of Nahant, the stripe of Revere Beach, the lumpy islands of Boston Harbor, and beneath our approach the rest of it, Wright's Pond, St. Ray's, Elm Street, the Sandpits where I had kissed Tina Spector. Our altitude miniaturized it and made it look like a map of the past, the way it was in my memory.

We banked, Massachusetts was tipped on its side, we came in low over East Boston and Orient Heights, and it seemed—as it always does to people landing at Logan—that we were landing in the harbor chop. There was only blue water beneath us. Just before we touched down in the sea the runway appeared like a breakwater, and I was happy—my heart lifted. Every landing I made in America was a homecoming, something to celebrate.

I was first in line at customs, which looked like a supermarket checkout.

"Bags?" the customs officer said, as I handed him my declaration.

"I don't have any."

He looked up. He had the Boston face—an Irish face, with meaty cheeks and a small mouth, thin lips, a close policeman's haircut, narrow shoulders, and a big solid belly pushing his belt buckle down.

He scratched his hairy forearm and started to intimidate me. He had blue unfriendly eyes and pale eyelashes.

I put my book down. It was Arthur Waley's translation of *The Secret History of the Mongols.*

"Is this all you have?"

"Yes."

He clutched my customs declaration with stubby fingers and leaned over the counter to see whether I was lying.

"This is all you have?"

I hated nags who repeated the same question.

"I just answered that," I said, and seeing his neck shorten in sudden anger I added, "Right. A history book. Thirteenth century."

"Where are you coming from?" He flipped the pages of his thick book, looking for my name on his wanted list.

"London."

He scribbled on my customs declaration, not looking up.

"Business or vacation?"

"Both."

"How long were you away?"

"Two months."

He looked up again and took a sip of air through his small mouth.

"You're away two months and you don't have any bags?"

"I have a house in London."

"Yeah?"

"I have everything I need there."

"What's this address in Barnstable?"

"My house," I said. "My other house."

He looked angry in anticipation, and envious—his envy showing in his small bunched-up mouth, as though he had been thwarted in something he wanted to eat.

"You don't even have a toothbrush."

"I own two toothbrushes."

He was still looking at me in that hungry and disgusted way, and I hated him for being obstructive. This is my country, I thought. I am home.

"That's nice. You got two toothbrushes."

"I have two of everything," I said. "One here, one there."

"That's very nice," he said. "What business are you in?"

"Writing. I write books."

"Have I heard of you?"

"Obviously not."

But he hesitated. "What kind of books? Thrillers—stuff like that?"

"Not exactly."

He was still initialing my customs declaration. He glanced aside and saw that arriving passengers were waiting.

"My wife's the reader," he said, and lost interest in me. He hammered my passport with a rubber stamp and slipped the customs declaration inside it. "Give that to the officer at the door."

I pushed my book in my pocket and went outside, where it was clear and cold, with a faint kerosene tang of airplane fuel in the air. I cut across Central Parking to the Eastern Airlines terminal and caught the early afternoon PBA flight to Hyannis—just me and a noiseless Yankee woman and her bulging L.L. Bean canvas shopping bag in the eight-seater plane. The Osterville Taxi was waiting in the deserted parking lot.

When I gave the driver the address and some directions he said, "I've driven you before."

"Right."

"Big house. Top of the hill."

"Right."

"Nice spot."

I disliked his showing an interest in my privacy, so I said no more. I cracked the window open and smelled the air—pine needles and salt marsh and damp leaves. The creamy dunes showed like surf across the marsh under a blue sky.

The driver knew the way. When I paid him he said again, "Nice spot."

It always made me apprehensive when strangers praised the house. I feared their interest, because I knew they would always remember it. It was that sort of towering house on its own hill. I wanted it to remain secret.

I watched him go, so that he wouldn't linger, and then I went inside. Everything was as I had left it. It was warm from the sun through the huge windows, my book was on the table where I had been reading, my slippers by the front door, my teapot and teacup next to the sink, the refrigerator door ajar. I tore two months off the calendar, and I called Eden.

"I'm here."

She let out a little scream of delight and said, "Oh, Andy, it's so wonderful to hear your voice. When can I see you?"

I unrolled the carpets and squared them off. I carried the framed Japanese prints that were stacked in the library and rehung them. I dug out the statues from the attic—the gold Tara, silver lama and bronze Buddha—and set them on their pedestals. I opened the windows, dusted the tables, and made the bed. I switched on the refrigerator and the hot water heater. I walked around the yard—picked up a few fallen branches and threw them into the woods, swept the pine needles out of a storm drain, picked some pebbles off the muddy lawn and tossed them on the path. I examined the shrubs. The magnolia blossoms were just blowing open, the tulips were rising, the azaleas were in bud. And there were small, hard, blood-colored buds on most of the bushes and trees. I unlocked the garage and looked for signs of mice: there were no corpses and yet all the poison had been eaten from the trays I had set out in January. I took the canvas cover off my rowing skiff, I pumped up a soft tire on the boat trailer. I reconnected the battery in the Jeep and let the engine run, while I cleared the spiders from the Jacuzzi. By then the household water was hot. I filled the tub and sat in the turbulence, easing my muscles; and then dressed in my Cape clothes—a sweatshirt and blue jeans, and moccasins that were cool from the closet.

I found a beer in the pantry and lay on the chaise lounge facing west and reading *The Secret History of the Mongols.* I became engrossed in the career of the Ong Khan, the supreme ruler of a people called the Keraits. He was a resourceful and imaginative leader and I began fantasizing about him and seeing myself on horseback, urging my warriors forward and ranging over great tracts of Mongolia. I wondered why someone as powerful as the Ong Khan had not posed a greater challenge to Genghis Khan.

And then I knew. The Ong Khan was unexpectedly defeated in a short battle. He lost his horse and all his equipment. He hurried away empty-handed, but he was safe—and he believed there would be more battles. He traveled a great distance—I looked up and saw the sunset reddening over Sandwich.

The Ong Khan [I read] was thirsty after this long journey and was going down to the stream to drink when a Naiman scout called Khori-subechi seized him.

He said, "I am the Ong Khan," but the scout did not believe him, and killed him.

I stopped reading, I closed the book, I considered my life. I had not used it much in my writing. The sunset was still in my face, and I watched it, thinking of the Ong Khan and myself, until the daylight was gone, until the last drop was wrung out of the sky by the night, and my house was in darkness.

In that darkness, without a book, I watched for Eden. At the foot of the hill was a distant solitary streetlamp, and its old-fashioned blob of light showed on the road. It was an austere and moody Edward Hopper, like the undecorated gas station down the road, like the white clapboard house on the marsh to the north. I listened to the foghorn from the Cape Cod Canal entrance—one low hoot every fifteen seconds. For the moment it all seemed perfect—my solitude, the sky full of stars through the high windows of my house, the streetlamp standing like a single daffodil, and the foghorn sounding in the blackness beyond it while I lay, propped up on one arm and drinking. I had forgotten the Ong Khan; I was thinking only of Eden. To me anticipation was bliss, and nothing was better than waiting in the warm shadowy house for this woman to arrive. It wasn't anything like repose. It was all motion, like a vivid journey, producing wave upon wave of fantasies and sensations.

In a random and disorderly world of hectic days and long nights this was a sure thing—certain happiness. The foretaste was so sweet that I became wistful when I saw the lights of Eden's car in the long drive and knew that the thrill of my wait was over. The two wheels with golden cogs that had been turning against each other in my mind slowed and stopped.

In the stillness I went out to the car.

"Why didn't you tell me when you were arriving?" Eden asked as we embraced in the driveway. "I would have met you at Logan."

"I didn't know what flight I was on until just yesterday."

I wondered in a little shudder why I had told her this lie. Was it because I wanted to arrive at the Cape alone and savor the moments of anticipation?

"You never plan ahead," she said gently. "You never have any idea what you're going to do from one minute to the next."

I clutched her and said, "I know what I'm going to do with you."

She said, "Anything," and kissed me long and hard, and began to cry—I could feel the sobs through her body. "I missed you," she said.

"I missed you, too."

Everything I said I examined for its truth. I told myself that this was true, as we went into the house, holding hands.

"Why did you stay away so long?"

"I had so much to do," I said, thinking: That was not it at all.

"Don't go away again, please."

"No," I said. "Never."

I was restless and somewhat self-conscious in the house with Eden, and time seemed to snag against us. I sensed us faltering. I kept asking myself: What would I be doing if I were alone? What would I eat—where would I go?

Eden said, "I want to cook you something."

"There's no food."

"We can get some—let's go shopping. Aren't you hungry?"

I did not know. If I were alone I would know, I thought.

"I ate on the plane," I said. "Let's have a drink."

"Then you'll conk out on me," Eden said. "You always do when you have jet lag."

It was still dark in the house. I had not bothered to put the lights on. I poured the wine in the dark and we drank at the window by starlight, watching the single streetlamp down on the road and listening to the foghorn from the canal.

"We have to talk about India," I said.

"Do you still want me to go with you?"

"Of course I do."

When I said that she came to me and crawled into my lap and nuzzled me. Her skin was soft and had the odor of flower petals, and I could feel her warmth against my eyes. She touched me and my mind went dead, my tongue became thick and stupid, and something deep within me came alive—a circuit that began to throb—whipping up my heart and my blood.

She said, "I was asking someone about India and they said this was the best time to go."

She spoke in a casual way but there was something in her tone that was anything but casual. It was vibrant enthusiasm and relief that the matter seemed settled. She was planning on this, she had been counting on me. When I was away I often forgot her intensity, and I had to be this near her to be reminded of how her life was connected to mine. But which of my lives was she depending on, and who had she told about India?

"Wait till you see it—the temples, the ruins, the rice fields, and the black trains chugging for days under huge hot skies."

Eden sniffed and said almost tearfully, "I'm so happy—you've made me so happy."

I kissed her and smiled in the dark, and I watched the tipsy stars, their streaks of light as they sprawled trying to move.

"I have something to show you," Eden said. She got up quickly and left the room.

She returned saying, "Can you see me?"

A match flared in her hand and she lit the candle and brought it nearer.

She was wearing a short black slip that reached to the top of her long white legs. Her lips looked black—she had put on lipstick, and in the starlight and the leaping candleflame her skin shimmered. She was like a night bloom, and when she knelt to put the candlestick onto the floor her pale white buttocks protruded as her slip tightened. Then she stood up and the candlelight shone through the silk showing her slender naked body. She approached me and stroked my outstretched leg and locked my knee between her thighs.

"Am I a bad girl?"

She squatted like a child playing horsey, chafing herself on my knee.

"Yes," I said eagerly.

She sighed and crept forward and sat on my lap, holding me and crushing her breasts against me. Her thick hair was in my mouth, her saliva on my lips, and my hands full of the black silk that had been warmed by her skin.

"If I'm bad you'll have to put me to bed," she said.

We went upstairs, clumsily holding each other. We made love blindly at first, and then we grew very sure of each other, and with that confidence in each other's flesh it was like seeing in the dark.

I came awake in the dark and the glowing clock showed that it was just after five. Eden lay asleep beside me, sleeping compactly, her body drawn up against mine, and her shoulders seeming to enclose her head. I slid out of bed and went downstairs in the woolly darkness and dialed London on the phone in the library.

"Jenny—is that you?"

"Darling," she said—she was surprised and pleased. "I didn't think I'd hear from you so soon. What time is it there? It must be the crack of dawn."

"Five-fifteen. I couldn't sleep."

"Is anything the matter?"

"No. Just jet lag."

"Your voice sounds so strange."

"I'm tired, I guess."

"You poor thing—get some rest. You'll be all right in a few days. You must be very excited about India."

"I don't know," I said. "I've got so many other things to think about."

"Anything I can help you with?"

"Not really—no," I said quickly and then, "I have the guidebook I used ten years ago. I'm taking the same route."

"Wouldn't it be amazing if it were just the same?"

"It won't be," I said. "It can't be."

"Jack misses you, too. He's nagging me skinny about buying him a computer."

"Buy him one," I said.

It seemed so innocent to want something that could be bought with money. I was going to tell Jenny that when she spoke up.

"I wish I were going to India with you," she said. "But I'd just get in your way. And I know you have your heart set on going alone."

All this time the dawn was breaking, like a tide turning, and as it ebbed rinsing the darkness out of the sky. I put the phone down in the whitened room and heard Eden call my name.

* * *

Three weeks later I rolled up the carpets, disconnected the battery, put the statues away, shut off the water, took down the pictures, and all the rest of it. I locked the house, and we left.

2.

Eden was tall and slender, with thick black hair that hung straight down, and pale skin that gave her a gaunt indoor look. And yet she was athletic. She had been a dancer—and she still practiced her steps for exercise and still stuck to her dancer's diet. It was only late at night, when she was hungry or amorous that she pouted and became a little girl. The rest of the time she was an elegant and intimidating woman with jangling bracelets and gray-green eyes like a fox.

I told her she was perfect. I described her carefully, praising her hair and eyes, to show her I noticed everything.

"I dye my hair. It's a color called 'Night-shine.' I use makeup, I use lip gloss. My contact lenses are tinted." She smiled. Was she taunting me? "I saved the first money I made to have my teeth capped. I have huge feet—haven't you noticed?"

This unexpected honesty only made her more appealing to me.

"I'm impossible," she said. "I'd drive you crazy."

Only women used those expressions, and I had always felt that when they did they must be believed—that they knew best.

But Eden made herself comic by exaggerating her faults, and she was happy to let me disprove her self-criticism. I loved her vitality, the way she always said yes, her willingness, her energy—she could spend a whole day swimming or hiking and the rest of the night making love. She took pleasure in cooking—clipped recipes out of gourmet magazines and we made the dishes. We shopped at the big supermarket in Hyannis and bought fresh fish and vegetables and went back to my house and prepared it. I associated her with fresh air and good food and rowdy sex, and I never felt healthier than when I was with her.

There was often a slight suggestion of *What now?* or *What next?* in her face or voice. She was thirty-four. She had never been married.

Some months after I had met her she became depressed. I asked her what was wrong. At first she said nothing, but her mood did not lift.

"I just wonder where all this is leading," she said.

I felt oddly ensnared by the sentence, yet wasn't the answer to that always *Nowhere.* Most women I had known had needed to look ahead—the future was always on their mind, the sense of time passing was strong in them; if I listened closely to any woman she seemed to tick like a clock, and even the silliest of them made plans. Eden thought about growing old.

In that same mood of depression she said, "What would you say if I told you I've been seeing someone?"

I've been seeing someone was inevitably an oblique sexual admission. It meant everything.

I couldn't speak or answer her—my mouth was too dry.

She said, "I was just joking. I wanted to find out whether you cared."

"I do care." It came out as a pathetic croak.

She became very serious. She could see that she had shocked me.

"You really do, don't you?" And she kissed me. "I'm sorry, darling. I shouldn't have said that. I'm a very bad girl." Her voice changed and softened to that of a small girl. "You should put me straight to bed. You should punish me."

That day she was naked underneath her short skirt and green cashmere sweater. She came alive when I touched her, and so did I.

She sometimes wore knee socks when we made love, or a lace collar—nothing else—or a ribbon in her hair. She always wore something—a silk sash, a leather belt, a pair of high-heeled shoes. "I feel more naked that way." Once she wore a mask. She was never completely dressed, nor completely undressed.

If she was vain about anything it was her stylishness, her flair, the way she presented herself—and this look was reflected in the way she wrapped presents, always so beautifully, with glossy paper and multiple bows. She took a pride in such things, as she did in styling her hair or wearing the right color contact lenses; but as with the gift-wrapping I had the impression she was calling attention to something that she happened to be good at. That was why it was vanity—because it didn't need emphasis. And also I suspected that she faintly despised the sloppy way I dressed or my casual gift-giving—I seldom wrapped anything. I felt like a buffoon putting a ribbon around anything except her neck when we made love. But we got along: she allowed me to be a brute and I encouraged her in her stylishness.

That awareness of the look of people and things probably came from her job. She was assistant editor of a Boston magazine that specialized in antiques and decoration, and she lived not far from me, in Marstons Mills, in an old house that she had restored. She had the skills of someone who had become self-sufficient by living alone. She had a vegetable garden, a good one full of healthy plants; she preserved fruit and froze vegetables; she made jam, she stewed tomatoes and kept them in mason jars. She had painted her whole house alone, wallpapered it, sanded the floors and varnished the planks. She had hooked her own rugs, sewn her own curtains, made her matching cushion covers. She was a painstaking cook, and like a lot of brilliant cooks was not a great eater—she loved watching other people eat her food, her sculptured vegetables.

Why hadn't she gotten married? If she had married she probably would not have mastered all these skills, but there was also another answer. She did not like children much. She was frequently childlike herself—a characteristic of some people who don't have kids. And she told herself—she told me—that she still had time to choose whether or not to have any.

We were on the plane out of Logan, flying east in the darkness, the pilot giving us details of our flight path over Newfoundland.

Eden wasn't listening. She tore a page of out a magazine. "Doesn't that look delicious?"

A good cook looking at a recipe is like a musician looking at a music score—the simplest notation suggests everything they need to know, and just glancing at a line their senses are aroused.

[429]

I read *Chef Bernard's Lobster Bisque.* It was a three or four hour operation; it contained wine and cream and several items I had never heard of; and it was made in about ten separate stages. Step seven, I noticed, was pulverizing the lobster shells to give it the right pinky color.

Eden rested her head against my shoulder and took my hand in hers. She said, "We'll make it on the Cape when we get back from India. We'll bake some bread. We'll have profiteroles for dessert."

She was expert at making the lightest puffballs of choux pastry—she knew that, too. It was another part of her vanity, but forgivable because she took such pleasure in cooking for other people and working hard to please them.

But why, I wondered, were antique fanciers and restorers nearly always lovers of gourmet food? Was it part of an ingenious attempt to live well, or was it all conspicuous and self-boosting pretension and the narrowest, most intolerant snobbery?

Yet Eden would have been the first to admit that she was like one of the objects she meticulously restored, or something she went to great trouble to prepare. The difficulty was that she had the gourmet cook's fastidious pedantry. That could be inconvenient.

As we talked about this great meal we were going to cook when we got back from India we were served a tasteless, overcooked airline meal that had the faint stink of baked plastic, and only surface color—when you scattered the peas they were no longer green. The chicken was wet and fibrous and coated with wallpaper paste, and surrounding it were sodden rice grains, brown-flecked salad, cold bread, and a cube of dry cake.

"Garbage," Eden said, and ate an apple from her handbag.

The food was terrible, but hunger gave me patience. Nevertheless, I felt so self-conscious eating a meal she had rejected I could not finish it. I resented her severity—the fact that she couldn't joke about this stuff. She was so certain that she made me doubtful, and I could not understand why.

A moment later she said, "We've never been on a plane together—we've never really traveled, have we?"

That was it—that was the reason. We had only known each other on the Cape, not in the world.

The movie *Trading Places* came on after the meal but I fell asleep in the middle of it, and just before dawn we flew low over London. I looked down at the pattern of yellow lamps on the city's irregular streets. I kept my face at the window, picked out the river, and then the larger parks, and finally as we dropped lower I could spot York Road and check our progress through southwest London, over Wandsworth and Putney and Richmond. We arrived at Heathrow in light brown morning light as rain plinked in puddles on the runway.

"Now that we're here I can ask you why we came this way," Eden said. "Wouldn't it have been simpler to go to India via the West Coast?"

"This is more direct," I said, and when she looked doubtful I added, "Because you don't cross the International Date Line."

She seemed to accept this. Well, it was six o'clock in the morning—not an hour that encouraged lucid discussions.

She said, "But isn't it strange being in London with me?"

"We're not in London," I said, evading the real question. "Didn't you know the airport's in Middlesex?"

We sat in the Transit Lounge for a while, and then she excused herself. She was away for about twenty minutes, but when she returned she had a newly painted face. She was fragrant and looked refreshed. She had the knack—it was makeup, and clothes, and something about her hairstyle—of being able to renew herself throughout the day.

Our Air India flight was not leaving until noon, and so I bought the London newspapers and read them over breakfast. I enjoyed eating and reading, and not saying much. But Eden was restless and more talkative than usual.

"It's all grease," she was saying of the eggs and bacon. "And what's this supposed to be?"

"Fried bread," I said, glancing up. "It's a big English thing." "Yuck."

She ate dry toast and an orange which she peeled with her own knife, and she drank Earl Grey tea—which she asked for by name.

"Tea bags," she said contemptuously, because she always made tea in a pot with loose leaves. "What is this country coming to?"

That was another thing about antique fanciers—besides being

gourmets they were usually anglophiles, and like the worst anglophiles they weren't just lovers of England but they were very critical and class-conscious, too. It seemed a characteristic of such people that no matter where they had come from in America they always included themselves with the English upper-middle class.

"What's wrong?"

I was frowning—disgusted with myself for noticing these characteristics in her.

"Nothing," I said. "I'm sorry you're disappointed in England. But remember this is just the airport. All airports are identical. We might as well be in Tokyo. Even cities are getting similar— the big capitals resemble each other more and more."

"All countries have a different smell," she said.

Had she read that somewhere? She had not traveled much, only to vacation places like the Caribbean and Mexico and Florida. I guessed that she was rather intimidated by foreign parts. She wanted to know more than she knew, she wanted to be expert. In her way she was a perfectionist, or tried to be, which was why she was such an energetic self-improver. She was good at tricky things, but she was self-conscious, and so she seemed amateurish no matter how skillful she was. I felt that at Heathrow she was noticing everything and would mention it all later—the peculiar telephones, ashtrays, carpets, signs, spellings; the shoes people wore, their hats, the way they smoked and ate.

We dozed in the chairs of the Transit Lounge and when we woke I showed Eden the Duty Free Shop.

"Please buy something for yourself," I said.

"You look so serious!"

"Because I want you to buy something."

"I don't want anything in the Duty Free Shop," she said. "I just want you."

She did not leave my side, nor would she let me buy her a bottle of perfume.

"Shall we get some vodka? In India it's—"

She clutched me and kissed me and said how happy she was to be with me, and I was all she would need in India.

"And all Jumbo jets have a different smell," she said, as the Air India flight filled with passengers—skinny parents with fat children and more hand luggage than I had ever seen on a plane.

It was nine hours to Delhi—two meals, another movie, and what they called "high tea." Eden found the meals acceptable— she chose the vegetarian menu, when she saw the other high- caste orthodox Hindus doing the same. She snuggled up to me and slept for part of the flight with her head on my shoulder. She said she felt very cozy. I did not tell her that she was preventing me from sleeping, because I was glad to see her so serene. Besides, it fascinated me to see this tall person folded up and fast asleep.

We arrived in the middle of the night at Delhi Airport, were jostled by the other passengers and pestered by porters, and eventually found our way through the grubby terminal. Then we were driven through the darkness and the empty streets to our hotel. The night was cool, but the battered taxi smelled of dust. And there was at the window the mingled smells of dirt and vegetation, cowshit, rotting fruit, woodsmoke, and diesel fumes.

Eden took a deep breath and gagged.

I said, "You'd know you were in the Third World even if you were blindfolded."

She seemed either angry or unhappy—she said nothing, only frowned.

"Poverty always has a bad smell," I said. "But India looks better in daylight."

The long drive into the city made her uneasy, and I could tell she was spooked by what she glimpsed from the window, and the odors, and the chattering and whine of the cicadas. Her nervous- ness made her sharp with the taxi driver.

"Why didn't you put the meter on?"

She had to repeat this.

The driver said, "Meter broken, mahdhoom."

"I'll bet it is!"

I didn't intervene. I had been told at the airport that the standard fare was 120 rupees, and I knew that Eden would be calmer at the hotel, reassured by the style of the place, its look of a mughal stage-set—marble floors, and flowers, vases of pea- cock's feathers, and chairs like thrones; the fountain in the lobby, the men in gold turbans and uniforms waiting anxiously to be flunkies.

And that was how it was, and it had its effect. When she was calmer Eden was more compassionate, but in the queenly way of a prosperous person in a poor country.

"Don't you wish you could take a couple of these little kids home with you?" she said as we were walking through the Red Fort the next day.

"They seem pretty happy here," I said.

The children were scampering among the stalls and shops.

"Think of all the things you could do for them," she said. "I'd like to gather up that little girl and spirit her away."

She made it sound like an abduction.

"Would you be doing that for your sake or for hers?"

Eden became formal and ungainly when she was angry. In a deliberate and wooden way she turned away from me, stumbling slightly.

"I keep forgetting you've got a child," she said. She was still walking with a ceremonial step, as though in a procession. She was still angry, her voice became poisonous when she added, "And a wife."

"Eden, relax. It's just that these children are happy as they are."

"Are they happy? I wouldn't know. I don't have any children."

"And this is *Hathi Pol*," the guide was saying. "This is place where elephant can enter Red Fort, carrying *howdah* on back. Sometime being clad in silk and jewels."

Big ragged crows perched on the battlements of russet stucco, cawing at us as we tottered on the uneven cobblestones. We visited the Moti Mahal and the Throne Room and the Marble Pavilion.

"That is *ghat* where Mahatma Gandhi was cremated," the guide said, pointing over the parapet and beyond the wall to the memorial on the banks of the Jumna River.

"I feel dizzy," Eden said, sagging slightly. "I must get back to the hotel."

"Memsahib is poorly?"

"Yes. Memsahib is poorly," I said, thinking how anywhere else in the world the word was absurd, but here *memsahib* suited her perfectly.

Later, by the pool, she said, "What bothers me is that everyone seems to be reaching out and nagging—beggars, guides, taxi drivers, hustlers, people selling postcards and souvenirs.

Even the birds—the sparrows and starlings and those horrible crows. They're all pestering." She sipped her tepid fruit juice and said, "God, I wish I had a real drink. We should have bought some duty-free booze."

My friend Indoo met us at the hotel the next day. He was a journalist who had become a travel agent and publicist. He liked the glamour of travel, and dealing with foreigners—finding them always jet-lagged and compliant—suited his bossy nature. But he was, like many other Indian men I had known doing non-Indian jobs, more a big nervous boy, whose tetchiness made him a taskmaster. He told me frankly that he was in the business because he got cut-price tickets and was able to fly all over the world.

"It is a pleasure meeting such an attractive woman," he said to Eden, and I knew that her height—she was a foot taller than him—unnerved him. And his charm had become more mechanical with each passing year.

I was surprised by the effect it had on Eden. She clearly enjoyed hearing this formula being repeated to her. I was embarrassed both by the flattery and by her reaction.

"I am at your service," Indoo said, seeing instantly that she was susceptible. "I can see that you will want to be shown something very special of India."

She was beaming—she was the *memsahib,* he the *chowkidar,* her servant.

"One of its many fascinating secrets," he said, and glanced at me with a wan smile, perhaps hoping that I would not interrupt or mock him.

Eden said, "You're very kind. But I think I've done all the sight-seeing I want to."

She had told me that morning that she did not want to see Humayun's Tomb, or the mosque in Old Delhi, or the lovely tower on the outskirts of the city, called the Qutub Minar. So we had taken a taxi and made a round of the antiques shops. In the course of browsing and buying she had learned some new words that she had already begun to use—*company paintings, mughal, Rajasthani.* She was full of questions. Three times that morning she asked shopkeepers what a particular stone object happened to be, and each of the men wagged his head and gave her the same answer: *It is a lingam, madam.* By lunchtime she had bought some painted wallhangings ("company period"), a carved chest ("mughal motifs") and some brightly woven cloth ("Rajasthani"). I had been on the verge of complaining about all this tedious shopping when she bought me a brass inkstand and kissed me—much to the delight of that shopkeeper.

Indoo said, "She is right. Why look at ruins? It is all tourists and disfigurements. Adventure tours are the big thing now. Thrilling, I tell you. Special—we go tomorrow." He showed his teeth. "Adventure tour."

"Do you want to, Andy?" Eden said. "It's up to you."

"I'd like to try," I said. "What are we in for?"

Indoo, being very positive, semaphored with his head. He said, "White-water rafting on the Ganges. Bring your bathing costume. I shall provide a hamper and all other requisites."

We left Delhi by car at four-thirty the next morning, Indoo sitting in front with the Sikh driver, Eden and I in the back. We slept on the way, jogging along in the dark, and it was sunny when we woke up at Roorkee—Indoo wanted to show us the canal and the carved lions. We stopped for tea and bananas, and then drove on—the Sikh honking incessantly at cyclists and bullock carts.

"This is a holy city," Indoo said at Hardwar, and when the Sikh hesitated, perhaps thinking that some sight-seeing was expected, Indoo said firmly, "Carry on."

He pointed out Rishikesh ("The famous Beatles visited here") and we drove on. The road began to rise and curve above the river, but after a few miles the Sikh turned sharply right and we traveled down a narrow track to the riverside.

"This is the camp."

There, among thin-leaved trees and twittering birds, was a pair of stone buildings. Two sturdy Indians wearing shorts and T-shirts sat with their backs against the warm stone, drinking tea in the sunshine. Just beyond them was the Ganges, thirty yards wide and frothing over smooth brown boulders. This alone was a surprise: I had always thought of it as a flat silent river, mud-colored and turgid. This was more like a mountain stream.

The two Indians scrambled to their feet when they saw us. Indoo shouted to them in Hindi and they hurried into one of the buildings. Ten minutes later they served us a late breakfast of fruit and a burned oily omelet. Eden made the motions of eating but did not eat.

The Indians were caretakers, they were cooks, they were drivers and boatmen. While we ate they tidied the gear, sorted the equipment and began inflating the raft.

Eden said, "This is fantastic. I can't believe I'm here. I feel excited, like a little girl on her first expedition." She clutched my arm and said in a squeaky voice, "I'm so frightened!"

"If you don't want to come with us you can stay here," Indoo said. "We have all necessary facilities."

"I'm going with you," Eden said in a different and intimidating voice, as though her courage had been impugned. "Do you think I'd let you leave me behind?"

Indoo was rattled by the severity of her reply. He turned to me and said, "It's so good to see you, Andrew!"

We strapped the raft to the car roof and drove along a bumpy road to a point several miles upriver, where there was an unoccupied villa. We parked in the grounds of this big empty place and changed into our bathing suits in its musty carriage house. Here the river was wider than at the camp, and not so turbulent, but Indoo said there was white water just around the bend, where there was a dome-shaped stony hill.

We walked to the rocky riverbank and in bright sunshine put on our life jackets.

"There's something about putting on a lot of uncomfortable equipment that makes me nervous," Eden said, buckling the straps.

"And crash helmet and gloves," Indoo said.

"Oh, Jesus. See what I mean?"

Indoo stood at the water's edge and showed us how to paddle—the techniques of slowing down, and turning, and speeding when it was necessary to power the raft out of a hole in the rapids.

"Why don't we practice in the raft?" Eden said, and it was clear that she felt foolish standing on dry land flipping her paddle back and forth, attempting the correct strokes.

"We cannot," Indoo said. "When we are on the raft there will be no time. River will be flowing too fast. Remember, this is Ganga!"

"Mother Ganga," one of the boatmen said eagerly.

"Oh, Jesus," Eden said under her breath.

"You don't have to come," I said, speaking casually, so as not to make an issue of it.

But Eden was insistent. "I'm not staying behind," she said, and to Indoo, "Show me that turning stroke again."

"That is the spirit," Indoo said.

Six of us knelt in the big rubber raft—Eden and I in the bulgy bow—and we pushed off from the bank. The raft seemed an ungainly thing, like a misshapen rubber tire or a beach toy, but in the first set of rapids I saw that it was a useful shape. Its sides were cushions—the best protection against the sharp rocks in the shallow rapids—and the whole raft lifted and flexed and squeezed itself through the turbulence, as Eden screamed. The rushing water drowned the sounds of her fear.

The Ganges here was not a sluggish silent thing. It was blue and loud and very cold, reminding me of the melting glacier that was its source in the foothills of the Himalayas.

When we got through the first white water, Indoo gasped with pleasure and said, "If you fall out, protect your face and swim for the bank if you can. Otherwise we'll pick you up."

"Now he tells us," Eden said, and I knew from her bad temper that she was really scared.

In this quiet reach in the river, Indoo gave us instructions for the set of rapids up ahead. We were to use the draw stroke, and when we entered the boiling hole beneath the rock we were to paddle with all our might in order to propel the raft out of the whirlpool—otherwise we would be hammered down by the force of the water, and kept there.

"Beautiful," Eden said in a toneless voice.

The rushing water was as loud as a cataract and had the same rhythm of a pounding engine. The Indians at the stern were howling to keep their spirits up. It was a shattering minute of cold water and loud noise and frantic paddling. I looked aside and saw Eden's mouth open, and her drenched face and white teeth.

And then we were out of it: we surfaced in the warmth and silence of another river bend.

"I'm cold," Eden said. "I'm exhausted."

One of the Indians squawked in Hindi, and the other replied. Indoo said, "They see something."

There was a sandbank ahead with a loose pile of dark drift-wood on it.

We paddled towards it, the men talking in their own language.

"What are they saying?" Eden asked.

"It is a body," Indoo said, as the raft swept onto the sand, a few feet from the jumble of bones.

His way of saying it, *a bhodhee,* made it seem especially like a carcass. The thing was leathery and ill-assorted, like a smashed valise, which in a sense it was. Only the skull gave it away: its teeth and its yellowed dome were the human touch.

"Let's move out," Eden said. "I don't want to look." Her helmet was off, her hands over her face. "Just leave it."

The two Indian boatmen were talking solemnly.

Indoo said, "They are saying we must bury it."

"How far do we have to go down the river?" I said.

"A mile," he said.

"Are there any more rapids?" Eden asked.

"It is rapids, rapids, rapids, from here to the camp."

"Oh, Jesus," Eden said.

Indoo looked soulfully at me and said, "An unburied body is a terrible thing."

But Eden was looking downriver in a desperate way and saying, "If we don't go now—"

"It is not a matter for discussion," Indoo said. "We have no choice. And remember this is Mother Ganga."

Indoo saw Eden glancing back at the boatmen, who were standing over the scattered bones and chanting.

"They are doing *puja,"* he said, and smiled to reassure her.

"And you're just standing there," Eden said to me. She sounded disgusted and victimized, but what had I done to her?

As we were talking we had stepped ashore and tethered the raft. Eden turned her back on us and walked quickly along the sandbank. When she had gone some distance and we no longer felt self-conscious from her disapproval we lifted the bones onto our paddles. The four of us moved slowly along the sand to the highwater mark, balancing the bones on the broad paddle blades. We used the paddles to dig a hole and we eased the skeleton in—the Indians murmuring *Ram! Ram! Ram!* in their *puja*—and we covered it all with the largest boulders we could find.

None of us said another word. It was as though we had known that dead person, and from the way we had found it we sensed that the person—woman or man—had died violently and alone. No rites had been observed, the corpse had not been burned, and until we had seen it on the sandbank it was just part of the trash on the river. It could have been Ong Khan; it could have been me.

It had been upsetting, but the exertion of carrying and digging calmed me, and the reverence of the others impressed me. They had gone to some inconvenience to bury the human remains and keep them safe from dogs and fish and carrion crows. In a world of ambiguity and cross-purposes this was indisputably a good deed. I liked it best for having been carried out in such a solemn and dutiful way in the full knowledge that there were no witnesses and that it would never have been recognized or acknowledged. We might have simply paddled past the carcass, but of course we couldn't. I did not want to die as Ong Khan had.

I remembered how as an altar boy at St. Ray's serving at three funerals earned us a wedding. There was no relation between that empty ritual and what we had done this morning, which had been like taking the first awkward steps towards inventing a religion. It was the first sign I had ever had that I might find my way back to believing.

As we began to launch the raft I felt elated, recalling how we had carefully packed the pathetic bones and skull into the hole. It was like being in the presence of grace, the old confessional thrill of truthfulness and hope that I had felt as a child. It was a sweet Easter feeling.

"We dug the hole with our paddles," I started to say.

"Don't tell me," Eden said—and she kicked the raft. "I don't want to hear about it. I just want to get out of here. I'm freezing."

Indoo understood. He said, "We are a bit short of time. We will take the quick way back. No rapids."

"Thank God for that," Eden said.

The day ended abruptly and not as we had planned. We stopped in Hardwar for *puris,* and on the way made stops for Indian sweets and ice cream.

Indoo said, "When I go on these trips I do all the things I

never do at home. I eat snacks. I drink colas. I take ice cream. I am happy."

"I know how you feel," Eden said.

"Maybe."

"I hope you don't think I overreacted to that dead body," she said.

Indoo wagged his head, saying yes and no. He liked being enigmatic and I knew he was enjoying himself when he said to Eden, "We Indians say the world is *maya*—illusion. It does not exist. Truly. The secret lies in letting go of things."

"That's lovely," Eden said.

"Some other day we will come back to the Ganga."

3.

A day or so later in Delhi I was in the hotel bar looking through Murray's *Guide* and I saw Eden enter the lobby. I had mixed feelings about men staring at her. I was proud of her beauty, but I hated the stupid greedy way that men stared, doing it not in appreciation but with a kind of possessiveness. I particularly resented Indians doing it, because it was forbidden for anyone to stare at their women, and because I knew that they regarded most western women as brainless whores and bitches. I saw that hunger and contempt on their faces and hated them for it.

"Those men were eyeing you," I said, when she came into the bar.

"They probably don't have anything better to do," she said. She wasn't insulted; I wondered whether she had actually been flattered.

"Where have you been all afternoon?"

"Out," she said, pursing her lips in a small girl's mischief-mouth.

I had to admire her resourcefulness. True, this was only Delhi, and it was easy to get a taxi and go anywhere in the city. But she had never been to India before: this was all alien and some of it threatening.

"Have a drink," I said.

"I'd love some *lassi,*" she said.

Liquid yogurt, served cold in a glass: where had she learned about that? I decided not to ask her.

The salted *lassi* was brought. Eden took a sip and then set the glass down. She was perspiring slightly, her hair was damp, her skin glowed, her blouse clung to her breasts. She smiled at me and touched her throat, a graceful gesture, smoothing her nails against the pale skin of her neck. Watching her fingers I saw that she was wearing a new necklace.

"What's that?" I said.

She drew sharply away and smiled at me.

But I had seen—I'd had a glimpse of a bone necklace of tiny carved objects.

"Is it skulls—one of those crazy Tibetan things?"

The carved beads were yellow against her skin.

"I'm not going to tell you," she said, and her hand moved from her neck to her breasts, lightly encircling them. "If you want to find out you'll have to come upstairs."

And she finished her *lassi,* licking the flecks of foam from her lips. She got up and left the bar, moving slowly with a lovely swing that made her hips seem thoughtful, and not noticing anyone as she passed through the lobby.

I was still seated. I called for the bill, and followed her; but she was already upstairs.

To be playful, I knocked on the door. She did not answer. I waited a moment and then knocked again. A small voice said, "Come in."

When I opened the door she stepped from behind it. She was naked for the whole of her lovely length. She kissed me and began to fumble with my shirt. She was wearing the necklace—one moment it was squeezed into her cleavage, and the next it was looped around a breast. It was as I had thought a string of small skulls, carved from bone, staring with empty eye-sockets and grinning without lips.

Eden took hold of me and pushed me down to the bed. She sucked me, more with eager greed than pleasure, and then squatted on my nodding cock, fitting it into her with one hand, as her necklace of little skulls shook in my face. As I came she grunted and thrust harder and threw her head back, the necklace still rattling.

"It was a present," she said later, when we woke from our sudden doze. And then she explained. She had found a shop that sold antiques—good ones, she said, real ones, the scarce one-of-a-kind that seldom reached the United States. She told the Indian owner ("a crazy little guy in a skullcap") about her magazine and said she wanted to feature his shop in the Destinations section.

"The shop is full of great stuff," she said. "Some of it is funky and some of it is incredible."

"I know exactly what you mean."

She said, "Are you putting me on?"

She would do an article, she said, and commission an Indian photographer to illustrate the piece. The shopkeeper had accepted the idea.

"Did you think he might object?"

And he had sent her away with the necklace.

"He just took it out of a drawer and hung it around my neck," Eden said. "He refused to let me pay him."

"Do you find that strange?"

"You're being really sarcastic, Andy. I can't stand it when you run people down."

She was right. I had vowed that on this trip I would simply wander with her and say nothing, and I had broken that vow.

I said, "They're yak bones. Tibetan refugees carve them. I've seen them in Darjeeling."

Eden dug into her bag and brought out two other objects.

"He also gave me this and this. One's a flute and the other's a drum, I think."

"They're Tibetan, too."

"You say it with such certainty. How can you be so sure?"

"Because Indians would never make any object out of human bones. That flute is a legbone—looks like a femur," and I stroked her thigh. "The drum is made from a human skull."

Eden started to laugh, as though she had just been made the butt of a mild joke.

"I told you he was crazy!"

I looked at the bones and saw a whole human head in the little drum and a skinny brown leg in the flute. I began to grieve for the way they had been mocked: they were lying on the thick white marble table with a copy of last week's *Time* magazine and an empty bottle of Campa Cola and some torn rupees that looked like dead leaves.

"Are you going to keep them?"

"I suppose you want me to bury them."

"It wouldn't be a bad idea," I said, and thought of how we had laboriously dug a hole with canoe paddles at the edge of the upper Ganges for bones just like these.

Eden laughed again and stood up. She was still naked. She had a piece of lopped-off cranium in one hand and a length of legbone in the other, and clicking at her throat the yellow necklace of skulls on a string.

She climbed onto the bed, still standing, and I saw little pearls of dew glistening on the hair beneath her navel, the neat beard pointed and dark and damp from our lovemaking. She straddled me, and then put one foot on my chest in a clumsy conquering way.

"What are you looking at?" she said in a tone of fierce teasing, as she moved her legs apart.

We made love again, and she was even more active than before. Afterwards we lay exhausted on the bed with the Indian sun just before it set piercing the curtains and leaving a bright hot stripe across our bodies.

"At least meet the guy," she said. "You might change your mind."

He was a starved-looking Kashmiri named Ismail. He had a bony face and bloodshot eyes. I distrusted him for his quivering politeness and the way he praised Eden and deferred to me. He seemed on rather familiar terms with her, though he had only met her that one time. I disliked his attentiveness, his furtive scrutiny, his subtle pressure, and his habit of bending double to spit silently onto the floor. Most of all I detested his air of confidentiality, the way he whispered and pretended to be conspiring with us when he mentioned prices. Someone had taught him the word "maximum." "It is maximum value," he said. "In Europe it will fetch maximum price."

I said very little. Ismail talked a great deal. When I spoke I could not keep the sternness and the impatience out of my voice. This made Ismail all the more deferential, and his whisper became a hiss.

"I can give you maximum advice," he said. He offered us *lassi*.

He clawed through trays of moonstones, and trawled with his fingers in boxes of silver chains and anklets, and when he ducked under the counter for more I suggested to Eden that we leave the next day for Agra.

We took the Janata Express, one of the slowest trains in India. Eden sat suffering on the wooden seat, groaning each time the train stopped—which was often—and glancing up at me in a blaming way. The Janata was a steam train, and so soot and smoke blew through the windows.

"I hated to leave that hotel."

"You can't visit India without seeing the Taj Mahal."

"We had such a beautiful room," she said. "I loved being with you there."

"There's a good hotel in Agra."

She looked doubtful. Her face was damp, there was a smudge on her cheek, her T-shirt was dusty and so were her feet in her sandals. I had never seen her dirty. It made her look youthful and reckless and even desirable. When I tried to tell her that she accused me of mocking her.

The Indians stared at her. None of them was traveling very far. They crowded into the coach, they stood and jammed the corridors and they sweated, and after a few stops they fought their way out and were replaced by others, looking exactly the same—just as lusterless and tired.

A man pushed towards us with a wooden box on his shoulder.

"Ess crim. Ess crim. Ess-ess."

He flipped the lid open and showed us the melting contents.

"It looks like poison. It's probably rancid," Eden said. "You'd better be right about that hotel in Agra."

We traveled in descending darkness past ditches of noisy frogs and bushes screeching with cicadas. Eden put her head down and seemed to be holding her breath to make the time pass.

We arrived at Agra Fort Station and were jostled by Indians

with bundles as we made our way along the platform. People were shouting, women shrieking, men heaving crates, children howling, as the train gasped and slavered. We were pushed from behind by impatient bony fingers.

"Sah, sah."

This man pushing me was trying to get my attention.

"I carry your bags, sah. I have taxi."

He was a small and slightly popeyed Indian in a torn white shirt. His hair was spiky and oily. One of his front teeth was missing, but the violence suggested in the gap made him seem more like a victim than a bully. He badly needed a shave.

"Take hers," I said.

"Please, missus," he said, and lifted Eden's big bag onto his head.

His taxi somehow matched him. It was a small black jalopy with brown fuzzy upholstery and a broken grille. Its headlights were close together like the Indian's eyes. The window cranks were unusable. One window wouldn't open, the other wouldn't close.

"I am Unmesh," the man said, taking his seat next to the driver. He rested his chin on the seat back and faced us.

We said nothing.

"I am know everything."

"That's good, Unmesh."

"This man is my employee," Unmesh said, of the man at the wheel. The man resembled Unmesh: whiskers, red teeth, torn shirt, damp eyes. "This is my driver."

"Isn't this a taxi?" Eden said.

"This is vehicle of tour company," Unmesh said. "Vanita Tourist Agency." He smiled and wagged his head with pleasure. "Vanita is my daughter."

The picture of the little girl was suddenly in his skinny hand: an astonished tot in a frilly dress.

"I call this automobile Vanita, too."

The seats were broken and lumpy—I was sitting on the bulge of a spring. The driver swerved without slowing down as we passed clopping tongas. The rising dust was like dense fog as it shrouded the lanterns of the roadside fruitstalls.

"I am managing director of Vanita Tourist Agency," Unmesh said. "I tell you, I am know everything."

We entered a long driveway lined by hedges. Eden looked out—hers was the open window. We came to a portico, a marble doorway, a bright foyer, and an Indian in a turban, looking like a maharajah, opened the door of the car. He wore white gloves. From behind the hedge came the wail of a peacock.

"This is more like it," Eden said, and got out.

Unmesh lifted his chin from the seatback and said, "You want to see Taj Mahal? I take you. I show you. I am know everything."

"Be here tomorrow at nine o'clock," I said.

Unmesh looked very surprised, almost shocked; and then he recovered and said, "Thank you, sah. Thank you. Oh, thank you," and pressed his hands together before his nose.

Eden had a bath and a drink and was happy. And after we ate she was relaxed and amorous.

"I love you," she said. "I love being here with you. I'm sorry I was so cranky on the train."

"Were you cranky?"

"I think I was," she said. "But I'm not cranky anymore. I'm going to be a good little girl from now on."

"Prove it."

"Put me to bed and you'll see," she said, and she breathed, "I want you to make love to me. Wait here—give me five minutes."

She was wearing a sari when I entered the bedroom. She turned slowly and let me unwrap her, but not completely. We made love in a tangle of silk.

She laughed the next day; she said "Where did you dig him up?" when she saw Unmesh. But she was friendly to him. We sat in the broken back seat and were driven to the Taj Mahal, as Unmesh told us about the Emperor Shah Jahan and his beloved wife, Mumtaz Mahal. They were so passionate they were joined as one flesh, Unmesh said.

Eden held my perspiring hand.

"Are you married?" she asked, interrupting Unmesh.

"I am married and I am having one daughter, Vanita," Unmesh said, and out came the snapshot again.

Eden smiled sadly. She hugged me, she looked out of the window and I knew she was thinking of children.

"How many kids, sah?"

"We don't have any children," I said carefully. "Not yet."

Eden squeezed my hand and looked sorrowful; yet I knew she was happy.

"I am show you Taj Mahal," Unmesh said. "I am tell you all about it. I am know everything."

But we dismissed him. We walked hand in hand through the gateway and looked past the narrow reflecting pool at the small exquisite building. In the early morning light it was pink and princely and so delicate it was like a seashell, with the slenderest minarets and the most precise windows and marble screens. It had a fresh and almost tremulous beauty, as though it had just been made, just finished that morning—like a newly blossomed flower with dewdrops on it.

I started to speak, but Eden squeezed my hand in a cautioning way that stopped me.

She was crying—tears running from beneath her sunglasses and her lips curled.

She turned to me to say something, but the effort to speak convulsed her and made her choke. And then her face seemed to swell and she began to sob. She kept her face turned to the Taj Mahal and she sobbed in a sad hiccupping way.

I took hold of her. I had never loved her more than at that moment. I hugged her and said, "I love you."

"Oh, Andy, I love you so much."

There was a sort of passionate relief, like a long sigh, as she said it, and she stopped crying.

She pressed her face against mine, and said "Please—" but went no further, for at that moment Unmesh appeared.

He grinned and showed us the gap in his stained teeth.

"I am not having ticket," he said, gesturing at the ticket window inside the main gate. "That ticket seller is my friend. He is knowing me."

I stared at Unmesh as Eden turned away and wiped her face.

Unmesh straightened and frowned and said in a reciting voice, "This is Taj Mahal built by twenty thousand men ordered by Shah Jahan, emperor, son of Jahangir, father of Aurangzeb. This Shah Jahan was a great collector of precious gems and jewels as we can see in world-famous Peacock Throne and even inlaid walls of Taj itself—go closer and you will see multitude of gems and jewels and semiprecious stones of every variety, and even so fascinated with jewels was Shah Jahan that on one occasion when *nautch* girls were dancing for him, almost naked and showing immodest and shameless posturing, Shah Jahan said nothing and coolly continued to examine some gems and jewels and semiprecious stones that had just been presented to him, taking no further notice of dancing girls. Shah Jahan—"

"Please, Unmesh," I said. "We just want to look around."

"I am show you," Unmesh said. "I am know everything."

But we left him behind and strolled on to explore the Taj itself.

"He's so sweet," Eden said. "Poor guy."

She had become tolerant. Amorousness made her forgiving, and I loved her for her kindness. The magical place had transformed us and made us better people.

I was going to tell her what Aldous Huxley had said about the Taj Mahal when he had come this way in 1926—that the Taj exhibited "poverty of imagination" and that the minarets were "among the ugliest structures ever created by human hands." Aldous Huxley, who of course knew about beauty because he lived in Los Angeles. He died the day Kennedy was shot, and so he was never mourned.

But Eden groaned softly and began to weep again, and I knew I couldn't tell her any of this.

We spent an hour or more looking inside at the various chambers, and she photographed the semiprecious stones inlaid in the marble—small carved gem chips arranged in flower patterns. The Taj looked immaculate at a distance but up close it glittered with borders of flowers and leaves.

We walked in the gardens, up the side of one triangle and down another, under the trees and the twittering birds.

"Please don't go away again," Eden said, holding my hand tightly. "I'm so miserable without you. I try to be brave, I do my work, but I think of you every second. I don't think about anything else."

I kissed her to calm her, but she resisted and said, "Missing you that much isn't healthy—it makes me crazy. Andy, we have to be together or else—"

She sniffed and breathed hard as though she was going to cry again. She was silent for a while, seeming to hesitate, as we walked past the fountains and more green boughs that hid screeching birds.

"It's a kind of death without you," she said. "I'm dead inside." She turned back to look at the Taj Mahal and pushed a damp strand of hair off of her forehead. "It's both love and loss. It's that"—and nodded at the lovely mausoleum in the sunlight. "I understand that."

As soon as we left the enclosure her mood changed, and on the way back to town she laughed and joked with Unmesh. He brought us to a marble carver, where I assumed he was paid a commission to include this on the tourists' itinerary. The work was extremely good. We bought an inlaid marble slab that could be used as a tabletop.

"This is for our house," Eden said, her face shining with pleasure.

We walked to the car in silence.

Our house, she had said, and I saw it vividly—a hot morning in California, in a dry landscape of cactuses and high white skies, in a place where neither of us had been before, our fresh start. I saw our life under the thick palm trees. Eden was sitting by a swimming pool, painting her toenails, taking her time, and she was framed by a carved door which left me in shadow. Our house was low and lovely—Eden had done most of the furnishing, found the antiques, the mission furniture, the paintings. She had done the curtains, made the candles, potted the plants, woven the rugs. There were no children or animals, but there was a sizable live tree in the lounge, standing near the marble slab from Agra. The kitchen was enormous, and although we seldom entertained, Eden often cooked gourmet food. I was fully alive in this heat and light, all my senses alert—a new place, a new life. I felt younger, I exercised, and we made love all the time. I had turned my back on the past. That was painful: the ache, the emptiness, the sense of failure. But I was writing about new things, about that ache, about the derangement of life. Eden and I always talked, we touched, we went to restaurants. Eden became terribly upset when my gaze wandered from her, when I seemed to be staring at another woman. We studied Spanish; she had been pestering me to take up tap-dancing—it seemed absurd but I was tempted.

"What are you thinking?" Eden asked, looking into my eyes.

It was always, to me, a devastating question, because my answer was always *Everything*.

"About you," I said. "About us."

And then she took my hand.

4.

"This place is magic," Eden said, stretching naked by the window the next morning. Her obvious happiness had made her seem physically different—stronger, bright-eyed, more relaxed and sexier. I had not realized how fretful and nervy she had been in the States until I saw her happy in Agra. But it was not only the Taj Mahal that put her in a good mood; she also loved the hotel, its pool, its fruit juice and its food, its bedrooms and its hot showers. And she was with me every minute. I wondered whether I should tell her that I felt slightly oppressed by our constantly being together. Wouldn't she understand? After all, she also knew a thing or two about solitary pleasures.

Unmesh drove us to Sikandra to see Akbar's Mausoleum, a big red crumbly palacelike place with an echoing chamber under the dome. Unmesh howled inside and we timed the echo. He took us to Fatehpur Sikri, the magnificent ghost-town in the desert. We ate stale cheese sandwiches and drank milky tea. Eden said she didn't mind at all. She had no complaints.

"I like roughing it," she said.

"This isn't roughing it."

She looked at me suspiciously, perhaps wondering whether I was mocking her. Didn't she know that having a picnic in the splendor of an abandoned Moghul city, among the mynah birds on a sunny day, was luxury?

Unmesh's car was stuffy and dusty. On the way back it jolted us into every pothole. It was prone to misfire and gasp, and then to chug and hip-hop on the road. Unmesh had a temporary remedy for his car's convulsions. He pulled over and blew into the fuel line. "Rubbish," he said, gasoline shining on his lips. About ten miles outside Agra the car began to jog—a flat tire.

"Sorry," Unmesh said, and swore at the driver in Hindi. The driver replied by kicking the tire.

"Don't be sorry," I said, and I meant it.

"The imperturbable Andre Parent," Eden said.

"That's me."

We were standing by the side of a hot dusty road. The road was made of broken slabs of soft tar.

"We could camp here," Eden said.

A cyclist went past and cleared his throat and spat a squirt of red betel juice at us, just missing Eden's dress. Eden did not see it as hostility. The man was just a bumpkin on a bike.

"It's so quiet," she said.

It was the sorrowful dead-quiet of the plains in summer that always reminded me of stinking shade and stagnant water and cholera.

"There is a willage that side," Unmesh said. "I am know this place."

"You see?" Eden said. "We'd be all right. We could live here in a little hut."

The driver knelt and struggled with the rusty nuts as Unmesh hectored him.

"I want him to hurry," Eden whispered to me. "I want to go back to that wonderful hotel and make love to you. I want you to use me—just use my body. Do anything you want. Give me commands, make me your slave, tell me what to do."

I turned to Unmesh and said, "Couldn't he change that tire a bit faster?"

The following day, when I told Eden we were moving south to Madras, she said, "Do we have to?" in the small-girl's voice that she affected to win me over.

But I had woken in a state of agitation, worrying that I had made so few notes. I said, "This isn't a vacation, you know. I have to write an article. I haven't done a thing so far."

"Have I kept you from working?" Eden said, looking hurt.

I said nothing. I shrugged. It was my own fault for not insisting on being allowed time to myself.

She said, "You have plenty of time for working when I'm not with you. How long have we been together this time? Two or three weeks on the Cape and ten days here in India. And you're surprised that I want to be with you?"

"Take it easy," I said, because I knew what was coming.

"Your wife has you all the rest of the time. Months, years! And I have nothing!"

This was another subject that stifled me and made me silent.

"And you have the nerve to accuse me of keeping you from your work," Eden said, in a poisonous voice.

She was backing towards the door.

"Okay," she said. "You want to work? Go ahead and work!"

She snatched her handbag and went out banging the door so hard the wall shook. And another door banged shut in my head.

I sat down at the table by the window and stared at my blank notebook with my head in my hands. I doodled awhile, sketching in the margin, and then I tore out a page and wrote a letter that began *Darling Jenny* . . .

The Madras Express arrived just after midnight at Agra Station. Unmesh stayed with us on the platform. He looked mournful, more ragged than ever. He brought out his snapshot of his daughter Vanita, and a tiny picture of his wife, just her face, like a mug shot. He produced two bottles of Campa Cola, and two straws.

The driver stood behind Unmesh, urging us to drink. It was too late to ask him his name.

Eden said, "These guys are starting to get on my nerves."

When the train began to pull out we lingered in the doorway next to the conductor, crowding the vestibule. Unmesh stood to attention. The driver did the same. They wagged their heads sadly at us.

"You come back, sah. I am taking you. I am showing you. I am know everything. I have good business then." Unmesh looked at me imploringly and repeated, "*Please.* You come."

We found our two-berth compartment and were rocked to sleep by the motion of the train.

In the morning I rolled over and saw Eden sitting gingerly at the edge of my berth, near my feet. I suspected that she had been sitting there for quite a while, waiting for me to wake.

"Good morning, darling." And she kissed me.

I could not help but think that those words and that kiss were for lovers alone. Did married people say *Good morning, darling,* and kiss each other at the crack of dawn? I didn't, and when I tried to picture it the effect was absurd and precious. Most people woke up and muttered *Aw shit.*

"Why are you smiling?"

I could not tell her why.

"I just remembered where we are," I said. "Did you sleep all right?"

That was another lover's question, and so was *Can I get you anything?*

"Like a log," she said.

I pushed the windowshade up and was blinded for a moment, dazzled by the brightness—not only the sunny sky but the brilliant green of rice fields and tall slender palms. I turned away and saw Eden's face—sallow, with lank hair and pale lips and swollen eyes in the same truthful and scorching light of the Indian plains. She had hardly slept; perhaps her little lie was her way of appeasing me.

She said, "I'm sorry I was cross with you yesterday. But you provoked me."

"Maybe I should apologize in that case."

She made a face and said, "I hate your sarcasm. I've just apologized, for Christ's sake. Why don't you accept it?"

I said nothing. We passed a station and the signboard flashed on the mirror at the back of the door. We clattered over a set of points and shimmied sideways onto a different line, and the motion made Eden's cheeks shake.

I started to get up. I swung my legs out of the tangled sheet and gathered myself to rise and dress.

Eden said disgustedly, "That's it. Run away. You always do that when we have an argument."

"I'm not running away. I'm getting out of bed."

"You completely ignored what I said."

"I didn't ignore it."

"It was a fucking apology! What more do you want?"

She began to cry, looking sick and sleepless, in her rumpled blouse—and then her face was creased and rumpled, too, from her weeping. "I think you enjoy tormenting me," she said.

I embraced her and as I did so glanced at my watch. It was seven-fifteen. I wanted to lie down and go back to sleep. I felt rattled and tired, though I had woken feeling wonderful. Holding Eden I sensed energy being drawn from me. There were some people I had known in my life who weakened me with their presence; something in their dependency drained my strength away, and they became frisky as I went limp.

After a moment Eden batted my arms away.

"Leave me alone. I can do without your sympathy."

She hunched over and became a figure of grief with bent shoulders, looking sadder because of the bright sunlight on her pale skin and black hair.

Without another word, I left the compartment and went to the toilet, a damp cubicle of metal and battered gray paint, with a hole in the floor—the blurred tracks rushing past—and a cracked porcelain sink. As the train raced on I braced myself and took an inaccurate piss, and then washed—my feet, my face, and stuck my head under the faucet. I brushed my teeth using toothpaste but no water. NOT FOR DRINKING a sign said in two languages over the sink. I looked into the mirror and was surprised by my grouchy hedgehog face: I hated being shouted at in the morning. I took two aspirin, swallowing them without water, and lingered there looking at my face—trying to see my other face in those features—until someone urgently rattled the door handle.

My compartment was locked. I tried it and pushed the door.

"Who is it?" Eden's voice was suspicious.

"It's me," I said, and I was going to say more when I heard the bolt being shot.

"Hurry up," she said, snatching the door open.

The shade was drawn, the compartment was in semidarkness, with only cracks of light at the margins of the window. Yet there was enough light to see her. She wore a T-shirt and high-heeled shoes, and nothing else.

"Lock the door," she said, and as I turned to do it, she hugged me from behind and ran her hands over me, and said, "I'm in charge. I'm a wicked filthy woman and you're my sex slave. You have to do whatever I want you to." She chewed my ear and moved her hands again and said, "This is mine, and this is mine, and this—this belongs to me." She sat on the edge of the lower berth, with her legs parted. "Get on your knees."

The dark compartment and the deafening noise of the train made her reckless. She insisted we make love again in the afternoon, but that time it was my turn, and I took all my cues from the games she had taught me in the morning. That day on the train was broken into many parts—eating, sleeping, making love, looking out of the window, and she read Emily Eden's *Up the Country* while I scribbled notes. My notes were like an explorer's, details of the weather and the distance and the landscape, and nothing about Eden, or about taking turns being slaves for each other in the hot compartment. We entered Andhra Pradesh and at nightfall were at Warangal, among glowing huts and chirruping rice fields.

"The second night on a train you always sleep better."

"God, I hope so," Eden said in her bunk.

We were brought tin trays of food—vegetables and rice and dhal, and three sodden chapatis, which had the discouraged look of failed tortillas.

"I can't eat it," Eden said. "I think I'll just read."

Within minutes she was asleep. I switched off the light and locked the door, but left the window open and the shade up, so that I could see the stars and the stations flashing past. And then I was asleep, and dreaming of my other life.

I woke hot and guilty in the bright sunshine of an early morning in Madras.

The Hotel Vishnu was old and hot and badly lit. It had the rotting carpets of all poor hotels in India: the carpets simply decayed in the damp shadows. It was airless and stank of mildew. The bathroom floor was wet, knobs were missing from the bureau drawer, in the closet were two misshapen wire hangers. The picture on the wall, cut from a calendar and framed, was of Mount Matterhorn, with a Swiss village in the foreground, a man in leather shorts, a woman in a bonnet and apron, some muscular cows.

Eden said, "It could be worse. At least I can have a shower."

But when she had stripped and turned on the faucet there was no water.

She swore and then she began to cry. She said, "I haven't had a bath for two days. I've had a bath every day of my life!"

I complained to the manager, a kindly man named Thumboosamy, with a black ratlike face. I had asked him whether that was his first name or his last, and he had replied, "Both!" He clucked and assured me that if we waited the shower would work. We had to be patient, he said.

"Water will come," he said in the odd prophesying way that Tamils adopted when they were being badgered.

I heard the shower bubbling and spitting as soon as I entered the room, and Eden was under it slapping soap on her thighs.

"It's cold but at least it's wet," she said. "It started just after you left the room."

She apologized for having made a fuss; and I said nothing.

She said, "It's all right, as long as we're together."

Later on, we bought oranges and bananas at a stall and ate them on a bench just off Beach Road.

"Why did we come here?" Eden said.

"For my Indian story. It's been over ten years since I was here last. I'm going to all the places I visited before, to see what they're like now."

"What's your conclusion?"

"I'll let you know," I said. "I'm also trying to see what I am like now."

Eden said, "Maybe I'm the one who should be writing this story."

"You're helping," I said.

"No, I'm not," she said. "All I've done is obstruct you. I haven't helped you at all. I'm ashamed of myself—but I'm desperate to be with you. I know you'd be traveling much faster without me, and probably seeing more. You'll never cover all those places you visited before."

"I know. I'll have to come back in July."

"That's when we plan our Christmas issue," Eden said. "I'll never be able to get any time off then."

"I'll go alone."

"I'll think about you," she said. "Now that I've seen you in India I'll be able to picture it."

Sometimes, speaking that way, she sounded sad and settled, like a widow.

"I'll imagine you walking around in the heat. You never perspire. You never get sick on the food. You never miss a night's sleep."

"You sound as though you resent it."

She gave me a blank look and said, "In a way I do. You never suffer."

"I did once or twice when I was younger, and it was so awful nothing has seemed very bad since."

"Everything seems awful when you're young."

"No. I was happy most of the time. I am talking about real fear. It was always other people. It was like a fatal illness."

"Tell me about it."

"I couldn't even begin to talk about it," I said. "Maybe I'll write about it someday."

"I'll see your picture in the paper. I'll read a review. I'll buy the book and read all about it."

She had begun to talk herself into a rueful mood, like an excluded mistress. Some of those words I had heard on the radio that very morning, when an Indian economist, talking about the recent bear market in Europe had said, *If you make the market your mistress you have to put up with its moods.*

I had something specific I wanted to do with her, though I approached it in the most casual way. After lunch, I said, "Want to go for a drive?" and took her in a taxi south of the city to the township of Tambaram, where I had a friend.

I had warned Mahadeva of my visit, but I had not wanted to involve him in the expense of meeting me in Madras. Anyway, we had first met here in Tambaram in 1973, at his little hut, and I wanted to repeat the encounter. He was a tailor, and he worked at his sewing machine on the veranda of his hut on the narrow road east of the market.

"We'll walk," I said to the taxi driver on the main road, because I had walked the first time. "Wait here for us."

"You're being very mysterious, Andy."

The sky had become heavy and gray, with hot clouds hanging like old sheets. I felt scalded by the humidity. Eden was so absorbed in her own hatred of the weather that she did not notice that it also affected me. We walked slowly down the road, past the vegetable and fruit sellers, and I told Eden the story of how I had first met Mahadeva and how he had made me a shirt.

"What's so special about him?"

"He refused to charge me," I said. "He made the shirt for me for nothing. He said it was a matter of friendship—a gift. Afterwards I sent him a twenty-dollar bill."

"So he got his money after all."

"He was terribly insulted, of course," I said. "He gave the money to charity. And there's one other thing that's special. I'll tell you later."

Mahadeva jumped up from his sewing machine when he saw us approaching. He wiped his hands and called to his wife and rushed towards us exclaiming, "I could have met you in Madras!"

He was noticeably older, unshaven in a gray bristly way, and though he was rather thin with spindly arms and legs, he had a perfectly round potbelly. His wife appeared beside him, and she was haggard as well. They drew the slack flesh of their faces into smiles and led us inside.

"Please sit down. You will have a drink."

He sent his oldest boy next door to the shop for cold drinks. His other children gathered at the door and stared in. There were four of them, very thin and with large eyes.

Mahadeva was chirpy—how was I? What had I been doing? He had seen an article about me in *The Illustrated Weekly of India*—he had sent it to his brother in Vijayawada.

While we chatted Eden fell silent, beholding the monotony and boredom of poverty. And I saw her staring at the colored pictures on the wall, of Ganesh the elephant god and Hanuman the monkey.

"I want to make you another shirt," Mahadeva was saying. "I can make a nice frock for the lady, eh?"

But Eden looked hot and inattentive.

We were brought palm leaves. They were set before us, and Mrs. Mahadeva ladled a mound of rice and a dollop of vegetable curry, some bright yellow potatoes and grated coconut. We ate with our hands, and Eden ate what I ate—the same food, the same quantity.

Mrs. Mahadeva said something to her husband in Tamil, and he turned to me and asked, "How many children?"

Before I could speak, Eden said rather sharply, "We're not married."

Mahadeva conveyed this information to his wife.

"I'm not drinking this water," Eden said.

Mrs. Mahadeva came and went. She did not eat. She did not speak. The children stared. They all seemed a bit afraid of Eden. I wondered whether it was because we were not married. It was not logical that we should be traveling together—and in letters I had spoken to Mahadeva of my wife and my child. I could not explain anything to him now. I did not try. It was better that we should be a mystery and that Eden should sense their bewildered scrutiny.

"Palm leaf is very sanitary—we just throw it away," Mahadeva said, because even in India it was regarded as a bit strange to eat off a leaf.

We sat and talked inconsequentially, to enact the ritual. It was a poor house, the man and woman looked unhappy and somewhat haunted, the children stared and the smallest, whom I suspected of being ill, just sat and squalled. There was a kind of sullen incompleteness about the place. The house smelled like a tomb, and the man and woman seemed too old to have such young children. To be poor was to be very uncomfortable, and I had wanted Eden to see how uninteresting it was too, how horribly inconvenient and hopeless. It seemed almost a contradiction that Mahadeva could be so spirited, but that was the whole point and one of the saddest aspects of the trap.

When we left and were walking back to the Tambaram road, Eden said, "What's the other special thing?"

"He's exactly my age," I said. "And Mrs. Mahadeva is exactly your age."

"That old woman?"

"That old woman is thirty-four."

Eden was quiet and reflective the rest of that hot day. Something in the compactness of her posture told me she was thinking about herself.

She said, "They didn't like me. Did you see the way they stared at me? They think I'm a whore."

That night she cried in the Hotel Vishnu. She slept badly and didn't eat breakfast. She said it wasn't the Hotel Vishnu—it was something else, she couldn't explain. We moved to the Hotel Taj Coromandel the next day. It was a fine hotel with large bright rooms, a coffee shop, a good restaurant, potted palms in the lobby, a swimming pool. Eden cheered up, and talked about her magazine, an article she wished to write, a meal she wanted to cook for us. She was happiest talking about the future. Mentally she had already left India, though there was more I wanted her to see.

We looked at the old ice house and the banquet hall, and all the other architectural relics of the Raj. We drove into the countryside and marveled at the rice fields. We went in a hired car to Mahabalipuram, the temple on the sea. It was a great ruin of carved elephants in stone next to the dumping surf, where black Tamil boys screamed and splashed in their ragged underwear.

Eden was wearing her skull necklace. The gusting wind pushed her hair aside.

She said, "I could learn to really hate this place. Maybe after I get home it will all seem wonderful. I wish I had the power to destroy it and build it all over again. You have that smile on your face."

I heard that but I was hardly listening to her.

She said, "Tell me you love me."

The waves came very fast, one crashing on the back of another, blown by the wind.

"I love you."

"I wish I hadn't asked you," she said. "Now it's too late."

That night in the hotel room I was lying on the bed reading the Madras daily newspaper, *The Hindu,* as Eden took a shower. With the sound of rushing water was another murmur. Was she speaking to someone? Was she singing? I put down the newspaper and went to listen at the door.

She was crying—and not just crying but sobbing, a slow struggling sound that rose and fell.

"Are you all right?" I called out.

She did not hear me. She went on sobbing. But soon the shower stopped and there was no sound from her. When she came out of the bathroom she looked relaxed—very calm, almost serene.

"I heard you talking in the shower," I said.

"I was crying," she said, but in a voice that indicated that whatever sadness she had felt had long passed.

She saw me still staring.

"I always cry in the shower," she said, stating a fact and smiling at me for not knowing it.

She always cried in the shower?

In the plane on the way back to Delhi she said ruefully, "I

wanted you to make love to me one more time." She took my
hand. "I wanted you to take me by force." And then she became
self-conscious. "I guess all women have rape fantasies. I'm
pretty conventional that way."

"Conventional meaning you have rape fantasies?"

"Of course," she said, in that same fact-stating and smiling
way.

"I'm forty-three years old, and I never—"

All women have rape fantasies?

But in Delhi, we did not stop, there was not time, I did not
take her by force or test this fantasy. We changed planes and
flew for nine and a half hours into the sun.

In London, at Heathrow, she looked suddenly alarmed, as
though remembering, and said, "Oh, God, you're leaving me."

"You'll be all right," I said.

"I'm all right now. But when you turn that last corner in the
terminal and I can't see you anymore, I'm going to cry."

5.

Then I was on the train, between two lives, hurtling from Eden
to Jenny, and I was alone.

It was a thundery spring morning of blackish blowing trees
and clouds the color of cast-iron marbled by yellow cracks. The
window beside me was made so opaque by the storm that I could
see my face in it—another person. But this one after a ten-hour
flight and no sleep looked like a zombie who had risen from a
hole in the ground to push his haunting face through the world.
Around me were people on their way to work, reading newspapers and books. My impression was not that they were hard-
working and virtuous people but simply that they were better
than me. Yet when I considered that they too had deep secrets
I realized how alike we were.

On my own like this I closed my eyes and held my breath, like a man dropping into a well. I no longer asked myself whether I was happy. It hardly seemed an important question, and there wasn't time to answer it with any clear reply. I inhabited this space, all this hissing air, going from one life to the other believing I was unchanged. I had lived like this for a long time. But today (I had no idea why it had not occurred to me sooner—perhaps it was the sight of my face in the glass) I had an intimation of another self within me, someone lurking, and I thought: *Who are you?*

I was living two lives, and I knew I was a slightly different person with each woman—lied to each of them, or chose a different version of the truth for each of them; remembered what to include and what to leave out. We were lovers. They invented me; I invented them. But for each of us there was a more complete person beyond all that fiddle. Wasn't I a new man when I was alone?

I did not want to make myself conspicuous on the train by writing, and so I mumbled to myself: Maybe I am living my life like this not because I want to enhance it with the intensity of two of everything, but rather because I am afraid to be alone. I am fearful of meeting face to face and having to give a name to that odd solitary man; I am afraid to see him whole.

But this rainy morning passing through Hounslow I saw there was a third person. He was the observer, the witness to all this, like the inspector who had just entered the coach to examine tickets: not a word, not a murmur, only the nibble and bite of metal punch. This third man was the one who stood aside and made the notes and wrote the books. His life was lived within himself. He was silent, he seldom gestured, he never argued, he dreamed, he saw everything, and so he was the one who suffered.

He rode his bike in traffic, he watched from the top deck of buses, he sat in the corner seat of trains and his reflection never stared back at him—his eyes were always fixed on other people. He was the one who read items in newspapers entitled *Bloody End to Love Triangle Riddle* and *Private Life of Jekyll-Hyde Writer Revealed on Piccadilly Line.* He took long solitary walks. He made excuses about urgent meetings and hurried away from demanding friends to eat fish-and-chips in the park and feed the leavings to the ducks. He picked up discarded letters and read them, foraged in the wastebasket at the main post office for first drafts of telegrams that people threw away—all that passion in a few lines; and he stared intently at the way women's clothes fit their bodies. If a woman glanced at him he went away; if ever he caught anyone's eye he looked askance and moved on. He was a letter writer. He killed time at the movies. He went to museums. He sat alone at concerts. He loitered in libraries. In the early darkness of winter he paused at the lighted windows of houses and looked in. He ate lunch standing up and seldom went into good restaurants. If there was a fight on the street, or an argument in the next room, or a crossed line, or someone punishing a child, he was transfixed, and he listened. He was alert, he was alive—not an actor waiting in the wings for a cue that would bring him onstage. This was his real existence, and there was no time to waste, because his life was passing and it was no more than a bubble the size of a seed pearl rising to break at the surface of the liquid in a tumbler, and then it would be over.

Being alive is being alone, I wrote, concealing my small notebook behind my hand. *Being alone is being alive.*

The only way of his understanding the world was in this intense and lonely concentration, seeing the stations pass, as he had once seen the Stations of the Cross at St. Ray's. But these were plainer and more misleading names, from Osterley to Boston Manor to Northfields. And did that man do the *Times* crossword every day and fold his paper in that same way? And what did that woman next to him feel when she read (as he could see, and it was still only eight-fifteen in the morning at Acton Town)—*then, once on deck he embraced her and covered her mouth with his and heated her lips and she felt his hard manhood throbbing against her as the yacht heeled in the wind*—when she read *throbbing* did she throb and what did she see?

The train slowed and stopped. The doors rushed apart. Two passengers alighted, a man boarded—he stood. The doors shut. The train shuddered and resumed, gliding on the tracks, picked up speed, rattled, slowed, stopped, and that man alighted and four more people pushed in; and on and on.

I had two lives but I had intimations today that because there were two they were both incomplete. I lived in the cracks between them—had only ever lived in that space. Outside it, among others, I was not myself, and so no one knew me. Was that everyone's condition—that we were each of us unknown? I did not talk. I listened. I watched. And in my silence I became invisible.

I thought: As soon as someone else's eyes are on us we are diminished—made into ugly miniatures of ourselves—which was why when someone looked at me I turned away. When I was invisible I felt vast and efficient, and I sensed that I saw everything.

And that morning, of all mornings, memorably, a young woman took a paperback of one of my books out of her bag, and flexed it and opened it and held it like a thick sandwich. A paperback that has been carefully read actually looks it—it swells and fattens and its spine wrinkles and cracks, and the reader's interest has had a physical effect on it. This copy, I could see, had been enjoyed. I watched the woman read on and I took pleasure in it—not watching the book but her face, her eyes. She was wearing a black coarse-knit cardigan over a blue blouse, and a bluish pleated skirt and white shoes and pale tights. She had big soft curls and her lips were pressed together in concentration, and sometimes they relaxed in amusement, slightly parted, as though she had seen something or someone approaching from the page. Eagerly, she turned the page with a neat plucking motion of her fingertips.

I could have watched her for twenty hours, and I might have missed my stop, except that at Earl's Court a voice piped up. It was a voice that sounded as though it came from the squawkbox of a synthesizer.

"Mind the gap . . . Mind the gap."

And then I changed trains.

6.

Jenny still had not woken. But the sky had mostly cleared, the high wind having pushed the thunderheads east and under the blue sky of an April morning the air had been freshened by the storm. The streets were damp and, rain-washed, looked blacker. And these few weeks were the only time of the year when London had any fragrance—the traffic fumes of the city were actually modi-fied if not overpowered by the masses of pink and white blos-soms—the flowering trees of an English springtime.

The house stood tall and detached on the quiet Clapham road, its white windows looking bright against the soot-soaked brick, and the brick itself no recognizable color—not red or black or brown, but the hue of an old tree trunk, senile and scorched, with the texture of porridge or tweed. The laburnum at the front had just come into flower. I was fascinated by the beauty of a living thing I knew to be poisonous.

I mounted the stairs but did not ring the bell. I used my own latchkey, quietly, and when I was inside I took off my shoes and some of my clothes and crept into the dark room and slid into bed with her.

"I heard you come in," she said, and kissed me.

Her limbs closed around me, her body attaching itself to me like a sea plant to a stone. The sheets were warm and moist from her deep sleep: she slept motionlessly, glowing in her still slum-ber.

"Your feet are cold," she said, and pedaled with her legs, and yawned. "What's the time?"

I said I didn't know, because if I told her she'd say *It's so late* and would get up. I wanted to lie there with her for a while.

"Are you glad to be home?"

"Yes."

"Did you miss me?"

"Yes."

"Did you have a good time?"

I did not reply, I hummed equivocally, and finally said, "I might have to go back."

"Oh, God!" Jenny said and took a breath, and her body hardened against me.

"You could come with me this time," I said.

She did not speak. She sighed and her body softened again.

"Yes, take me with you," she said, and kissed me. "But I know what it will be like. All your trip. All your plans and arrangements. You'll be big and bossy, and I'll have to follow you around like your mistress."

She then clung to me.

She said, "Do you have a mistress, Andy? No, don't tell me—I don't want to know. Listen, are you serious about taking me to India?"

"This is the first proper meal I've eaten since you left," Jenny said.

I had made her an English breakfast—eggs and bacon, grilled mushrooms, porridge and—just to see her reaction—fried bread. She drank coffee, and I had brewed a pot of green tea for myself. We were sitting at the table by the window—Jenny dressed for work in a flower-patterned dress that resembled the clematis in the back garden, pinky white blossoms on a background of pale green.

She said, "Did you notice I lost weight? I hardly bother to eat when you're away. I eat cheese and biscuits, I watch telly and eat sausage rolls, I drink too much. Sometimes I think I'm turning into an alcoholic. You didn't miss me, did you? Oh, never mind—it's so good to have you home. Are you going to see Jack?"

"I might meet him this afternoon for tea," I said.

"He'd love to see you," Jenny said. "He misses you so much when you're away. He gets pale and goes all quiet and he snaps at me when I try to be nice to him."

And she gave me the other news: the car was buggered and wouldn't start, the skylight had sprung a leak, the charlady hadn't shown up for almost a week, there was no food in the fridge—she said there hadn't seemed any point in shopping, since Jack was home only at weekends, I had missed the best of the daffodils, and my messages and mail were stacked on my desk.

"I couldn't be bothered taking detailed messages," she said.

"It's such a bore, and what's the point? I told everyone I didn't know when you'd be home." She shook her head and frowned. "They feel sorry for me when you're away. They treat me like a widow. I hate that. And some people get so obsequious when they find out I'm married to you. I had one the other day. I told him my name, and spelled it. 'Like the author,' he said. His mother reads your books. It's pathetic. I'd like to change my name."

"Why—are you ashamed of me?"

"No," she said, "but I'm a person, too. I'm intelligent, I read books, I have opinions, I even have my own name."

"One would never know you have opinions," I said.

She smiled and then began to laugh, and stood up to go. "That was a lovely breakfast, but you've made me late for work."

I was still thinking about these obsequious people she met. I said, "You'll see—travel is hard. India isn't a vacation. It's work."

"Don't lecture me, Andy, please," Jenny said. "I need a little time to think about this. And don't think you can come back and start ordering people around. I'm not going to drop everything I'm doing to go to fucking India. I've got a job too, you know."

She had been putting on her coat and growing flustered and fiercer as she fumbled her arms into the sleeves. I just watched her, saying nothing.

At the front door she said, "Oh, God, look at your face. I've said the wrong thing. Give me a little time, Andy. I got used to your being away. And now I have to get used to having you back."

She kissed me and snatched up her briefcase and was gone.

I unpacked my bag. I took a shower. I made more green tea and opened my mail: friendly readers' letters, invitations to seminars, requests for me to give lectures, demands for autographs, appeals for comments on bound proofs—four of them, with the sort of letters my publishers had once sent out soliciting endorsements, so how could I chuck them aside? And bills, Jack's school fees, tax assessments, and seven more including a phone bill for £600—a grand's worth of telephone calls to Eden in Marstons Mills. It would take two days to work my way through this stack, but that was another penalty of being away.

The car was out of gas, which was why it wouldn't start for Jenny. I bought a gallon for my gas can and then drove to the station and filled the tank. Three light bulbs were blown in the house. I replaced them. I went shopping in Vauxhall and filled the fridge. I made more green tea.

I sat by the window, looking out onto the Common, drinking Chinese tea. Clouds filled the sky and sank. I felt motionless and complacent—a sense of homely peace that was akin to inertia, as though in being at this house I was tethered to a slowly dragging sea-anchor, not at rest but steadied and safe. I had had this identical feeling in my other house. This was a lovely view and this was a comfortable chair; but I had treetops there, too, and a similar chair. I had a wide desk here and a wide desk there, a razor here and a razor there; books here and books there—two atlases of the world, two sets of Dickens, two Boswells, two Shakespeares, two *Obras Completas* of Borges. A bicycle here and one there; two canoes; two pairs of binoculars; two shortwave radios, two toothbrushes, two sets of clothes—a suit here, a suit there, and everything else, down to the bottle of Tabasco Sauce in each cupboard, in each house, in each country. This house was a different shape but its contents were an exact counterpart of my American house: two of everything.

Except—and with that hesitating word I saw children on the Common and remembered Jack.

The clouds now filled the sky, and a light rain was falling. I dressed for bad weather—a felt hat with the brim tugged down, a leather jacket and thick trousers. I wheeled my bike out of the garden shed and rode it downhill to the river, and along Chelsea Embankment to Pimlico, thinking how much better this bike was than my American one. The river was full and flowing backward with a spring tide, and a cormorant disappeared into it as I turned into Bessborough Gardens. I was shocked to see workmen tearing the houses apart, the ones that faced the square, because in one of them Joseph Conrad had written his first words as a novelist. And now that house was a stack of broken bricks. One of the greatest things that writers did, I thought, was to isolate an event, and light it with the imagination, to make people understand and remember; and not just events, but people and their passions. Forgetting was much worse than failure: it was an act of violence. For all writing aimed at defeating time. No one could become a writer—no one would even care about it—until he or she experienced the impartial cruelty of time passing.

I cycled past the rubble of Conrad's house, crossed Vauxhall Bridge Road and cut behind the Tate Gallery and took back streets to Smith Square and Great College Street. There I locked my bike against the railings of one of the school buildings, and I lurked.

I was always reminded, waiting for Jack, of how I had helplessly waited for my girlfriend Tina Spector, when I was fifteen, near her house on Brookview Road. Lurking, I felt an obscure sense of guilt, as though I was about to be found out and accused. And with Jack I felt awkward and vulnerable, because I had been away so long.

He seemed not to recognize me when he appeared from the doorway to the schoolyard, walking quickly to his house. He wore the school uniform—a black suit, a black tie, black shoes. His shoes were scuffed, his suit too tight—he was growing. His hair was spiky, he was pale. He looked tired and rumpled. He carried a briefcase. He looked like a serious little overworked Englishman.

He made quickly for me but did not greet me—did not look at me. He stood near me, and he turned his head away, staring across the grass that was enclosed by the old school buildings.

"Take that hat off, Dad. Take it off. Please take it off."

"It's raining, Jack."

He had started to walk away. I was losing him. He said something more in that same desperate and insistent voice, but I could not catch it.

I took off the hat, stuffed it into my jacket, and followed him.

"And the bicycle clips," he said.

I had forgotten those. I removed them.

" 'Hatless, I take off my cycle-clips in awkward reverence,' " I said.

"We're doing him," Jack said. "We're doing that poem."

"Who else are you doing?"

Now I had caught up with him. He was walking quickly, heaving his briefcase, and taking a roundabout back way towards Victoria Street.

"Everybody—Chaucer, Jane Austen, Conrad. Two Shakespeare plays." He spoke in a weary and almost defeated way. "Don't ask me—I have so much work to do. I'll never get A's on these exams."

"It doesn't matter if you don't get A's."

"It does, or else what's the point of taking them?" He was disgusted at being forced to be logical because I was frivolous. "Besides, no university will look at me if I don't get A's."

"What Conrad are you doing?"

"*Heart of Darkness.* Where did you get that stupid hat?"

"Don't forget to read 'An Outpost of Progress'—that was the original of the story. And my favorite, 'The Secret Sharer.' When I was riding through Bessborough Gardens, I was thinking—"

"Dad, why—?"

"Listen to me. I was thinking—the first thing to understand is that time passes."

He had hesitated to listen. His face was pale, a smudge of ink on his cheek, raindrops clung whole to his hair. I could see in his eyes that he would remember what I had said.

"Dad, why did you have to come on a bike?"

"It's quicker. I can never find a parking space around here for the car. Why—does it embarrass you, like my hat?"

He said nothing, he continued walking, and then more softly he asked, "How was India?"

"Interesting," I said, but I could tell from the angle of his head that he wasn't listening, didn't care, was only changing the subject.

"I might be going back with Mum."

He hadn't heard.

He said, "I've got history and Russian to prepare for, too." We had turned into Victoria Street.

I said, "Is there anything you need—anything we can buy?"

"Batteries for my Walkman."

"That's all?"

He shrugged, but it was not a large considered gesture—it was his body wincing towards his head, briefly burying his neck.

I was annoyed and frustrated, because I wanted him to want something that I alone could give him. By not wanting anything, or perhaps refusing to tell me, he was making himself powerful.

He was fifteen, and yet he seemed very old. His leather brief-case was battered and cracked, and seeing it and his loose fallen-down socks and his white ankles, I became sad. He was not a big boy but rather a small man, and he looked weary and harassed in his shabby black suit. Walking along I felt younger than him, in my blue jeans and leather jacket.

I said, "Is there anything wrong, Jack?"

He shook his head, meaning no, but too quickly, telling me yes.

We went into a small cafe run by an irascible Italian just off Victoria Street. Condensation sweated upon the front windows, the tea urns gasped, and the smell of frying hung in the air with a clinging odor of boiled vegetables. Jack waited for me at the table, and I bought two cups of tea and two cakes. Once he began eating, Jack revealed both his hunger and his mood. Eden sometimes ate that way—the slow, sour, and disgusted way that people ate when they were depressed.

"It's your exams, isn't it?" I said.

His silence meant yes, just as his no had meant yes, and I thought then how if he had said yes I would not have known what he meant. "Maybe I can help. Please let me."

Only then did he raise his eyes. I saw cold resentment in them.

He said, "Do you speak Russian, have you read Pushkin in Russian, do you know standard deviation in advanced maths?"

I smiled fatuously at him, and seeing me draw back he became more insistent.

"What about the Avignon Papacy? What did Charles the Fifth contribute to the recovery of the Valois cause in the Hundred Years War?"

He looked as though he was going to cry.

"I have to write an essay on that for tomorrow," he said. "Four sides of foolscap. I haven't even started."

Then I remembered how I had been sententious with him and said, *The first thing to understand is that time passes,* and I said, "Maybe I could help you with your English."

"I don't want help," he said. "I just want to get it over with."

He drank his tea in silence, the moment passed.

"I'm hoping Mum will come with me to India," I said. "Do you wish you could come?"

"Why do you ask me that, when you know I have to stay here and take these exams?" he said, being logical again in a way that shamed me.

"I never took exams like that in the States," I said. I thought of myself at his age, of my rifle, of being an altar boy at St. Ray's, of Tina Spector at the Sandpits, of three funerals equals one wedding; of the whale steaks a few years later. "I wish you didn't have to."

He clawed his tie and said, "Then you shouldn't have sent me to this school."

His expression was of someone who has been double-crossed. He had been trying to please me in studying hard. What right did I have to undermine him by insincerely wishing it otherwise? He was truer than I was.

He said, "What does Manichaean mean?"

"Something to do with duality—seeing that good and evil are mingled," I said. "Good in the spirit, evil in the body and material things. Something like that."

"Where does the word come from? Is it Greek?"

"From the name of the prophet—Manes. He was a Persian who kept being visited by an angel whom he realized was his double. He was also a painter. He was killed. His followers fled to central Asia. Why do you want to know?"

"It was one of the heresies that the Papal—oh, never mind. It doesn't matter," he said, and pushed his cup and plate aside and put himself out of my reach. "I have to go back now. Thanks for the tea, Dad."

We left the cafe and I had the sense that the owner was staring at me, as though I was a pederast.

Jack said, "You don't have to go all the way back with me."

Was he embarrassed or ashamed of me? I didn't know for sure, but I guessed he was. We passed a shop window selling clerical vestments and in the reflection I saw Jack dressed like a mortician and myself in the drizzly monochrome of London dressed like a cowboy, with wild hair. No wonder Jack felt conspicuous.

I walked with him to the large stone archway, which was a side entrance to the school, and Jack hesitated. He didn't want me to go any farther.

I said, "After you've finished these exams you'll be through with school. We'll go to the States and have fun. You can take driving lessons."

He looked up excitedly for the first time that afternoon and said, "I can hardly wait. I really want my license. Will you let me drive your car?"

"You can *have* my car, Jack," I said. "Anyway, I've got two of them."

Then I saw him behind the wheel, driving away and vanishing on an American road.

He looked energized, still pale and tired but with spirit in his eyes, the vitality inspired by wanting something, even if it was years away. His wet hair was plastered against his head.

"Thanks for the tea, Dad," he said. "It's really good seeing you." He was smiling—thinking of driving a car.

I could not restrain myself from taking him in my arms. I hugged him—he was so thin. He stiffened slightly in surprise but he allowed me to hold him. Then I kissed his cheek, and in the way he returned the kiss I sensed the affection that I had not heard in his voice. He was like me and so he had a horror of revealing it.

"I'm sorry I've been traveling so much."

"I don't mind," he said. "As long as you come back."

He picked up his briefcase and passed his fingers through his wet hair.

"But when you were away Mum was depressed and quite upset," he said.

"I think I know why."

"Please don't tell me," he said, and I knew he feared having to bear the burden of knowing that story. It was a burden enough to be my son—to try to please me without being overwhelmed by me, without being a lackey. "Dad, I really have to go."

He was suddenly self-conscious and urgent again. He said " 'Bye" and broke away from me. Would he ever know how much power he had over me—how in my love for him I needed his encouragement and approval, perhaps more than he needed mine? I watched him until he got to the end of the walkway and had grown small, like a figure out of my past. It was still raining. I put on my old hat and went to my bicycle.

7.

"Does it seem strange, going to India with another person?" Jenny asked in the taxi on the way to the airport.

I said truthfully no.

"I know how you prefer to travel alone," she said.

I said nothing. I smiled at her. I was grateful to her for coming. I took her hand but she was too nervous to be conscious of the gesture. Her hand went dead when I touched it and she did not notice what I had done until I let it drop. She was agitated at the prospect of a ten-hour flight, worried that she might not have brought the right clothes, fretful that she had left inadequate instructions for her replacement at work.

"Imagine. India. So soon," she said. "I'm going to be a little out of my element."

"We'll have a good time," I said. "All I have to do is get enough for my article and then we can enjoy ourselves. Our only problem will be the heat. This month and next are the two hottest in India."

"I don't care. It's been a horrid spring in London. I don't mind missing Wimbledon. And it's a good thing you didn't insist that I go with you last month." She was half talking to herself, fussing, murmuring, smoothing her skirt. "That would have been out of the question. Budget Day. The Chancellor had a few surprises for us, I can tell you."

Jenny was an accountant with a large firm in the City, having left the bank which had been her first job. Her work was as remote from mine as it could possibly have been. Its remoteness and its obscurity perhaps made it bearable for me. I had very little idea what she did. It wasn't tax. She analyzed corporate expenditure. I sometimes saw the results—her name on reports. And she saw mine on books. But she had never seen me write one, no one had, no one—not even another writer—knew how a particular book was written. It had nothing to do with fluency. It was a clumsy, messy, and mysterious process that was done in the dark.

Jenny did not have the severe look of an accountant. You

might have taken her in her casualness for an art teacher or magazine editor. She was browny blonde. She dyed her hair so regularly with Born Blonde that I did not know what her natural color was now. Perhaps underneath it all she was going gray. She had greeny-blue eyes, and sometimes wore thick glasses and sometimes contact lenses. I hated knowing how a woman achieved an effect of stylishness or beauty; I did not want to hear about wires or makeup. I wanted to see the final result.

She seldom dressed fashionably, but she had conviction which was possibly a greater asset. Her clothes were large and loose, and she always looked comfortable. I had first been attracted to her by her looks, and she had not lost her beauty.

There was something in the way she sat, and in her loose clothes and big bag, that suggested she needed space—elbow room. She seldom held my hand, she recoiled slightly when I hugged her. If I touched her or took her arm she always smiled, and then her arm seemed to go dead. I often spoke to her and saw her smile; but she was not listening to me—she was smiling at something in her mind. She had a powerful memory and she sometimes lived in it, outside my reach. She reminded me of Jack in her seriousness. She was logical and at times very quiet, and those times I imagined her heart fluttering and her breathing very steady and that she was unaware of what was happening around her. She was intensely alert but not particularly watchful. She walked fast and had no sense of direction. She was defeated by the simplest mechanical object and always had trouble with so-called childproof caps on aspirin bottles. She laughed at the thought that she might have to apologize for her eccentricities. "That's the way I am," she said. She did not find fault with anyone who was different. Her own oddness had made her tolerant. But she could be very impatient.

This compassion in her, this logic and intelligence I relied on and needed. She had English good sense and English modesty, and was without the English envy. I was deficient in all her strongest qualities, and I knew it. Because of that she had become a part of me. Was there anything in me that she valued? I think she was fascinated by my various weaknesses and my self-assurance. She had told me that she wondered: How could someone like Andre, so incomplete, be so bold? She had once thought it was because I was an American. But no, it was because I was a writer. That conundrum had made me a writer.

She knew me well and could be very quiet beside me, or else could read my mind. We had been married nearly sixteen years. She hated the word "wife."

In the Transit Lounge of Terminal Three at Heathrow I said, "The plane's not boarding yet. Let's look at the Duty-Free Shop. I want you to buy something for yourself. Will you do that?"

"Of course, if you insist. I think I'll buy a diamond wrist-watch."

I stood by with my credit card but all she bought was a liter bottle of whiskey.

She said, "Someone in the office had one of those fake Rolex watches. She bought it in Singapore for about twenty quid. It was actually quite nice—so nice, in fact, that it put me off the idea of ever buying a real one." She clasped the bottle. "This is all I need. I've heard you can't get the stuff in India."

She held my hand as the plane taxied to the runway, and she squeezed it tightly until the plane took off. But just as we passed over Windsor Castle she let go. When I put my arm around her she said, "Please don't, Andy. I'm so hot. Oh, God, are you offended?"

Night came on quickly because we were flying east. We ate, we slept, we were woken for breakfast; and we landed in hot early morning, in blinding light. It was much steamier than on my previous visit, and because I was mentally comparing it I found it harder to bear than Jenny. I had not expected it, but she had been ready for anything.

The heat made me bad-tempered. When the taxi driver told us that his meter was broken I laughed sarcastically. I said, "Anyway, I know the fare is a hundred and twenty rupees."

"One fifty, sah," he said. He was unshaven and thin, and another grubby man sat with him in the front seat of the jalopy.

I tried to insist.

"Don't make a fuss," Jenny said. "You're always trying to get a bargain. You should be ashamed of yourself, haggling with this poor man."

After we checked into the hotel and were shown to our room, Jenny stood at the window and said softly, "It's a moral dilemma, isn't it—the luxury hotel in the poor hungry country?"

She turned to me and laughed in a helpless and self-mocking way. "It's wickedness."

"So what should we do about it?"

"I don't know about you, but I'm going for a swim," she said, and she pulled off her T-shirt.

I said it was too hot to swim and that it seemed almost perverse for people to sunbathe in a tropical country.

"You used to criticize me for swimming in Uganda."

"Yes, at the swimming pool, with all the Africans hanging on the fence."

"Don't be absurd," she said. She changed into her bathing suit quickly and efficiently, hardly conscious of her nakedness, as though she were alone. She was healthy and had a good figure—in fact, she was beautiful, with a youthful bloom still on her clear skin. But she was frowning at herself in the mirror. She said, "I've just been through a beastly English winter and some sun is just what I need. You can sit here and sulk and feel virtuous."

While she was swimming I called Indoo at his agency. He said that we must meet—that he had some plans for me.

"I'm here with my wife," I said. "That woman you met—Eden—was not my wife. You understand?"

"Don't worry, old boy," Indoo said.

Later that day I took Jenny to the Red Fort. I showed her the Moti Mahal, the Throne Room; we walked on the battlements. I said, "That's the *Hathi Pol*—the elephant gate."

"This is fun," Jenny said. She wore a straw hat she had bought at a stall, and a blue dress and sandals. "I can't believe I'm really in India. If it weren't for the smells and all these ragged people I would find it hard to believe. It's splendor and misery together, isn't it?"

An Indian man was following us. He had a stack of postcards which he showed us and then held in Jenny's face, obstructing her.

"I don't want any postcards, thank you," she said.

But the mere fact that she had spoken to him was taken by the man to be a sign of encouragement and he began grunting and whining and shuffling the cards.

Jenny ignored him and tried to walk on.

"Muddhoom, muddhoom—"

"No," Jenny said, and smiled stiffly at him. But he made the mistake of trying to put a postcard into her hand, insisting that she buy it, and she snapped, "Pack it in!"

This made some children playing nearby turn to us and laugh. Jenny's expression softened.

She said, "Do you remember when Jack was that age?"

She became serene with reflection, and she seemed impervious to the heat. The temperature was in the nineties and the afternoon sun was cruelly slanted, striking from just above the rooftops into our eyes.

"So sweet," she said as the children continued to laugh in a hiccupping way. "We're not too old to have another child, you know." She was still smiling. "And they can be such a damned nuisance, too."

We moved on, to the alleys of the fort that had been converted into a bazaar. I kept stopping at the stalls and looking at the brassware, the antique jewelry, the carvings, the leather goods and woven bags.

"You and your knickknacks," Jenny said, laughing impatiently. "You can buy that stuff in London, you know." She went ahead. "I'm going to look at the marble screens."

"Aren't you tired of sightseeing?"

"Not yet. I want to finish looking at this place. I don't want to have to come back here tomorrow. That's for somewhere else—the mosque, I think."

Another postcard seller approached her and began gabbling.

Jenny stared at him and in a level voice she said, "Bugger off."

The next day we met Indoo at the bar of the hotel. He looked rather stunned, and I wondered whether he was drunk, but then I realized he was just being respectful, because of Jenny. He did not remark on her beauty—it was regarded as unseemly to speak that way of a man's wife. I wasn't flattered—I was annoyed that he had taken a liberty in gushing about Eden on my last trip.

"Perhaps you would enjoy meeting my wife," Indoo said. He spoke to Jenny in the solicitous tone that he might have used for an invalid.

"I'd love to," Jenny said. "Only we don't have a lot of time."

"She would show you all the shops in Delhi," he said. "The best-quality ones. You could indulge yourselves in shopping sprees."

"I'm afraid that's not my line," Jenny said, smiling pleasantly.

Indoo—his idea rejected—became even more formal. He said, "I understand perfectly" in a way that suggested he did not understand at all.

To lighten the mood I said, "Indoo doesn't really approve of material things. He probably agrees that shopping is a sinful waste of time."

This made him smile. "True," he said. "But India needs hard currency. So I make an exception."

"Tell Jenny about *maya*," I said.

He lifted one finger, the way bores do when they lecture you, and he said, "We Hindus believe the whole material world is *maya*—illusion. The secret lies in letting go of things."

Jenny merely stared at him, her head slightly tilted in disbelief.

Indoo was trying to look pious. He held his glass primly and in a soulful voice said, "I myself believe this is so."

"Then what's that in your hand?" Jenny asked. "Is that whiskey or an illusion?"

Indoo laughed slowly and insincerely. "Jolly good," he said. "I like that. I forgive you for that."

It seemed to me that this little get-together was not working at all.

Finally, Indoo said—as though for the first time—"I tell you what I would like to do very much indeed. White-water rafting on the Ganges. Bring your bathing costumes. I shall provide a hamper and all other requisites."

"That's an interesting idea," I said.

"Yes," Indoo said. "I will collect you in my car early in the morning—say, four or four-thirty. We will drive northward to Hardwar. There we take a back road to my agency's camp on the Ganges. The river is very swift at that place. I have four chaps onsite who will take us downriver. You put on life jackets and paddle like hell through the rapids. I tell you, it is jolly exciting, especially when raft twists and turns in water. Adventure travel is the thing these days. This is a full day's adventure. What do you say?"

This produced a silence, and then Jenny said calmly, "Excuse me, are you talking to me?"

"Indeed," Indoo said, and I saw he was miserable—just the way he tried to wink at me made him seem pathetic. "What about it? White-water rafting on Mother Ganga."

Jenny smiled at him. She said, "You must be joking."

But she agreed to go with us the next day as far as Hardwar, where she got out, holding Murray's *Guide.*

Indoo and I had breakfast at the camp. He seemed to relax as soon as Jenny was gone. Was it because she was my wife and he had had to keep a pretense of formality? Or was it that he felt part of a deception? I was surprised that he had any reaction at all, since I had always taken him for a fairly easygoing hypocrite.

"It is better this way," he said, buckling on his life jacket. "Women are not at home on rubber rafts, you know."

He paddled just behind me in the rear seat, shouting and screaming in the rapids and yelling to his men to go faster. When we came to the reach in the river where we had seen the corpse, he laughed and said, "Remember?"

The water brimmed where we had buried the bones. After seeing that I lost my taste for the rapids and couldn't paddle very hard. I wasn't grieving—I simply became heavy and thoughtful, and I kept looking back, as though in burying those bones I had buried something of myself.

I wanted to tell Jenny this when we met her later in the afternoon at the bridge in Hardwar. But I did not want to burden her with a lugubrious thought: she was smiling, she was happy, she said she had had a wonderful day. I'd tell her tomorrow.

"We must see Roorkee," Indoo said, but he forgot to tell the driver, and he was sleeping when we came to the turnoff, so we kept on the direct road to Delhi. Indoo slept crookedly beside the driver, his head at an unnatural angle, and it flopped forward, waking him briefly, each time the driver touched the brake.

I told Jenny about the white-water rafting. I did not mention the corpse; only the rapids, the cold water, the hike afterwards.

"I would have hated it," Jenny said. "You know who you sound like? One of those boring scoutmasters, always rabbiting on about fresh air. One of those tedious middle-aged men who walk around in shorts showing their knobbly knees. The next thing you'll say to me is that I need more color in my cheeks!"

But this was mischief, not malice. She was hugging me as she spoke, and then she kissed me.

"I'm glad I came," she said. "And I'm glad you had a good time. You don't really need me to hold your hand, do you?"

"How did you spend the day?"

"I wandered around Hardwar. I had a cup of tea and then I had lunch at a filthy little place. The food was quite decent. I took some pictures and looked at the temples. You know Hardwar is a holy city? Then I got a taxi and went across the river to Rishikesh. Do you remember how the Beatles used to go there, to see the Maharishi? I wasn't expecting much—I was prepared to mock it. I walked around and watched the people praying and washing in the river and"—there was a catch in her throat—"don't laugh, but I felt a kind of holiness come over me."

She stopped, suddenly self-conscious in the jogging car.

"Go on," I said, holding her.

"I looked at all the skinny people traipsing round the town, and I began to cry—from the sheer joy of seeing them. They looked so innocent, and their happiness made me happy. It wasn't pretty, but there was a logic to it all. They had found a way of being happy in this strange world. I was thinking about there being order in the spirit of things, that holiness was order, and it all seemed so far from my accounting in London. The sun was slanting into the river, and I thought how your friend"—she nodded at the crumpled, sleeping figure of Indoo—"called it Mother Ganga."

She paused again, and swallowed, and I thought she was going to cry.

"I was moved," she said. "I felt like Mrs. Moore in *A Passage to India*—something wonderful and weird was happening to me. Maybe this is what people call a religious experience, except that it sounds so bloody pompous. But I loved it without even understanding it. I didn't want to leave. I just wanted to stay and see those people washing themselves and praying, and the children praying, and that glorious late-afternoon sun striking the river." She made an odd honking noise and I realized that she was laughing. "I kept thinking, 'I want to go on living.'"

"That's good," I said. "I love you."

"You don't have to say that. Just show me that you do."

Soon after, Indoo woke and insisted on stopping for ice cream.

"I enjoy going on these trips," he said. "It means I can eat whatever I want." He ordered a Campa Cola and a chocolate bar and a vanilla ice-cream cone. "I never eat this stuff at home. My wife doesn't like it."

Did he remember that he had told me that before? I doubted it. When people repeated things to me it made me feel that they didn't know me—didn't remember—didn't care who they were talking to. They existed and I didn't.

Indoo was smiling in a way that irritated me and made me feel that he could be very stupid. I looked out of the window, but I could not make any sense of the mass of rough stars that cluttered the sky. They were so bright they deflected my eyes to the thick blackness that surrounded them. The road turned dusty and what looked like rising fog was this same dust, with lights glaring in it, and those shaky orange headlights that always seemed to belong to old dangerous buses.

"It's been a perfect day," Jenny said at the hotel after we made love.

I agreed, but I also thought of Eden and felt that I had somehow to explain my absence to her. What better time than late at night when everyone was fast asleep? What better place than by the marble fountain in the lobby of this hotel, on hotel notepaper? But after I mailed it and was on my way upstairs I could not help feeling that I had spoiled the day.

8.

When I suggested taking the Janata Express to Agra the day after we arrived back in Delhi, Jenny said, "What's the hurry? We haven't seen Delhi properly. I want to see the Red Fort again. You didn't tell me that Shah Jahan built it, and his daughters built mosques all over the old city. And we British built New Delhi. Don't you think I have a right to be interested in that? And there's a tomb here that was a sort of clumsy prototype for the Taj Mahal."

"Humayun's Tomb."

"That's the one," she said, and snatched up the guidebook

and read, " 'Its plan was that afterwards adopted at the Taj, but used here without the depth and poetry of that celebrated building.' So don't put me off. I'm doing my homework. And what about this?" She flipped one of the page-marking ribbons and read, " 'The erotic carvings are notorious but possess religious significance for Hindus. Visitors need not see them if the attendant is discouraged from pointing them out.' "

"Where are they?"

"Benares," she said, and laughed. "Bad luck!"

She was a patient and thorough sightseer. If the guidebook called attention to the scrollwork or the screens, or if it said, *There is a unique Persian inscription in Kufic in the mihrali,* she was on her way. "Which way to the mihrali?" I heard her asking a bewildered Indian at one of the Delhi mosques. She evaluated the guidebook's praise and once, scrutinizing some carved flowers on a gateway glanced into the guidebook and said, " 'Unusually good' is a bit much, I think."

We stayed two more days and worked through each tomb and tower, each mosque and church, paragraph by paragraph. I found myself in such circumstances distracted from the architecture by the crows or by picnickers, and at the Qutub Minar Jenny said, "Notice the corbeled balconies and angular flutings" as my eye traveled down the flutings and fixed upon a black and scabby cat that scuttled among the ancient russet flagstones. I preferred looking at tourists to looking at ruins. Jenny did not mind, nor did she lecture. "I'm sure I'll never want to come back here," she said, "that's why I want to be thorough and see everything now."

Late on those hot afternoons I went to Connaught Circus and haunted the antiques shops. I was more acquisitive than I had been on my previous visit because a painted wall-hanging (of Rama and Sita on a swing fixed to a mango tree)—one that I had wanted to buy—had been sold. That disappointment had made me decisive. I bought another wall-hanging—inferior to the one I had wanted, but it was the best they had; a silver bracelet; a brass head of a goddess; and a dagger for Jack.

Jenny reluctantly accompanied me one evening when I was debating whether to buy an old decorated door from Orissa. It had four panels and was carved and in fine detail was painted with scenes from the Ramayana.

"If you think you need a door," she said, "then by all means buy it."

"This isn't any old door," I said.

"I think I'll buy some postcards," she said, and when she saw me hesitating she said, "Oh, buy the silly thing if you want it, but for God's sake stop asking my opinion. Do you think you need my permission?"

"I suppose I secretly suspect that you disapprove."

"Of course I disapprove," she said. "You have so much that you don't need. You've got two houses and they both look like museums. I've never seen so many carpets and statues and carvings. I hate people who are always snaffling up trifles and saying 'This is a nice piece' or 'It's very old—there's a story behind this door.'"

"People are staring at you."

"Let them stare," she said. "Look, you want to know my opinion? I think people who go in for buying antiques and surrounding themselves with ancient junk are very insecure and desperately acquisitive, and all of them—for some reason—hate kids. If you don't like my opinion, don't ask for it." Then, in a tone of suffering and apology, she added, "Christ, I'm hot."

I decided not to buy the door from Orissa. It wasn't only Jenny's scorn that put me off. It was also because I couldn't face the tedium of making out shipping orders in triplicate. It was simpler to walk away. This had a chastening effect on Jenny, slightly shaming her for making her think that she had discouraged me.

Deeper in the bazaar that last day we passed Ismail's shop. I paused at the window, where the yak bones and the carvings were arranged on pedestals.

Jenny was frowning at them. She said, "Do you think they kill animals especially to make this stuff?"

Inside the shop Ismail was beckoning, moving his arms in a conjuring motion, as though trying to call up spirits from the deep.

"Come in. You are welcome. Please. Maximum value."

I followed Jenny into the shop, but already Ismail had opened the drawer. He took out a necklace of dark stained bones and held it up. Then, facing Jenny, he slipped it over her head.

"It is yours, Madam."

Jenny went rigid, her neck stiffened, her arms straightened at her sides, and her fingers began to curl inward.

"Take that thing off my neck," she said.

The yellow in Ismail's eyes was the color of his fear. He hesitated, and winced, and then he obeyed.

The train was hotter and more crowded than I had remembered it, and it seemed much slower and dirtier too. India was full of unexpected delights, and the people were capable of grace and generosity; but this particular train contained everything that was to be detested in the country—bad tempers, filthy floors, poisonous toilets and dust, and the poorest food imaginable. It was a microcosm of the worst in Indian life, even to the way it seemed to petrify time.

Jenny said, "Is this the only way to get to Agra?"

"It seemed a good idea—get to know the people," I said. " 'Janata' means 'people' in Hindi. This is the Janata Express."

"It's dreadful," Jenny said, almost in disbelief at how bad it was, and she looked around the coach with a look of curious loathing. She then became apologetic. "I'm sorry for complaining. It must be such a bore for you. But if another person treads on my toes I'll scream."

She got up and paced, and I followed her. I wondered whether she would scream. She didn't—on the contrary, she became quieter and more compact in an attempt to endure this strenuous trip. She sat and scowled for a while, and when I looked up (we were passing through Muttra—I was reading about it in the guidebook) she was smiling. Across the aisle an Indian woman was holding a small baby on her lap. Jenny was watching, half in envy, half in bliss.

"Look," she said.

The baby was a small, scalded-looking creature, pink from yelling. It wanted to be picked up and hugged. That was the instinct of a human baby, because it was so fearful and helpless. The human mother's instinct was to respond, as probably the father's was as well. Why didn't I want to do anything to soothe this baby? Perhaps the instinct was exclusive, and we were so selfish and competitive as humans that we were indifferent to other people's children—I was, at any rate.

I told Jenny this. I added, "I can't think about children in the abstract."

"But babies are so sweet," she said. "Look at it."

"You don't even know whether it's a boy or a girl," I said. "It's odd, you know. If you asked me whether I liked babies I think I'd say no."

"You used to make such a fuss over Jack."

"Ah, my own baby—that's different."

She became quiet once more, seeming to concentrate on the Indian baby.

"What if we had more children?"

She was ambiguously talking to herself: it wasn't a question.

"I'm still young enough for it," she said. "Maybe you want someone younger. There are lots of women who would marry you. You could raise another family. Jack wouldn't even miss you. He's old enough to understand."

She looked piercingly at me.

"Why don't you?" she said.

I said, "Maybe I prefer you."

"I'm such a shrew."

"But you don't mean it," I said.

"I really don't, you know."

"It's only bad when people overhear you," I said. "It sounds awful. You sound terrible sometimes."

"Poor Andy," she said.

"I love you," I said.

"Do we have to tell each other that?" she said, and then added, "Sorry. I reckon we do."

We held hands after that, but hers grew damp and drifted away from mine.

At nightfall, with the darkness a mood descended on us. I imagined that we were all old in that railway carriage. The lights didn't work. There was no water. There were no empty seats. We sat in the dark, very tired; and it was too noisy from the rackety wheels for anyone to hold a conversation. It was a spooky ride, all of us silent people riding into the dark, as though we had turned into spirits on this ghost train.

So deeply had the mood taken hold and possessed me that when we arrived at Agra Station I had the strong sense that I had never been there before. Unmesh was nowhere in sight, though

I had counted on seeing him—missing him was also a part of my feeling of alienation.

We took a taxi to the hotel—the same hotel—and Jenny said, "It looks posh."

We had a room with two single beds. I lay in mine considering her provocative question on the train, *Why don't you?* I wondered why I didn't choose.

Unmesh was at the hotel the next morning. That name perfectly suited this faltering, ramshackle man. I was expecting him. I had sent a message through the bell captain, a vast and murderous-looking Sikh whose yellow gloves matched his turban, and before I finished breakfast I was sent word (a note delivered on a silver plate) that Unmesh was waiting for me in front, *At your service.*

He greeted me like an old friend, pumping my hand and smiling wildly, perhaps terrified that he might be going too far in this familiarity. It was a sort of sideways reunion, and his expression was that of a man who at any moment thinks he might be rebuffed. Yet he was chattering the whole time. He brought greetings from his wife. He had told his daughter Vanita all about me. She wanted to go to America. She wanted to see me. She was at school. The driver—Unmesh never used the poor man's name—remembered me, Unmesh waved at him, and he stepped forward, jerking his head, and trying to show me that he was pleased to see me.

Jenny appeared on the hotel steps in a white dress, the sun blazing in her blonde hair. Visitors to hot countries—women especially—seemed either much older or much younger than they were—something about the light, or the way they responded to the heat; some wilted, others bloomed. Jenny seemed even younger than the thirty-eight that she was.

I said very distinctly, "Unmesh, this is my wife, Mrs. Parent."

"Thank you, missus," Unmesh said and looked truly fearful as he clasped his hands in a *namaste* in front of his nose.

"He knows everything," I said.

Unmesh's eyes were close together and when they grew small and serious, as they did now, they seemed even closer.

"I am know everything," Unmesh said.

"We want to see the Fort and the Palace this morning," Jenny said. "This afternoon we will visit the Taj. Will you take us?"

Unmesh began uncertainly to hiss *yess, yess,* and said that he would show us. Then in his telegraphic way he said, "Taj. Morning. Better."

"All right then, you know best."

"I am know everything, missus."

This now sounded to me like a declaration of utter ignorance.

"Let's go," I said.

"Not yet," Jenny said, and turned to Unmesh. "I have one or two things to do. I want to buy some stamps, and then listen to the Financial Report on the BBC World Service. Depending on what I hear I might have a telex to send. And then we can meet and go to the Taj Mahal. I've heard it is very romantic. I will be ready at nine-fifteen. Perhaps you could explain this to your driver? Thanks so much."

All this she said as though to an old trusted colleague. Unmesh listened with white flicking eyes, perhaps amazed that he understood it all.

We left at the time Jenny had specified. Unmesh was anxious, not knowing whether Jenny or I were in charge—he always glanced frantically at me when Jenny spoke to him. But he started his spiel about Shah Jahan and his beloved wife and his love for gems and jewels as soon as the car drew into the parking lot. He was still at it—about Shah Jahan's incest with his daughter, his making the Peacock Throne, his death in prison: maybe Unmesh really did know everything—still yakking, as we walked to the ticket window in the mighty archway. He kept on, reciting dates, describing stonework, while I bought our tickets.

I said, "We'll see you later, Unmesh."

"I come. No charge. I show you this and that. Hither and thither. No charge. No money."

"Don't bother."

But Jenny said, "Yes, I think that's a good idea."

"We don't need him," I said.

"I want him to come along," Jenny said and I knew from her tone—though no one else would have known—that she was insisting and on the verge of losing her temper if she was thwarted. "I want him to tell me about it." She turned to Unmesh. "Come along, then. Tell me about this pool and these trees. Do you know about those?"

"I am know everything, missus," he said, and he gestured.

"Cypresses, missus." The sibilance made him gasp like a beach toy losing air.

I walked ahead. I had wanted Jenny to be alone with me and to stand still for her first look at the Taj. But she was glancing between the guidebook and the Taj, comparing the description on the page with the building in the hazy sunlight; and she was listening to Unmesh tell her that Taj was a corruption of Mumtaz, the name of the beloved wife. I had not known that simple thing, and so I walked alone, and my annoyance dissipated.

I was distracted and overwhelmed by the experience of looking up at the Taj Mahal and seeing a different structure from the one I had seen before. It was not just different in form—it was bigger, for example, its minarets were thicker and taller; it was also a different color, as though it had been made from a different sort of marble, or a different stone altogether—harder and shell-like. It was rosier, not so white, and it glowed a golden color where the sun struck it. But its shadows were blacker than before. I saw its sturdiness now and wondered where its frailty had gone. New revelations, new secrets: it was very disturbing to me. It was a hotter day than before, and a different hour, but how could the same building be so changed in six weeks? It did not look so fresh as it had. It was mellower, and with its look of perfection—so strange in this country of ruins—was a look of everlastingness. And something else—an unmistakable vitality, something alive and breathing there.

"What do you think?" I said, because Jenny had not said anything.

"It's fantastic," Jenny said behind me, and I knew she was not thinking about what she was saying. She was gabbling, because her attention was fully engaged. "I've honestly never seen anything like it."

She peered at it, her expression growing more serious with her scrutiny. She nodded and said no more for a long while, lost in reflecting on it and no longer looking at the guidebook.

"Incredible," she said, muttering to herself.

"It taking twenty-two years to build, missus."

"I'm not surprised," Jenny said, though she was hardly listening. She smiled at me. "It's just what it's cracked up to be. To tell the truth I was expecting something of a letdown. But I like this."

I told Jenny what Aldous Huxley had said about the Taj ("poverty of imagination . . . minarets among the ugliest structures ever created"), and she shrugged.

"Rubbish," she said. "But he was blind, you know. I mean, literally—legally. He went limping and bumping all over the place. He couldn't see. What do you expect?"

Unmesh said, "I am show you inside, missus. I am know everything."

I thought, Oh God, and traipsed after them as he went yakketing up the marble steps. His explanations were long and muddled. Jenny said, "Is that English? Are you speaking English?" and asked him to repeat himself. Each time I caught up with them and started to speak, Unmesh interrupted, eagerly pointing, as Jenny cued him.

"Where is this 'marble trellis-work of exquisite design'?"

Inside, under the dome, Unmesh shushed us and told us to be very still. And then without warning he howled in a strangled doglike way: *How-ooooohhh—*

When he finished he said it was a forty-second echo, and that we could time it if we wished. I left as he howled again. In the poor light Jenny raised her wristwatch to her eyes to count the seconds.

We were walking in the gardens towards the rear of the Taj for a view of the rust-colored river when Unmesh approached, breathlessly conveying information.

Jenny said, "That's enough, Hamish. We're just going for a walk."

"His name isn't Hamish."

"Whatever. Hamish is a perfectly good Scottish name, and I think it suits him." She was fumbling in her purse. She pulled out a pink ten-rupee note.

"Don't give him that."

"What do you mean?"

"He's our guide—our driver. I'm paying him for that," I said. "He told us that he was coming into the Taj as a favor. I didn't even want him to come. Anyway, let's take him at his word and not tip him."

"I want to tip him," Jenny said.

Unmesh was listening, his face darkening with anxiety.

"You heard him," I said, and this time I turned to him. " 'No charge. No money.' "

Unmesh twitched and smiled in eagerness for Jenny to reply. "I didn't hear him say that."

"He said it. You said it, Unmesh, didn't you? He won't look at me!"

"I don't care what he said. If I want to tip him, I'll tip him—"

Unmesh's shirt was dirty. It was the same one he had worn when I first met him, the only shirt I had ever seen him wear. It was torn at the shoulders, there were stabbings of a ballpoint pen at the pocket, the tails flapped. It had aroused my pity once; but now I wanted to hit him for wearing it and not washing it.

"—and it's no business of yours what I do," Jenny was saying.

"He said he didn't want the fucking money!"

"It doesn't matter whether he asked for it or not. I know he wants it. You have no right to tell me what to do!"

We had silenced the birds in the trees above us, a few children wandered over to listen, and still Unmesh lingered, staring hard at Jenny, his fingers at the level of her money.

"This is ridiculous," I said, becoming self-conscious as I saw the Taj Mahal glaring behind Unmesh's wild hair.

"Take it," Jenny said, pushing the ten rupees into Unmesh's eager hand and adding five more to it.

Unmesh became courtly. The money relaxed him. He closed his eyes and touched the money to his forehead, bowing slightly as he did so.

"You said you didn't want any money," I said, nagging him. But Unmesh wouldn't look up. He was averting his gaze, his head twisted towards Jenny, who was walking away.

"That's you all over," she said, tramping up the path to the riverside. "Bossy. Mean. Trying to get the better of that pathetic little man. Trying to push me around." She turned and said, "Don't you ever tell me who I can tip. If I want to give him fifty quid I'll do it, and you have no right to stop me. It's nothing to do with you. Now get away from me. You make me sick."

With that she pulled her hat brim down and walked on, in the strict geometry of pathways that led back to the beautiful Taj Mahal. It was becoming mottled now in the cloudy light of midmorning.

Unmesh was lurking behind me.

"I thought we were friends," I said.

He looked down and seemed to shrink in a posture of apology. Was he doing this deliberately to make me feel ashamed?

"Oh, forget it," I said, and when I laughed he seemed reassured.

After the Fort and the Palace and lunch we went to the marble carving workshop. By then Jenny was calmer. She did not allude to our argument at the Taj until I mentioned it, saying that Unmesh probably got a tip here for bringing us, and wasn't he lucky he met gullible tourists?

"He's not lucky at all," Jenny said, glancing back at him. "And you were completely in the wrong. You just refuse to admit it. But I don't want to hear anything more about it."

We were taken through the workshop and shown the boys preparing the marble slabs, smoothing and polishing them, and the skilled men carving scrollwork into the stone or setting bits of semiprecious stones in the surface. They were making paperweights and tabletops and chessboards, in the same patterns of inlaid flowers that occurred on the walls of the Taj.

"Shall we get one?" I said. I pointed to a slab that would serve as the top of a coffee table.

Jenny said mockingly, "A little piece of India to take home with you. Must you?"

"It would make a lovely table."

"Don't be silly, darling," Jenny said, in a gentler way—perhaps self-conscious because of the watching marble carvers. "It's lovely but it's useless. We'd just get tired of it and put it in the attic, like all those other useless treasures you've bought. Andy—be honest—haven't we got enough already?"

9.

Jenny said, "I think we've absolutely done Agra—let's look at something else," and we went to Sikandra, five miles up the Muttra Road, to look at the mausoleum of the Emperor Akbar. It was a vast and glorious mosquelike building with a big dome, in red sandstone, and when Jenny said, "where are the boldly pierced grilles," and laughed, Unmesh dashed ahead and pointed to the flanking walls. And he claimed there was a wonderful echo under the dome—not quite as long as that in the Taj but long nevertheless, particularly when it was a human howl. Unmesh obliged, Jenny timed it—thirty-four seconds—and she handed him ten rupees, which he touched to the red juicemark on his forehead before he closed his skinny hand over the crumpled bills.

"I don't want to hear a word out of you," Jenny said, taking my arm. In a sweeter voice she added, "Let's not quarrel. This is such a lovely place—and there's no one else here. I know I was a little sharp with you yesterday, but don't you see that you were totally in the wrong?"

We passed a small white pillar. Jenny, who still held the guidebook, said that the Koh-i-nur diamond had once been set into it, before becoming part of the Peacock Throne.

Listening to her read from the guidebook I felt very tender towards her and asked, "Do you love me?"

She smiled. "Yes," she said. "Very much. And I love traveling with you. I want to go on doing it."

When she said that I had the clearest vision of Eden looking alarmed and saying *When you turn that corner I'm going to cry.*

We went to Fatehpur-Sikri. Jenny in her floppy hat went with Unmesh from street to empty street identifying the buildings. I exhausted myself climbing to the top of the five-story Panch Mahal, and after that stayed in the shadows of the doorways, breathing hard and watching for snakes. I did not want to know the exact temperature—I was sure it was well over a hundred, and could have been a hundred and twenty. It was a withering parching heat. Even the crows had dry pleading caws. When the crows were gone nothing moved in the blinding sunshine and the only sound was that of locusts, a high-tech whine that pierced the heat like the point of a blade.

Unmesh unpacked the lunch in the shade of a familiar-looking building: it was the same spot where we had had our lunch before.

"Pignig," Unmesh said.

Jenny and I sat together on a stone seat. "Tell me what is in this sandwich, Hamish."

"Cheej," Unmesh said.

"Delicious," Jenny said. "This is heaven."

"Maybe too hot for missus," Unmesh said.

"Let's not talk about the weather," Jenny said. "What is the name of this building?"

"Khwabgah," Unmesh said.

"Meaning?" I asked.

"House of Dreams," Unmesh said.

"How wonderful," Jenny said. " 'House of Dreams.' "

"Because they sleeping inside."

"You see, Andy? He really does know everything."

Her praise fired Unmesh and he said, "And that is Panch Mahal where mister was climbing. Panch meaning five. Five levels."

"Punch—the stuff you drink—has five ingredients. That's why it's called punch," I said.

"You see, Hamish? My husband knows everything, too."

"Yes. He knowing everything," Unmesh said, and then perhaps fearing that Jenny doubted him he pointed with his sandwich and said, "That Daftar Khana, that Rumi Sultana, that Jodh Bai's Palace, that Jami Masjid—"

"He *is* a bit of a bore," Jenny said, when I found her alone later on. "But he's awfully sweet."

"Where is he?"

"I sent him off to find me a nice cup of tea."

"Tea? In this heat?"

"Don't be so ignorant," she said. "Tea is just the thing. It makes you sweat, and that cools you. Ask anyone. And you're supposed to be the great traveler!"

She laughed as she always did when she said something dismissive—but it was a gentle laugh. She was not malicious. She was simply preserving her own identity, distancing herself, testing my ability to be challenged or defied. I secretly admired her for standing up to me, but it annoyed me when she was in the wrong or when she went too far. And I could not stand arguing in public, particularly in front of Unmesh. I felt she owed it to me, out of solidarity, if not to agree with me at least not to bully me when Unmesh was present. He had no right to see us argue. But I knew her well enough to be able to phrase her reply for her: What right did I have to win an argument, simply for the sake of appearances?

Our petty dispute over Unmesh's tip lay unresolved, but I felt she was paying for it in the way Unmesh tagged along after her and babbled and howled, believing that at the end of it there would be more baksheesh.

There was no more. He did not know Jenny as I did. And as always she spelled it out.

"I know you want another tip, Hamish. But I've given you quite enough already. You should be happy with what you've got."

Still he persevered, hoping to impress her, and just before we left he hurried us urgently to the south wall of the mosque, where there was an enormous gateway and a long flight of steps.

"Gate of Victory Buland Darwaza," Unmesh said. "Look, look." He was gesturing to an inscription in Arabic script. "I am read it." He traced the script by moving his skinny finger through the air and said, "Issa, peace be on him, saying, 'World is bridge. Pass over bridge but do not build house on bridge. World lasts one hour only—spend it by praying.' "

"Who is Issa?" Jenny said.

"Jesus," Unmesh said.

"Our Jesus?"

"Your Jesus!" he said triumphantly.

He looked hopeful, but there was no reward.

On our way back to Agra on the rutted road I prayed for something to go wrong with the car, as it had when I had traveled this way with Eden. The car was just as wrecked-looking and noisy, but rattled along without an engine failure or a flat.

So at a certain point, I said, "Stop the car, Unmesh. I have to make water."

"What a quaint phrase," Jenny said.

I slipped out as Unmesh's face—his big brown nose, his close-set eyes, his spiky hair and narrow head—rose up from the front seat.

"Are you making water, missus?"

Her gaze went straight through his head and she did not reply.

I took my time by the roadside. It was late afternoon and the air was sultry and unbreathable, with the accumulated heat of the day. Dust clung to my damp arms. The fields next to the road were dried out and looked cracked and infertile. Voices carried from nearby huts—children's laughter and the chattering of women. Where did they get the energy to raise their voices?

A young man approached the car. He looked in at Jenny with curiosity, his mouth open, and then put his tongue out and cringed and whined.

"He wanting money, missus," Unmesh said.

"What is he saying?"

"He say he is very hungry."

Jenny seemed undecided. She looked at him through her sunglasses.

I reached into our picnic basket and took out a slender cucumber and handed it to the young man. He screwed up one side of his face and muttered twice and stepped into the crumbly field.

Jenny called him back and gave him five rupees. He groaned, thanking her, as Unmesh looked on resentfully.

"You are such a jackass," Jenny said to me softly, almost with affection.

I was still standing by the car, on the broken road.

"How would you like to live here?"

"You mean *here* in this scruffy little place, or in India in general?"

"Here—in that village over there."

"I am know this willage," Unmesh said.

But Jenny was laughing. "What a silly question!"

We left Unmesh at Agra Station one hot night. The darkness was like a thick blanket lying suffocatingly over us. Unmesh's gesture of farewell was to show us snapshots of his daughter, Vanita. Jenny said, "She looks just like you," but he protested, saying "Not at all!" as though this was an unwarranted slur on the little girl.

Two trains pulled into the station at once from opposite directions. This sent Unmesh into a passion of explanation.

"Over here Up-train. That one Down-train. This for Gwalior, that for Madras Express. Two bogies, four coaches freight, sleeping coach this one—"

At last I relented and gave him a tip to calm him. And he and the driver stood on the platform perspiring at us as we boarded.

Jenny said nothing about him until I asked her.

Then she replied, "He's a funny little person, isn't he? Do you suppose he's a bit simple?"

The Madras Express was not air conditioned, but the scorching draft that blew under the raised window shutters was only part of our discomfort. There was no bedding, the compartment was dirty, the mattresses stank of bug shit, and we were told that there would be no food until tomorrow morning.

"This compartment has taken away my appetite," Jenny said. "And I'm so tired I don't think I'll notice the lack of sheets. But God, sometimes you have the silliest ideas, Andy."

She wrapped herself in a length of cloth she had bought in Delhi and she went directly to sleep. I lay awake cursing the train but also thinking that with Jenny this was a different trip. I had not decided whether it was better or worse; it was like a trip through an altogether different country. The hotels did not seem the same, the people were altered, Ismail was not Ismail, Indoo was not Indoo, and even the Taj had changed. The merchandise in shops—the antiques and crafts—seemed less exotic and rather crude. The weather was different, so hot I felt feverish, and the noise made it seem hotter still.

"It will be cooler in the rains," the conductor said the following morning. "The monsoon is late."

Dawn had come early and suddenly, the sun rising—an extraordinary size and shape from the simple flat fields. Then the whole sky filled with light and turned bluer, until at noon the day was drenched with heat under a white sky.

I watched black buffaloes submerged to their nostrils in the wallows beside the track, and I envied the naked children leaping from the top of culverts into ditches of frothy water.

That day Jenny hardly spoke. She said she was too hot to eat much. She read a novel she had brought from London, a plotty and pretentious spy story. "My holiday book," she called it.

"Why do you read him?" I said, irritated by the serene way she sat on her berth turning pages.

"Don't be jealous," she said. "Write another novel and I'll read it. In the meantime, please don't bother me. This is a bit overwritten but it's not bad. Just childish in the way that spying is childish. It's a game that men play, isn't it?"

"Who cares?" I said, and turned away as the train jogged along through the heat. "My next book's going to be travel."

"I hate travel books," Jenny said. "Oh, don't be offended. You know what I mean. What's the point of them? It's usually just second-rate writers waffling on about themselves and looking for trouble. They have absolutely nothing to say."

"Are you talking about me?"

"This is a discussion, Andy. It's not personal," and she smiled sweetly. "My feeling is that travel writers are like bitchy reviewers. They go to a place and review the weather, then they review the people, then the sights, then the hotels. That's what travel writing is—it's all bitchy reviews."

She said this with such fluency and certainty that I found it funny, and as soon as I laughed, she faltered. She said, "They all write well these travel writers—that's what's so pathetic about them—" and then she stopped. "I'm hot," she said.

She did not return to her book. Some minutes passed and then she said, "By the way, I've been watching you ever since we left Delhi."

The train clunked across the points in a junction and then swayed as we passed a freight train. Jenny began to speak again, but she knew she would not be heard and so she paused until the noise subsided and we were in the open again.

"I hope you don't mind that I've been observing you," she said. "I couldn't help it. I mean, it's so obvious."

"What are you talking about?"

"You haven't really looked at any of the sights. You hardly glanced at the Taj Mahal—and that was gorgeous. You just plopped down at Fatehpur-Sikri as though you had dropsy or something. And for the past two days you've just been mooning around with your mouth open."

Perhaps that was how it seemed, yet how could I admit that I had been observing her?

"Forgive me for asking," she went on, "but don't you have any work to do?"

"I've been making notes," I said lamely.

"I'm not asking you for an explanation," Jenny said, "but your attitude does seem extraordinarily casual." ·

Then she went back to her book. We traveled all that day in the dusty train, on a route that seemed longer than it had a month before. I murmured to myself a line from a poem I loved, as I looked at a stupa painted white in a village at the center of some drowned rice fields: *What spires, what farms are those?*

I wished that Jenny had been reading something I had written.

I thought of the tube train that morning I arrived in London, when I had seen the young woman reading a book of mine. Just watching her turn the pages was such a pleasure for me that time had passed quickly and I had almost missed my station. I loved the look of absorption on the woman's face, her occasional smiles; she was a friend and she knew me intimately.

Watching Jenny read someone else's boring book made time pass slowly. But it was my fault for not being busier. I should have been writing—making notes, at least. I was doing nothing, and I was agitated. Jenny always looked serene when she was idle, and she was happiest in repose. Her own contentment helped me: she did not require my constant attention, she never said, *What are you thinking?* which always meant *Are you thinking about me?*

I now knew how being married to her had freed me. What we were today we would continue to be, and so I could see clearly this same scene, but on the Cape, one afternoon under a cloudy sky left by a severe winter storm. We were in our house, the same house as ever, but it was warmer, cozier, quieter. Jack was going to call tonight from London, where he lived. In our silence we were anticipating that—his news, his mood, his new life. There was a kettle of stew on the stove, bread in the oven, the makings of a salad on the butcher's block. We were so used to one another we hardly talked, and our lives were somewhat separate—we each had a car, and Jenny did some consultancy work in Boston. As ever she protected me from people I did not want to see, and I used her as my excuse. This was the life I had been tending towards for years, and this was the house I had planned, filled with my artifacts from India and China. Jenny had made a place for herself in it, though she occasionally complained of being an alien—in America, in this house. At intervals, short or long, like a sudden fit of sobbing that gives relief, we made love.

She saw me watching her.

"This book isn't half bad," she said. "I mean, it's rubbish but it's fairly readable."

Then she looked out of the window of the train, at the evening sun dissolving into a flooded field of rice.

"God. India. Still there after all the miles we've gone."

That night, still traveling, we shared a sticky meal.

"I've had better Indian food in Clapham," Jenny said.

We turned in, climbing into our separate shelves, and we lay there in the heat, listening to the clatter of the wheels and every so often passing a station on the line and being raked with the glaring yellow lights of the railway lamps.

In the darkness, Jenny said, "Do you suppose anyone ever makes love on these trains?"

I said nothing; she was still murmuring.

"You'd probably dislocate your back."

"Do you want to make love?" I asked, whispering from the lower berth.

"Not now. I'm too hot," she said, and after a moment, "I'd rather have a nice cup of tea."

Mr. Thumboosamy, the manager of the Hotel Vishnu in Madras, was anxiously watching Jenny's face for a reaction as she took a deep dramatic breath. The door to Room 25—I had requested that one—had just been opened, but Jenny had hesitated on the threshold, Thumboosamy beside her with her bag in his hand.

"Yes," Jenny said, and sniffed again.

Thumboosamy looked eager.

"That's the smell of my mother's house in Balham," Jenny said, turning to Thumboosamy. And now she smiled. "Mice. I hate mice. I'm not superstitious. I'm not frightened of mice. I can't stand them. They're dirty. They spread disease. They crawl over you when you're asleep. I'm not staying in this place."

"This room, darling?"

"This hotel," Jenny said.

"It's the only hotel in town with rooms free," I said.

Mr. Thumboosamy confirmed that this was so. Madras was packed with tourists, he said.

"There must be something," Jenny said.

"Not available," Mr. Thumboosamy said, making it a cluster of consonants, like a Tamil phrase.

"That's absurd," Jenny said. "Madras looks a hideous place. And this is the hot season. Who would want to come here? There must be lots of hotels with empty rooms."

I said, "What if there aren't any?"

"Then I'll sleep under a tree," she said. "Anywhere but here."

We went to the Taj Coromandel, the luxury hotel just off

Mount Road, and were told they had plenty of spare rooms. "This is more like it," Jenny said of our clean pleasant room with its view over the city. She did not jeer at me, as I guessed she might, but simply said that perhaps I didn't know as much as I thought I did about traveling in India.

"Maybe I should come along with you more often," she said. "Aren't you glad I found you a nice place to stay?"

We rested that day—had a nap, made love, and then swam in the hotel pool. The water was uncomfortably warm and after the swim I felt limp and exhausted as though I had been stewed.

Our room overlooked a mosque, and in the early evening there was a call to prayers. We watched the muezzin climbing into the minaret. Jenny had been reading her spy novel. She put it down and crept to the window, when she heard the muezzin clearing his throat in the loudspeaker.

Below us the faithful were gathering. I watched Jenny's intense concentration and admired her reverence. She picked up her camera quickly and fingered it and focused. But she did not shoot a picture—out of respect, I felt. She said nothing, only watched, and I kept looking at her, the way she scrutinized the scene at the mosque. I thought how travel was composed of moments like this: discoveries and reverences separated by great inconvenience. These encounters, taken together, added up to one's experiences of a place—the inconvenience had to be forgotten and displaced by the epiphany—like this call to prayer.

I had never seen Jenny so patient, and I felt the same love for her that had welled in me when I had seen Eden in front of the Taj Mahal sobbing for the beauty of it.

I joined Jenny. I took her hand. She held mine a moment and then dropped it.

In the courtyard of the mosque, as the muezzin howled, a solitary muslim was bent double, worshiping Allah.

"He's praying," I said.

"I know that."

"They do it five times a day."

"I know that, too."

We stared at the praying man.

"I just remembered something," Jenny said. "Isn't it awful when someone says a striking thing that you know is unfair? The way it sticks in your mind, as though it's true?" Her eyes were still on the muslim crouched in prayer. "I admire that man's piety. My vulgar Uncle Monty fought in Mesopotamia. He was a war hero, so we could never contradict him. When they pray, he used to say, they look like a dog fucking a football."

Mahadeva was watching us from his little wooden porch. We had taken a rattly train from Madras to Tambaram. Mahadeva had suggested the train when I came the day before by taxi to explain that I would be returning with my wife—and I gave emphasis to the word.

He called out and clapped his hands when we approached his house, and three of his children rushed up to us, the smallest and dirtiest plucking at Jenny's bag.

Mrs. Mahadeva was apologetic and shouted for the older girl to take the child away.

"Please don't worry," Jenny said. "All children are the same. Mine used to be like that. It's good—it means they're not afraid of strangers."

"You are having?" Mrs. Mahadeva said.

"Just one. A little boy," Jenny said. "Not so little!"

Mahadeva listened to this exchange and smiled. He said, "Let us leave these ladies to entertain themselves."

Jenny was marveling at the older daughter's gleaming hair.

"We are applying coconut oil to it, sometimes on a daily basis."

Mrs. Mahadeva spoke English!

When I saw Mahadeva relaxed I realized how fearful he had been when I had brought Eden here. His fear had made him seem poor and beaten. This time he was expansive. He had little experience of a single woman; but a wife and mother he understood.

As we ate—and this time we ate together, the four adults sitting around the table—the older girl served and spooned seconds onto our palm leaf plates. And she sometimes missed the leaf: she had been staring at Jenny, and she kept glancing back at her.

It was clear that she had made Jenny self-conscious, because Jenny began to speak with her. The girl was sweet and inattentive, and she went on serving in her clumsy way until her mother muttered at her.

"What is your name?" Jenny asked.

"My name is Annapurna."

She was very thin, with bony hands and bony feet, and large sunken eyes, and she was wrapped in a faded sari. But the name was that of the mightiest mountain ridge in the world.

"This food is really delicious, Annapurna," Jenny said, squelching the rice into a little ball and wiping it through the puddle of smashed lentils and conveying the sticky mass to her mouth.

Jenny's dexterity with the food was remarked on by Mahadeva—and still his daughter Annapurna stared. Why did this make me so uneasy? The rest of them were talkative, complimenting Jenny on her pretty dress, her sensible hat, her sturdy shoes, her lovely hair; and they said how lucky I was to have her with me.

"I hope, before we leave Madras, that you'll come to our hotel and join us for a meal," Jenny said.

Mahadeva was pleased and flattered to be asked, and it was obviously a novelty for him to be negotiating this with Jenny and not me. Out of deference to Jenny he consulted his wife, and out of deference to us they discussed the matter in English.

"But there is impending arrival of Subramaniam," Mahadeva said.

"We have ample of time before then to make preparations," Mrs. Mahadeva said.

"I think he will be left cooling his heels," Mahadeva replied.

This went on for a while, and at last, with profuse apologies they said they were forced to decline—and they used those words.

"What about next time?" Mrs. Mahadeva said, and she went on to say that she looked forward to seeing our son.

Still Jenny ate and still Annapurna stared.

Mahadeva said, "We will go to Mahabalipuram. We will bring a picnic hamper."

It did not matter that this was fantasy and probably would never happen. It brought consolation to them. Or perhaps it seemed to them that I was making regular visits to Madras—I had been to their little house twice in six weeks.

Sensing Annapurna's eyes on her, Jenny said, "My husband

hasn't finished his rice. I hope he did better than that the last time he was here."

"Oh, yes," the girl said slowly, folding her skinny arms together. "But the other auntie did not eat the food as you do."

A silence swelled in the room and solidified like lead, and stifled every noise. And then the Mahadevas, husband and wife, spoke at once.

"Annapurna, hurry and get the container of pickle!"

"Our children will play together in the sea," Mahadeva said. "In Mahabalipuram."

Jenny had only momentarily lost her smile.

"I look forward to that," Jenny said. "To coming back and seeing you."

"And I hope you will bring your hubby," Mrs. Mahadeva said.

Jenny was rising from the table. She gathered her palm leaf and mine, and some of the tin bowls and cups and she made for the kitchen.

"That's up to him," she said, just as she disappeared behind the door.

I rose to follow her, but Mahadeva waved me back.

"Never mind. We will talk."

But all we did was sit, and I tried to hear the whispers from the kitchen. Jenny stayed there a long time with Mrs. Mahadeva and Annapurna. Nothing said was audible, though once I heard Jenny laugh—and the others did the same in a nervous respectful way.

"You see? It is all right," Mahadeva said.

When they emerged, Mrs. Mahadeva said, "Your lady wife was adamant about helping me."

When it was time for us to go, I was moved by the tenderness of Mrs. Mahadeva's farewell to Jenny. She seemed genuinely sorry to see Jenny leave, and I wondered perhaps whether they shared a secret. Again, we were made to promise to return soon.

"Both of you together," Mrs. Mahadeva said, stepping in front of Annapurna. And she repeated it, "Both of you together!"

"What was that all about?" I said.

We were walking back to the main road through the deadening heat and noise of the Tambaram bazaar.

Jenny said, "Don't mock her. I liked that woman."

"You'll never guess how old she and her husband are."

"Let me try," Jenny said, and guessed at their ages and got them both.

"She must have told you," I said. "When you were talking all that time in the kitchen."

"No. We were talking about something else."

Jenny faced me to see my reaction to this, and encouraged by it—I could not hide my curiosity, I could not mask my mounting sense of dread—she said, "I was seriously wondering whether the world is just illusion. Does the secret lie in letting go of things?"

In that moment I thought again of Eden. *The other auntie.*

Jenny simply stared at me, and when I said, "Is that all?" she laughed and took my hand.

"That is everything," she said quietly.

We found a taxi at Tambaram Station that would take us to the temples at Mahabalipuram. I showed Jenny the temple that stood amid the crashing waves. Jenny was just behind me. I turned towards her. Was that grim expression on her face an effect of the strong wind, or was she thinking about us—our marriage? I didn't know how to ask. The surf broke and pushed its suds up the shore. Fishermen wearing wet pajamas knelt in clumsy black catamarans and cast their nets downwind.

Jenny put her arm around my shoulder, the way she often did with Jack. But there was almost no weight to her arm, no pressure to her hand, and she did not lean on me. Yet I was weakened by the gesture.

The monotonous surf kept collapsing on the shore near the temple.

"Or letting go of people," she said, in a different voice, as though finishing a thought.

She spoke to the crashing waves.

For a moment I had not the slightest idea what she was talking about in this broken-off sentence. And before I could say anything she let go of me and left me. When I looked around she was gone—lost in the crowd of Indians on the beach.

I stood awhile and thought of Eden, of a particular moment—naked, wearing the skull necklace and standing over me, looking like Kali, looming above me with her legs apart. The memory rattled me. Feeling guilty I went in search of Jenny. I found her up the hillside standing near the grand bas-relief that was dense with the carvings of elephants and dwarfs and monkeys and birds.

A barefoot Indian in a pin-striped jacket and wraparound *lungi* was saying, "—depicting all the gods and humans and animals observing Lord Shiva who allowing River Ganga to flow through his tangled hair, so that it spills gently—"

Seeing me, Jenny said, "I reckon that's why my husband didn't tip his raft over."

"Is this gentleman your husband, madam?"

"What's left of him," Jenny said, and then turned back to the gray stone cliff-face and its carvings. "That's a beautiful story," she said, as though the thought had just struck her.

She was silent as we visited the other *raths* and pillared caves and did not speak again until we were in the taxi back to Madras. She said, "But India is full of beautiful stories, isn't it? That's probably why it's such a desperate shambles."

The taxi was traveling down a narrow road of soft and broken tar, past parched fields.

"Letting go of me?" I asked.

At first she wouldn't answer. Then she said, "Would that worry you?"

She smiled pityingly at me in my discomfort.

"What did that woman tell you?" I asked.

At first she shrugged, and then she had an answer.

"What I've known for ages," she said.

I had not expected this at all. I did not know what to say. And it angered me that I did not know whether she was teasing me. And which was worse, the teasing or the truth?

At the hotel, Jenny said, "I hated that story the Indian told me about the Ganges. I kept thinking about that dead body you told me about—the one you buried."

We were walking through the cool lobby.

"Whenever you see something dreadful here someone has a beautiful story to explain it," Jenny said.

Another couple was waiting to take the elevator. The man was one of those bearded individuals whose hairy face is like a hedge—he peered at us silently across this barrier. The woman was small and blonde and wore a brick-red dress.

Seeing us they took a step nearer each other and held hands.

"Isn't this weather something?" I said, to be friendly.

"It's a lot hotter than this where we're going," the man said, and it seemed like a boast. "Thanjavur," he said, unnecessarily giving the place its ancient name and then he explained, "Tanjore."

"Where the bull is."

"The Nandi, yes," he said, and the woman looked anxiously at him, averting her eyes from me. The man was still talking solemnly through his beard. "In the Pagoda of Brihadi-Swara. They anoint it every day with oil—the whole thing."

"What a splendid idea," Jenny said without raising her voice.

The man went silent, perhaps wondering whether he was being mocked. And when the elevator came we got in and ascended in silence.

"Another beautiful story," Jenny said in the room. Then she smiled. "What a funny couple. I'll bet you anything they're not married. Americans can be so pedantic."

"Why don't you think they're married?"

Jenny shrugged. "Something in the air. There was an atmosphere around them. They were edgy and bored and formal and a little too polite."

"And holding hands?"

"That too. Another auntie."

I hated the word—it was worse than *wife*. We had taken the word away with us from Mahadeva's, and since then it had developed into a presence—not a person, but a specter. There were three of us now.

That night over dinner Jenny was raising some food to her mouth when she stopped her fork in the air and said, "I suddenly want to be out of here. I want to be home, in a mess I understand."

We stayed two nights in Delhi in order to rest for the long flight back to London. Jenny said she wanted to see the place where Gandhi had been cremated, and so we went to Rajghat on the Jumna and mingled with the pilgrims. Her voice came out of that mob.

"What bothers me most is that I've been involved in some drama without knowing it. That I'm a character in a plot. That I'm a fool."

She walked on, buying some flowers and strewing them over the Mahatma's funeral ghat.

would shock him and make him sweat; how he would begin to dissolve, all the while staring at me—imploring me to act.

"I know exactly what to do," I said.

And I was pretty sure I did, you know.

East Sandwich–Shanghai–London
1985—1988

About the Author

PAUL THEROUX was born in Medford, Massachusetts, in 1941 and published his first novel, *Waldo*, in 1967. His subsequent novels include *The Black House, The Family Arsenal, Picture Palace* (winner of the Whitbread Prize for fiction), *O-Zone, The Mosquito Coast*, which was made into a hit movie starring Harrison Ford, the critically acclaimed *My Secret History*, and *Chicago Loop*. His bestselling and highly successful travel books include *The Great Railway Bazaar, The Old Patagonian Express, Riding the Iron Rooster, To the Ends of the Earth*, and *The Happy Isles of Oceania*.

us.

slept with this ghost, we ate with it, the ghost hovered between she hadn't scolded. She knew that I was thinking *What now?* We though she had dealt with it obliquely—she had not blamed me, shared the same ghost. She didn't want this thing in her life, secrets. But I had been found out: now, in India, Jenny and I And I believed in ghosts—in my ghosts. They were powerful secret, the life I led beyond all these others. I was never able to give a name to the process. It was my deepest ness and joy—every emotion; and after I wrote, it was real. But I needed order. My writing came out of confusion and loneli-

''Good. It's too hot for that.''

''I don't think I have one.''

''I don't know. Are you going to tell me your theory of art?''

I said, ''If silence is truth, then what's writing?''

We had wandered to the river to find some shade under the trees.

All this time I felt that Eden was listening to us, and it made me feel guilty, because Eden believed in beautiful stories. She believed in me, she depended on me, she was waiting.

''Then was broken by the memory of Jenny saying to Indoo, ''Then what's that in your hand?''

truth and the whole world was *maya*, all illusion. But the mood mood I could easily work around to the view that silence was certainty was nearly always false—it was self-deception. In this There had to be a ragged element in the best of them, because I began to understand why Jenny doubted beautiful stories.

''Well, silence *is* truth, isn't it?'' she said, and walked on without waiting for my reply. ''And I'm not a fool.''

She was still walking slowly and then she let go of the last of her flowers.

''You're being very enigmatic,'' I said.

''It's my way of being honest,'' she said. ''Only writers believe that life has a plot, that stories have an end.'' She was still tossing marigolds onto the dusty ground. ''Don't think I'm not glad we came here. It's just that if I stayed longer I think I'd turn into Forster's Mrs. Moore and start talking obscurely about the riddle of the universe and the irony of death—that silence is truth.''

There were three of us, and it was awful, and I believed it was worse for me. We made love wildly one night, and Jenny was both passionate and remote, with that self-absorption and eagerness of which lust is the mainspring. It was as though I was a stranger she had taken home from a bar, someone she was using for her pleasure. She tied me to the bed with silk scarves, and held me captive; she sucked me and sat on me, and ardently caressed herself in my face, uttering long adoring sighs, while I watched, fascinated, wondering what fierce eroticism she kept in her mind. In the morning she was cold, she didn't remember, and I was the stranger from last night who was expected to leave after breakfast. I felt mute and stupid and guilty.

I said, "I think we should see Indoo before we go."

He took us to his club—Indian golfers, lots of handlebar mustaches, waiters with sashes and turbans. I liked the Greek pillars, the potted palms, the aquatints on the walls, the cool interiors and the dusty tigerskins.

A black Indian in a white dinner jacket sat straight in a chair next to a palm, playing a violin. His hair was parted in the middle, and a nearby lamp made his hair oil gleam. The very sight of him thrilled me. I wanted him to play "Beautiful Dreamer."

Indoo said I should make this request of the violinist—he was most obliging. Then Indoo excused himself. "The Gents," he said.

Perhaps the violinist didn't understand my accent. He stood up to ask me to repeat it, and—standing—he looked conspicuous and out of place this hot night, holding his fragile, misshapen instrument.

I named the song again.

"You hum it, I play it," the violinist said.

I liked that. I turned eagerly to Jenny.

"That's my theory of art," I said. "That's what I do."

She was not smiling, and yet she looked very calm. She first glanced in the direction in which Indoo had gone, and when she had established that he was not on his way back, she turned to me and spoke without emotion in simple declarative sentences.

"I know there's someone else, Andy. I won't put up with it. You will have to choose. If you don't I'll leave you."

The violinist had not heard her. But I imagined how the words